GOWER HANDBOOK
OF MANAGEMENT DEVELOPMENT
Third edition

Gower Handbook of Management Development
Third edition

Edited by Alan Mumford

Gower

© Gower Publishing Company Limited 1991

First published 1973 as *Handbook of Management Development*
Second edition 1986
Third edition published by
Gower Publishing Company Limited
Gower House
Croft Road
Aldershot
Hants GU11 3HR
England

Gower Publishing Company
Old Post Road
Brookfield
Vermont 05036
USA

British Library Cataloguing in Publication Data
Gower handbook of management development. –
    3rd ed.
    I. Mumford, Alan, *1933–*
    658.4

ISBN 0–566–02907–3

Printed in Great Britain by
Billing & Sons Ltd, Worcester

Contents

PART IV   MANAGEMENT DEVELOPMENT IN ACTION

List of illustrations

Editor's preface

In my preface to the 1986 edition of this Handbook I said that the book was based largely on the definition of management development offered by the Training Services Agency in 1977. This was: 'an attempt to improve managerial effectiveness through planned and deliberate learning processes'. This new edition again focuses on the kind of planned and deliberate processes used by most management development advisers and personnel directors. My own research and experience has been increasingly concerned with an expansion of the meaning of 'management development' so that we can incorporate the relatively accidental processes, not even always recognized as a development or a learning process, which managers call 'learning by experience'. It seemed to me, however, that at this stage the proposition I have offered about the nature of management development, and which I discuss in my introductory Chapter 1 for this Handbook, is not yet widely accepted. So although readers will be introduced to the concepts, and to my model of management development, in that chapter (and can follow the argument in more detail in my other books) I have restricted my attention here to formal management development processes.

Chapter 1 discusses learning **from and about the reality of management**, compared with attempting to learn from simulations or descriptions of it. It also emphasizes the significance of understanding and working on **learning processes** themselves. It provides, therefore, a statement – both conceptual and practical – about what I believe management development to be. It also covers a great deal of the ground which otherwise I might have asked another author to cover in Part III, which deals with learning processes.

In Part II, the chapters by Tony Vineall and Andrew Stewart (Chapters 2, 3 and 4) respond to the need for 'planned and deliberate' processes. They represent an editorial judgement also, in that another editor might have chosen to include much more on the mechanics of management development. Clearly, the relatively small number of chapters I have allocated to this subject reflects my priorities – and, by implication, those that I am suggesting to readers. I do not regard the mechanics as unimportant, but in past years too much attention was paid to formal management development systems and not enough to questions such as: 'Management development for what?', and 'How do managers learn more effectively?'. The chapter by Charles Margerison (Chapter 5) offers some innovative ideas on managing careers; Andrew Mayo in Chapter 6 gives a detailed case study describing how management development plans can be based on the strategies an organization has chosen for its own further development.

The substantial section on learning processes is certainly different from any other collection of management development articles I have seen. For many years management developers, trainers and educators have based their activities either on a single management development process regarded as the only way to develop managers, or on a catholic menu through which managers are exposed to a variety of processes. In the latter case, there was at least a recognition that some managers learned better from one process than from another, but there was no attempt to identify **what processes suited which managers**. Part III offers exciting insights into the characteristics of the individual learner by Peter Honey and Ian Cunningham (Chapters 7 and 8). John Morris in Chapter 10 looks at the same kind of issue from a slightly different perspective, by discussing learning as an **organizational**, as well as an individually determined, process; readers may also usefully turn back to my own Chapter 1 at this point. Don Binsted in Chapter 9 is concerned not so much with individuals as with the contribution the new technologies are making to our understanding of learning processes.

Part IV describes some applications within management development. Bruce Nixon in Chapter 11 gives a fascinating insight into the development of improved answers to management development problems over a period of time. Jean Lawrence, previously one of the few original workers on action learning in the UK not to have written about it, has contributed Chapter 12, which is stimulating both in form and in content. John Teire in Chapter 14 provides an admirable statement of a process which has passed the stage of being 'flavour of the month'; as editor, I am particularly pleased to see how much emphasis he has given to the issue of **how people learn from outdoor training** – not a priority in many outdoor courses. Jim Butler in Chapter 13 describes with both conceptual clarity and specific detail the design of some senior management courses; again, readers will notice the emphasis on how managers are helped to understand **how** as well as **what**, they are learning.

Part V deals with a number of issues which do not readily fit into any of the first four Parts. Bob Garratt in Chapter 15 discusses organizational culture and its impact on the development of managers. The relationship between management development (MD) and organization development (OD) – the subject of much confused debate in the 1970s – remained important even when people ceased to write about it; Graham Robinson's Chapter 16 will help practitioners understand more clearly what they might achieve, depending on their objectives. The chapters by David Ashton and John Crosby (Chapters 17 and 18) take up the perennial issues of handling multicultural management development. Finally, Judi Marshall in Chapter 19 proffers some challenging views on the issues involved in developing women managers.

We revert to more general questions through Alun Jones's review of the role of the management trainer and Peter Bramley on evaluation (Chapters 20 and 21). Then follows a chapter by Bill Critchley and David Casey (Chapter 22) which contains stimulating comments on the important issue of whether the development of particular skills for a particular process may be good management development, but not very effective in terms of *managerial priorities*. Because the choice of resources depends on the objectives of management development, I have left to the end the chapter on this theme by Mike Abrahams (Chapter 23), who at my request wrote it as a consumer rather than as a provider.

When I set out to specify the contributions for this third edition, I reviewed the extent to which there might have been new developments which ought to be incorporated. My conclusion was that there was no single major new thrust which required a chapter to itself. Over the last six years the movement has, however (if we judge by articles and speeches at conferences), been towards **more specific, tailored management development** – certainly as far as courses are concerned. There has also been an increase in the number of articles referring to the use of **diagnostic instruments** to help managers understand their own learning processes. Two reports – by Charles Handy and by John Constable – attracted a great deal of attention when they were published in 1987; it is, in my view, unfortunate that the good features of those reports, especially that of Charles Handy, quickly turned into a debate about management qualifications, and to an associated volume of work on managerial competences. These issues intially seemed to overwhelm the other ideas contained in those reports, particularly on the improvement of management training, and the use of on-the-job development. I had originally planned to include a chapter on management competences, but finally decided that whatever we might offer stood the risk of being outdated by developments. Those developments might be positive, in the sense of helping the competence idea forward, or negative – the possibility that the competence movement will collapse under the weight of its own paper. As my own Chapter 1 indicates, I am in favour of the appropriate use of competences, but I am concerned about generalized national standards.

I did not think it right to force all contributors to adopt one way of recognizing that there are both male and female managers; in some chapters, therefore, 'he' is used instead of 'he/she'.

Alan Mumford

Acknowledgements

The editor and publishers wish to thank the following for permission to reproduce copyright material.
British Postgraduate Medical Federation, for Figure 8.1, from an idea in J. Heron, *Dimensions of Facilitator* Style (1977).
Economist Publications, for Figure 15.1, from A. Campbell and M. Devine, *A Sense of Mission* (1990).
Management Education and Development (1984) for the original version of Chapter 22.

Notes on the contributors

Michael D. Abrahams (*Choosing resources*) was Management Development Manager at Marks & Spencer Plc for fifteen years. He is now a consultant with Brind Associates, a consultancy specializing in designing and resourcing management development initiatives. He is a Fellow of the Institute of Personnel Management.

David Ashton (*Handling cultural diversity*) became the first holder of a Chair in Management Learning in a British University in 1986, based in the Department of Management Learning at the University of Lancaster. In 1987, he became Dean of the Management School at Lancaster. He had previously held a senior corporate-level management development post in the BAT Industries Group; earlier academic posts included Senior Lecturer and Director of the Management Development Unit at the Durham University Business School. He was also McKinsey Foundation Fellow at the Graduate School of Business, University of California at Berkeley. He has published several books, continues to edit international journals in his field, and has a wide range of consulting experience.

Don Binsted (*New ways of learning*) had an industrial career with ICI (twenty-one years) where he held a variety of posts in line and staff management, training and organization development. In 1974 he became founder/director of the Management Teacher Development Unit at the University of Lancaster (now the Centre for the Study of Management Learning, CSML). Latterly he became director of distance learning, with his research focusing on the use of technology to facilitate learning. In December 1987 he became self-employed but had the honorary post of senior fellow in CSML.

Peter Bramley (*Evaluation*) was a trainer for some ten years (in the

Army) and also worked for about ten years as a training consultant. Since 1981 he has been lecturing in training and development in the Department of Occupational Psychology at Birkbeck College and has set up within that department a small research and consultancy group, the Centre for Training and Evaluation Studies.

Jim E. Butler (*Learning design for effective executive programmes*) is currently Director of Studies (Management Education/Development) at BAT Industries Group Management Centre. He has held senior management development posts in both the public and private sectors of industry. Immediately prior to joining BAT Industries in 1984 he was the Management Planning Manager for Burmah Oil plc and before that the Management Development Manager of the National Water Council, UK. He is a member of the British Psychological Society, the Institute of Personnel Management and the Association of Management Education and Development and has special interests and expertise in management and organization learning. He has written a number of papers and contributed to other published texts on this subject.

David Casey (*Team-building*) started his working life as a teacher, and a deep interest in creating learning environments has been a leitmotif throughout his career. His interest in management began with he went to manage the R & D laboratories of Berger Paints and later the training function for part of Reed International. He now spends his time creating learning environments for managers. Since 1971 this interest has led to a broader focus than the individual manager – he now creates learning environments for management teams and whole organizations, in the private and public sectors in the UK. He is an Associate at Ashridge Management College.

Bill Critchley (*Team-building*) is a Business Director of the Ashridge Consulting Group. As an organization consultant he works with companies in both private and public sectors to bring about improvements in organizational performance and capability, working with top teams to help them review their managerial style and practices, and their critical impact on the organization's culture. He specializes in helping organizations identify and overcome the main blocks to effecting major change and has presented papers to conferences on this theme. He holds an MBA from Cranfield and the Diploma of the Gestalt Psychotherapy Training Institute of Great Britain in Organisational Consulting and Clinical Psychotherapy.

John Crosby (*Developing local nationals*) is Director of Group Personnel, BAT Industries plc. He joined BAT Co. in 1976, initially as the company's Personnel Advisor for its Sub-continent and South East Asian companies and subsequently was a member of the company's Board with responsibility for personnel, administration and security. Previous posts have included personnel management appointments with EMI Ltd and the Costain Group of Companies and, from 1968–76, he was a senior management consultant with Hay-MSL Ltd. As a consultant he led assignments in many major British companies, as well as overseas in Pakistan, Tanzania and Zambia. He was President of the Institute of Personnel Management from 1985–7 and is currently a Governor of the Centre for International Briefing (Farnham Castle), a Council Member of VSO and a Trustee of the Overseas Students' Trust.

Ian Cunningham (*Self-managed learning*) is Director of Roffey Park Management College. He has in the past been Managing Director of Metacommunications Ltd, a Senior Research Fellow at Ashridge Management College, a head of division in a regional management centre, a manager, a management trainer and a research chemist.

Bob Garratt (*The cultural contexts*) is an international strategy consultant operating out of London and Hong Kong. He specializes in the simultaneous development of business strategy and people strategy, particularly the development of directors. He is Chairman of the Association for Management Education and Development, and of the multi-media company Media Projects International Ltd. He is Visiting Fellow at the Management School, Imperial College, London University. He has written *Creating a Learning Organisation* (Director Books, 1990), *The Learning Organisation* (Fontana, 1987), *China Business Briefing*, with Sally Garratt (Hawkeshead Communications, 1987), and *Breaking Down Barriers: Practice and Priorities in International Management Education*, edited with John Stopford (Gower, 1980).

Peter Honey (*Styles of learning*) has been a freelance psychologist and management consultant since 1969. He specializes in anything to do with people's behaviour and its consequences. He divides his work into designing and running courses on interactive skills, team-building, creative thinking, problem-solving and self-development; consultancy projects on such subjects as customer satisfaction, assessment centre criteria, management training needs, staff attitudes, behaviour in meetings and groups. Peter Honey is a member of the British Psychological Society, the Institute of Management Consultants and the ATM, and a Fellow of the International Management Centre from Buckingham and the Institute of Training and Development.

Alun Jones (*The role of the management trainers*) is an independent consultant and was formerly Director, Research and Development, of The Industrial Training Services Ltd, an international consultancy in the development of organizations and people. He is a research chemist who was a training manager in the chemical industry before joining ITS. Dr Jones is a Fellow of the Institute of Training and Development.

Jean K. Lawrence (*Action learning – a questioning approach*) left Manchester Business School in 1982 to open the Development Consortium. As a managing partner she works with organizations to develop them and their managers through 'in-company' and 'inter-company' work. A visiting member of staff at Henley and Oxford (The Strategic Leadership Programme), she also works regularly overseas; in recent years, she has worked with top African managers from many countries. Jean managed the production of assortment at Cadbury Bros and was a senior consultant with Anne Shaw before joining the Manchester Business School in 1967. Her topic there was project management and she developed skills in providing learning opportunities in small groups, particularly in association with the Tavistock Institute, for whom she has directed conferences. In the 1970s, she was chairman of AMED (then ATM), a founder member of ALP International formed to work with GEC on the first UK management development programme based on action learning. Extensive experience in many forms of action learning programmes followed, and led to her current Chairmanship of The International Foundation for Action Learning.

Charles Margerison (*Managing career choices*) is a Professor of Management at the International Management Centre and the co-creator of Margerison McCann Team Management Systems. He was previously Professor of Management Development at the Cranfield School of Management. His work as a management educator is recognized internationally with such organizations as Mobil Oil, Shell Corporation and Citibank, while in Australia he has conducted major assignments for Australian Airlines, ACI, ICI and other organizations. He is a graduate of the London School of Economics and did postgraduate work at Liverpool University and Bradford University where he obtained his doctorate. He is currently International Vice-President of International Management Centres. His other interests include writing for various journals and he is the current Editor of the *Journal of Management Development*. He is the author of several books, including *Team Management – Practical Applications*, Mercury Books, 1990, *Managerial Consulting Skills*, Gower, 1989, *Conversational Control Skills for Managers,* W. H. Allen, 1987, and *Shakespeare and Management*, MCB University Press, 1988.

Judi Marshall (*Women managers*) is a Senior Lecturer in Organizational Behaviour at the School of Management, University of Bath. Earlier in her academic career she studied managerial job stress and published extensively in this area, including *Understanding Executive Stress* with Cary Cooper (Macmillan, 1978). Her current research interests are women in management, developing feminist contributions to organizational theory, organizational cultures, and developing post-positivist research approaches. She has also published *Women Managers: Travellers in a Male World* (Wiley, 1984).

Andrew J. Mayo (*Business strategies and management development*) is Director of Personnel, ICL Europe at STC-International Computers Ltd., a European-based information technology company operating in some seventy countries. He is currently responsible for Human Resources for all ICL operations in Western Europe, as well as some based in the UK. He was until recently Director of Manpower Development for the ICL Group, and in this role his responsibilities included resourcing and development policies for the company worldwide, majoring in international management development. After degrees in Chemical Engineering and Management Science he served his management apprenticeship with Proctor and Gamble in several line and staff positions. His career has taken him through various companies in the chemical process and electronics sectors, in personnel, marketing and general management positions. He is a Fellow of the Institute of Personnel Management.

John Morris (*The learning spiral*) is Emeritus Professor of Management Development at Manchester Business School and a managing partner of the Development Consortium, a consultancy specializing in action learning and organizational change. He pioneered action learning programmes at Manchester Business School, and was awarded the Burnham Medal of the British Institute of Management for contributions to management development. He has worked on development assignments in many leading organizations, including Willis Faber, Thorn EMI, Yorkshire Water, and the National Health Service. He has also served as a member of specialist panels of the University Grants Committee and the Council for National Academic Awards.

Alan Mumford (*Effectiveness in management development*) has been Professor of Management Development at the International Management Centres, Buckingham since its inception. In that role he is responsible for developing the Centres' approach to improving management performance through effective learning processes. He has worked with senior managers and directors in a variety of organizations including Ford of Europe and Pilkington. Professor Mumford's previous experience in management development has been exceptionally wide. It included periods with John Laing & Sons, IPC Magazines and International Computers Ltd and a spell as a deputy chief training adviser at the Department of Employment. For six years he was Executive Resources Adviser to the Chloride Group. Professor Mumford is a Companion of the Institute of Personnel Management and was its Vice-President (Training and Development) from 1971–3. He has published numerous articles and books on management development including: *The Manual of Learning Styles* (Honey, 1986), *The Manual of Learning Opportunities* (Honey, 1989), *Developing Top Managers* (Gower, 1988), and *Management Development: Strategies for Action* (IPM, 1989).

Bruce Nixon (*An in-house senior programme and organizational change*) is an independent consultant. For several years he was Training & Development Manager with Sun Alliance and prior to that he worked for several different organizations in the UK and overseas. His main professional interests are helping trainers develop tailor-made in-house programmes for managers and working with teams (line management or trainers) on their vision, their strategy and whatever they have to do to achieve it. With associates he offers an annual programme for leaders of organizational change and development and leadership programmes. He is a fellow of the Institute of Personnel Management and the ITD and a member of AMED.

Graham Robinson (*Management development and organization development*) is a Director of Kennedy Robinson Business Development Ltd, a company specializing in providing advice to top managers on the implementation of major organizational change and in the provision of education and learning programmes to support such change. He has worked in this field for twenty-five years, both as purchaser as Personnel Director of Sperry Information Systems in the early 1980s and as a provider while a researcher with Ashridge Management College and the Institute of Social Studies in the Netherlands. He has worked with a wide range of private and public sector organizations in the UK, Africa and the Far East and is author of a number of publications in the field of organization and management development.

Andrew Stewart (*Diagnosing needs, performance appraisal*) is Managing Director of Informed Choice, consulting industrial psychologists. He lectured at Aberdeen and Surrey Universities and was Personnel and Management Development Officer at IBM (UK) and Senior Fellow at the Institute of Manpower Studies. He is co-author (with Valerie Stewart) of *Practical Performance Appraisal* (Gower, 1978), *Managing the Manager's Growth* (Gower, 1978), and *Managing the Poor Performer* (Gower, 1982).

John Teire (*Using the outdoors*) has been a training and development consultant since 1975, designing and conducting in-company programmes for managers, teams and company development. He makes use of the outdoors as a complement to other learning activities which include company workshops, residential courses and business simulations. He is a member of AMED, the Group Relations Training Association and the Business Graduates Association.

Tony Vineall (*Planning management development*) is Deputy Head of Personnel, Unilever. He has held personnel management positions for Unilever in the UK and abroad and his responsibilities now include development of senior managers for all Unilever's operations. He is a Fellow of the Institute of Personnel Management, a Council Member of the Industrial Society, and Vice-Chairman of Governors, the Centre for International Briefing (Farnham Castle).

PART I
SETTING THE SCENE

1

Effectiveness in management development

Alan Mumford

In 1984, I wrote a paper, which was subsequently published in the second edition of this *Handbook*. In revising that chapter for this third edition I have found the main themes I put forward then still to be appropriate. My own work, and my reading of the work of others, has led to a greater emphasis on one theme – **effective learning processes**. There has also been some additional work on effective managerial behaviour, which has added to the options available for defining what this may mean.

There has been one other significant change from my views in the mid-1980s. I was then still defining management development as 'an attempt to improve managerial effectiveness through a planned and deliberate learning process'. I have now come to the view that a great deal of Management Development is not 'planned and deliberate', and probably never can be. In two books (1988, 1989) I have developed and illustrated the idea that Management Development must be considered to include **informal** and **accidental** processes, as well as those defined as planned and deliberate. Of course, most personnel directors and Management Development advisers reading this *Handbook* have operated to a planned and deliberate definition, and advised formal planned and deliberate processes which they have understood to be, uniquely, 'management development'. While in this chapter I shall be giving much more emphasis to formal processes of Management Development, the additional material I have given on effective learning processes particularly brings out the point that a great deal of the development of managers is brought about by activities which have not been influenced at all by planned and deliberate interventions in the traditional sense.

The question of our definition of Management Development and of the areas in which we as advisers choose to intervene, is of course vital in considering issues of effectiveness: however effective our interventions may be on formal processes, if (as has largely been the case) we do not intervene in those informal accidental day-by-day activities through which managers learn, their effectiveness is both reduced and partial. Reduced because we may succumb to the temptation of dealing only with those managerial issues which we can **understand** and **influence**; partial because we are acting only on a small and often **highly untypical** part of the manager's life – a big decision about a job move, or the occasion of attendance on a course. So part of the case made in this chapter revolves around the idea that we must embrace a wider vision of what we understand 'management development' to be, in order to expand our contribution to the manager's learning and development capacity. That wider vision is expressed in the following definition:

An attempt to improve managerial effectiveness through a learning process.

THE THREEFOLD NATURE OF EFFECTIVENESS IN MANAGEMENT DEVELOPMENT

Effectiveness in Management Development is best achieved when we bring together three different aspects of effectiveness:

- A contingent definition of effective **managerial behaviour**
- A developmental process which emphasizes **activities** in which managers are required to be effective, rather than emphasizing the **knowledge** necessary for action
- The identification of learning processes which are effective for the **individual or group**, rather than economical and convenient for tutors or trainers.

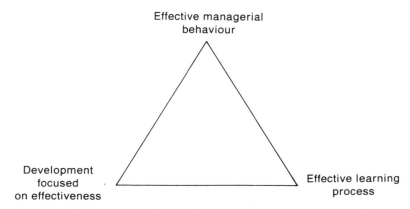

Figure 1.1   Effectiveness triangle in management development

It should be noted that in 'the effectiveness triangle' shown in Figure 1.1, the triangle is **equilateral**: this means that all three aspects are equally important. Moreover, the particular presentation offered in Figure 1.1, which could be interpreted as showing two contributors to 'effective managerial behaviour', is not the only way of representing the triangle. In some situations, the triangle could be moved round so that effectiveness was seen as depending on a triangle resting on a single point – effective learning processes. As presented in Figure 1.1, the triangle gives emphasis to the desired end conclusion – effective managerial behaviour.

EFFECTIVE MANAGERIAL BEHAVIOUR

It is, of course, absolutely fundamental to recognize that the prime purpose of Management Development is effective managerial behaviour: it is not just knowledge, or attitudes, although these clearly can often be significant contributors to effective behaviour. As anyone with experience of management knows, there are managers who have been extremely knowledgeable who have not been effective, and managers with appropriate attitudes who have not been effective. An 'effective manager' is one who does the right things in the right way – and it is the emphasis on 'doing' which is the key requirement for a manager, as distinct from a researcher, writer or academic. Unless we also recognize the necessary features of what effective managers **do**, and what proportions of emphasis are appropriate in different situations, then the purposes of Management Development will be as badly aligned as they will be if we give too much emphasis to issues of knowledge and attitude.

For many years the formal process of MD followed what might be called the 'classical view' of the nature of management. A familiar version of this could be summarized under five heads:

- Forecast/Plan
- Organize
- Motivate
- Coordinate
- Control.

These terms, and the concepts and misunderstandings underpinning them, still survive in some formal courses. Rosemary Stewart (1976), Henry Mintzberg (1980) and John Kotter (1982) have provided research which shows that the basis of these concepts is unscientific. All three authors have also argued strongly that these inappropriate statements have led to structures for developing managers which have been unrealistic, and therefore unhelpful. Since each has then proceeded to his or her own statement of key managerial activities, it might be argued that their demolition of one list of managerial tasks and its replacement by another is simply due to differing perceptions and personal preferences when describing those managerial activities.

In fact, for Management Development purposes an even more significant common theme is that any generalized statement about managerial activities, including their own, is likely to be at least partially (and possibly substantially) incorrect for any particular manager or group of managers. They found substantial variations in required managerial behaviour in different organizations; the managerial activities in which any individual had to be effective were seen to depend on the specific kind of function and job, or the manager's interpretation of that job or role, and others' interpretation of the manager's role and responsibilities within that job. The main features of their analyses are conveniently spelled out in Mumford, (1988).

It still seems to be the case that these discoveries have not had the impact on Management Development processes that they ought to have done; the more intellectual courses probably include such analyses as important and thought-provoking contributions to the debate about what managers do. The consequences of their discoveries do not, however, seem generally to have been used to develop the course itself. Take as an example the importance given by Kotter and Mintzberg to the way in which **networks**, and their **effective use**, can contribute to effective managerial performance. Many courses will include sessions about interpersonal relationships; how many include sessions on the effective use of networks? Even more important, as we shall see in the next section, how many include practical work on the effective use of networks?

While the generation of more appropriate generalizations, and their incorporation into appropriate management training, seems not to have been fully carried through some improvement does seem to have been made in producing more organization-specific training. It is still unfortunately true that in many (probably most) organizations needs analysis is relatively superficial and leads to the facile adoption of training courses whose content differs remarkably little from one organization to another. There have been two problems in adopting a more rigorously analytical approach. Even where the professional Management Development adviser knows what he ought to do, there can be considerable obstacles in terms of actually engaging line managers in the analytical process. The definition, and interpretation, of what is meant by 'effective behaviour' takes time and energy, which managers on the whole would rather give to some other activity. This is most obviously true for a demanding process such as the repertory grid; although well used by some organizations, it has not been adopted as an appropriate approach by most of them.

The alternative approach receiving most attention in recent years has been that of management competences. Originating with the work of Boyatzis (1982) and being more widely aimed through the revived national Management Development debate in the UK in the late 1980s, this is an approach found helpful by a large number of organizations. It has the advantage of not requiring managers to start totally from scratch, as with the repertory grid; it is possible to start with the list produced by Boyatzis, or (in the UK) a list produced under the aegis of the Training Agency. A debate about the appropriateness –

or, as many would see it the inappropriateness – of a national list of competences may produce two not wholly intentional consequences. The first is to make organizations think specifically about what managers in those organizations need **to be able to do**, and the extent to which a nationally agreed list is appropriate. The second is to focus attention on the actual **content** of the competences, which has sometimes appeared to be a rather strange conglomerate of skills, attitudes and end results.

Although there has been this shift in at least some organizations towards what managers need to be able to do, the shift has in many not gone far enough, if it has even started. It is slightly surprising to see surviving into the 1990s one cause more understandable in the 1960s and 1970s – an over-emphasis on developing managers for the future instead of working on issues of **current requirements**. While organizations have certainly helped to sustain this emphasis, the argument applies with even greater strength to many training and educational institutions offering taught experiences outside the organization. The identification of the nature of effectiveness in management has scarcely influenced the design of their programmes – as distinct from making a contribution to parts of the syllabus. The traditional business schools, all of whom now offer in-house programmes, have not on the whole shifted themselves substantially towards issues of effectiveness. They have stayed in the areas which they understand – those of knowledge, particularly **conceptual or theoretical knowledge**. With few exceptions, their in-company programmes have largely mirrored such 'open' programmes where there has been an inevitability about the generalized views of management processes on offer. Although there has been some shift to the design of specific material for particular companies, it has been relatively cosmetic; again, one looks in vain in many programmes for sessions designed to help managers to define and improve their own **effectiveness criteria** rather than sessions designed to convey only generalized management knowledge.

If we look, as we should, on the traditional business schools as the intellectual leaders in defining effective managerial behaviour, we see them largely still locked in the confusion between efficiency and effectiveness described by Peter Drucker in 1974: 'Efficiency is concerned with doing things right. Effectiveness is doing the right things'.

DEVELOPMENT PROCESSES EMPHASIZING EFFECTIVENESS

Just as too much Management Development has been based on an inappropriate view of what managers need to be able to do in their specific organizations (an intellectual failure), so there has also been a complementary failure of a different kind. Management Development processes have too often been detached from the reality of the **perception and understanding of managers themselves**. With rare exceptions, managers are not concerned about the knowledge possessed by a boss, colleagues or subordinates; their characteristic judgement on a manager's effectiveness is whether or not he or she can get things done. The fact that they are not aware of, and tend to be impatient about, the knowledge and skills required to enable a manager to get things done is not of course in itself an argument for not providing these things. It is a practical and psychological argument from two sides of the same coin – for starting from the reality of **where managers are**, rather than imposing on them our views about what they need.

Since effectiveness is defined clearly by managers in terms of the results actually secured, and not by the knowledge someone possesses, it would seem sensible to concentrate in our processes on helping managers to learn from **actions undertaken**, rather than providing them with conceptual statements of what managers ought to do, or with analytical experiences of what other managers have done (or might have done). Instead of giving emphasis to the provision of knowledge and asking managers to interpret and use that knowledge in subsequent action, it would be both more appropriate and more likely to be successful if we gave attention to issues of **action**, and only secondary attention to issues of the required **knowledge**: knowledge and the capacity to analyse and produce solutions to problems are necessary but insufficient contributors to effective action. Primary attention to managerial skills may similarly be misplaced although not inappropriate: the first stage of attention should be on a **desired managerial result** rather than the skills required for managerial activities.

In the UK, of course, the original definition of the benefits to be derived from working through real past experiences was provided by Reg Revans (1982) and then by John Morris.[1] My own research (1988, 1989) follows their ground-breaking statements by putting forward views about the kind of development experiences it is possible to identify, and to use effectively.

It may be inevitable that good ideas are sometimes misunderstood and later watered down. The original work of Revans and Morris has frequently been misinterpreted simply as being about the use of a defined project by an individual, or the creation of a group of managers discussing their own projects; so, increasingly, management training and education courses have included projects as part of the syllabus, and in such cases projects have been yet another interesting variant within a set menu. Virtuous though this may be in programmes otherwise suffering from a surfeit of conceptual and analytical exercises, it is not an adequate representation of what is meant by using 'real-life experience'. Similarly, the view that managers ought to work on some kind of direct problem-solving, presented as a simulation of effectiveness issues in management, is a misunderstanding of what is desirable and possible. Whatever the arguments for introducing bridge-building with lego bricks, or outdoor experiences requiring managers to bridge chasms and climb cliffs, they are stronger as arguments directed to providing variety in learning activity than they are to using real work issues for development.

Courses which give primary attention to managerial skills such as interviewing, negotiation or interpersonal relationships, or to skills involved in dealing with information technology, can be significant contributors to the improvement of managerial performance. This will, again, be more likely to be true if such courses are built on a proper analysis by the organization – and preferably by the managers themselves – of what they have to do, rather than on someone else's judgement that all managers need to be good at some given list of skills.

Four cases are now given, illustrating the kind of shift of emphasis in which I have been involved, and where I find other organizations working with what I believe to be an inappropriate idea of what can be achieved.

Case 1

The final stages of a two-week programme were geared to the participants reviewing the corporate strategy of the group for which they worked. The intention of the sessions, which included a presentation to the chief executive, was that participants should be more familiar with the reasons for the corporate strategy, instead of just criticizing it from their own level in the business. In later programmes we made a significant change, since it seemed to us less relevant that participants should know the corporate strategy than that they should be encouraged to **take action on strategic issues affecting their own business**. They were instead asked to make proposals on a significant business problem currently affecting most of them: one example was the nature of, and possible reactions to, competition from Japanese manufacturers. While they could not do anything about corporate strategy – except perhaps understand it better – they could do something in their own companies about the Japanese 'threat'.

Case 2

A company which had revised its sales objectives and organization structure had some concern that the managers involved might not have the skills necessary to achieve the changed objectives. As a result of analysis with them it became clear that although probably a number of them were lacking in some skills, the larger problem was that, although apparently committed to the revised objectives, they had not fully set up the action necessary to **implement** them. The prime effectiveness was not therefore the skills of sales management, but the identification of specific actions to implement the broad objectives agreed.

Case 3

A company which had changed the composition and structure of its marketing function found that a number of those involved would be unable to produce what was required because they were not fully equipped with marketing skills. In the course of discussion with them the emphasis was shifted from the **acquisition** to the **implementation** of skills. An in-house marketing programme was devised which, in addition to giving managers the necessary tools, took them through to the identification of specific marketing projects which needed to be undertaken. The programme was designed to meet general marketing skill requirements in the organization, the specific requirements of the projects which had to be undertaken, and the completion of real work to meet the needs of the business.

Case 4

MBA programmes normally provide participants with a better understanding of the various functional areas of management such as marketing, finance and production. The expectation is that managers who have acquired this knowledge may be able to manage these functions better, or may through a better understanding have an improved relationship with other departments. IMC's MBA programme starts at the other end of the process, by requiring our associates to analyze the nature of **relationships between their own function and others in the business**, and to make proposals for improvement. While we believe that it may be important for most managers to 'understand finance better', we see it as at least as important that they should be helped to take specific actions relevant to their own needs in dealing with other functions.

As I have shown, some of the central principles of action learning have been misunderstood and misapplied. Another problem has been that the simplistic generalization that 'all managers should learn through doing a project' has too often been expressed entirely in terms of **doing** the project, and very little in terms of **learning from it**: learning processes concerned with effectiveness must always deal with the reality of the manager's job, and always involve her or him in action on it. A manager will, however, not learn enough simply by taking action, and it is clear from most of the literature on action learning that this is not sufficiently understood, and certainly is given too low a priority. The emphasis has been on projects and action to the exclusion of any serious discussion of the learning process while people are **undertaking the project**.

One other opportunity for development processes related to concern for effectiveness is now beginning to emerge. Managers have always expressed themselves in the cliché that: 'I have learned from experience'; it is often clear in fact that their learning has been partial, inefficient and ineffective – though that may not be always clear to them. One of the reasons is that learning from experience at work is very rarely designed, and even more rarely discussed; while formal Management Development processes will, for example, highlight the relevance of a particular job move from one function to another, from one country to another, or from one product to another, very little will have been done to make sure that effective learning occurs **within those experiences**.

We encounter now the essential paradox of Management Development which is that Managers claim to learn from experience; they talk about the jobs they have done, the projects they have completed, the bosses they have worked for and even about the courses they have attended (see Mumford, 1988). Yet Management Development because, as I argued at the beginning of this chapter, it has seen itself as being concerned with formal processes – has paid very little attention to this. Management Development has been defined purely in terms of formal off-the-job training and education, and formal processes for moving people around. Not only have these schemes offered a prescription which does not meet the managers' realities; as already described, the processes themselves have given no help to managers in reinterpreting, and making better use of, their on-the-job development opportunities.

Clearly if we actually want to focus our development on effectiveness, rather than purely on discrete knowledge or skill, the on-the-job experiences present the prime vehicle. What we need is both a conceptual understanding that Management Development must embrace those accidental informal opportunities, previously ignored by most Management Development advisers, and practical processes for integrating real work experiences and formal schemes of development. A great deal of that integration will be accomplished by managers and their bosses with no intervention from the Management Development educator or trainer, except perhaps through some introductory sessions on a course or the use of some reading material or workbook.

Our understanding of the opportunities here, first illustrated on a large scale by Revans and Morris, is now being enhanced by more recent work. In the USA the work of McCall and his colleagues (1988) describes and analyzes the kind of experiences to which managers are exposed. My own work with my colleague Peter Honey (1989) builds on my original 1988 research work in spelling out how managers can actually engage successfully in learning terms with the opportunities open to them. The use of learning experiences at work is by far the greatest area for attention for productivity in Management Development: it meets the criteria suggested by centring on what managers actually have to do, and on issues of their personal effectiveness; it removes the problems of simulation and of transfer of learning. Increased recognition of such opportunities – whether at the design level by Management Developers, or by individual managers for themselves – will nevertheless not necessarily lead to effective learning. It is one of the most potent criticisms of formal Management Development schemes that in proposing to provide additional development opportunities – whether through courses or job assignments – we have largely assumed that **learning will necessarily follow**.

The argument of this section has been that formal Management Development processes can (and should) be focused on and operated through effectiveness issues, but that Management Development must also embrace the ways in which managers **learn to be effective** – learning by experience, largely outside normal schemes. The model I have developed to describe this view of Management Development is given in Figure 1.2.

EFFECTIVE LEARNING PROCESSES

If we manage to work successfully on the issues of managerial effectiveness in the ways described, we create the potential for a virtuous learning circle (see Figure 1.3). It is clear that for many managers involvement in formal management development processes off-the-job has created a vicious learning sequence (see Figure 1.4). Modern motivational theory tells us that behaviour which is not rewarded is not willingly engaged upon again. Some managers have had training or educational experiences they regard as useful or interesting or stimulating, and they are willing to return to similar experiences subsequently; others are relatively unwilling to attend in the first place and/or experience nothing like stimulation or utility during the course. All too often this can be traced back to the failure of courses to deal with the issues of what managers really do, and to deal with them in the ways most related to their normal managerial work processes. If trainers and educators have grappled successfully with the issues of **evaluation**, then corrective steps could have been taken to improve results; either the programme could have dealt with effectiveness issues in the ways I have recommended, or if they did not they would at least have dealt with broader issues of knowledge or skill in a

Type 1   'Informal managerial' – accidental processes

Characteristics
- occur within managerial activities
- explicit intention is task performance
- no clear development objectives
- unstructured in development terms
- not planned in advance
- owned by managers

Development
consequences
- **learning is real, direct, unconscious, insufficient**

Type 2   'Integrated managerial' – opportunistic processes

Characteristics
- occur within managerial activities
- explicit intention both task performance and development
- clear development objectives
- structured for development by boss and subordinate
- planned beforehand or reviewed subsequently as learning experiences
- owned by managers

Development
consequences
- **learning is real, direct, conscious, more substantial**

Type 3   'Formal management development' – planned processes

Characteristics
- often away from normal managerial activities
- explicit intention is development
- clear development objectives
- structured for development by developers
- planned beforehand and reviewed subsequently as learning experiences
- owned more by developers than managers

Development
consequences
- **learning may be real** (through a job) or **detached** (through a course)
- is more likely to be **conscious, relatively infrequent**

Figure 1.2   Types of management development

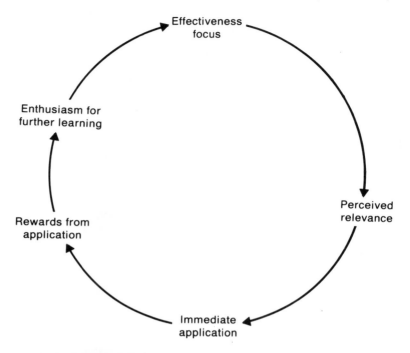

Figure 1.3   The virtuous learning circle

more effective way. The absence of evaluation is particularly ironic in that, for those programmes which do emphasize the acquisition of knowledge or skill, evaluation is not only necessary but achievable (see Easterby-Smith, 1986); emphasis given to effectiveness issues makes the evaluation more difficult to separate for evaluation purposes. It is also probably less necessary; if you design a process actually to engage people in action you **reduce** the requirement to **test the extent to which they have applied that which they have learned**: I use the verb 'reduce', not remove.

The whole shift of emphasis to action-based learning helps us to remove one of the traditional problems of management education and training. It is a logical oddity that having created a situation of unreality (i.e., a structured off-the-job learning experience), and then having done in many cases very little about directing attention to those issues of real personal concern to managers, tutors and trainers have then complained and written learned articles about the problems

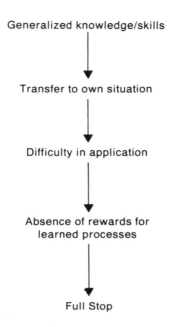

Figure 1.4   The vicious learning sequence

of transfer of learning. If we create unreality and do not deal with issues of effectiveness, we ought not to be surprised that managers have problems in transferring what they are supposed to have learned back into their real job situation. Nor should we be surprised that the boss and colleagues to whom they return from the off-the-job experience gives no welcome to the kind of learning which the managers brings with them.

Concentration on those issues which are relevant to the manager and his colleagues in the real-life situation certainly reduces the transfer problem, both because of the perceived reality of what the manager is engaged in, and because there need literally be no 'transfer' in the sense that he can be involved in projects and real-time problems **drawn from his own work** which do not then have to be 'translated'. Where learning activities are not primarily and directly based on the manager's own work, we should tackle the transfer problem on our programmes instead of leaving it to the manager to resolve on his own on his return to work; this means less time on teaching, and more time on how the manager will **implement** what he has learned.

Emphasis on effectiveness and reality will nonetheless not, as some writers seem to assume, in itself completely overcome the need for careful choice of effective learning processes. Management Development has been far too subject to 'flavour of the month' approaches, each of them claiming to be uniquely appropriate to developing managers. Over the years we have been told that T-groups, grid training, coaching, self-development, action learning and now outdoor training were, successively, the answer to our management development problems. In my view, the adoption of any single technique as the predominant answer to our management development problems is lazy and incompetent; nor is the answer a further proliferation of Management Development processes. In his most helpful book, Huczynski (1983) identifies around 300 Management Development techniques. While in no way wishing to inhibit future creativity, it is my view that productivity in Management Development will derive from the appropriate methods already relatively well-known and tried, rather than the identification of new processes. I take this view because the application of Management Development methods is at the moment so clearly both inefficient and ineffective; we have failed to fit our processes to the **needs of the learner**. Just as we have not satisfactorily dealt with the reality of how a manager **manages**, so we have not dealt with the reality of how a manager **learns**. Just as we have swept aside the common perception of managers that they learn through on-the-job processes (a matter of common experience apparently too simple for researchers to cope with), so we have ignored the reality that different managers actually **learn differently from the same process**. It is an extraordinary fact that educators, trainers and developers know very well that if Brown and Jones both have the same need to improve an aspect of their managerial performance, and both are taken through the same learning experience, Brown will learn and Jones will not. It seems that most tutors having stumbled across this truth painfully, when an individual reacts badly to a learning process, then pick themselves up and hurry on as if nothing had happened. In designing courses the best that may occur subsequently is that the designers offer a catholic menu of activities, hoping everybody will get something out of the course. Thus the supposedly well-designed course will include role-plays, films, case studies, lectures, an afternoon in the resource centre: if you are bored by one, there is always tomorrow.

It is an extraordinary commentary on management education in both the UK and the USA that only in the years since 1980 has there been attention at any level of significance to differences in the ways in which people learn. The field was for a long time dominated by fundamentally sterile debates about the virtues of case studies, of business games, or of experiential exercises. I emphasize again the absence of action on the part of the traditional business schools because of their perceived dominance in the rest of the management development world. I cannot think of any significant university-level contribution in this field apart from the original innovative work by Kolb, and the work done by the Centre for the Study of Management Learning (CSML). CSML have made a considerable contribution in the literature on issues of the general design of different kinds of learning event, and the significance of the interaction between the tutor and the learner. Although much of their written work is understandably directed at the tutor I believe they would share with me the view that one of the problems is that the tutor has been given too great a prominence in the learning process: their efforts, quite rightly, are geared to helping the tutor be more effective by assessing the learning situation in which they are involved.

No doubt because I started from a different kind of environment my own concern has been as much with the learner as the tutor. Peter Honey and I have developed Kolb's original concept of the learning cycle, and have advised the designers of learning experiences how they need to pay attention to **all stages** of the cycle, designing total programmes, sessions within programmes, or particular kinds of on-the-job learning experience. We also took Kolb's original concepts of individual learning preferences, developed our own method of determining these, and then provided direct guidance to the learner on how to make use of this information (Honey and Mumford, 1986a, 1986b).

Honey and I have also argued that knowledge of the **learning preferences** of managers actually arriving on a learning experience can be used to provide a more appropriate experience. We think it is irresponsible simply to throw a ragbag of activities at a group on the assumption that their learning styles will be different. Our general proposition is, of course, that the experience should actually be designed as a **learning**, not as a **teaching**, experience. This undoubtedly increases the difficulties for the designers and operators of learning events, and perhaps it is the prospect of such difficulties which has deterred training and education institutions from actually thinking seriously about the learning process. Nor would understanding by designers and providers of development experiences, while helpful, go sufficiently far. It is surely another prospective leap forward in Management Development that we should share with managers our improved understanding of learning and cause them to recognize and improve their own learning processes: that is to say, that we should incorporate our improved understanding not merely in the design of a more effective event, but that we should treat learning as an **overt part of the programme**. Instead of being an implied and unstudied part of most management development activities, learning should be placed in the forefront as an explicit activity; nor should it be confined to an interesting session at the beginning of a programme, with perhaps some review of personal development growth at the end of it. We must provide time and resources to help managers consider their learning processes **during the programme itself**.

I have carefully used the word 'programme' rather than 'course', because I see this as being applicable just as much in the situation in which an advisor is counselling someone's development on the job as it would be where a tutor is running an off-the-job experience. The reason for this extended attention to the learning process is not merely a matter of logic – of the extraordinary fact that many programmes which claim to help managers to learn never actually address that issue – but also that it is essential as one of the ways in which we will manage to draw together on-the-job and off-the-job development experiences. If in our off-the-job experiences we give sufficient time and attention to engaging a manager in understanding his own learning, we can also help him to see how to apply this knowledge so that he **continues to learn** from similar or equivalent learning experiences when he is back on the job. Just as dealing with issues of effectiveness will help reduce substantially the problems of transfer of learning, so by giving substantial attention to the learning process itself we can reduce the notorious problem of managers seeing experiences as a series of one-off events, with no connection with each other in learning terms.

The phrase 'continuous learning' is now becoming popular; it will be no more than a promotional phrase if we do not provide the **learning processes** necessary to secure it. It seems clear that some of the people writing about continuous learning are really talking only about a series of training events, and not in fact about continuous learning at all; for learning to be **continuous**, rather than simply a series of events, we need to equip people to learn effectively **outside and around those events**: we need to do so for the obvious reason that for most managers most learning will occur – or not occur – **on the job**. Continuous learning and 'learning how to learn' will become empty clichés unless real effort is put into enabling individuals to understand what is involved, and to develop the necessary skills. In addition to our work on learning styles, Honey and myself have increasingly concerned ourselves with further practical exercises to facilitate an individual's understanding of his or her own learning (Honey and Mumford, 1989, 1990).

In the same way that definitions of managerial effectiveness are most sensibly couched in specific organization terms, effective learning processes are defined most appropriately by the **learner**, not by the tutor. In my experience, it is salutary for advisers and trainers to be exposed to an analysis of their own preferred approach to learning (see Chapter 7 below) and then to see how far what they offer – and how they offer it – is dominated by their **own preferences**, not by the individuals they are supposedly trying to help.

SUCCESSFUL MANAGEMENT DEVELOPMENT

I have used three different aspects of 'effectiveness' in this chapter. If we understood these issues better, and carried out our work on the development of managers more appropriately in relation to them, we would be much more likely to produce effective Management Development. Most specifically, we would increase the chance that we would be offering processes which managers themselves recognized as being effective and were therefore prepared to engage in for themselves and offer to others. I think we need to recognize that the continued unpopularity of Management Development (the formal process) is due at least as much to our failures as designers and implementers of formal processes as it is to unwillingness of managers to spend time and devote energy to formal Management Development.

Of course, there is more to successful Management Development than the three main themes I have mentioned here. Margerison (1982) offers a substantial review of causes of success and failure in Management Development; I agree with many of his items, but have expressed my own views as well (Mumford, 1988). It seems to me that too many Management Development schemes are dominated by issues about the 'system' and too little influenced by the needs, requirements and potential for growth of individuals. We will not have effective Management Development as long as we encourage systems which are in fact geared to processing people seen as a **concept**, rather than as **individuals** who can be assisted to develop. I shudder when I hear a personnel director or Management Development adviser say 'All our managers have been through . . .': it has become all too obvious that some Management Development schemes measure results by the number of people who have 'been through', rather than by **achieved results in development**.

I have already argued that we need a more substantial contribution from the organizations who ought to be leading Management Development. Definition of what effective managers do, and the identification of learning strategies and techniques – two out of my three areas of effectiveness – ought to receive much more attention. On the first, the marvellous work of Stewart, Mintzberg and Kotter surely cannot be the last word. On the second we need a substantial research effort from the business schools; perhaps the subject is too difficult for them to tackle, because it raises too many questions about the purposes of management education. I have argued for a focus on effectiveness, and the practice of most business schools certainly does not take them in that direction. (If they had a coherent philosophy, perhaps that, too, would inhibit them from pursuing the areas I have indicated.)

Although I have particularly strong views about the associated issues of learning and effectiveness, I am not alone in my criticisms. Over the last twenty years we have seen the views of Livingston (1971), who told us that formal management education 'tends to distort managerial growth because it overdevelops an individual's analytical ability, but leaves his ability to take action and to get things done under-developed'; this kind of criticism was repeated by Peters and Waterman (1982) and Behrman and Levin (1984). There has been no equivalent research and analysis of the output of UK business schools. This is not to say that we have lacked comment – from business schools vocal about their excellent contribution; from individuals such as Gordon Wills critical of that same contribution; and from the potential customers who have voted with their feet to be absent. An optimistic view would be that the debate largely engendered by the Handy and Constable Reports may encourage a concentration on issues of effectiveness. A pessimistic view would be that the traditional business schools will unconsciously follow the advice offered by Peters and Waterman, and that they will therefore stick to their knitting – offering programmes geared to a view of management education as essentially concerned with the identification and application of theory and concepts, with all too little emphasis on **application**.

NOTE

1. See John Morris (Chapter 10 in this volume).

REFERENCES

Behrman, J. N. and Levin, R. L. (1984), *Are Business Schools Doing Their Job. Harvard Business Review* (January).
Boyatzis, R. (1982) *The Competent Manager* (New York: John Wiley).
Drucker, P. (1974) *Management Tasks, Responsibilities, Practices* (New York: Harper & Row).
Easterby-Smith, M. (1986) *Evaluation of Management Education, Training and Development* (Aldershot: Gower).
Honey, P. and Mumford, A. (1986a) *The Manual of Learning Styles*. 2nd edn (London: Honey).
Honey, P. and Mumford, A. (1986b) *Using Your Learning Styles* (London: Honey).
Honey, P. and Mumford, A. (1989) *The Manual of Learning Opportunities* (London: Honey).
Honey, P. and Mumford, A. (1990) *The Opportunist Learner* (London: Honey).
Huczynski, A. (1983) *Encyclopaedia of Management Development Methods* (Aldershot: Gower).
Kolb, D. (1984) *Experiential Learning* (Englewood Cliffs, NJ: Prentice-Hall).
Kotter, J. P. (1982) *The General Manager* (New York: Free Press).
Livingston, J. S. (1971) 'The Myth of the Well-Educated Manager', *Harvard Business Review* (January).
Margerison, C. (1982) 'How to Avoid Failure and Gain Success in Management Development', *Journal of Management Development*, 1(3).
McCall, M., Lombardo, M. and Morrison, A. (1988) *The Lessons of Experience* (Lexington, Mass: Lexington Books).

Mintzberg, H. (1980) *The Nature of Managerial Work* (Englewood Cliffs, NJ: Prentice-Hall).

Mumford, A. (1988) *Developing Top Managers* (Aldershot: Gower).

Mumford, A. (1989) *Management Development: Strategies for Action* (London: IPM).

Peters, T. J. and Waterman, R. H. (1982) *In Search of Excellence* (New York : Harper & Row).

Revans, R. (1980) *Action Learning* (London: Blond).

Stewart, R. (1976) *Contrasts in Management* (London: McGraw-Hill).

PART II
PLANNING FOR MANAGEMENT DEVELOPMENT

2

Planning management development

Tony Vineall

The literature of management development planning has grown a great deal in recent years and with a more practical and less academically statistical slant. What this chapter aims to do is to answer the question which anyone who is believed to have some practical experience in the subject gets asked several times a year: How do we begin? The question usually comes from a senior executive who has been given the task of 'doing something about management development', usually in a medium- or large-sized group which operates in more than one country and in more than one product or service area. The group will often have been through several phases of management development. There will have often been a period in the past of excessive and over-structured activity, from which little remains other than a lot of forms collecting dust. Most commonly there is an active recruitment programme and some (not very long-term) succession planning for the very top jobs; and not much in between. The group wants to do something systematic to get a grip on its longer-term management resource situation. What follows charts a path to do just that: it will involve quite a lot of work, especially in the early stages, and serious commitment coming down from the top; but experience shows that the balance of what it can contribute over its demands in terms of inputs is such that it can rapidly become accepted as a valuable institution and be seen as just as indispensable as the basic financial accounting procedures or annual operating plans.

THE BASIC DISCIPLINES

Like all planning, much depends on the **quality of the basic data**. Certain preliminary activities have, therefore, to be carried out to provide the data on which all management development planning is based. Examples of such activities are as follows.

A systematic grading of jobs based on their content

Job classification based on **content** is usually first introduced primarily for determining salary scales. It is, however, equally important to management development, providing a ready common language to describe and group jobs according to content. Where management development is to be planned on an international group basis, the grading system should ideally be one which applies throughout the group. Where this does not exist, a series of **broad seniority bands** may have to be introduced for management development purposes, and local grades converted to them. One way or another there must be a clear and common perception of the **relative levels of jobs** before planning can begin – and job titles rarely suffice for this purpose.

A system of performance appraisal

Performance appraisal has also usually been devised initially for other purposes – to provide a basis for differentiating rewards; or for counselling the individual; (or, less happily, to build up a case for remedial action or termination). Appraisal systems should, however, also serve to ensure that there is a **regular recording of achievement on the job** which forms, especially over time, an indispensable foundation for management development. Management development is not just about performance, but if predictions about the future are not firmly rooted in what the manager has **actually delivered**, the whole exercise will fall into disrepute.

Potential assessment

Performance appraisal is, however, only a beginning. More specifically relevant to management development planning is the assessment of **potential** – the judgement of how far the manager may be promotable in the future. Such judgement has to be related to performance, but goes further, and is, of its nature, more speculative and more judgemental than performance appraisal. The relationship between performance and potential is not a simple one – the best performers are not necessarily those of high potential. The process of potential assessment has accordingly to be more complex: whereas performance appraisal focuses on what the manager achieved, potential assessment is equally interested in **how he achieved** it, and it must involve more people, such as the boss's boss or the head of the appraisee's function, and also the individual himself.

Most organizations include a brief assessment of potential as something of a footnote to the annual appraisal exercise and this is useful – although the form in which it is communicated to the individual needs care. It is also, however, desirable to organize more extensive potential assessment exercises at key stages of development. A few companies set up assessment centres, or use external ones; more commonly companies make some in-house arrangement to set aside time on specific occasions to think through, in a structured way, with the help of all those who are in a position to contribute, the likely future pattern of an individual's progress.

A system of development lists

The results of such potential assessment then need firming up in a form which can guide action and provide a useful input to planning. This is best done with a framework of **development lists**. Jobs are divided into three or four main levels, each therefore with a salary breakpoint about 50 per cent above the level below, and each of these main levels thus incorporating probably three or four normal salary grades. A development list will then be drawn up of those individuals in any one main level who are judged to have the potential to reach the next higher level within five years. If the main levels were termed 'junior management', 'middle management', 'senior management' and 'top executive', the first list would be those likely to be promotable from junior management to middle management within five years; the second list those promotable within five years from middle management to senior management, and so on.

Such a system of development lists contributes to management development planning in several ways. First, it focuses and sharpens judgement about potential by asking specific questions – judgement of potential can otherwise be sloppy, with too many people being vaguely 'promotable within a few years' without commitment to how many, or even how soon. Secondly, they provide the raw material for basic planning comparisons of promotable resources and known and likely future needs. Thirdly, they highlight training and development needs; challenging and testing opportunities, which are often in short supply, can then be directed to those on the lists. Finally, the system provides a useful language in which different parts of a large complex organization can communicate about the sort of people they want for a certain job.

People change and develop, and sometimes disappoint, and it is vital that names are **deleted** from lists as well as added to them. It may therefore be desirable not to tell individuals when they are put on such lists, lest the need to tell them that their names are being removed becomes a deterrent to actually deleting them.

These activities have been described as 'basic disciplines': they are to management development what the basic accounting records are to financial management. They do not themselves constitute or guarantee good management planning, but without them what follows will probably be in vain. It is now possible to consider the regular, usually annual, management development planning cycle.

MANAGEMENT RESOURCE PLANNING MEETINGS AT COMPANY OR UNIT LEVEL

Appraisals of performance have been completed, judgements of potential have been made. What happens next?

What happens next is the most central feature of a system of management development planning – **a review at unit level** (typically the operating company) which provides the focus for the appraisals and potential assessments and sets priorities and plans which will guide the individual appointments, attachments, training courses, etc. which will move the organization, and those who manage it, forward in the coming year. This is the crucial point at which, in respect of that particular unit, the organization 'gets its act together' in respect of management development – it is amazing how frequently the need for a well-prepared meeting of this kind is not appreciated.

The first thing to establish is who should attend, and that will depend on the structure of authority and responsibility in the particular business. For a subsidiary company the review is essentially between the chief executive and his boss – probably the director to whom he reports at group level. Indeed, together with the annual operating budget, this review is a key control for these two. Each will have his personnel executive with him, and where there is some other arm of the business closely involved with management development it should be represented also. The criterion is that anyone whose authority is needed to effect a major personnel change should be there.

This unit/company review should address the key areas of management development and ensure that they have a full picture of the management resources of the unit in the context of likely future needs. Accordingly, they will consider six areas:

1. **Major business plans** and any likely **organizational and establishment changes**. This link with operational planning is fundamental and should be clear and overt. For this reason, management development reviews can usefully be timed to follow long-term planning meetings. This will enable management development planning to accommodate the likelihood of a move into a new product area or an important technological change in the industry or plans to acquire subsidiaries in another country – or, indeed, a strategic withdrawal from a certain market segment.

2. An **individual review at the senior levels in the unit** – the level will be defined according to the individual unit, but as a guideline will, in an operating company, clearly cover the Board members and the level immediately below them. This review should be based for each individual on a simple sheet recording:

   (a) the basic **personal details** (age, service, qualifications, grade, pay, etc.)
   (b) a brief summary of the individual's **performance appraisal**
   (c) a statement of the individual's **potential**.

As the system becomes more sophisticated a statement of how the individuals feels about **his own career** is a useful addition.

Those conducting the review must first establish that they really understand and agree with what is being said about the manager: then they should determine what to plan for the next stage of his development. This may take the form of a recommendation that he should be considered for certain kinds of job move – to widen his experience; to fill a gap in his knowledge; to test him in a more demanding post; to extend his base by operating in another product area or country. Or it could recommend a training course. In other cases it may conclude that he is ideally placed for the time being and that the most important priority is that he should *not* be moved but should remain long enough both to contribute in, and benefit from, the job he is doing. Specific moves can be agreed in this way but that is not the main aim – what is basic is to establish agreement on the **priority for the coming year**.

3. A review, on the same lines, of those who have been included on the development lists because of their potential. It will also normally be at this review that individuals will be **added** to these lists. In the case of such people it is particularly important to identify **gaps in their experience**, and to plan moves which will enable them to develop and further prove their abilities.

4. Identification of possible **successors for vacancies** which are likely to arise at senior levels – because of retirements; or because the incumbents are likely to move; or because of organizational changes; or, where numbers are large enough, where past experience suggests that there may well be some losses to posts outside the organization. Such lists of possible successors are, of course, tentative, but like so much in this field, they begin to point the way to possible problem areas. The same few successors may keep appearing against several vacancies or in some areas all the candidates may look less than ideal. The reviewers will then want to reconsider the agreed plans for some of the successors in order to speed up or replan this development.

   Succession will not always – particularly at the most senior levels – be provided within the individual company, and this succession planning at unit level is only one part of a wider exercise: the personnel executives involved must ensure that the particular succession planning is related to the wider group situation.

5. At this stage it should be possible to take an **overall view of the company's situation**. No one can produce a checklist of precisely what should be discussed: in one unit it will be the lack of any managers of development potential in the engineering function; in

another it may be the unfortunate coming together in time of a series of top-level retirements and promotions, and how to arrange them successfully; elsewhere it may be the fact that none of the financial managers seems to stay in the job for more than eighteen months. The review paperwork will have provided the basic data to show up these issues, but there is a skill in spotting them. If this skill – essentially, though not exclusively, a contribution of the personnel specialist – is lacking, no amount of forms and checklists will compensate: a system of management development planning needs a lot of **managing**.

6. The meeting should be summarized quickly in clear **action notes**. The temptation will be to record everything that was said; succinctness with an emphasis on action will not only make it more likely that the notes are not immediately filed, but may actually result in **people moving**.

REVIEW OF RESOURCES AT HIGHER LEVELS

Even at the level of the individual company or unit the review will inevitably (and rightly) consider issues of balance of resources and needs; but planning will not always be viewed within the group context and imbalances in particular units are, to an extent, to be expected. It is therefore important that a further review is conducted at a higher level – probably for **all group resources in a particular country**. Thereafter, a similar exercise needs to be carried out for the **total group**. These reviews may well address themselves to the individual details of the highest levels of management and to succession at that level. They will certainly give priority attention to a more 'aggregated' approach to management development planning: to reviewing the promotable management resources in the light of likely needs as determined by the age structure of the existing management, business plans to change the management establishment in the future, and best estimates of patterns of leaving. The kind of basic information appropriate to this exercise is set out in Figure 2.1. This review should certainly be prepared in total for all functions and a similar exercise carried out for specific functions.

On the single sheet in Figure 2.1 can be found the signposts to most of the management development **problems** which will crop up over the

B. RECRUITMENT OF TRAINEES

Year	No. Recruited	Number In					
		Jun. Mgt.	Dev. List I	Upper Middle Mgt.	Dev. List II	Sen. Mgt.	Left the Coy
1980							
1981							
1982							
1983							
1984							
1985							
1986							
1987							
1988							
1989							

Plans
1990
1991
1992

A. REVIEW OF MANAGEMENT STRENGTHS, AGES, RESOURCES, ETC.

	Senior Exec.	Dev. List III	Senior Mgt.	Dev. List II	Upper Middle Mgt.	Dev. List I	Junior Mgt.	Total Mgt.
Under 35								
36—50								
51—55								
56—60								
61+								
Total								

Establishment forecast in 3/5 years								

Leavers (other than retirement) last 5 years								
Resigned								
Dismissed								
Redundant								
Died								

Figure 2.1 Human resources review

next few years. From an informed review of the data will come provisional conclusions, such as that:

1. There is a hump in the age distribution of senior executives and that those with potential to replace them (List III) are too few and, apparently, rather young.
2. The age distribution at the top (or at some other level) is such that, in combination with planned establishment reductions, there is going to be a shortage of promotion opportunities over the next five years, followed by a further five years of intense demand for replacements. How will the succession candidates be stimulated meanwhile? Or will they leave? Maybe someone should talk to them about it!

Once such problems have been identified, discussion must move to **specifics and individuals**. The review will have done the essential task of management development planning and drawn attention to a problem which, if nothing is done, is likely to creep up on the business.

Most large organizations regularly recruit graduates either straight from university or within a few years of graduating. The review just described will form the basis for deciding what the level of recruitment needs to be for the next few years. Such trainees are typically recruited with the intention that they should progress fairly rapidly through the ranks of junior management in their first five–ten years in the business. Accordingly, it is useful to have the information in Section B in Figure 2.1, which highlights the success in retaining and developing the recruits and gives a picture of how careers are actually **experienced by those who join**.

These overall reviews at higher levels will form the basis of plans for the coming period.

PLANNING OF INDIVIDUAL CAREERS

Some further comment is needed on what 'planning' means in terms of the **careers of individuals** – something which is often misunderstood. Clearly, management development planning does not prescribe in detail the future advance of an individual's career. The development lists focus on how far an individual looks capable of progressing in five years, and it is also reasonable to forecast the **kind of job** – e.g., a specialist rather than a generalist, someone who will be in a line job rather than an adviser. It is right for the individual to know this information, although it needs to be communicated with clear indications of its limitations – in particular, that any such forecast is dependent on **continued performance in the job** (and, equally importantly, on the **availability of appropriate jobs** in the future).

The organization also needs to think through typical career paths in the main functional areas – not to ensure that everyone's career slavishly follows the model but to plan that the careers of most individuals will meet most of the requirements. This will ensure that those who progress to reach the most senior positions, particularly in general management, will have passed through a range of the most appropriate experiences. The detail of such a model has to be worked out in every individual organization, but a typical checklist could well be:

1.   To cover the **full range of responsibilities in his basic function**. It could thus be appropriate to plan that engineers have experience not only on development and design but also in the management of ongoing engineering departments, including maintenance, etc. Similarly, it might be decided that accountants should have experience of both financial management and management accounting; that personnel managers have experience of both industrial relations and pay issues.
2.   To have operated in **more than one environment**, preferably at a reasonably early stage in a career. This means working either in a different market or in a different country.
3.   To have actually been 'in charge' with responsibility for 'hands on' management of a **distinct part of the business**. Few will have experience as general managers in an early part of their career, but it is important to ensure that careers do not continue permanently in headquarter organizations and that those of potential operate away from the company's base, perhaps running the accounts department or the engineering function at a distant site. Like riding a bicycle, this is something which has to be learnt in practice, and preferably when young.

It will never be possible to ensure that all careers meet all these criteria, but a regular analysis and the availability of the model as an objective can significantly raise the number of careers which meet most of them. Without such a model the tendency could easily be to use people's experience in further jobs which develop and further test only the same capacities. There is a huge difference between **ten years' experience** and **the same years' experience ten times over**.

CONCLUSIONS

These are the elements in a management development planning system. It is a 'system' in the sense that it is a series of regular tasks which highlights the shape of the present situation and points to potential problem areas. But how useful it is will depend on the **use made of it** – it will give no automatic answers. More than most planning systems, it will be a continuously rolling exercise, always an updated forecast, always open-ended, usually a bit untidy.

Three points are worth making in conclusion. The first is to restate the importance of the **middle levels** which are the most elusive in the process of getting a grip on the development of managers. It is very difficult – but vital – to plan and influence careers between the 'bottom-up' activities of recruitment and early training and the 'top-down' plans for top-level succession. One very experienced consultant who advised medium-sized companies in this field once put it more caustically when he said he usually found that management development consisted of 'an interest in young men and a sort of mafia surrounding the chairman'. It is usually because they are concerned to get more order – or less disorder – into that middle ground that groups want to institute management development planning, and it is by progress in that difficult area that it will in the end be judged.

The second point underlines a theme running through this chapter: that the regular systems are valuable to point to a **specific trend or problem**. Accordingly, there will be frequent occasions when it is right to follow this up by setting up ad hoc exercises: a senior working group to study the high turnover of engineers, or to look at the gap between well-trained accountants and their ability to move on to financial director jobs between which there are many discontinuities in the skill requirements, for example. Such exercises, as well as coming up with a good answer, can put the right political clout behind development programmes. The need to set up such ad hoc exercises is not a weakness of the regular system: the fact that the need for them is perceived is, in fact, the system's strength. It is, however, also important that such one-off exercises do not get incorporated into the regular procedures, involving continuing work long after it has ceased to be necessary.

The final point is the most important of all. It has been stressed that the planning systems must be seen as a support for – and useful only insofar as they support and contribute to – good decisions about **actual people and their careers**. This is a two-way relationship. The systems must usefully guide the individual appointments; in addition, the appointments must be seen to forward the overall objectives of the plan. There is also an even more important interaction and mutually supportive relationship with the **organizational culture** – those shared attitudes and values in respect of people and their development which exist in the organization. The systems will be frustrated if the culture does not incorporate a belief that it is right – for the business – to regard longer-term career development as important, and on occasions to make short-term operational level sacrifices to that end. This will come about only if the systems make it reasonable to assume that such sacrifices are not in vain – and, above all, that the systems bring benefits in terms of the availability of well-developed people as well as demands for the release of others. It is such a culture which marks the company which has really integrated its management development planning into the running of the business.

FURTHER READING

The Institute of Personnel Management publish pamphlets on many of the individual activities in the field. For a further and deeper treatment, reference could usefully be made to:
Bennison, M. and Casson, J. (1984) *The Manpower Planning Handbook*, (London: Institute of Manpower Studies/McGraw-Hill)
Hibch, W. (1990) *Succession Planning*, Institute of Manpower Studies
Walker, James W. (1980) *Human Resource Planning* (London: McGraw-Hill)

3

Diagnosing needs

Andrew Stewart

Managers often try to solve assessment or development problems by adopting new techniques; if those new techniques are seen not to be successful, the techniques themselves are blamed as being ineffective. The fault more probably lies with an inadequate or non-existent **diagnosis of the needs which the technique was trying to meet**: if the problem is not properly defined, a solution is likely to be elusive.

This chapter is primarily concerned with the training and development needs of individuals and groups, but there is another set of needs which should be established before specific training and development needs are addressed: these needs have to do with the **commercial or functional effectiveness of the organization**, and may be seen to exist at three levels:

- At the **strategic** level, the question is whether there are shortfalls in the performance of the organization – now or in the future – which can properly be traced to ineffective performance on the part of some managers of employees. In addition, new developments in the market or customer base may create a demand for different ways of doing things, which implies no criticism of current performance, but which will lead to difficulties if no change in approach occurs.
- At the **manpower planning** level, the question is whether the stocks and flows of people through and around the organization

are appropriate – both to current needs and to future trends. More importantly, perhaps, is the quality of individual concealed in the statistics such that the operation will be enhanced rather than held back for lack of talent?

- At the **individual** level, it is advisable to check whether there are people who are under-performing compared to expectation, and if so, **why**. They may have reached their level of incompetence; or they may simply be in the wrong job, or they may be perfectly capable of performing better with some developmental help.

These three levels of question are primarily concerned with the way in which the business of the organization is being conducted, whether this be in the commercial style of private enterprise or in the service-orientated style of the health service, local or national government. If it can be shown that the performance of individuals or groups is impeding the attainment of the organization's declared objectives, then it may be worth while to probe training and development needs in some depth to establish **what kinds of intervention** are going to yield the best pay-off. This chapter is primarily concerned to present a range of techniques for probing those needs.

TYPES OF TECHNIQUE

Training needs analysis techniques can be classified in two distinct ways. There is a distinction between **group** techniques and **individual** techniques; and there is another distinction between **deficiency**- and **ideal**-based techniques:

- Group techniques are particularly useful at a **macro level**, for strategic planning and for deciding training priorities; individual techniques are designed to make accessible the training needs of **single persons**.
- Deficiency-based techniques are aimed at discovering short-falls in **current performance** in order to design remedial action; ideal-based techniques are designed to achieve statements of what, in the best of all possible worlds, people **should be doing**, and then set out to help people to get closer to that ideal.

The trainer needs to know about both the ideal and reality, but the order in which this is achieved may be determined by the diagnostic techniques used. Most of the techniques presented in this chapter can be used in either group or individual mode; only some of them can be used in ideal mode, but most of them can help to uncover deficiencies.

CRITICAL INCIDENT

In this technique, the interviewer selects a group of managers who are representative of the target population, and asks them to talk about the most difficult problem they have had to deal with in the last period of time. This period can vary from around one week to not more than six months; memory for detail will fade seriously after this time. Six weeks is often chosen as a period of time which will be meaningful to most people, and the starting question might be: 'Can you tell me about the incident in the last six weeks which has caused you the most difficulty?' Follow-up questions might include:

• When?	One-off problem or regular?
• Why?	Your problem or someone else's?
• Who with?	What caused it?
• At what cost?	Will it happen again?
• How was it solved?	Any long-term effects?

After a number of interviews have been conducted, it then becomes necessary to **classify the information**. Some categories which have emerged from the data include:

- Alone/other people involved
- Technical/financial/managerial
- Type of product/service involved
- If other people involved, insiders/customers/suppliers/others
- If other people involved, senior/peer/junior/other
- Producing new ideas/servicing old ideas
- New problem/old problem.

Although it is more difficult, it provides a more accurate reflection of the data if the **interview content is allowed to dictate the categories**

into which it is sorted. In some other systems the interviewer comes with a prepared list of categories into which the data will be fitted; this seems to suggest that the content is already known, in which case it might be hard to justify the research.

Critical incident technique is fairly rough and ready, but will give fast information about priorities. For example, a service engineering organisation was putting about 80 per cent of its training effort into technical product training and 20 per cent into interpersonal skills. A critical incident survey showed that less than 15 per cent of the problems were generated by the equipment, and that all the rest required customer handling skills. A rapid shift of priorities could then be seen to be justified, together with congratulations to the technical trainers who had clearly been doing a good job.

Critical incident interviews do carry an implied commitment to those interviewed that something is about to be done about their problems; if no tangible results appear within a relatively short time those interviewed may well feel let down. Some form of **feedback and action** should therefore be made apparent at the earliest opportunity.

SELF-REPORT QUESTIONNAIRES

In self-report questionnaires managers are asked fairly straightforwardly **what training they think they need**. The manner of putting the question varies from providing a list of courses to tick to providing a list of skills to tick; sometimes the managers are simply given a blank sheet of paper. The problems with this approach are that the managers may not know their own training needs, may not know enough about the training courses on offer, and may regard the questionnaire as just another piece of paper to be filled in and leave it in their in-tray, or fill it in negligently.

Self-report questionnaires are more useful on the technical and financial side than on interpersonal relationships. A good questionnaire begins by providing some background information and asks the respondents to refer to their year's objectives or to think of their most recent critical incident. Then it asks respondents to tick relevant courses or to tick the skills and knowledge they feel they lack. Some typical answers include:

- Management training   Statistics

- Management of people
- Encouraging creativity
- Joint problem-solving
- Problem definition
- Management by objectives
- Experimental design.

Survey methodology
Finance
Negotiating skills
Interviewing
Technical updating
Influencing company policy.

These answers are not condensed, except in the area of technical updating. They are a good example of the lack of detail which most self-report questionnaires yield. The technique is very frequently used, but cannot seriously be recommended.

STRUCTURED INTERVIEWS

In a structured interview the trainer visits a number of managers with a standard list of prepared questions which it is hoped will throw light on their training needs. Clearly the questions will vary from company to company and from situation to situation, but once the list is prepared it should remain **constant across all interviews**, otherwise any differences that appear between interviewees may be due to the questions they have been asked rather than to any real differences. One typical set of questions is as follows:

1. What sort of things in your job give you most **satisfaction**?
2. What **changes** would be needed to make your job more **effective**? **Who** could make these changes?
3. What sorts of **activities** take up a lot of your time? Does this please you?
4. How far are you **responsible** for planning the way you use your time?
5. What proportion of your activities do you have **no choice about**?
6. Which aspects of your work **interest** you the most? Which the least?
7. Where is the work you do **initiated**?
8. Do you often come **under pressure** for quick results? **Where** does the pressure come from? **How** do you react?
9. How are your **standards of performance set**? By **whom**?
10. How do you get **feedback** on the results of your work?

11. How, and by whom, does the work you are doing get **stopped**?
12. How much **public presentation** of your work and your department do you have to do?
13. Do you find yourself working very much in **committees**?
14. How much do you have to do with the **data processing** department?
15. Do you have much to do with **unions or staff associations**?
16. Do you find the job **different** from what you were expecting?
17. Has any job you have been involved with **failed to reach completion** because of lack of technical knowledge or skill on someone else's part?
18. Have you any skills you feel are being **inadequately used**?
19. Where do you see your career going over the next **year**? The next **five years**?
20. What **training** have you **had**? Do you remember any training as particularly useful, or useless? Why?
21. What **training** do you think you **need**, either that you know is already available or that you would like to see introduced?
22. What kind of person would you advise the organization to recruit to **replace you** if you were to move on? What technical knowledge should they bring with them? What training and experience would you want them to be given in the first three months? What advice would you give them? What sort of mistakes do you think they would make at first?

Some questions will be more fruitful than others. Questions 9 and 10, for example, did not work with some technical/professional managers since they had not considered that setting standards of performance and organizing feedback systems was a useful activity: for them, the technical job set its own, unique, non-negotiable standards of performance. In the case of a company legal department it was held to be unethical and an invasion of privacy to even attempt such a thing, since it implied that their legal qualifications were in some unequal one with another and did not represent the ultimate statement of legal competence! Questions 18 and 22 usually unleash a great deal of information, regardless of occupation.

The results should ideally be **analyzed independently by two or more people**. In this way, any classification which emerges has the added reliability of having been arrived at by two or more separate individuals, and is less likely to be influenced unduly by one strong set of values. Generalization should wait until all the data have been sifted.

Structured interviews are usually better than self-report questionnaires for anything other than the most straightforward needs diagnosis, but they do take time. Only some of the questions will pay off, and it may be difficult to achieve standardized administration between two interviewers, or from the same interviwer on different days. The critical incident technique may yield more information faster, but carries a greater implied commitment to action.

DIARY METHOD

In this method, those involved are asked to keep diaries which **record their activities under a variety of headings**; this record is then analyzed to deduce the demands being made on the individual, and the skills needed to do the job. This form of analysis moves away from the identification of deficiencies towards the description of **actual** performance, and the deduction of **ideal** performance; this feature can help to obtain people's commitment to the work involved in making the record.

Diaries can be general (attempting to cover a whole range of potential needs) or highly specific (when one or two needs are to be examined in depth). For example, a supervisor in a garment factory was asked to keep a diary to assist in the introduction of new procedures under the 1974 Health and Safety at Work Act. She was asked to place a tick in the appropriate space each time she had to deal with one of the following:

- **Workshop tidiness**

    - materials obstructing free passage
    - made-up goods obstructing free passage
    - dangerous goods stacked at unsafe heights
    - personal belongings lying around.

- **Machine maintenance**

    - machines being serviced with power on
    - untrained people attempting to service machines
    - unsafe parts not being properly disposed of

- machines left uncleaned
- operatives transferring machines without permission
- machines not being switched off during breaks.

- **Personal**

  - long hair in danger of being caught
  - smoking in prohibited areas
  - liquid refreshment being passed around at work stations
  - shoes making foot controls difficult to operate
  - pregnant operatives lifting heavy weights.

The supervisor ticked each item and used a code to show whether she had taken action herself, told someone else to take action, or taken no action at all. She was not asked to state how long each incident had lasted, or who else was involved.

Much fuller diaries have been sought in order to obtain a broad picture of the activities carried out by managers. In the example below, managers were asked to record the length of time spent in each activity, who else was involved, and the degree to which the activity was planned.

- **Activity**:   Talking on the phone; with one other face-to-face; with more than one other face-to-face; and was the contact scheduled? touring (inspecting the work place); mail handling, other paperwork; lecturing; travelling; operational work.
- **Contact**:   Alone, with boss; with secretary; with subordinates; with colleagues (i.e., peers reporting to the same boss); with peers (i.e., people of similar level not reporting to the same boss); other senior; other junior; external (specify); new contacts.
- **Interruptions**:   In own office; other (specify).
- **Nature of activity**:   Crisis (drop everything to sort out); choice (need not have done that day); deadline (done for a definite time goal); new work (different from anything done before); recurrent task; urgent work; unexpected work.

In addition, mail in and mail out was analyzed, and the whole was supported by a detailed questionnaire. Results were classified into **choices, constraints, demands,** and **skills required**.

In designing a diary the following sequence has proved useful:

1. Conduct a **pilot investigation** to determine the greatest areas of interest, and whether they are general or specific to one or two skill areas.

2. Since the diary is intended to demonstrate the demands being made on the individual, some definition of the **specific demands to be investigated** should be made. Examples might include duration of activity, contact with others, amount of discretion in choosing the activities, need for information about the results of the activities.

3. Each of the desired categories is broken into codes – one for type of activity, one for contacts, and so on. If the length of time spent in each activity is important, then an appropriate breakdown should be offered. It is important to make the job of completing the diary as easy as possible by using ticks or some other simple code rather than seeking substantive written information.

4. A **questionnaire containing the diary** is then assembled, together with a statement of its purpose and instructions on how to fill it in. This is first piloted on one or two friendly individuals, and then sent to a small but representative sample of those from whom the final responses are sought. At this stage, irrelevant questions can be removed and those that have been found difficult to answer can be modified. The method of analysis should be tried out at this stage as well.

5. The full set of questionnaires is sent out, the returns analyzed, and a report prepared on the demands made on respondents, broken down into sub-groups if this is useful. Full discussion of these demands is then followed by **decisions about the needs revealed**, and the early stages of **planning to meet them**.

Diary method can offer a complete and well-aimed account of the key areas of individuals' work and the support they need to do it. It can bring to light the dull, day-to-day training needs that few bother to look for, and it can provide an informative contrast between what really happens and the job description. It does, however, take time to set up and run, and some statistical skill to analyze. Respondents may resent the time taken to complete it, particularly if there is no space to record the time taken filling it in. There is also a slight danger of asking questions because they look nice rather than because they will yield useful information about how the job is being done. Despite the labour, the diary method can be one of the richer sources of information about training and development needs in the organization.

PERFORMANCE QUESTIONNAIRE

This technique is useful particularly at the interface between **individual training needs analysis and organization development**. Having identified the level of individual whose training or development needs are to be investigated, a questionnaire is designed which contains a series of **bipolar statements** – describing, for example, managerial behaviour – with a five-point scale between the poles. Some items from a group of senior managers in an international bank included:

- Prefers to work in the field   Prefers to work in the office
- Is better at relationship   Is better as a technician
  skills
- Reacts   Anticipates
- Prefers action   Prefers evaluation
- Prefers the client to set   Prefers the bank to set priorities
  priorities
- Would rather explain a sit-   Would rather improve a situa-
  uation   tion
- Knows when to cut losses   Does not know when to cut
      losses
- More concerned with short   More concerned with long-term
  term (less than two years   (two years or more ahead)
  ahead)

The questionnaire is distributed to managers of the position under consideration, and if possible to current occupants of the position and those of their colleagues who have a close working relationship with them. Each is asked to think of the most effective holder of the given job they know, or have working directly for them, and to describe him or her on the questionnaire anonymously. Both **good and bad points** should be allowed to emerge. When the completed questionnaires have been returned a second set is sent out. These are exactly the same as the first set, but the instructions now ask the respondents to think of the least effective holder of the given job they know; anonymity is understandably even more important on this occasion. A simple statistical analysis of the comparisons between the two sets of returns will reveal which items discriminate between **perceived effective** and **perceived ineffective** performers. Other analyses will yield a list of items solely associated with effective behaviour, and a list of items solely associated with ineffective behaviour. (The analysis involves no more than counting the number of times each response option is used for each question.) There will be no particular pattern which emerges from some questions, and they may be discarded. In other cases there may be a clear pattern. For example, take the item:

- Reacts.   Anticipates

Suppose that fifty people have responded to both the first (effective) and the second (ineffective) administration of the questionnaire. The results might look as follows:

- (1st administration)   Reacts   0   0   5 15 30 Anticipates
- (2nd administration)   Reacts   20 25   0   5   0 Anticipates

The results are now weighted to reflect the extremity of view expressed. Thus the frequencies in the outside two columns are multipled by 3; the frequences in the next two columns are multiplied by 2; the centre column remains unaltered. The results now look as follows:

- (1st administration)   Reacts   0   0   5 30 90 Anticipates
- (2nd administration)   Reacts   60 50   0 10   0 Anticipates

The difference between the results of the first (effective) administration and the second (ineffective) administration are clear. The maximum frequency for the first set appears at the extreme right-hand side; for the second set at the extreme left-hand side. There is a clear picture of effectiveness in that virtually all votes went for anticipation; there is a clear picture of ineffectiveness in that the great majority of votes went for reaction. An unclear result is obtained when the votes are spread fairly evenly across all five options (a more detailed account of this procedure will be found in Stewart and Stewart, 1981b). The analysis of results thus yields the material from which a picture can be constructed, of both the effective and the ineffective holder of the position. In this way, both information about **behaviour for development**, and **behaviour to be avoided or trained** out can be obtained.

The items which make up the performance questionnaire can be brainstormed or produced by selective interviewing, but the best method seems to be to conduct a short series of **repertory grid interviews**, which will yield results already in bipolar format. This method is discussed later in this chapter. The performance questionnaire has the advantages that the information has been generated directly by those who are likely to be involved in any action for change that may follow, and concerns **real people and real events**. It therefore provides a good basis for asking whether the characteristics revealed should be perpetuated or changed. It also tends to generate information of a kind which is directly observable and amenable to change, rather than personality statements which make for difficulty in observation and may not be possible or proper to try to change. The main drawbacks are that it requires that there be at least thirty (and preferably fifty) respondents for the statistics to be reliable, and it is therefore unlikely to be of use to very small organizations or at the top layer of any organization, unless great care is taken not to try to generalize the results beyond the immediate group surveyed. Further, if the questionnaire is not couched in terms which are in the **language and culture of the people responding**, and if they are not asked to respond about real people, the result will be a poor response rate and resort to 'ideal' types. This in turn leads to **unrealistic or inappropriate statements of needs**.

CONTENT ANALYSIS

This technique presents the analyst with an unusual opportunity to conduct a diagnosis of training or development needs which does not impinge directly on those being investigated. This **non-reactive research** depends on obtaining access to written records of various kinds, and going through them systematically to extract training needs. It is possible to look for skills being exhibited, for deficiencies being shown, for demands being made, or for all three. It can be done on a group basis, or for an individual; since historical data are being used, no one in the field is being disturbed, nor will the information be faked for the occasion.

Sources of information for content analysis can include performance appraisal records, internal memoranda, letters to outside people (customers, suppliers, competitors), complaints, training literature, sales proposals – indeed, almost any written material can prove a valuable source of information. For example, despite the existence of an in-house written communication course, it was clear that the reports being produced by one particular research organization were failing to meet their twin objectives of communicating the research and maintaining a high profile in the market place. It was agreed to undertake a content analysis of a range of reports recently produced. It was also, unusually, possible to gain access to previous drafts of the final reports, so that not only could the finished version be seen, but the contributions of the various reviewers along the way could also be analyzed and training needs extracted. The following were found, with a note of the frequency of occurrence after each:

- **Strategic errors**
  - Facts not distinguished from opinion   7
  - Benefits not clearly stated   5
  - Context missing (and needed)   4
  - Purpose of report unclear   4
  - Political implications of work missed   4
  - Lack of awareness of readers' special needs   4
  - Statements made that could easily be taken out of
      context and misused   3
  - Too much claimed in the title.   1

- **Grammar and syntax**
  - 'Data', 'criteria', and 'media' used with a singular verb 21
  - Subject not agreeing with verb   17
  - Spelling mistakes   15
  - Inappropriate use of brackets   14
  - Misplaced apostrophe in possessive cases   14
  - Misplaced qualifying clause   7
  - Confusion between 'its' and 'it's'   5
  - Use of jargon abbreviations without explanation   4
  - Use of quotation marks to show emphasis   2

- **Presentation errors**

– Unreadable handwriting	5
– Tables too dense	5
– Terms not defined clearly	4
– Results given without mentioning sample size	3
– Paper, to be read verbatim, clearly too long for allocated time	2
– Inconsistent typestyles used on final document.	2

- **Editing and management errors**

– Paper too late for publication deadline	5
– Editor offers clarification; author responds with 'I know what I meant'	5
– Editor puts check mark instead of specifying what is not clear	4
– Editor, having asked for report, forgets why it was wanted.	3

Two courses were set up as a result of this analysis. One replaced the existing report-writing course, which clearly either made assumptions about basic competencies which were not justified in practice, or failed to meet its objective to teach them. The second course was specifically aimed at editing skills. This was partly because they were clearly needed, and partly because senior managers were flattered to be invited on to an editing course whereas they would be insulted by the implication that they needed help with writing skills. It is also worth mentioning that correspondence files were reviewed, revealing the fact that over 50 per cent of replies to external letters began with some variation on 'I am sorry for the delay in replying to your letter . . .'. The improvement in style produced a dramatic change in the management of **customer relations**.

It may require some imagination to trace the places where information truly relevant to the diagnosis of training and development needs may be found, but because it is non-reactive, can be checked, uses historic and usually unfaked data, and can be fitted into odd time corners, content analysis is an attractive technique. New trainers can also be inducted into their jobs by offering them some content analysis in order to help them find their way round the organization and some of its problems. However, care needs to be taken about breaching confidentiality, so that personal records should be used with considerable discretion, if at all. The day-to-day paperwork of the organization will generate enough information for most needs.

BEHAVIOUR ANALYSIS

Behaviour analysis is a special case of content analysis in which **people's actions and statements** are categorized in a **running analysis performed by themselves or by the trainer**. The behaviour of each individual, either alone or in a group, is monitored under a series of simple headings, and a check mark made every time one of the list behaviours occurs. The exact headings will vary with the area of need under investigation, but for a course in general interactive skills the following might be appropriate: proposing, supporting, building, disagreeing – criticizing, seeking information, giving information. The trainer looks for the **overall contribution level** of each person (too high? too low?), and the **relative importance** of the various kinds of behaviour. Building behaviour is usually important in developing a cohesive team, so people low on this behaviour may need help to increase it. People with a high level of proposing and giving information may need help in learning to listen.

Using different categories of behaviour, some ratios can yield useful information. The ratio of **caught** proposals to **escaped** proposals (those that get some attention even if only rejection, and those that get none) can be useful when helping someone to get their ideas accepted; the ratio of **bringing in** to **shutting out** behaviour can be useful for developing teamwork skills – it is frequently observed, incidentally, that those who profess most vehemently the virtues of participative management are those who most seriously exhibit shutting out behaviour. The ratio of **defending–attacking** behaviour to admitting difficulty can demonstrate a person's way of coping with challenge. For help with committees and other groups operating to an acknowledged formal structure, the ratio of **backtracking** to **jumping the gun** behaviour can be useful in helping control and to distinguish between (a) going over old ground or (b) leaping ahead to matters that are not yet ready to be dealt with. Feedback of the ratios, together with charting of changes in the ratios as the training progresses, can provide both an elegant diagnosis and a direct measure of change in the one package.

A full account of the use of behaviour analysis in training will be found in Rackham and Morgan (1977). To make the most effective use of behaviour analysis, simple category systems should be used with very few assumptions about what right and wrong behaviour look like; value judgements occurring too early will impede flexibility of styles and accuracy of self-analysis. **More than one person should be observing**, and the results should be frequently checked against one another. Feedback should be given early and often, as soon as the observations can be shown to be reliable. It should then be possible to depart in a controlled manner from the original training programme to address new needs as they emerge.

TESTS AND QUIZZES

One simple way of assessing training needs is to ask people questions and discover how many right answers they give. In technical areas, this is a useful and neglected approach to analyzing training and development needs.

For example, as part of the diagnosis of training needs of personnel managers, questions could be asked along the following lines:

1. How many warnings must an unsatisfactory performer be given before dismissal?
2. How long must a woman have worked for employer before she is entitled to maternity leave?
3. Give two examples of conditions of employment that might be construed as indirect discrimination against women.
4. Joe has been on the hourly paid staff for five years and four months. How much notice is he entitled to, should we wish to dismiss him?
5. Consider the following list of our suppliers. Tick those that operate a closed shop agreement. Name the main unions recognized by each of them.
6. On average, how long must a newly recruited salesman stay with the company before the cost of recruiting and training him or her is recovered?
7. An executive aged 55 dies while in our employment. His salary was £40,000 plus £5,000 profit sharing last year. What is the payment due to his widow?

It is not difficult to see how this kind of exercise can serve as a diagnosis of training needs, especially if it is self-scored and used from time to time as a progress check, perhaps involving a parallel-form version at the end of whatever remedial work takes places.

In order for this approach to work, the quiz constructor requires a clear idea of the **ground the training needs analysis must cover** and of the **objectives** of any course to which it is linked; the more open the question, the more difficult it will be to score. Interactive skills are less amenable to this approach, since questions which pose a hypothetical situation and then ask 'what would you do?' tend to receive answers of the kind that the respondent thinks are required rather than a genuine response; to make matters more complicated, the respondent may not know that he is doing this. Where factual information is concerned, therefore, the quiz can perform a valuable role; where interact skills or matters of opinion are involved it is less effective and may actually be misleading.

PSYCHOLOGICAL TESTS

There is a mythology about psychological tests which it may be useful to dispel. A test is no more than a **conversation, frozen into a standard form**, so that as near as possible the identical 'conversation' is held with everyone who enters the situation. In this way, any differences which are detected between individuals are likely to be genuine differences and not caused by differences in treatment. That is all. The rest is merely technology to try to ensure that the tests work.

Tests are designed to provide answers to three levels of question: the more interesting the answer, the more difficult it is to provide. At the lowest level, tests provide answers to the question 'Has this person actually done or learnt what he claims to have done or learnt?' These are the **achievement tests**.

- At the next level, tests provide an answer to the question 'Could this person do the things we want him to if we gave him the task and trained him?' He has not done it yet, and has no relevant track record. These are **ability and aptitude tests**.
- Finally, there are tests which try to answer the question 'If we gave him this to do, would he choose to do it?' These are **personality and attitude tests**. They yield the most interesting

answers, and are the most difficult to construct, administer and interpret.

Achievement tests will indicate at once whether there is a training need. Ability and aptitude tests will give an indication of whether the person has the brains or inclination to learn what has to be learnt. Personality and attitude tests (or, more properly, questionnaires, since there are no hard and fast right answers) may help to decide what likelihood there is that any training, development or appointment to a position may be successful.

Achievement tests are simple to score in that the person either produces a performance (typing speed, colour vision acuity, etc.) of the kind claimed, or he does not. Ability tests are fairly straightforward in that a person achieves a score which can be compared with that achieved by other people, and conclusions can be drawn about the probability of his ability to do the job; perhaps for reasons of self-flattery, the level of ability judged necessary to perform many jobs is over-estimated. Personality questionnaires represent a quite different order of difficulty in interpreting. A questionnaire will permit some form of classification of an individual into a particular personality type. This enables the interpreter to say that some occupations will be more congenial than others, or that there may be a preference to tackle situations in one way rather than in another. But there are no absolutely right or wrong answers; there are simply new pieces of **technical information** upon which an individual or a manager has to make some judgement.

Tests and questionnaires are very high-profile techniques and are easy to challenge. It is both technically proper and tactically wise to ensure that the instruments used are properly validated for the kind of people upon whom it is intended that they are to be used. Such tests should have fairly bulky manuals containing a wide range of statistical information about both reliability and validity over a number of different groups of people; instruments which cannot offer this information, and whose proponents are making no systematic effort to produce such information, should be avoided. The best indicator of all is how easy it is to **obtain access** to the instrument; if it is freely available for a fee or licence, then it may not meet the necessary standard. If, on the other hand, the supplier insists that the potential user shows evidence of being qualified to use such an instrument, then it may be worth considering.

REPERTORY GRID

Most kinds of interview carry with them the danger that the results will be **contaminated in some way by the views of the interviewer**. The repertory grid approach is designed to go some way towards preventing this. A grid interview begins with the selection of the topics for discussion, called **elements**. These are concepts, items, people or behaviours representative of the area of interest. Examples of element lists might include:

1. Accidents, to discover the training needs of a safety officer
2. Brand names of competing products or services, to discover the training needs of a marketing manager, or indeed some of the marketing needs of the organization
3. Names of managers occupying the level for which replacements are ultimately to be sought lower down the organization
4. Job activities undertaken by those managers.

Eight or nine elements is usually enough, although it is possible to use the technique with as few as three elements.

The interviewer checks that the interviewee is reasonably familiar with the elements on the list. Then the elements are taken, three at a time, and the interviewee is asked: 'Can you tell me some ways in which any two of these elements seem like each other to you, but different from the third?' If managers' names have been used, the interviewee might say that two of them are usually to be found in the field while the third is normally in his office. Another two might be thought to be approachable while the third was difficult to get to know. Yet another two might be described as fast workers while the third is thorough. Each of these bipolar distinctions is called a **construct**. It is the constructs which yield the information that is sought in a needs diagnosis.

By constant repetition of the process, long lists of constructs can be obtained. The interviewee is then asked to go back over his or her list and to indicate which end of each construct is the preferred choice for effectiveness as a manager, or as an attractive feature of a product or service, or as having importance for a safety officer to deal with. At the end of such discussions with a number of interviewees, the interviewer will have accumulated lists of constructs with value judgements indicated by most of them. It is then possible to group the results in such a way as to produce a picture of the kind generated by other techniques. It is also possible to translate the bipolar constructs quite directly into bipolar items for a performance questionnaire. Note that the interviewer contributes no **content** at all, but merely **guides the process** along set lines.

This technique can be used to accumulate data from a range of people, or it can be used to interview a very few exhaustively. Only construct elicitation has been described; to go on to a full grid requires some more steps in the logic, and may not always be a cost-effective approach for diagnostic purposes. Construct elicitation will often suffice. A fuller discussion of repertory grid and its uses in business will be found in Stewart and Stewart (1981a).

CONCLUSION

A number of techniques for diagnosing training and development needs have been presented in this chapter. They have in common that they are intended to provide a statement of what **people could do better**, expressed in **measurable terms**. The depth to which it is thought worth while to probe, the type of need to be investigated, and the breadth of coverage intended all influence the choice of diagnostic technique. The better the diagnosis, the easier it is to design the subsequent evaluation of the training or development, since the measures will already have been suggested. It has been indicated that desired **behaviours and performance** should be considered first, and translated into **training needs** afterwards; care should be taken not to present needs that are beyond reasonable efforts to accomplish; prospective trainees should participate in the diagnosis, and not have the results suddenly thrust upon them.

Finally, attention may well be given to something strangely seldom addressed when training needs are being considered – the preferred **learning style** of the individual about to be trained or developed. Honey and Mumford (1986) have developed a simple instrument to enable an individual to detect his or her preferred learning style: **activist, reflector, theorist** or **pragmatist**. Most people have elements of all four in their approach, but one or two are likely to predominate, and it is possible for training or development to be designed to take account of the learner's preferred style of acquiring information or skills: it seems unwise to spend a great deal of time and effort in diagnosing training or development needs if no effort is put in to making the subsequent experience 'user friendly'.

REFERENCES

Honey, P. and Mumford, A. (1986) *The Manual of Learning Styles*, 2nd edn (London: Honey).
Rackham, N. and Morgan, T. (1977) *Behaviour Analysis in Training* (London : McGraw-Hill).
Stewart, V. and Stewart, A. (1981a) *Business Applications of Repertory Grid* (London: McGraw-Hill).
Stewart, V. and Stewart, A. (1981b) *Tomorrow's Managers* Today (London: IPM).

FURTHER READING

Guion, R. M. (1981) *Personnel Testing* (London: McGraw-Hill).
Miller, K. M. (1975) *Psychological Tests in Personnel Assessment* (Aldershot: Gower).
Stewart, R. (1982) *Choices for the Manager* (London: McGraw-Hill).

4

Performance analysis

Andrew Stewart

A great deal has been written about performance appraisal; a great deal more has been said. It is odd that, despite all this attention, so few organizations say that they are satisfied with their particular way of conducting appraisals of employee performance. It is all the more strange since the task is, in principle, very straightforward. Two people, one the manager and one the managed, sit down together perhaps once during the year, in order to find answers to the following four questions:

- What did we **set out to achieve** during the year?
- Have we **achieved** it?
- What are we going to do **next**?
- How will we know **if we have done it**?

Anything more elaborate than the above could be said to be complicating a simple matter more than it merits, to the confusion of all concerned. This chapter presents some of the approaches that have been adopted to trying to obtain satisfactory answers to these four questions.

First, some of the more usual varieties of appraisal system will be described, together with a discussion of the performance criteria associated with them. Some comments will be offered about system design, and this will be followed by an account of some of the ways in which organizations try to train their managers to use their systems. Ways in which systems can be monitored and controlled will be presented, and then two further issues will be explored which often cause difficulty: **assessing potential**, and **problem performers**. Some future trends will also be discussed. Finally, there will be a simple checklist to help managers to ensure that all the necessary steps towards a successful performance appraisal interview have been carried out.

VARIETIES OF SYSTEM

People do not learn unless they are given **feedback on the results of their action(s)**. For learning to take place, feedback must be both **regular** and **frequent**, should register both **successes** and **failures**, and should follow soon after the relevant action(s). In the daily rush of getting things done, much of this can be forgotten or not put into effect. Performance appraisal schemes give people the chance to learn how they are doing, to correct their mistakes and to acquire new skills. Since manager and appraisee are together reviewing past performance and planning to meet the needs of the future, it should follow that some of the necessary conditions for the **successful management of change** are also being met. A performance appraisal scheme can also offer the opportunity to consider and agree longer-range targets for achievement, thus making positive growth more likely for the organization, and avoiding the trap of doing nothing more than daily 'firefighting'. Finally, since employees are expensive, it makes sense to try to encourage their best efforts. A performance appraisal interview can be one of the most motivating events in an employee's year; badly handled, it can be a disaster.

There are usually four parties to an appraisal: the appraisee, the appraiser, the central planning and personnel departments, and external bodies such as training boards, trade unions and bodies set up in the interests of equal opportunity legislation. The interests of the first two parties should dominate; if the main focus is either planning or defence, then the chief objective of the exercise may be lost.

Appraisal systems may be used for three main purposes: **remedial, maintenance** and **development**. A system should have a mix of all three; systems become out of balance if any one purpose predominates. If the **remedial** purpose is foremost, then the appraisal interview may become a disciplinary interview, and the form a charge sheet. If

maintenance is the main objective, then the process can become a short, skimped, perfunctory ritual. If there is too much emphasis on **development**, then the focus falls on the next job rather than the one presently in hand, and the interview may be construed as a promise of future progress.

Above all, the appraisal interview is a time for **listening**. The appraisee probably has a good idea of how his performance appears to him, and this is unlikely to be badly at variance with his manager's view: indeed, there is some evidence that an appraisee is likely to be harder on himself than his manager intends to be.

Many variations in appraisal systems have been tried in order to support the basic purpose of **looking backwards in order to look forward**. The chief ones appear to be:

1. **Eligibility**: all staff, or managers and salaried staff only
2. **Appraiser**: immediate line manager, technical specialist, personnel specialist, 'grandfather' or 'grandmother' (manager's manager)
3. **Employee access**: employee sees all the form, some of the form, or none of the form
4. **Self-appraisal or preparation for counselling form**: used, or not used
5. **Past performance only**: or past and present performance measured
6. **Measurement against**: performance targets or objectives, rating scales of performance, rating scales of personality, or no measurement criteria specified
7. **Rating scales**: present or absent, together with variation in the number of divisions on the scale
8. **Opportunity to set targets for future performance**: or not
9. **Discussion of training and development needs**: for present job, for next job, or for longer term
10. **Potential rated**: on a one-dimensional scale, a multi-dimensional scale, or no formal rating of potential
11. **Discussion of salary**: forbidden, mandatory, or optional
12. **Appraisal interviews**: frequency and regularity
13. **Disputes**: resolved by appeal to manager's manager, or personnel, or no procedure
14. **Appraisal forms: who may see**: and for what purpose

15. **Use of forms: for central planning** purposes
16. **Use of forms: for day-to-day management** and **coaching** purposes.

Each of these variations is held to be helpful by different practitioners, depending on the circumstances in which they are working. It is not possible to offer a single best method, merely a selection from which a choice may be made. The area which seems to cause the most anxiety, however, is the link with salary. If salary is seen as compensation for work done, then perhaps the link with performance is more tenuous. If salary is used as an incentive – to reward outstanding work and to encourage rising standards – then some form of link seems inevitable. If salary review and performance appraisal occur at the same time, there may be a tendency to drift the rating unjustifiably upwards in order to be able to offer a satisfactory increase. One way to prevent this is to have both performance and salary rated on the same scale and in the same way, but to have the events occur **six months apart**; in this way, all concerned understand the system, but managers have the freedom to vary the salary rating if the employee's performance has either improved or worsened since the performance review.

PERFORMANCE CRITERIA

In order to be satisfactory, both to those directly involved and to the law, the criteria for a performance appraisal system should be **genuinely related to success or failure in the job**, and should be as far as possible amenable to objective (not subjective) judgement. In addition, it is helpful if they are easy for the manager to administer, appear fair and relevant to the employee, and strike a fair balance between sensitivity to the needs of the present job and applicability to the company as a whole.

Most appraisal systems offer some guidance to appraising managers on the way they should measure performance. There are two major kinds of measure: **personality** measures and **performance** measures.

- **Personality** measures have largely fallen into disuse. They are difficult to apply reliably, depend too much on the quality of personal relationships rather than employee performance, and if the employee is judged deficient on a personality measure there may be little incentive or ability to change. Their use is now generally discouraged.

- **Performance** measures have replaced personality measures in most cases. They have two main forms. There are **rating scales**, which are generally printed on the form and held to apply to all employees. There are **objectives**, which are an individual performance measure, agreed between manager and employee. Rating scales allow the measurement of change in one employee over time; they also allow comparisons between employees. They are therefore necessary if the appraisal records are to be used for any kind of central manpower audit, leading to the planning of salaries, careers or succession. They have the disadvantage that not all scales may be equally applicable to all employees, and that managers may not share similar standards in the use of the scales. Objectives give greater freedom to both manager and employee in deciding how performance will be measured. They may also have a greater motivational effect by demanding that standards be discussed and understood by both manager and employee, whereas rating scales can be imposed without the opportunity for understanding. The disadvantage of objectives is that no common yardstick may exist between different appraisers and appraisees. It may be possible, and desirable, to have both rating scales and objectives in one system.

Personality measures might include such items as drive, loyalty or integrity. Performance measures might include accuracy, clarity, analytical ability. Objectives might include 'sell x widgets by y date to z customers'. Clearly these measures are offered in increasing order of precision; some systems have aimed at maximum precision at the expense of measuring what is important but not easily quantifiable. Under these circumstances, a **qualitative** measure, the meaning of which is clear to both parties to the interview, is probably preferable to a **quantitative** measure which assesses with great accuracy something which is not important.

The derivation of performance criteria demands research. A specification for the universally effective employee does not seem likely to be a realistic target. Each organization should evolve its own performance measures, and should monitor them continuously to ensure their relevance. The needs of organizations, and of individuals, **change**: if the performance criteria do not change as well, preferably a little ahead of the need, then the appraisal system will serve no useful purpose, and may even do damage by insisting on performance measures which no longer relate to the work in hand. A variety of methods for establishing performance criteria will be found in Chapter 3 on diagnosing needs.

SYSTEM DESIGN

Each of the four main parties to an appraisal has different but overlapping purposes, all of which have implications for system design.

- The **appraisee** will wish to make a contribution to the appraisal process, which implies a face-to-face interview. If acceptance of the appraiser's **evaluation** is to be indicated, or at least evidence that the appraisee has seen the comments is required, then the appraisee may need to sign the form at the end of the interview. If there is to be an opportunity for **long-term guidance**, then the system will need to provide for planning or objective setting for the future, together with discussion of ambitions, training needs, and abilities not yet evidenced in the work currently being done. If appraisal is to be used for **self-development**, then goals will need to be agreed during the interview, some variety of preparation for counselling form might be helpful, written objectives should be retained by both manager and appraisee, and there should be further mini-appraisals during the year.
- The **appraiser** will want the employee to work to agreed goals, which implies the setting and recording of objectives and personal goals. These goals may need coordinating with those of other employees, which will require control over the timing of appraisals from the top of the organization downwards, with the minimum time lag possible between appraisals at top and bottom, and fairly close coordination and control of appraisals from the centre. Coaching the employee will require the setting of specific performer targets, as much as possible suggested by the employee, including both targets and measures, and both parties will need to keep records and use them for frequent and

regular reviews. To encourage the appraiser to listen to the employee, a preparation for counselling form should be strongly encouraged, and the appraiser may wish to record the employee's comments separately, possibly for later integration. In order to make the early detection of problems more likely, general, open-ended questions should be used concerning aspirations, unused skills, constraints on performance and other self-rating techniques. The preparation for counselling form can be a vital aid here, as can the need for the grandparent to sign-off the appraisal form before the interview takes place. In this way it is also possible to achieve some measure of equity between employees. The management information system can also be used to detect broken trends or unusual patterns if rating scales are being used. If the training of subordinates is to be controlled, then there needs to be a record of both training needs and the extent to which they are being met. If money is being used as compensation, then a salary increase may be communicated at the appraisal interview, since pay and performance are not directly linked. If money is being used as an incentive then, as suggested above, the salary review should be a separate but related exercise.

- **Central planning and control** may have a wide range of purposes, but some of the most common are mentioned here. A manpower skills audit will require that there are some common performance criteria across all employees, and that there be central collation of measures on these criteria. For manpower planning purposes the form may need to record not only the employee's performance as measured on required characteristics, but also information about age, job history, mobility and family circumstances. Succession planning also requires that some form of assessment of employee potential takes place, as objectively as possible, and that information about employee aspirations, judged suitability, and current performance is coordinated. Salary planning may require that the manager gives an overall performance rating across all characteristics, and central collation will be necessary, either with or without intervention, to produce conformity to agreed norms. A record of training needs will be required if overall decisions about training priorities are to be taken on an informed basis. Equity between employees can be monitored by defining and communicating the scope of the scheme to all concerned, by grandparent signing-off appraisal ratings, by central monitoring of both quality and promptness of appraisals, and by a formal system for handling unsatisfactory performers. Problem and grievance detection and handling becomes easier if the employee signs-off the completed form, if the employee is invited to comment on the form, if grandparent or central personnel have the power to intervene in critical situations, and if there is a formally defined and agreed procedure for improving the performance of those judged to be unsatisfactory, followed by a declared system for asking them to leave the organization. Finally, downward transmission of organization objectives can be achieved by centrally coordinated cascading of appraisals, so that no manager is put into the position of having to agree objectives with a subordinate in the absence of his own agreed objectives.

- **Outside parties** can also have interests which impinge on the appraisal system. Local, industry or national codes of good practice can usually be adhered to by ensuring that the performance criteria are relevant to the job, that no group of employees is given special treatment, and that appropriate guidance is offered on the use of appraisals with poor performers. Pay restraint has often been a feature of the political climate; in this case, the system needs to ensure that both immediate parties to the appraisal understand clearly any restrictions on the manager's discretion, and increased use needs to be made of the remaining motivational characteristics of appraisal. Finally, privacy or right of access legislation may require that forms be designed so that the employee can see the whole form, adequate safeguards are in place against misleading interpretation – such as employee sign-off and comment space, a formal grievance procedure is in place, and there is a clear policy about who has access to appraisal data and for what purposes, together with location and duration of storage of records. This is now a particularly sensitive area where any part of the records are stored in a computer.

Rather than approaching this set of problems in terms of the various purposes of the parties involved, it is very common to spend much time and effort designing the paperwork: given the strong arguments sometimes put forward for a blank piece of paper being the ideal appraisal form, some of this enthusiasm may be misplaced. Assuming, however, that the purposes have been thoroughly investigated, certain specifics then need clarification. If **individual objectives** are to form the core of the process, then a common form is simply a blank piece of paper divided down the middle, with objectives on the left-hand side and standards of performance on the right. It is important to offer some guidance so that managers do not try to set too many objectives, try to set objectives to cover the whole job, or set as objectives only those things that can be measured quantitatively.

If narrative summaries are to be used, then the form will contain a list of **key words** – such as accuracy, speed, cash control, or timing – and the manager will be asked to write a two-line summary of the employee's performance on each of these characteristics. This method has the advantage that it does apply **common yardsticks** across large groups of people, but does not demand undue precision. Differences may occur in the way in which individual managers interpret and judge these characteristics, however.

Rating scales require that the appraisee is rated on each characteristic, using a scale with a number of divisions. While useful, rating scales carry some issues which need resolution. There is no point in offering more than five divisions on the scale. Scales with seven, nine, or even thirteen points have been seen, and managers tend to use them as if they were slightly vague five-point scales. There is often dispute about whether there should be an odd or even number of points on the scale. It is possible to avoid this discussion entirely in the following way. Label the points on the scale, avoiding the use of the word 'average', so that the first four are concerned with above-the-line performance and only the fifth records below-the-line work. For example:

- Exceeds in all respects
- Exceeds in most respects
- Exceeds in some respects
- Meets basic requirements
- Fails to meet basic requirements.

In this way, ratings are being made against the **requirements of the**

job and not against colleagues, and the scale can be described either as a five-point scale, or as a four-point scale with an extra box for the unsatisfactory performer. It can also be helpful to offer a separate 'not applicable' box. Any overall rating should follow the separate rating scales, preferably at a distance. It may also be useful to consider a separate column to record **immediate past performance**. This emphasizes the fact that the appraisal is supposed to be a review of the entire previous year, and allows any recent changes in performance to be noted without unduly affecting the rest of the year's evaluation.

Perhaps the most important consideration in system design is to ensure that the system **responds to the developing needs of all those using it**, and to avoid the situation in which an entrenched system dictates inappropriate behaviour by those upon whom it is inflicted.

TRAINING

Appraisal training falls into three parts. They need to be kept distinct and to be carried out in the sequence shown, otherwise confusion and ineffective implementation are almost certain to occur. The first stage involves obtaining manager's **commitment**. The second stage trains them in the **formal systems and procedures**. The third stage trains them in the **necessary interview and interpersonal skills**.

Commitment is best obtained by holding a series of meetings at which all those who will be affected by the system have an opportunity to hear what is being proposed, and to discuss it. It may be helpful to lobby one or two key managers in advance; there should be a clear statement about the purposes of the appraisal system and there should be a readiness to negotiate about system design, but it is better to avoid being side-tracked into form design. This should follow as simply as possible from the agreement of purposes. It may also help to de-emphasize the judgemental role of the appraiser and to stress the benefits that employees will gain from being appraised – in other words, help them discover what they will be able to do as a result of appraisal which would otherwise have been difficult or unlikely. If no such benefits are apparent, the value of the system as proposed must be questioned.

Training in the systems and procedures should occur only **after** commitment has been obtained, otherwise much time will be consumed trying to answer the question 'why' when the training is designed to answer the question 'what'. This stage of the training should include the history of the appraisal system and the organizational problems it is supposed to solve, what actually happens in the interview, how the form is filled in, when, and by whom, who receives the form, what happens to the information, and whose responsibility it is to see that actions recommended on the form are actually carried out. Special emphasis should be given to ensuring that managers understand the **grievance and poor performer procedures**. Practice in handling and completing forms should be offered, together with the opportunity to criticize and spot mistakes in forms already completed. This stage of the training responds well to some form of programmed instruction, either in text form or on a computer.

Training in **skills** depends on successful completion of the previous two stages, otherwise disruption is highly likely. Three training techniques may be worth considering.

- **Role play** is used automatically by many trainers. It can have many drawbacks, including the passivity of most of the audience and the fact that participants can always opt out by stating, correctly, that it is not real life; poorly-chosen role plays can compound these difficulties. Role play can be useful, however, particularly where **attitude change** is important. Trainees can be asked to play the part of someone whose attitude they need to understand, such as someone passed over for promotion. They can also be useful in unfreezing people by trying on a completely new appraisal personality.
- **Real-life counselling** involves one participant counselling another about a genuine work or personal problem, while the remaining participants observe. This certainly lacks the artificiality of role plays, but can get a little sharp. For this reason, perhaps, it is generally a better vehicle for learning counselling skills than the normal role play.
- **Live appraisal of real** tasks involves the following sequence:
  1. A participant performs an **appraisable activity** while the remainder of the small group observe
  2. All prepare to **appraise the volunteer**, who prepares to be appraised
  3. One person then **appraises** while the rest observe

4. All prepare to **appraise the appraisal**, while the appraiser prepares to be appraised
5. One person then **appraises the appraisal**, while the rest observe.

This module can be repeated as often as necessary, and concludes with a general review. The exact nature of the kick-off task is relatively unimportant, so long as there is enough to appraise. Subsequent appraisals quickly become surprisingly real, and the whole approach can be highly successful at making apparent issues of objectives, standards and measurement. **Rich feedback** is essential, and should be as accurate as possible, backed perhaps by videorecording the entire episode. **Objective matters** should predominate, such as the balance of talking at various points of the interview, the amount of time devoted to extremes of performance versus the amount of time used to talk about the regular performance, the use of open and closed questions, and the amount of positive versus negative feedback offered.

An interesting variant is to offer training in **being appraised**. This has worked particularly well where managers have been reluctant to appraise or to be trained. The prospect of their subordinates being better equipped than they are has sometimes led to both appraiser and appraisee being better equipped to fulfil their roles.

The most common issues arising in the skills training stage include:

1. Knowing one's own **biases**
2. Being prepared to discuss both **good and poor performance** in a straightforward manner
3. Using **open, closed** or **reflective questions**
4. Handling **conflict**
5. **Listening** and **summarizing** skills.

The most common pitfalls encountered in appraisal, which therefore require to be looked at in training include:

1. The **halo effect**
2. Creating **extremes of rating**

3. **Talking** too much
4. Failing to support opinions with **evidence**
5. **Inadequate briefing** of the appraisee
6. **Pre-judging** performance
7. Not allowing **adequate time** for the interview
8. Choosing the right **environment**
9. Basing assessment on **feelings** rather than facts
10. Over-stating **weaknesses** or **strengths**
11. Failing to take account of **special circumstances**
12. Basing judgements on **too short a time span**
13. Making **false assumptions**.

Understandably, looking at that list, skills training can be a fairly intense experience which has benefits far beyond the immediate task of the appraisal interview.

MONITORING AND CONTROL

All appraisal systems need constant **monitoring**, and from time to time they need **alteration** of some kind. In the early implementation of a system the designer should look out for two main kinds of misunderstanding.

- Misunderstanding of **terms** may occur, particularly such common ones as 'objective', 'job description', 'man specification', 'training needs', 'development needs', 'counselling', 'personality', 'performance' and 'behaviour'. These may well be familiar to trainers and management developers, but many line managers have no real idea of what is meant by them, or may have developed some eccentric definitions.
- Misunderstanding the **system** will be shown by forms going to the wrong place or being filled in late, inadequate coverage of certain employees or groups, peculiar use of rating scales, or partial completion of the forms.

Later on, as part of a more general research programme, some other types of monitoring may seem possible and appropriate. Appraisal action may be checked by following up the actions recommended on the appraisal forms to see if anything has **actually happened** as a result; the types of **objectives** set can also be reviewed as part of this process. Appraisal predictions, particularly of potential, can be checked to see if they are actually proved to be **correct in practice**. Employee attitudes can be checked, either with a purpose-designed survey or as part of a larger **attitude survey**. Examples of some items that have proved significant indicators of effective interviews in the past include:

- I had a clear idea of his/her career path
- He/she and I had the same idea about the direction of his/her career
- My manager agreed with my rating
- My rating came as no surprise to him/her
- She/he accepted my rating of her/him
- My manager agreed with my rating of her/him
- She/he fitted in with the rest of the work group
- We wanted the same outcome from the interview
- I could visualize him/her as my manager some day.

Whether the interview was conducted in the office or outside, and whether the manager had selected the employee for the job initially or not, were not significantly related to the effectiveness of the interview.

As any survey of employee options will **increase their expectations**, there should be a policy about feedback of results, a method of feeding back locally useful results fast, and a commitment by top management to action should the results indicate a need for change.

IDENTIFYING POTENTIAL

Performance appraisal, as we have seen, is designed to **look backwards in order to look forwards**. The best predictions of potential, using performance appraisal as the basis, are made when the next job is not greatly different from the previous one. The greater the proportion of new demands, the less likely that track record alone will suffice. Performance appraisal seems to be essential but insufficient as a predictor of future performance.

Objections to the use of performance appraisal records for the prediction of potential include the following. Single-scale measures of potential, such as most systems still use, are too simple to permit a full statement of what the employee may be able to do. Although supported with words, it is the number that goes into the manpower planning system. In addition, a statement of the kind 'ready for next move in x months/years', if seen by the employee, can be construed as a promise. Managers' confidence in their ability to make ratings of potential is usually very low, and they are very rarely trained in using the potential assessment part of the form. They thus receive the least support at precisely the point where they feel they most need it. Managers find it difficult to assess potential for positions much above their own or in parts of the organization with which they are not familiar. Promotion solely on the basis of past performance almost inevitably leads to promotion to the person's level of incompetence. Discontinuities in the system will occur, where past performance is a particularly poor indicator of success in the next job – for example, the first move from a non-management to a management position.

Poor performers who are in the wrong job are difficult for the system to detect. For them, appraising potential on the basis of past performance is doubly unfair. Finally, in the absence of experience, the appraisee has no basis for judging whether the post under consideration would appeal to them. The more people know about the job for which they are being considered, the more likely it is that they will succeed in it.

There are many alternatives and adjuncts available to performance appraisal as a means of identifying potential. These include assessment centres, psychological tests, assignments, secondments, peer- and self-assessment and action learning programmes. Ideally, ratings of potential should involve the use of more than one criterion or trait, more than one assessor, and more than one technique. In this way, a more reliable judgement may be reached.

If the performance appraisal system is to play a useful part in the prediction of potential, then it should ensure that appraisal is on the basis of **performance**, not personality; and the performance criteria should be related to success in the job for which potential is being assessed. Appraising managers should be trained to use this part of the form and to extract appropriate information during the interview and at other times. Promises of specific jobs should neither be made nor implied. Preparation for counselling forms should be used. Ratings of potential should be checked as a matter of course, rather than as part of the grievance procedure. There should not be sudden and major discontinuities in the requirements for jobs in adjacent grades. Finally, there should be a buyer's market for important staff.

Unsupported by other techniques, performance appraisal can be seriously misleading as a predictor of potential; but the information which it yields is a vital component of any decision reached by whatever other methods may be used.

PROBLEM PERFORMERS

People perform unsatisfactorily for a wide variety of reasons. The first task is to discover which particular combination of reasons applies in the specific case. The problem may lie in a number of factors:

- **Intelligence** – too little, too much, specific defects of judgement or memory
- **Emotional stability** – over-excitable, anxious, depressed, jealous, sexual problems, neurosis, psychosis, alcoholism, drug addiction
- **Motivation to work** – low motivation, low work standards, lack of organization, frustration, conflict
- **Family situation** – domestic crises, separation from family, social isolation from peer group, money worries
- **Physical characteristics** – illness, handicap, strength, age, endurance, build
- **Work groups** – fragmented, over-cohesive, inappropriate leadership, wrong mix of personalities
- **The organization** – inappropriate standards, poor communication, too little investment and management support, span of control too large, responsibility without authority
- **External influences** – employment legislation, consumer pressure, safety legislation, changing social values, economic forces, changes in location.

The appraisal system can be used as part of the process for dismissing people who do not perform satisfactorily. Alternatively – and preferably – it can be used to **manage those people so that their performance improves**. This can be achieved in a number of ways.

- **Counselling** – self-appraisal, preparation for counselling, some form of job climate questionnaire, vocational guidance, mid-career guidance, medical help, financial counselling
- **Training and development** – as a reward and encouragement, not punishment, set up with precise, measurable objectives, careful monitoring and close follow-up
- **Changing the job** – physical layout, timing, induction, responsibility without authority, no feedback on performance, late or distorted feedback on performance, too many figurehead duties, little or no control over the job content, insufficient warning of changes, shared management of subordinates
- **Termination** – which does not have to be rushed or graceless, can take proper account of financial arrangements, time off to look for a new job, vocational guidance, interview training and exit interview.

Note particularly that there is an option to change jobs **within the organization**. Several appraisal schemes specifically exclude this possibility; the options there are either to improve performance in present post to an acceptable standard, or to dismiss. This runs the serious risk of sending away someone who could do a perfectly satisfactory job if he or she were in the right place. While the logic of not wanting managers to shuffle poor performers around the system instead of addressing uncomfortable issues cannot be denied, it seems potentially wasteful to make a rigid rule that prohibits trying an employee in a different role.

There are particular groups who perform badly simply because they are unhappy or bewildered in some way. These people may include new graduates who are experiencing a mismatch of abilities and assigned task with inadequate induction. Old employees may be feeling that they have reached their ceiling or be experiencing difficulty with the slower learning patterns that can come with older age groups. People without clear career paths will appreciate information and options; people with a sad history in the organization need help to discover whether the problem is real and not merely a reputation which is following them around without justification. The performance appraisal system should be able to generate information, objectives and controls to assist with most of these situations, making the unhappy necessity to dismiss for poor performance rarer, but more sure-footed when it does occur.

FUTURE TRENDS

The only certain thing about today's business environment is that it is changing rapidly and somewhat unpredictably. It follows that no performance appraisal system should expect to be the same in five years' time as it is now. There is therefore a need for continuous monitoring and control of the **relevance of the system to the organization's shifting requirements**. Some of the primary influences on change as it affects performance appraisal include increasing public scrutiny of performance criteria, coupled with open record systems. It does, after all, seem perverse to deny access to information about someone when that someone is the person who might benefit most from knowing it – quite aside from the ethical issue about whether there is any right to deny access to information about an individual to that individual. **Self-appraisal** is a growing component of many systems, and is a logical outgrowth of the open record. The increase of on-the-job training and self-development, wherein people take responsibility for their **own learning**, increases the inevitability of self-appraisal, and matrix management makes the older, hierarchical approach to performance appraisal almost unworkable. Pressure towards professional and technical career paths to parallel the more traditional managerial career progression also puts pressure on performance appraisal systems. Managers have to be better informed about the technology they are managing, or have to hand over some of the responsibility for appraising performance to those who do not manage but do perform a technical or professional function. Special efforts need to be made to counsel those who are experiencing mid-career change, possibly coupled with a personal life crisis. The phenomenon of middle managers who feel that their worth is in question, reinforced maybe by redundancy, is more common. Many more people are now questioning whether they are pursuing the right path, and would welcome informed advice about alternatives. There are pressures to bureaucratize. While it is true that some of these pressures can legitimately be traced to the door of government at various levels, more come directly from within the organization. The first reaction to difficult trading conditions is often to tighten controls and to administer more effectively what is already there, rather than to go all out to discover new ways to do things, or new things to do. Under these circumstances, negative feedback and talk of where people are failing becomes the norm, and the appraisal system become the vehicle for **stifling initiative and motivation** rather than a stimulus to new directions and originality. There is a feeling that smaller business units may be helpful; some organizations have become too large to manage, and breaking up the monolith into more viable pieces needs to be accompanied by local control and adaptation of the appraisal scheme. It may be necessary for the large unit to put things on to a computer, but a manual system may be perfectly adequate for the smaller organization; the move to smaller units offers an encouraging chance to simplify over-elaborate systems. Finally, there is a greater inclination to treat people as valuable investments, not merely as units in a card index or computer file; the return to an organization on investment in good recruitment, selection, induction, appraisal and assessment of potential practices is now more rarely questioned. Performance appraisal systems are being seen as less concerned with discipline, control and record-keeping, and more orientated towards development, self-development and growth. This seems to me to be an invaluable trend.

APPENDIX: PERFORMANCE REVIEW SEQUENCE

The following is offered as a rough guide to the sequence of events which a manager may wish to initiate in order to be fairly sure that nothing of importance in the performance appraisal process has been overlooked.

1. Agree a time and date for the review **well in advance**
2. Arrange for the location to be **private** and **free from interruptions**
3. Set aside **at least an hour and a half**, and possibly two and a half hours
4. Bring **all relevant results and information** concerning the appraisee's performance in his/her area of responsibility
5. Ask the appraisee to review his/her performance in the work situation **point by point**

6. Ask the appraisee about any **problems** which might affect performance
7. Ask the appraisee about the **implications of any problems or events**, and their effect on the individual, the team and the work
8. Ask the appraisee what needs to be done by either of them to help **improve performance**
9. The appraisee should ask about anything which he/she feels is **affecting his/her performance**
10. Agree the **key result areas**
11. The **appraisee** should **set/agree standards of performance** for the next review period
12. The **manager** should **set/agree standards of performance** for the next review period
13. Agree future action
14. Close with a firm date for the **next interim review**.

FURTHER READING

Boyatzis, R. E. (1982) *The Competent Manager* (New York: John Wiley).
Fletcher, G. and Williams, R. (1988) *Performance Appraisal and Careers Development*, (London: Hutchison).
Gill, D., Ungerson, B. and Thakur, M. (1973) *Performance Appraisal in Perspective* (London: IPM).
Handy, C. A. (1977) *Understanding Organisations* (London: Penguin).
Long, P. (1986) *Performance Appraisal Revisited* (London: IPM).
Margerison, C. (1976) 'Turning the Annual Appraisal Systems Upside Down', *Industrial Training International* (February).
Stewart, V. (1983) *Change: the Challenge for Management* (London: McGraw-Hill).
Stewart, V. and Stewart A. (1978) *Practical Performance Appraisal* (Aldershot: Gower).
Stewart, V. and Stewart, A. (1982) *Managing the Poor Performer* (Aldershot: Gower).

5

Managing career choices

Charles Margerison

The importance of a career today is accepted, just as acquiring a trade
was recognized in the days when craftsmanship was the basis for
securing lifetime employment in a prestigious role. The concept of a
'career' now goes well beyond the original legal, medical, educational
and religious professional positions which were the major professional roles prior to the emergence of modern industrial and commercial organizations. Today, when there are a vast number of people
in universities and colleges acquiring qualifications in everything from
accounting to zoology, there is a tremendous pressure for the development of a wider base for **career mobility**. The chief focus for this
pressure is the work situation, and in particular the medium and large
industrial and commercial organizations, together with public service
bodies.

People who have acquired qualifications and skills in a particular
area want to go on and use these and acquire roles in an organization.
However, there are simultaneously the organizational problems of
coordination and management. This brings to the fore different
aspects of career work than the original technical specialization in
which a person qualifies. In developing a career many people have
therefore to look at the extent to which they pursue particular roles
which concentrate more on administration and management rather
than their original specialization.

The concept of the **managerial career**, in contrast to the craft and technical career, has become established only over the last thirty to thirty-five years. The predominance of the managerial role in terms of the status and rewards associated with it has, however, overshadowed the other equally important career roles in industrial and commercial organizations. This chapter concentrates on career roles related to organizational levels and performance criteria. Van Maanen and Schein argued that we should indeed examine 'the person within the total life space and throughout his lifetime' (van Maanen and Schein, 1977); it is important to identify the different **career roles** people can play in the modern organization and the transitions that need to be made for success at the different levels.

A number of approaches have been taken in the literature to the study of careers and career development. Several theories exist which explain careers in terms of **life cycle stages** (Miller and Form, 1951 ; Erikson, 1963 ; Levinson, 1978 ; Schein, 1978). Schein (1978) 'identified' three distinct models: biosocial life cycles, family–procreation cycles and work–career cycles. Within this last group the focus of attention becomes the stages through which managers move as they pursue an organizational career (Super *et al.*, 1957 ; Hall and Nougaim, 1968 ; Schein, 1971). In a different approach Holland (1973) distinguished six major orientations to work. Margerison (1980) showed that British chief executives ranked themselves in priority order as enterprising, social, conventional, investigative, artistic and realistic, in that order on Holland's scale. In looking at managerial career prospects, however, we need to examine the **key role factors** that should be used to assess **career progress** at both the technical and managerial levels.

As the traditions of long service, loyalty and the gradual evolution to a senior executive position in Western industrial organizations have declined, an increasing emphasis has been placed on **performance review and appraisal**. The essential aim of performance appraisal has been to assess people on their merit, and to ensure that promotions and pay reviews are related to a review of performance against agreed criteria. Alongside this has emerged the assessment centre method (Bray and Grant, 1966 ; Byham, 1970) for identifying in particular those with executive potential. These trends reflect the increasing competitiveness of organizational life.

In contrast to these developments are a number of organizationally-orientated problems which have a direct bearing on the development of careers. Van Maanen (1977) identified areas of concern such as the changing values relating to work life and leisure, alienation from work, reduced organizational effectiveness and lack of understanding of adult identity and development.

Too often, the study of careers concentrates exclusively on the managerial or executive role. However for an organization to function adequately it needs to have policies and practices reflecting people's different roles and different expectations. This chapter therefore provides a model for comparing career roles at different levels and functions.

MANAGERIAL CAREERS AND ORGANIZATIONAL ROLES

There are many individual roles in organizations, which enable people to develop their career paths. Careers, according to Hall (1976), are 'the individually perceived sequence of behaviours over the span of the person's life'. However these experiences and activities take place through recognised professional bodies and in employing organizations based on particular roles. The significance of roles at the general level of the organization has been well documented (Katz and Kahn, 1978). In the career context Louis (1980) has developed a typology of **career transitions**, comprising two main categories – **inter**-role and **intra**-role transitions.

Concern has been raised at the extent to which modern organizations force people to **leave their technical specialization role** in order to get promotion within the organization and the reasons for this (Jennings, 1971; Beckhard, 1977; van Maanen, 1977; Vardi, 1980; Veigi, 1983). While financial rewards and higher status may result, they are often achieved at the expense not only of a person's original career interest, but also of **individual and organizational performance** (Peter and Hull, 1969; Jacques, 1976).

A key aspect of this process is the relationship of technical to managerial work. While each person has a personal career line, there is an overall trend which can be seen in Figure 5.1.

When a person starts in the workforce it is usually in jobs at levels that are primarily **technical**.Gradually, the person who is successful is asked to take on more responsibility; this usually involves supervizing the work of other people and therefore involvement in the process of

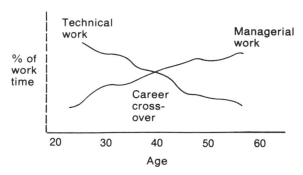

Figure 5.1   Career choice model

management is initiated. More time is spent at the next level in allocating and delegating work, reviewing that work, sitting on committees, ordering resources, budgeting and the various other tasks associated with management. There is for many therefore a definite **role transition** from a technical to a managerial job in terms of the time spent, although clearly the technical background knowledge and experience is usually essential to do the managerial task. Nevertheless as the role of senior managers has been examined in depth only since the mid-1970s, (Mintzberg, 1975; Lau and Pavett, 1980; Kotter, 1982), the task of explaining the **personal processes** of such role transitions is not fully developed.

Driver (1979) postulated that individuals have one of four basic approaches to their organizational careers and personal development – transitory, steady state, linear or spiral, and has drawn on Schein's 'career anchor' scheme of career motivation (Schein, 1978) to develop further an **active passive sub-type** within each main career concept type.

What seems to be missing from previous research are the critical factors that govern a person's **career prospect**. Is it possible to reduce the complexity associated with career assessment to two central factors: **competence** and **achieved capacity to manage**. If we extend this to identify the factors underlying promotion through various roles to a senior managerial position then we should relate achievement specifically to the capacity to manage factor (Jacques, 1976; Stamp, 1981), and competence to a person's experience and expertise.

The capacity to manage others involves not only the desire but the

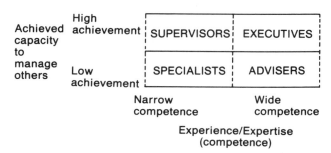

Figure 5.2   Types of role within organizations

ability to **exercise influence in a managerial role**. There are many people who would desire to reach a senior organizational level and have lots of people reporting to them. However, many do not have the interpersonal skills and ability to tolerate ambiguity while at the same time giving direction for action and achieving results through people. It would appear that the capacity to manage others is a very difficult concept to measure. However, most people know what it means. There are few people who voluntarily indicate when they have reached what they believe to be their preferred level; it is always the temptation to take on more than we can do, if only because the incentives – such as the rewards, the status and the fringe benefits that tend to go with managerial roles – are attractive. However, as Jacques (1976) indicated, there are individual differences in capacity and this relates to management as much as it does to any other aspect of life.

Likewise the achievement factor can be applied to the managerial role capacity just as much as it can be applied to a sporting role such as a golfer or tennis player. Figure 5.2 outlines the factor of managerial capacity contrasted with the competence (experience – expertise) factor. This produces four specific roles which have been named the **specialist**, the **adviser**, the **supervisor** and the **executive**.

The specialist

The specialist is a vital part of any organization. Specialists usually have very **narrow experience in a particular area**, such as a research chemist working on one product, or an engineer on one machine. In so far as they have penetrated their particular discipline or function to a considerable degree they do it within narrow boundaries. Very often they have **low inclination to manage others**; their key interest is in pursuing that which they know best. They often like to do their work in their own way and with the minimum of interference. Very often they will not wish to have the responsibilities of administration or of managing others.

Such people are very important in research and development, in planning jobs and in other technical work requiring concentrated endeavour assessing specific issues in depth. While such work must be done and must be done well, it is unlikely that people with such an orientation are likely to make successful managers: they have neither the interest in doing so, nor the experience. While they may be highly achievement-orientated in their own discipline, their achievement level in terms of management is low. Where a specialist shows an interest in managing others his experience and work allocation will need to change in order that he gains opportunities as an adviser, a supervisor and an executive.

The adviser

The adviser usually also has a **low concern for managing others**. However, in contrast to the specialist who acts within a narrow field, the adviser operates on a very wide basis of experience and knowledge. The very nature of his job involves him in working with a variety of clients in different parts of the business. The accounting or finance person will usually, for example, have a wide understanding of the systems applying to production and sales and be able to make a substantial contribution to the personnel department in terms of wage costs. Through his own discipline he therefore picks up a very wide understanding of the overall business. This stands in contrast, for example, to the specialist chemist whose area of expertise does not facilitate the **crossing of organizational boundaries**.

The adviser, therefore, may have wide experience but little interest in managing subordinates. While his achievement-orientation in terms of managing is usually low he may have high personal needs for achievement within his discipline or function. If a person who is in an adviser role shows interest in the managerial role then it is important he or she gain a leadership position in a supervisory role, and if successful then in an executive role to test his abilities and achievement.

The supervisor

The supervisor is a generic term to cover those people who have a **high capacity to manage others**, but only within **narrow functions and disciplines**. They enjoy taking on integrating and administering tasks but do so within specific and limited areas of knowledge and experience. These are usually confined to their traditional area of technical training; they have not usually gone beyond that knowledge and training to acquire the language and skills of other functions. An example could be the foreman in charge of the engineering maintenance area. However it could also apply to an accountant who reaches a high level inthe organization but still has experience of managing people only in the financial area. Where a person shows an interest and ability in managing it is important to assess their performance by widening their range of experience and developing their competence; this can come only through real experience on different jobs.

The executive

The executive is the person who understands the three roles that we have mentioned and brings about an **overall approach** to what has become known as **general management**. He will have a high capacity for gaining achievement through managing others. He will have acquired wide experience and expertise through various job changes and self-development activities. His competence is therefore widely based so he can assess organizational issues on a broad front.

Executives develop a wide picture of the organization through gaining personal experience in managing different functions and tasks. They intially have team leadership experience in a specific area, but then move to manage a **cross-functional team** of people from different backgrounds. From there they often move into a role whereby they manage a part of the organization where they have **profit and loss responsibility**. Beyond this, they can, in large organizations, move to corporate roles involving the strategic management of many profit and loss units or divisions.

The executive role therefore demands widespread competence and understanding of the legal, financial, marketing, operational and personal aspects of organizations, combined with a high achieved capacity for managing others.

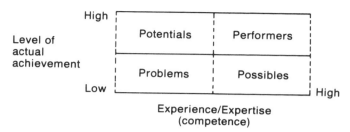

Figure 5.3   Model of perceived career prospects

IDENTIFYING PEOPLE'S CONTRIBUTION PROSPECTS

In addition to the four main career roles identified it is also important to identify how well a person **works in a given role**. It is rare for a person to take on a role and immediately perform to a high level; normally there is a **learning period** during which adjustments are made. In choosing a person for a role we are always taking a risk that they will not learn and adapt quickly enough to perform the duties as required.

How do we assess whether a person can make the transition from one role to another? Organizations use a variety of means – interviews, psychological tests, temporary postings, special project assignments and other means. However, one of the key tests is how well a person is performing in his **present role**. This may or may not have any bearing, however, on a person's output (for example) if moving from a specialist role to an executive role, or from a supervisory role to an advisory role.

Given the significance of the factors of achievement and competence that have already been identified it is useful to outline a simple model for assessing a person's career situation within any role. Figure 5.3 shows a model designed to indicate the **perceived outcome of several role influences** on an individual, regardless of the level in the organization at which he or she is located. It is based on two criteria: the **level of achievement** that a person exhibits in a particular role and the **experience–expertise** (competence) that a person possesses. It is these two factors that are central to effective individual action. The model therefore produces four ways of viewing a person at a particular point in his or her career – namely, as a performer, potential, possible or problem. Let us examine each of these terms.

Performer

Those people who have a **high need for achievement**, and produce results based on a **wide background** of experience and expertise within particular roles.

Potential

Those people who have shown a **high need and level of achievement** but so far **do not have the range of experience or expertise** to do a wide range of work in their professional area.

Possible

Those people, by contrast, who have been exposed to a **wide range of experience** and have **expertise** but have yet to show **commensurate levels of achievement** in a particular role.

Problem

Those people who within particular roles have shown **little achievement** and have a **low level of expertise–experience**.

In any organizational position or level at which a person finds themself, the sum total of the role influences to which he or she is subjected may thus take on any one of the four dimensions.

MERGING CAREER PROSPECTS AND ROLES

Although the roles described provide a general framework for the analysis of organization positions and the skills associated with those positions, they indicate only half of the total picture. People can have a high desire to manage others and wide experience, but they may not have the **interpersonal skills** or **political awareness** to carry out their managerial role as an executive. It is thus essential that the concepts developed from Figure 5.3 be integrated with the roles developed in Figure 5.2.

Role	Role assessment			
	Problem	Possible	Potential	Performer
Specialist				
Adviser				
Supervisor				
Executive				

Figure 5.4   Model for assessing role performance

A person can be a performer in an executive position but may be a problem in terms of his or her contribution to another role such as a specialist. This may be because the person has not occupied the role of specialist for twenty years, during which time the type of work in the area in which they originally qualified has radically altered. This could place the executive performer in the position of a problem specialist if they had to revert to that role. Likewise someone on a specialist role can be a performer in that role but may be a potential in one of the other roles, such as an adviser, through lack of experience–expertise in that role. In assessing people's careers we thus need to examine their **strengths in relation to particular roles**. As shown in Figure 5.4, for every role we need to assess a person's work.

This approach differs from that of Driver (1977) in that it applies regardless of the type of organization concerned or the level at which the individual operates within that organization. A trainee chemist in a bureaucratic organization may thus be a performer in that role but have difficulty in being a performer in a supervisory or executive role. A general manager in a multinational public company may be perceived as a problem in that role despite the fact that in his career he has successfully been a performer at the specialist, adviser and supervisor roles.

Figure 5.4 therefore provides a basis for making assessments within particular roles and a guide for manpower planning. People who wish to progress in their careers are normally expected to show performance in **specialist roles** before becoming advisers. Equally there is usually an expectation that an executive will show prior performance as a supervisor and perhaps as a specialist and an adviser before an executive appointment. However, it is possible that people who can excel in an executive role may not be performers as specialists or advisers. It is therefore important to discriminate when making career promotions. Equally there are dangers in appointing supervisors and executives from people who succeeded as specialists or advisers. The oft quoted example of the best salesman being promoted and becoming a poor manager can be replicated many times with chemists, engineers, computer specialists, teachers, accountants and others.

This is why it is important to identify the capacity to manage amongst those people who are to be promoted into supervisory and executive positions. The work of Ghiselli (1971) is instructive here as is the work of Jacques (1976) and Stamp (1981) on managerial capacity. Essentially those people who will become performers at supervisory and executive levels must have the desire and determination to influence others as well as the competence of experience and expertise.

Margerison (1980) asked chief executives what were the primary influences that had helped them develop as a manager; they cited the following seven items in order of importance:

1. The ability to work with a wide variety of people
2. Early overall responsibility for important tasks
3. A need to achieve results
4. Leadership experience early in career
5. Wide experience in many functions prior to age 35
6. An ability to do deals and negotiate
7. Willingness to take risks.

The chief executives therefore recognized too the capacity to manage depended heavily on the ability to work and influence others combined with wide experience and expertise plus high achievement. However, the important point emerging from this research is that the executives stressed the importance of **early leadership** and **wide responsibility at an early age**, building on their personal need for achievement.

Many specialists and advisers have high achievement but either do not wish to or are unable to, influence people appropriately in the managerial role. It is increasingly recognized that career paths must be charted for such people so that they obtain the status, prestige and rewards that go with senior positions of a non-executive or supervisory level nature. A number of important organizations have now established such specialist–advisory career paths. This is akin to what happens already in hospitals where a specialist surgeon does not need to become chief administrator to gain similar rewards or status, or in a university where a professor can be a specialist or adviser and a senior member of the organization. There is a danger that in business organizations we will lose people who perform as specialists and advisers because they feel that career progress will cease if they do not become executives.

CAREER PATHS AND POSITIONS

Some implications

Clearly, a person's interpersonal/political skills and their leadership style have a lot to do with their overall success as a manager. However, far more attention needs to be paid to the person's **individual desire to manage** and **capacity to achieve** in that role as a basic measure of potential. Few organizations when selecting new managers from outside put sufficient emphasis on these issues. Alongside this there needs equally to be the recognition of experience being related to **outputs**, rather than just a series of involvements with different kinds of work.

It is possible to deduce from current research a number of strategically important issues which organizations need to address if they are to obtain the people who are best equipped to contribute to the organization in the future. It is also important to have a policy which enables the lessons of such research to be put into practice. This would certainly include many of the following points:

1. People should be **tested through experience in various roles** and enabled to gravitate to that which is their strongest role.
2. The **reward structure** of the organization should provide status as well as financial comparability to those who excel in specialist and advisory roles as well as supervisory and executive roles.

3. The organization should enable people to **assess themselves** as specialists, advisers, supervisors and executives through direct experience, through projects, task forces and other limited-term activities.
4. The organization should be sufficiently **decentralized** to enable people identified as executives at a young age to have a profit and loss responsibility to test their capacity to manage.
5. Opportunities should be provided for people who have been identified as supervisors and executives prior to the age of 30 to have an early chance to take on leadership positions where they will have the various **inter-personal issues** to manage.
6. The organization **structure** should facilitate the movement of people to meaningful jobs in different parts of the business where competence at a wide level can be tested through experience.
7. The organization should establish a **career development structure** that is taken as a serious part of managing at all levels, so that appraisal and counselling form an integral part of management practice.
8. The organization should recognize people's **strengths** and enable them to work in roles where they can perform best without having to change for salary or status reasons.
9. A consequence will be that **specialist and advisory roles** are given equally high status as supervisory and executive roles.
10. The assessment of people for supervisory and executive positions should assess their capacity to **manage others**, rather than just technical performance in a previous role.

REFERENCES

Beckhard, R. (1977) 'Managerial Careers in Transition: Dilemmas and Directions', in Van Maanen, J. (ed.), *Organizational Careers: Some New Perspectives* (London: John Wiley).

Bray, D. W. and Grant, D. L. (1966) 'The Assessment Centre in the Measurement of Potential for Business Management', *Psychological Monographs*.

Byham, W. C. (1970) 'Assessment Centres for Spotting Future Managers', *Harvard Business Review*, 48 (July–August).

Driver, N. C. (1979)'Title', in Katz, R. (ed.), *Career Concepts in New Dimensions in Human Resource Management* (Englewood Cliffs, N.J.: Prentice-Hall).

Erikson, E. H. (1963) *Child-hood and Society*, 2nd edn (New York: W. W. Norton).

Ghiselli, E. (1971) *Explorations in Managerial Talent* (Santa Monica, Cal.: Goodyear).

Hall, D. T. (1976) *Careers in Organizations* (Santa Monica, Cal.: Goodyear).

Hall, D. T. and Nougaim, K. (1968) 'An Examination of Maslow's Need Hierarchy in an Organizational Setting', *Organizational Behaviour and Human Performance*, 3, pp. 12–35.

Holland, J. L. (1973) *Making Vocational Choices: A Theory of Careers* (Englewood Cliffs, N.J.: Prentice-Hall).

Jacques, E. (1976) A General Theory of Bureaucracy (London: Heinemann).

Jennings, E. E. (1971) *The Mobile Manager* (New York: McGraw-Hill).

Katz, D. and Kahn, R. L. (1978) *The Social Psychology of Organizations* (New York: McGraw-Hill).

Kotter, J. P. (1982) *The General Managers* (New York: Free Press).

Lau, A. W., and Pavitt, C. M. (1980) 'The Nature of Managerial Work: A Comparison of Public and Private Sector Managers', *Group and Organizational Studies*, 5, pp. 453–66.

Levinson, D. J. (1978) *The Seasons of a Man's Life* (New York: Knopf).

Louis, M. (1980) 'Surprise and Sense Making: What Newcomers Experience in Entering Unfamiliar Organizational Settings', *Administrative Science Quarterly*, 25(2).

Margerison, C. J. (1980) 'How Chief Executives Succeed', *Journal of European Training*, 4(5).

Miller, D. C. and Form, W. H. (1951) *Industrial Sociology* (New York: Harper & Row).

Mintzberg, H. (1975) 'The Manager's Job: Folklore and Fact', *Harvard Business Review*, 53(4), pp. 49–61.

Peter, L. J. and Hull, R. (1969) *The Peter Principle* (London: Souvenir Press).

Schein, E. H. (1971) 'The Individual, the Organization and the Career: A Conceptual Scheme', *Journal of Applied Behavioural Science*, 7, pp. 401–26.

Schein, E. H. (1978) *Career Dynamices: Matching Individual and Organizational Needs* (Reading, Mass.: Addison-Wesley).

Stamp, G. (1981) 'Levels and Types of Managerial Capability', *Journal of Management Studies*, 18 (3).

Super, D., Crites, J., Hummel, R., Moser, H., Overstreet, P. and Warnath, C. (1957) *Vocational Development: A Framework for Research* (New York: Teachers College Press).

Van Maanen, J. and Schein, E. H. (1975) 'Improving the Quality of Work Life: Career Development', in Hackman, J. R., and Suttle, L. (eds), *Improving Life at Work: Behavioural Science Perspectives* (Washington, D.C.: Department of Labor Monograph Series, 2).

Van Maanen, J. (1977) 'Summary: Towards a Theory of the Career', in Van Maanen, J. (ed.) (1977) *Organizational Careers: Some New Persepctives* (New York: John Wiley).

Vardi, Y. (1980) 'Organizational Career Mobility An Integrative Model', *Academy of Management Review*, 5(3), pp. 341–55.
Veigh, J. F. (1983) 'Mobility Influences During Managerial Career Stages', *Academy of Management Journal*, 26(1), pp. 64–85.

6

Business strategy and management development

Andrew J. Mayo

There is an air of grandeur about the phrase 'management development strategy'. If you asked me what my management development
strategy was, I would probably describe a series of activities – in
training, appraisal and succession planning. Related to the business
objectives? 'Well, not specifically, of course, but since all these things
are important in getting better managers, they must contribute to the
business mustn't they?'

But 'investing in people' is as important an investment as any other,
for people are our most precious resource. Just as we would not allow
a product strategy in isolation from a market strategy, so surely our
organization and people development strategy must be integrated,
too. A strategy is a chosen route to meet objectives we have set for the
future; within it will be programmes and activities that take us along
that route.

Self-evident, then, are the conclusions that:

1. We must clearly understand current business objectives and be
   able to interpret their **implications** – for skills, experience, organization, etc.
2. We must assess the **routes open to us** to get from here to there
3. We must **choose** a strategy, **articulate** it, and **integrate** it as part of
   the business plan

4. We must define **programmes** and **activities** which make the strategy **happen**.

Our eye is primarily on the future, not limited by today. In ICL, this is the result of an evolutionary process. This case study is a story of a Managing Director and his team becoming convinced that management development was a necessary and positive contributor to the achievement of new business objectives, and to the guarantee of a future.

ICL – BACKGROUND

ICL was born in 1968 from the merger of ICT with English Electric Computers. In 1976 it increased its small systems capability and geographical presence by the takeover of Singer Business Machines, and in 1984 it merged with STC. It is today a fourth autonomous division of Fujitsu, trading as ICL PLC. Its turnover today is some £1600 million, it employs 20 000 people and operates in 70 countries. With an established reputation and expertise in mainframes and independent of government finance, its strategy in the late 1970s was based on high revenue growth. But in 1980 a series of factors – strength of sterling, inflation, interest costs and a cost base too large for a falling revenue growth rate – led to a crisis.

NEW DIRECTIONS

It is at such a point in a company's history that a revolutionary change is required, and as is frequently the case it is **new leadership** that gave the driving force for change for ICL. A completely new way of thinking – on technology, on markets, on collaborations, on competition – was needed, and fast. A more or less completely new team was brought in at the top including the Chairman, Peter Bonfield and, based on a strategy of succeeding on our own, the work of change commenced. A new mission was set for the company implying significant changes in direction – defined as 'ICL is an *international* company dedicated to applying *information technology* to provide profitable high-value customer solutions, for improved operational and management effectiveness'. Objectives were set designed to build strength as a major European player in information technology (IT) and to focus on specific markets – to be known as a system integrator with a reputation for quality. Key strategies were to be built around:

- High-value solutions to **defined markets**
- Commitment to **open systems** – providing customers with greater flexibility in choice of manufacturer and confidence for the future
- **Collaborations** – to gain market or technical leverage
- **Organizational responsiveness** – to react to the fast-changing market
- Focus on **systems and solutions for the customer**, and on providing real added-value for the customers in running their businesses.

All these were put together by the new team with speed, energy and commitment.

NEED FOR A NEW 'MINDSET'

But to quote the new Managing Director:

> I gradually realized that I lacked the levers to transfer my strategic insight into the hearts and minds of the organization so that they shared the imperative. They had to know why, not just what. An impressive programme of communication was not enough. I got immensely frustrated – thousands of bright people all working hard but not buying in to the directions.

The new Managing Director also used the well-worn Second World War saying of a US General: 'I have seen the enemy and he is us'. He came to the conclusion that the ICL 'culture' was going to beat him if he did not do something about it. An approach which was rather more subtle than confrontation was needed. ICL had to be led to change its company culture, and integrate its strategic thinking with an organization capability that could match the challenges of the changes needed. In other words, part of the business strategy for change had to be in the development of the **thinking and capability of the management group,** in resetting the cultural values of the organization, and in creating an environment where change could be managed and high individual performance achieved. What were the changes required?

Shifts were needed in the way that people **thought,** made their **decisions** and conducted their **lives** in the company. For example:

Movement	Goal
• In outlook from being **technology-led**	to being **marketing-led**
• From **tactical** and **short-term** reaction	to strategic, **long-term** planning
• From a focus on **internal** problems	to **external** focus
• From trying to do **everyting**	to concentrating on **specialized target markets**
• From people operating on a **parochial level**	to having a **company commitment**
• From being **procedure-bound**	to being **innovative** and **open minded**
• Away from being a UK exporter	to being a **global competitor**
• From a **bureaucratic** ER (Employee Relations) dominated **reward system**	to paying for performance on an **individual basis**

But, in the early 1980s, although the company had a new strategic vision and knew it had to change, it had a legacy of values, beliefs and ways of doing things – partly due to its multi-merger history – that prevented a quick response to that vision. It urgently needed a purposeful approach to changing direction. As a start, there was a need for an **explicit and common statement of values,** so (in 1982) this was prepared and fully publicized to all staff as 'The ICL Way'. On the front cover was the statement 'The Way We Do Things Around Here'. Inside were a set of seven commitments for all staff and obligations for managers designed to set out the way that ICL wanted to run its business. It was greeted with a predictable mixture of support and cynicism, but it was the beginning of a completely new cultural

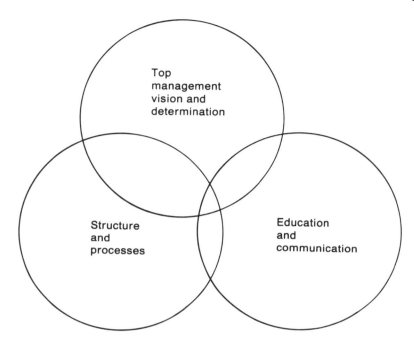

Figure 6.1   Culture change

framework. The symbolism of publishing such a document was probably more important than the detail of its content. The seven
commitments provided a reference and guide for activities within the
Company.

In itself, publishing the ICL Way with the values and beliefs we
wanted was just a start, a signal of interest. It was a statement of the
environment we wanted, but it could not in itself **create that environment**.

ACHIEVING TOTAL CULTURAL CHANGE

What is needed to achieve the reality of change? Not for the first time,
I find the simple model of three interlocking circles very helpful (see
Figure 6.1). In the first is 'top management vision and determination':
a truism always worth repeating. Organizations take their cue from
top management; they are the symbols of 'what counts', the most

critical role models. How many companies have been shaped by the vision of a leader? In ICL, we were at the starters' line – this whole programme was **initiated by** (not sold to) **the top**.

The second circle is in Figure 6.1 'Education and communication': and everybody has to understand **why** we are doing what we are doing, to know **why** they have to shift their thinking. At a time when many companies would have said: 'Training is a postponable expenditure', major educational programmes were commissioned. Entitled 'Core Management Development Programmes', the objective was to communicate the strategic vision, and the rationale behind it, to all managers in ICL, and to reinforce the values of The ICL Way. The four levels in the programme were strategic management at level 4, business management at level 3, work unit effectiveness at level 2 (for first-line managers) and then for new managers, management induction at level 1. On to this core could be grafted individual or sub-group training needs and solutions.

To put this into place, ICL engaged C. K. Prahalad of the University of Michigan and Gary Hamel of the London Business School. They immersed themselves in ICL and its strategies and, together with internal resources, developed the top-level and most critical programme – 'Developing Strategic Capability'. Level 4 was particularly significant, as it was aimed at that group of managers who never felt they needed or had time for training. The Managing Director insisted that the Board attended – and they did: a one-week event studying global competitiveness, strategic resourcing, organizational options with world-class tuition and time to apply the learning from case studies to real ICL issues.

These core programmes began to address overall management capability; at the same time we introduced a Marketing programme. Using Insead's MARKSTRAT model, and working with professors from Tulane University in the USA, we instituted a six-part course in professional marketing to introduce the vital element of **customer focus**. In the mid-1980s, we commenced a third major cultural education programme for all employees, based on 'Quality as a way of life', again in support of the business objective to be known for **quality** and **reliability**.

No one could be in any doubt that top management was serious. Never in the history of the company had the Board not only backed such a training programme, but actually attended themselves, nor had it ever been the case that any programme was mandatory for managers. There was (and is) no doubt about the credibility that the programmes attracted, especially and significantly at the senior levels. The programmes became the core of our management development and training portfolio.

The third circle in Figure 6.1 is 'Structure and processes'. You can help people to think differently, but if you maintain the old processes – the cement of the organization – you will soon crush the brave new world. You cannot tell everybody about strategic management and then review them only on the current quarter's revenues. Existing **processes, structures** and **systems** must be re-examined, and new ones created overtly to support the new directions.

We will here focus particularly on those that are relevant to **people, growth and development**.

MANAGING FOR PERFORMANCE

ICL has invested significant amounts in establishing skills and standards in the areas of objective-setting, creating specialist career structures, effective employee appraisal, career management and making organization–people issues an integral part of the business. The appraisal discussion between an individual and his or her boss is the foundation stone of people development, and ICL has given it particular attention.

I find it interesting that 'elementary' management processes like objective-setting and appraisal are always on the agenda – our determination that a high-performance environment was needed left us no choice but to make them real for everybody, every year: we could shift from traditional annual negotiated general pay increases to individual management discretion – with each increase being based on performance, commitment and contribution – only if we did so. In the process, we needed to maintain good union relations. In 1988 we launched a worldwide 'consolidation' of our experience in these areas entitled 'Investing in People'. Consisting of four handbooks for managers – 'Managing for Performance', 'Developing Individual Capability', 'The New Employee' and 'Planning' – and an employee handbook, it put into a set of coordinated processes all we had been working on during previous years. What made it different was the linking together of these people processes into an **integrated**, attractively packaged whole. Each of these handbooks was backed up by extensive training materials designed to equip all managers with the necessary knowledge and skills.

Our reward systems for managers were made to include sharply focused individual incentive schemes. These are used ruthlessly to reinforce 'what counts' in the organization. Although bonus is partly dependent on business results, an equal part is dependent on achievement of **personal objectives** – which frequently include organization or management development issues. We also use the concept of thresholds as a 'forcing function' to kick-start the organization on certain key issues. We were deeply concerned at the low hit-rate on employee appraisal, so we put an **appraisal threshold** into the bonus plan – if you don't get 95 per cent of your unit with quality appraisals in each year – no bonus! This particular threshold supported very effectively the broader drive on 'managing for performance'. Put simply, it underscored the cultural value we wanted to instil – that the manager is the person solely accountable for his or her staff: their performance, their reward, their development and so on.

RESOURCE PLANNING

What practical link is there between **manpower planning** (organization flow and movements) and **individual development planning?** Some questions worth answering are:

- What is the effect of **internal promotion policies** on manpower planning?
- How many people with potential can an organization **cope with effectively?**
- How can the company plan for **adequate succession** in the longer term?
- How should the company plan careers for **'high flyers'?**
- How can the company tell that its organization is 'healthy' in terms of building the **quality** of its future manpower needs?
- Is there a rational way of determining the intake of **young people** each year?

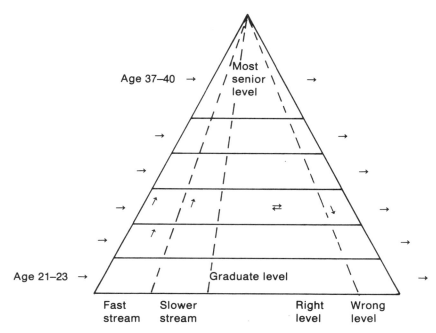

Figure 6.2   Resourcing an organization for the future

These questions go beyond the traditional short-term approach to succession planning.

The model I am going to describe has the following outputs:

- Ratios of people with upwards potential to others in a 'healthy' organization.
- Annual input of young entrants.
- Expected annual resourcing plans at each level.
- A basis of comparison with today's reality leading to actions in resourcing and development to come closer to the desired position.

Manpower planning is traditionally concerned with relatively **short-term flows in, out** and **within** an organization. Its time-scales are significantly shorter than those we want to think about in career planning. How can we look at resourcing in the longer term? A summary of the model that has been developed is shown in Figure 6.2.

Based on visualizing an organization as broadly pyramidal, and dividing it into levels of accountability, the first question one must ask is: 'What ratio of internal versus external resourcing meets the need of our business?'. This may not be the same at all levels in the pyramid: for example, many organizations would say that whereas they wish to hire and train all their own young people, they do not want to bring in externally at the top. They would, however, like perhaps a 10–20 per cent replacement rate at mid-levels from outside. Others, of course, are 'cradle-to-grave' companies, who try to avoid any external recruits above the bottom two levels and promote entirely from within. (The effect of a 100 per cent internal promotion policy is very significant for the number of people needed to be available for promotion).

Every loss from the organization (or sub-set if we are looking at a part of it) requires replacement from without or within. An internal replacement will come – eventually if not immediately – from a promotion up the ladder of accountability. Modelling requires therefore some division of the population at each level into bands of 'potential'. This is shown in Figure 6.2: on the left-hand side is an A stream which includes people perceived at the time of assessment to be able to go at least two levels further forward, and to move relatively fast. The second, the B stream, is that which includes others with 'upwards' potential – maybe not more than one level, and generally moving slower. The company believes that everyone at any time has potential to grow; however people will grow in different ways. The next two classifications are those who have reached their right level (as currently perceived) – and the majority will have 'lateral potential' (i.e., will be able to move sideways or take greater responsibility). There will also be a group who are truly 'the round pegs in the round holes', and want to stay that way. Lastly, few organizations escape from having a few people who have, according to Professor Peter (Peter and Hull, 1969) reached their level of incompetence.

Let us now go through the model in thirteen steps, and using a worked example.

Setting up the resourcing plan (see Figures 6.3 and 6.4)

Step 1   Choose a **discrete population of statistically significant size** (>100); this could be a unit, a function, or a whole organization.

POPULATION:

DATE:

ORGANIZATION RESOURCING

LEVEL / GRADE	NO. AT THIS LEVEL	'A' STREAM				'B' STREAM				C/D STREAMS ALL LOSSES	ANNUAL RESOURCE REQD				TARGET RATIO A:B:C+D	ATTRITION RATE (%)
		Entry age	Promotion p.a.	Other losses p.a.	No. required	Entry age	Promotion p.a.	Other losses p.a.	No. required		Total	% INT	INT	EXT		
2	40	38				45										5
3	150	34				40										7
4	600	30				35										10
5	1800	27				30										10
6	3000	24				25										12
7	5000	21				21										15
8																

A   Substantial potential; 2 levels min   B   Some potential; 1/2 levels further   C   Sideways potential   D   Right job, right level

Figure 6.3   Steps 1–4

POPULATION:

DATE:

ORGANIZATION RESOURCING

LEVEL [/] GRADE	NO. AT THIS LEVEL	'A' STREAM				'B' STREAM				C/D STREAMS ALL LOSSES	ANNUAL RESOURCE REQD				TARGET RATIO A:B:C+D	ATTRITION RATE (%)
		Entry age	Promotion p.a.	Other losses p.a.	No. required	Entry age	Promotion p.a.	Other losses p.a.	No. required		Total	% INT	INT	EXT		
2	40	38	1 (to Level 1)	1		45	–	–		1		100				5
3	150	34		3		40		3		4		80				7
4	600	30		20		35		20		20		80				10
5	1800	27		60		30		60		60		70				10
6	3000	24		120		25		120		120		80				12
7	5000	21		250		21		250		250		0				15
8																

A Substantial potential; 2 levels min   B Some potential; 1/2 levels further   C Sideways potential   D Right job, right level

Figure 6.4 Steps 1–7

Step 2   Define the **'levels of accountability'** (i.e., real promotional rungs), and determine the number of jobs at that level. (It is of interest to do the model both with the existing number and that projected by the traditional manpower plan for a time in the future.)

Step 3   Set the **'speed of progress' parameters** for the *A* and *B* streams. Figures should reflect the reality of the organization, or how it would like to be – e.g., the *A* stream might enter the most senior level at 40; the *B* stream top out at the next level down at 45 (on average).

Step 4   Determine the **voluntary attrition rates** for each level – the anticipated level based on the best information available. (This is an attrition rate requiring replacements, so should not include forced separations in redundancy situations.)

           Note: If this is a *sub-set* of the organization it must include transfers out of this sub-set.

Step 5   Estimate at each level what proportion of the annual losses might **typically come from each stream**.

           Note: Due to 'career plateauing', 'mid-career comfort', etc. above middle levels it is usually mainly people of potential who will leave voluntarily. It is useful to track this in the analysis of attrition.

Step 6   Determine the percentage of **internal promotion** that is desired at each level.

           Note: If we have taken a sub-set of the organization, 'transfer in' will count as external resourcing.

Step 7   Estimate the **average annual promotion rate** out of Level 2 to the top level. (Express as a decimal if necessary.)

Step 8   For Level 2, add all promotion and loss figures to give the **annual resource requirement** for that level.

Step 9   Based on the assumption in Step 6, split the annual resource requirement between **internal** and **external**.

Step 10   Cascade downwards by distributing the 'internal requirement' to the 'promotion p.a.' boxes of the *A* and *B* streams respectively at the next level.

Step 11   Repeat steps 8–10 until the bottom right-hand box is filled. This will be the **annual young entrant intake**.

Step 12   For each level determine the number required at that level in the A and B streams as follows:

N = (Promotion p.a. + Losses p.a.) × Average time between levels.

Step 13   Calculate the ratio of A: B: $(C + D)$ for each level.

In the example shown, it might be said the span of control (looking at the second level) is far too low and that there is a clear case to take out a level of management. However, this is not untypical of technical organizations where a number of specialists are employed who may or may not have small teams.

We could conclude from this example that this population of 10,600 people with the desired internal–external resourcing percentages shown:

1.   Needs a resourcing intake of some 1,170 p.a. at the bottom level
2.   Requires some 40 per cent or so at each level to be people with some potential
3.   Requires a recruitment plan as shown in the column headed 'EXT'.

1 and 2 would be reduced by lower loss rates, slower progression up the ladder, and a lower internal resourcing rate.

Such an exercise will have limited value without a **comparison with reality**. By undertaking an 'organizational audit' (i.e., assessing the potential of each individual) we can find the actual ratio of people with upwards to people with lateral potential.

The model was applied in three ways in ICL – to the overall UK organization; to each separate Division; and to the Personnel function as a whole. As a result, numbers of young entrants were increased substantially. Several weaknesses in parts of the company in respect of future long-term resourcing were discovered, and action was taken over a period to strengthen those parts. In understanding the 'speed of progress' dynamics we realized we were not accelerating high-potential people fast enough; frustrated ones left for greener pastures. So we brought the average age of entry to 'senior' management grades steadily downwards. Over the years 1986–90, we came much closer to

POPULATION:

DATE:

ORGANIZATION RESOURCING

LEVEL (/) GRADE	NO AT THIS LEVEL	'A' STREAM Entry age	Promotion p.a.	Other losses p.a.	No. required	'B' STREAM Entry age	Promotion p.a.	Other losses p.a.	No. required	C/D STREAMS ALL LOSSES	ANNUAL RESOURCE REQD Total	% INT	INT	EXT	TARGET RATIO A:B:C+D	ATTRITION RATE (%)
2	40	38	1 (to Level 1)	1		45		-		1	3	100	3	-		5
3	150	34	2	3		40	1	3		4	13	80	10	3		7
4	600	30	6	20		35	4	20		20	70	80	56	14		10
5	1800	27	35	60		30	21	60		60	236	70	165	71		10
6	3000	24	90	120		25	75	120		120		80	420	105		12
7	5000	21	240	250		21	180	250		250		0	-	1170		15
8																

A Substantial potential; 2 levels min B Some potential; 1/2 levels further C Sideways potential D Right job, right level

Figure 6.5 Steps 1–11

POPULATION:

DATE:

ORGANIZATION RESOURCING

LEVEL [/] GRADE	NO. AT THIS LEVEL	'A' STREAM Entry age	Promotion p.a.	Other losses p.a.	No. required	'B' STREAM Entry age	Promotion p.a.	Other losses p.a.	No. required	C/D STREAMS ALL LOSSES	ANNUAL RESOURCE REQD Total	% INT	INT	EXT	TARGET RATIO A:B:C+D	ACTUAL RATIO DIVN 1	DIVN 2
2	40	38	1 (to Level 1)	1	8	45	–	–	–	1	3	100	3	–	20:0:80		
3	150	34	2	3	20	40	1	3	20	4	13	80	10	3	13:13:74		
4	600	30	6	20	104	35	4	20	120	20	70	80	56	14	17:20:63		
5	1800	27	35	60	285	30	21	60	405	60	236	70	165	71	16:23:61		
6	3000	24	90	120	630	25	75	120	975	120	525	80	420	105	21:23:56		
7	5000	21	240	250	1470	21	180	250	1720	250	1170	0	–	1170	29:34:37		
8																	

A Substantial potential; 2 levels min   B Some potential; 1/2 levels further   C Sideways potential   D Right job, right level

Figure 6.6 Steps 1–13

our 'preferred' balance of internal promotion vs external hiring at senior levels.

The model clearly lends itself to a spreadsheet format and this is to be strongly recommended. It is dynamic, and needs review every six–twelve months to ensure the validity of the assumptions. Using different assumptions we can measure **sensitivity** in various areas. For example, taking out a whole level of accountability in organizational design will have a significant effect.

Why is this approach so helpful?

- It focuses attention on **future resourcing**, beyond the normal horizons of manpower planning. It looks at long-term succession capability
- It models an 'ideal' organizational dynamic, and comparison with the **actual situation** provides a basis for intelligent resourcing strategies
- It works against a **stop–go policy of resourcing**, particularly with young entrants.
- It disciplines an organization to concentrate on **potential**, and regularly assess it
- It can show relative strengths and weaknesses across parts of an organization and lead to actions for a **better balance**.

THE LINKS WITH MANAGEMENT DEVELOPMENT

There are two truths that must be recognized when thinking of the individual:

- Most real development comes from **experience**
- Growth through experience is a **time-consuming** process.

There is of course a continual requirement for **training**: everybody needs it to provide individual growth and meet the needs of the changing business. But the **management of experience to develop potential** is the real task. We should therefore take a longer-term view of individual growth in parallel with the organization resourcing model described above.

Is it obvious which stream people fall into? By no means. Will the high flyer naturally develop himself or herself consistently with the future business needs? Again – not necessarily, even though many will say 'the best people look after their own development'. Career management is a **mutual responsibility** between the company and the individual.

How, and when, should one assess potential? This is, of course, an ongoing process based on appraisal and development discussions, but there are three formal points where some special assessment may be made. These are:

1. on recruitment
2. two–three years in, and
3. eight–ten years in.

At recruitment, of course, (particularly of young entrants), we are not just recruiting for their first job. We must always aim to recruit high-potential people, especially at the bottom end. In some companies, (Natwest, Shell) they start a high-flyer 'cadre' group here although at present ICL does not. Then, after the induction, settling period and some real work, two–three years on, comes the opportunity to set the first 'aiming point'. This is the first division in a technical company between those who look like being future managers and those who may become specialists. (Their growth and development is, of course, of critical interest, too, and we ask senior functional managers to take specific interest in 'specialist career streams' for which we have developed and published structures.) Then, six years or so further on is a time formally to assess 'general' management potential in the context of where the business is going and the skills that are going to be needed in the future. In our appraisal and development discussions, we encourage managers to discuss a career aiming point for the next five–six years, so that we can plan the skill and experience enhancements necessary to fill the gap.

We may make regular assessment of potential, but how often should we make a thorough study with an individual of his or her **career direction**? This will depend on the structure of career patterns in a particular organization. In an information technology company like ICL – and in many other similarly – there are a number of distinguishable technical–professional–specialist options, where documented and published achievement–experience–reward ladders have been put in place, leading to a level equivalent to senior manager. The majority in fact follow these; the danger, however, is that equal thought is not given to the management of 'general' careers, providing people with a mix of experience that will be needed in a general management role. It is important therefore to provide the opportunities for assessing career direction (see Figure 6.7), and not just – as in a typical appraisal discussion – 'what would you like to do next?'. Hence the concept of 'career aiming points' – where should you aim for over the next five–ten years? If we can get a good fix on that we can do something about managing the journey, and not rely on luck and opportunism (which will, however, still play their part in a turbulent world).

Every genre of job can be characterized by two parameters – the **skills** necessary to do it effectively, and the **experience** necessary in order to enter the job. These are normally defined in the context of the 'person profile' in a recruitment specification. With greater or less sophistication, selection procedures seek to assess them when a job is available. More difficult is to assess against the criteria for a job two, three or four levels higher than the current one, but more and more companies are now doing this. As can be seen from Figure 6.7, there are certain points at which it makes sense to assess whether the person should continue on a specialist path, or be trained more generally. Personal choice will come into it, but it is a service to all concerned to back up that choice with some more objective assessment, particularly if the path to general management is chosen. Such an assessment needs to be against the criteria of a **future job**. Thus one can take the experienced young entrant (after two–four years) and assess for junior management capability, and one can assess junior managers in a function against the criteria for general management.

In ICL we researched skills and experience felt to be important for a general manager in the environment of the mid-1990s. There are standard techniques for researching such areas, and we produced sixteen personal abilities and seven ideal areas of experience (these are shown in Figure 6.8 and 6.9). The personal abilities (or skills) were split into those that were readily assessable in the **current job** (e.g., team leadership, delegation) and those that should form the basis of attendance at an **assessment centre**. The design of this is standard, occupying two days with a requirement for a significant strategy paper prepared beforehand covering a competitor.

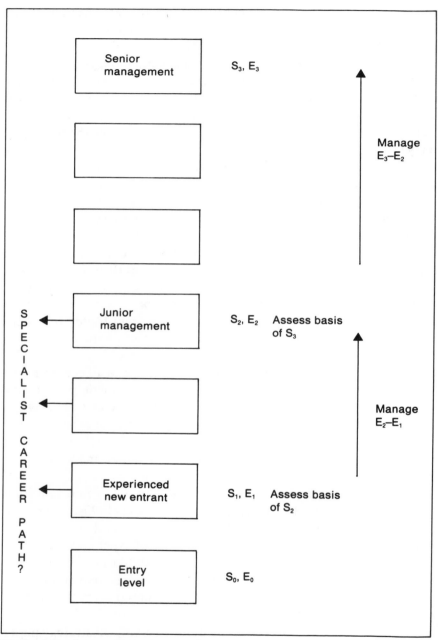

Figure 6.7   Assessing career paths

SKILLS AND EXPERIENCE REQUIREMENTS FOR GENERAL MANAGEMENT IN THE NINETIES

EXPERIENCE

E1   Line management accountability for specific deliverables relating to ICL business results

E2   Significant financial accountability on a P&L basis

E3   Significant man management accountability through at least two levels of subordinate management

E4   Commercial experience – personal involvement in customer or supply negotiations

E5   International experience – preferably through physically working outside the home country or extensive involvement in working with overseas countries

E6   Staff appointment – responsible for helping influence line managers to perform better in a particular function of their role

E7   Has operated within more than one division of ICL or other companies

Figure 6.8   Skills and experience research experience

PERSONAL SKILLS

S1   A good team leader, able to weld together and use complementary knowledge and skills towards common objectives

S2   A good strong people manager; fair/firm, balancing task/team/individual needs; known for developing staff

S3   Able really to delegate accountability

S4   A strategic thinker – demonstrates vision, sees the overall company as well as local need, formulates tactics within an articulated strategy

S5   One who sees and seizes opportunities within agreed strategies

S6   Able to multiprogramme a large number of issues at any given time, and keep all major accountabilities in progress

S7   Able to balance long-term requirements against short-term objectives

S8   Able to manage conflict constructively, with peers or peer groups

S9   Able to adapt his management style to different needs

S10   Skilled at communication, especially verbally

S11   A good probing relevant questioner, and a good listener

S12   Ready to take necessary decisions at the right time

S13   Able to cope with stress without loss of performance

S14   A controlled risk taker

S15   Has a personal presence that can command respect internally and externally

S16   Personal ambition – desire and drive to take senior accountability

Figure 6.9   Skills and experience research: personal skills

The centre is called a 'career guidance centre' and we ask Divisions to put forward for a limited number of places those they believe have the highest potential. Directors act as assessors and take part in a thorough verbal feedback together with the current manager and personnel manager, agreement on career paths and development steps are documented, and, finally, one of the Directors acts as mentor to each individual. To date about 60 per cent of those attending have been assessed as future general managers, the others as capable of a high level in particular functions. All attendees get the same treatment, thus creating some 'top level' ownership of a group of potential general managers for five–seven years hence.

Continuity of a programme such as this is critical; though exercises have been modified the events are now standardized and the assessors experienced. It is now the intention to extend the principle down to another level, and begin the assessing of more junior employees for junior management.

To return to the context of long term resourcing. We may conclude that there is a population of 'corporate interest' that should include the senior management group and also those who might be in the group in the future. We can now redraw Figure 6.2 and the shaded areas will show such a population (Figure 6.10).

Actually developing such people, once potential is identified, is the next challenge. Some key aspects are:

- Knowing what the **aiming point** is
- Planning the 'building blocks' of experience to **add-value constantly** – defining the skill and experience profiles of senior positions in the organization
- Planning the **use of training** – making sure it can be applied quickly in real life
- Keeping in mind the importance of **international exposure** – in building knowledge, personal skills and attitudes for people both in 'developed' and 'less developed' areas
- Setting up **growth opportunities within the job** – exposing people to new areas (e.g., junior management boards)
- Identifying 'development positions' and using them – positions where good people can make an **early contribution without specialist prior knowledge**.

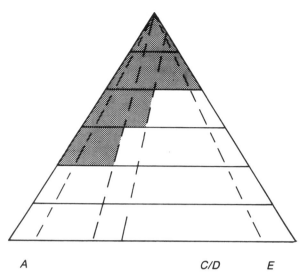

Figure 6.10   Population of 'corporate interest'

Let us now return to Figure 6.1. The extent of top management vision and determination was, as we have seen, clear. The programmes were very professionally put together, and there is no case on record of anyone feeling that a particular module was not extremely valuable to them – especially, and significantly, at the senior levels. These programmes were set up to **support the strategies**, and did so very successfully.

I have discussed some supporting processes in the 'professional personnel' area, but these were not enough; we needed some that were an integral part of the business. Most significant is a process we call the 'Organization and Management Review (OMR). There is a business review quarterly cycle with the Chairman and Managing Director, and each of these is followed with an OMR. The process is cascaded down at least two levels further throughout the world; it is entirely owned by line management. With particular focus each quarter, it takes stock of **where we are** and **where we need to move to** in terms of organization and skill needs, and highlighting the development of key individuals.

Secondly, there is a special meeting of the Management Executive called the 'Executive Review Panel'. Meeting monthly, and led by the

Chairman, it reviews all **major organizational and people policy changes**, and discusses all changes and movements in the top executive population of 150 or so. It recommends the adaptation of changes to people development policies, and members are involved personally in the career guidance centres referred to above.

HAS IT WORKED?

Culture change is a long-term process – one must work on a five–ten-year time-scale. There is no doubt that a common language and approach in the senior management group has been developed, and that the shifts in thinking mentioned earlier have happened. We need, however, to get more at the hands and feet, as well as the hearts and minds. A Phase 2 of the core programme has been developed, as well as an updating and extension of the original Phase 1 which was more 'education' than 'training'. Having put managers through a 'mind expansion' awareness programme, we are now focussing much more on **tools**. And so Phase 2 is about **processes** – literally 'The Way We Do Things Around Here' – and will be run with operational teams working out together how a particular ICL process (whether it be business planning, people development, communications, or whatever) can be made effective in each part of the organization.

Attitudes of staff and management in terms of individual reward have certainly changed. A major cross-company opinion survey is carried out every year and progress here measured. Is the company losing less good people? Attrition rates for senior management have dropped and the company is going less to the outside market. But we need longer to track this.

Can we relate any bottom-line success to the investment that has been – and is being – made? ICL would not pretend to do that; what has been done is an act of faith, a firm belief that clear strategies must be supported with the development of people. Nevertheless, the bottom-line results have been very encouraging, showing a steady growth in profit and in turnover through the recession, particularly through 1986–87, when a number of companies in the industry suffered quite badly; return on capital employed is one of the most respectable in the industry.

WHAT HAVE WE LEARNED?

- Success in business strategies is dependent on **people**, their **growth** and **development**
- You are unlikely to change business direction without reorientating the **knowledge, skills** and **thinking** of your people
- Management development and **manpower planning** must be linked
- Top management **vision** and **ownership** is essential
- **Processes** and **systems** must move **in parallel**, and are as important as education
- Management development people must be intimately in tune with **where the business is going**.

One is always conscious of how much more needs to be done, but ICL have tried to get strategy and management development linked. If we had not done so, we would not be where we are now. In the process, we have developed a number of techniques and approaches, which hopefully can be usefully applied elsewhere.

REFERENCE

Peter, L. J. and Hull, R. (1969) *The Peter Principle* (London: Souvenir Press).

PART III
THE PROCESS OF MANAGEMENT
DEVELOPMENT

7

Styles of learning

Peter Honey

In 1962, Chris Argyris wrote a piece where he predicted, amongst other things, a move

- **from** management development (MD) programmes that teach managers how they **ought to think and behave**
- **to** MD programmes with the objective of helping managers to **learn from experience**.

Argyris argued that this was necessary because 'no one can develop anyone else except himself. The door to development is locked from the inside'. He went on to say 'Emphasizing the *processes* of how to learn, how to diagnose administrative situations, how to learn from experience – these are timeless wisdoms'. His conclusion was that we needed less emphasis on developing **learned** managers and more on developing **learning** managers.

When I first read Argyris's words I agreed with them wholeheartedly, but I did not fully understand how to put them into practice. What exactly were the processes of learning from experience? How could management development be designed to give managers practice in these 'timeless wisdoms?' Was it just a question of exposing managers to different experiences and hoping they would learn from their successes and mistakes? Or did the **mechanics of learning** need to be understood and designed into management development as a deliberate strategy?

I confess I did not know the answers to any of these questions. Then I came across Kolb and Fry's Learning Style Inventory together with their description of the stages involved in the business of learning from experience. This was the spur for many years of work in conjunction with Alan Mumford which has resulted in our publication *The Manual of Learning Styles* together with its sister booklet *Using Your Learning Styles* (Honey and Mumford, 1986). In these publications we describe the full range of uses of learning styles information in the design of programmes, boss–subordinate relationships and selection of structured learning activities.

In this chapter I intend to concentrate on the use of learning styles by individuals for themselves. I shall:

1. Examine the **process of learning from experience** and the short cuts that managers characteristically take to truncate the process.
2. Describe four different learning style preferences and show how they affect the **sort of activities managers learn from**
3. Show how it is possible to develop an under-developed learning style, and thus become an **all-round learner from experience**.

THE PROCESS OF LEARNING FROM EXPERIENCE

Alan Mumford and I have developed a simplified version of Kolb's (1984) model, which looks like Figure 7.1.

It is rare to find managers who consciously discipline themselves to do all four stages as shown in Figure 7.1. Depending on their learning style **preferences** (this will be discussed later) managers are likely to take a number of liberties with this process. Some of the better-known ones are as follows:

1. **Indulging at stage 1** (i.e., rushing around have lots of experiences and keeping frantically busy but never bothering to review, conclude or plan). Such managers equate having lots of experiences with learning and conveniently assume that if they have experienced something they have automatically learned from it.
2. **Limiting stage 1**, by repeating familiar experiences over and over again and never going out on a limb and trying something new or different.

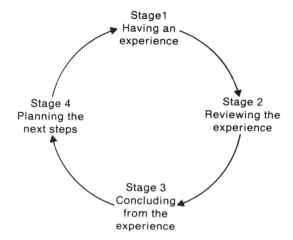

Figure 7.1   Learning from experience

3. **Avoiding stage 1**, by being a 'voyeur' and learning from other people's experiences rather than their own. This reduces the risks of making mistakes or making fools of themselves.
4. **Avoiding stage 2**, by having a stock of conclusions and forcing experiences to fit the conclusions rather than the other way round. This is closely akin to the well-known process of jumping to conclusions; the attraction is that it avoids the uncertainty of reviewing an experience and the hard work of reaching conclusions.
5. **Limiting stages 2 and 3**, by collecting ready-made ploys and techniques of the 'how to do it' variety. This avoids the hard work of discovering and creating practical ways of doing things via reviewing and concluding experiences.

Of course, all these short cuts are entirely understandable and all have their attractions but they, and others like them, all tend to erode the amount that can be learned from experience.

DIFFERENT LEARNING STYLE PREFERENCES

Kolb and Fry's Learning Style Inventory suggested that people develop preferences for different learning styles in just the same way that they develop any other sort of style – management, leadership, negotiating, etc. Naturally I did the inventory to discover my own learning style and started to include it on training courses I ran as a way of predicting who would respond in what sort of way and so anticipating learning difficulties. Unfortunately, whilst I bought the theory, I found some problems with the inventory itself (the predictions were not as accurate as I wished and the face validity was poor). Accordingly, together with Alan Mumford I started to develop a questionnaire that would do a better job.

After three years of intensive experimentation the result was an eighty-item questionnaire that takes ten minutes or so to complete and identifies whether someone is predominantly:

- **Activist** – what's new? I'm game for anything.
- **Reflector** – I'd like time to think about this.
- **Theorist** – How does this relate to that?
- **Pragmatist** – How can I apply this in practice?

The learning styles tie in with the four stages of learning from experience as follows:

- A preference for the **Activist** style equips you for **stage 1**
- A preference for the **Reflector** style equips you for **stage 2**
- A preference for the **Theorist** style equips you for **stage 3**
- A preference for the **Pragmatist** style equips you for **stage 4**.

All-round learners, or 'integrated learners' as they are sometimes referred to, are clearly best equipped to manage all four stages. However, most people develop learning style preferences that assist with some of these stages, and hinder others.

These style preferences very significantly affect the sort of activities that people learn best from.

Activists

Activists learn best from experiences where:

1. There are **new experiences/problems/opportunities** from which to learn

2. They can engross themselves in **short 'here and now' activities** such as business games, competitive tasks, role-playing exercises
3. They have a lot of the **limelight/high visibility**
4. They are **thrown in at the deep end** with a task they think is difficult.

Reflectors

Reflectors, on the other hand, learn best from activities where:

1. They are encouraged to **watch/think/chew over activities**
2. They are allowed to **think before acting**, to assimilate before commenting
3. They have the opportunity to **review what has happened**, what they have learned
4. They can reach a decision **in their own time** without pressure and tight deadlines.

Theorists

Theorists learn best from activities where:

1. They have time to explore methodically the **associations and inter-relationships** between ideas, events and situations
2. They are in **structured situations** with clear purposes
3. They have the chance to question and probe the **basic methodology, assumptions or logic** behind something
4. They are **intellectually stretched**.

Pragmatists

Pragmatists learn best from activities where:

1. There is an obvious link between the subject matter and a **problem or opportunity on the job**
2. They are shown techniques for doing things with obvious practical advantages **currently applicable to their own job**
3. They have the chance to try out and practise techniques with **coaching/feedback from a credible expert**

4.   They can concentrate on **practical issues**.

The dovetailing between learning styles and learning activities has led us to postulate some key questions that people can use to assess the appropriateness of different learning opportunities.

Key questions for Activists

- Shall I learn **something new** – i.e., that I did not know/could not do before?
- Will there be a wide variety of **different activities**? (I do not want to sit and listen for more than an hour at a stretch!)
- Will it be OK to **have a go/let my hair down/make mistakes/have fun**?
- Shall I encounter some **tough problems and challenges**?
- Will there be other **like minded people** to mix with?

Key questions for Reflectors

- Shall I be given adequate time to **consider, assimilate and prepare**?
- Will there be opportunities/facilities to **assemble relevant information**?
- Will there be opportunities to listen to **other people's points of view** – preferably a wide cross-section of people with a variety of views?
- Shall I be under pressure to be **slapdash or to extemporize**?

Key questions for Theorists

- Will there be lots of opportunities to **question**?
- Do the objectives and programme of events indicate a **clear structure** and **purpose**?
- Shall I encounter **complex ideas and concepts** that are likely to stretch me?
- Are the **approaches** to be used and concepts to be explored 'respectable' – i.e., **sound and valid**?
- Shall I be with people of **similar calibre** to myself?

Key questions for Pragmatists

- Will there be ample opportunities to **practise and experiment**?
- Will there be lots of **practical tips and techniques**?
- Shall we be addressing **real problems** and will it result in **action plans** to tackle some of my current problems?
- Shall we be exposed to **experts** who **know how to/can do it** themselves?

BECOMING AN ALL-ROUND LEARNER FROM EXPERIENCE

A knowledge of learning styles can either be used to help dovetail learning activities to suit learning styles or be used as a starting point for **self-development**. The latter option is the one I want to explore now.

The advantages of having a broader range of learning skills are that you become a more effective learner from life's events and, if you are a trainer as I am, you are more likely to be able to help a greater range of trainees by being a more effective trainer. I want to illustrate how I personally have made use of a knowledge of my own learning style preferences to become a more effective trainer, as a means of trying to encourage readers to develop their own learning skills and thus become better at helping other people to learn.

THE TRAINER'S LEARNING PREFERENCE

I have been a trainer since 1965 but it was only in the late seventies that the implications of my own learning styles really dawned on me. My own preferences are for the Activist and Pragmatist styles. This means that my strengths and weaknesses tend to be as follows:

- An an Activist, my strengths are that I am:
  - flexible and relatively open minded
  - happy to have a go
  - happy to be exposed to new situations
  - optimistic about anything new and therefore unlikely to resist change.

- As a Pragmatist, my strengths are that I am:

  - keen to test things out in practice
  - practical and realistic
  - businesslike and down to earth
  - keen on specific techniques.

That's the good news! On the other hand, my preference for the Activist and Pragmatist styles means that I have some important weaknesses.

- As an Activist, my weaknesses are that I am:

  - likely to take the immediately obvious action without considering alternatives
  - likely to take unnecessary risks
  - likely to do too much myself and hog the limelight
  - likely to get bored with implementation and consolidation.

- As a Pragmatist, my weaknesses are that I am:

  - likely to reject anything without an obvious application
  - not very interested in theory or basic principles
  - likely to seize on the first expedient solution to a problem
  - impatient with disorganised people who 'waffle'.

Clearly these strengths and weaknesses affect my performance as a trainer. For example, I am likely to design training courses that are packed with lots of activities and to sell people short on theory and basic principles. I am likely to warm to trainees who display activist tendencies and to have difficulties with trainees who hold back and are more cautious and less assertive. Also, paradoxically, the more I try to jolly along trainees who have Reflector–Theorist preferences the more likely they are to take fright and withdraw still further.

THE CHOICE OF SELF-DEVELOPMENT

Once I knew my own learning style preferences (the Learning Styles Questionnaire together with its score key come as a package with *The Manual of Learning Styles*) and realized their implications for me as a trainer, I had two choices. Either I could specialize and train only fellow Activists and Pragmatists or I could set out to develop my under-developed Reflector and Theorist styles so that I was better equipped to help a broader range of trainees.

The idea of specializing has some practical difficulties and having seriously toyed with the idea I dropped it in favour of self-development. The practical difficulties are not by any means insurmountable – indeed, on an in-company basis where there may be a team of trainers with various styles there is much to be said for more thoroughly matching trainer and trainee styles. It would require a system where trainee's learning styles were identified *before* they attended a training programme so that they could be catered for either by allocating them to courses designed to suit their styles or to trainers with compatible styles.

I decided to set about consciously strengthening my Reflector and Theorist styles so that, through an extended repertoire, I would be in a better position to adopt styles suitable for all types of trainees. More specifically, I set myself the goal of strengthening my Reflector style by becoming:

- More thoughtful, thorough and methodical
- Better at listening to others and assimilating information
- More careful not to jump to conclusions.

In order to strengthen my Theorist style, I set about becoming:

- More rational, objective and disciplined
- Better at logical (vertical) thinking
- Better at asking probing questions.

SELF-DEVELOPMENT PROGRAMME

Here are some of the things I did in order to strengthen my Reflector and Theorist styles.

1. Each month I sat in the public gallery at the Town Hall observing our local councillors during their meetings (for an Activist this is ideal, because you are not allowed to speak – only to observe). I

kept a careful record of what was said and later did an analysis of the arguments used, and the processes that led up to a decision.

2. A general election was called soon after I had embarked on my self-development plan: I bought myself copies of the manifestos for the three main parties and did a painstaking analysis of the policies each was advocating. Having done this, I designed a self-scoring questionnaire to help people decide which policies they agreed–did not agree with.

3. I put myself on a Rational Emotive Therapy (RET) course. RET is a rigorous form of therapy that brings out and challenges your irrational beliefs, and as such is an excellent vehicle for developing the theorist style in particular.

4. I read articles in the 'quality' newspapers and did a thorough analysis of the arguments they were using, and tried to identify and write down the fundamental assumptions they were based on. I compiled a list of probing questions that I wished to put to the authors.

5. I forced myself to compile lists for and against a particular piece of action. I tried this on domestic decisions not just work ones and it nearly drove my wife mad! Never mind, it helped me to think of alternative courses of action rather than revelling in instant (Activist) on-the-spot decisions.

6. I deliberately increased my serious reading. To give myself an incentive I volunteered to write reviews of books. This is an excellent way of forcing yourself to read the book in question carefully enough and analyze its good and bad points.

7. I took a list of criteria to be used as the basis for designing an assessment programme for middle managers and broke each down into a number of specific behavioural indicators. Previously, the criteria had been global and vague (leadership, flexibility, decision-making, etc.). I spent a concentrated day pinpointing six key behaviours for each criterion.

8. Finally, and perhaps most helpful of all, three times a week I make an entry in my learning log. The procedure I have devised is as follows:

   (a) start by thinking back over an experience and selecting a part of it (a 15-minute period or so) that was **significant** or **important** for you

(b) write a detailed account of what happened during that per-
     iod; do not at this stage put any effort into deciding what
     you learned – just concentrate on describing what actually
     happened
(c) then, list the conclusions you have reached as a result of the
     experience; these are, in effect, your **learning points**: do not
     limit the number, and do not worry about the practicality or
     quality of the points
(d) finally, decide what learning points you want to implement in
     the future and work out an action plan which covers what
     you are going to do and when you are going to do it; spell out
     your action plan as precisely as possible so that you are clear
     what you have to do, and that it is **realistic**.

I have been so impressed with the value of keeping a log like this that I
have introduced it as a twice-a-day feature on most of the training
programmes I run. Activists need some cajoling: Reflectors, Theorists
and Pragmatists take to it more easily.

STRENGTHENING THE ACTIVIST AND PRAGMATIST STYLES

Of course, none of my personal examples will help those who want to
develop their Activist and/or Pragmatist styles. Here then, taken from
The Manual of Learning Styles, are some 'thought starters' for people
in that position.

Self-development activities to develop the Activist style

1. At least once a week do something new, i.e., something that you
    have never done before. Visit a part of your organization that you
    have neglected, go jogging at lunch time, wear something outra-
    geous to work one day, read an unfamiliar newspaper with views
    that are diametrically opposed to yours, change the layout of
    furniture in your office, etc.
2. Practise initiating conversations (especially 'small talk) with
    strangers. Select people at random from your internal telephone
    directory and go and talk to them. At large gatherings, confer-
    ences or parties, force yourself to initiate and sustain conver-

sations with everyone present. In your spare time go door-to-door canvassing for a cause of your choice.

3.   Deliberately fragment your day by chopping and changing activities each half hour. Make the switch as diverse as possible. For example, if you have had half an hour of cerebral activity, switch to doing something utterly routine and mechanical. If you have been sitting down, stand up. If you have been talking, keep quiet, and so on.

4.   Force yourself into the limelight. Volunteer whenever possible to chair meetings or give presentations. When you attend a meeting set yourself the challenge of making a substantial contribution within ten minutes of the start. Get on a soapbox and make a speech at your local Speakers' Corner.

5.   Practise thinking aloud and on your feet. Set yourself a problem and bounce ideas off a colleague (see if between you you can generate fifty ideas in ten minutes). Get some colleagues–friends to join in a game where you give each other topics and have to give an impromptu speech lasting at least five minutes.

Self-development activities to develop the Pragmatist style

1.   Collect **techniques** (i.e., practical ways of doing things). The techniques can be about anything potentially useful to you. They might be analytical techniques such as critical path analysis or cost benefit analysis. They might be interpersonal techniques such as transactional analysis, or assertiveness or presentation techniques. They might be time-saving techniques or statistical techniques, or techniques to improve your memory, or techniques to cope with stress and reduce your blood pressure!

2.   In meetings and discussions of any kind (progress meetings, problem-solving meetings, planning meetings, appraisal discussions, negotiations, sales calls, etc.), concentrate on producing **action plans**. Make it a rule never to emerge from a meeting or discussion without a list of actions either for yourself or for others, or both. The action plans should be specific and include a deadline (e.g., 'I will produce a two-page paper listing alternative bonus schemes by 1 September').

3.   Make opportunities to **experiment** with some of your new-found techniques. Try them out in practice. If your experiment involves

other people, tell them openly that you are conducting an experiment and explain the technique which is about to be tested. (This reduces embarrassment if, in the event, the technique is a flop!) Choose the time and place for your experiments; avoid situations where a lot is at stake and where the risks of failure are unacceptably high. Experiment in routine settings with people whose aid or support you can enlist.

4.   Study techniques that **other people use** and then model yourself on them. Pick up techniques from your boss, your boss's boss, your colleagues, your subordinates, visiting salesmen, interviewers on television, politicians, actors and actresses, your next door neighbour. When you discover something they do well – emulate them.

5.   Subject yourself to scrutiny from 'experts' so that they can watch your technique and coach you in how to **improve** it. Invite someone who is skilled in running meetings to sit in and watch you chairing, get an accomplished presenter to give you feedback on your presentation techniques. This idea is to solicit help from people who have a proven track record – it is the equivalent of having a coaching session with a golfing professional.

6.   Tackle a 'do-it-yourself' project – it does not matter if you are not good with your hands. Pragmatists are practical and, if only for practice purposes, DIY activities help to develop a practical outlook. Renovate a piece of furniture, build a garden shed or even an extension to your house. At work, calculate your own statistics once in a while instead of relying on the printout, be your own organization and methods man, go and visit the shopfloor in search of practical problems to solve. Learn to type, learn a foreign language.

CONCLUSION

If management development is designed to provide managers with learning opportunities, then the process of learning from experience is an essential ingredient, perhaps the **most essential**. In my view, any respectable management development programme should offer explicit help with **learning how to learn**, by doing some or all of the following things:

1.   Help managers to know the stages in the process of learning from

experience and how their learning style preferences help (and hinder) them with parts of this process.

2. Help managers to work out how to develop an under-developed learning style so that they can aim to become better 'all-round' learners.

3. Provide managers with a safe haven where they can practise developing an under-developed style and help learning from experience to be a deliberate, conscious process.

4. Help managers to identify **learning opportunities** in their current jobs, and plan how to **utilize** them.

REFERENCES

Argyris, C. (1962) *Interpersonal Competence and Organizational Effectiveness*, (Homewood IL: Irwin-Dorsey).

Honey, P. and Mumford, A. (1986) *The Manual of Learning Styles* 2nd edn, (London: Honey).

Honey, P. and Mumford, A. (1986) *Using Your Learning Styles* 2nd Edition, (London: Honey).

Kolb, D. (1984) *Experiential Learning* (Englewood Cliffs, N.J.: Prentice-Hall).

8

Self-managed learning

Ian Cunningham

The phrase 'self-managed learning' (SML) was coined in order to distinguish this approach from close relatives (but relatives which are distinctively different). I was particularly interested in trying to meld together the advantages of various learning modes, whilst at the same time discarding their disadvantages.

LEARNING APPROACHES

Independent study

From work in the North East London Polytechnic, I wanted to use the idea that individuals can **plan and carry out their own learning programmes** (see Cunningham, 1981).

Action learning

The value of individual managers **assisting each other** in their learning (through the use of sets) was clearly demonstrated in various action learning programmes in which I was involved (e.g., GEC's Developing Senior Managers' Programme; see Casey and Pearce, 1977).

Autonomy labs

Harrison's (1974) work in creating courses where managers were free to do what they liked (almost) impressed me. Restricting the trainer role to providing **rich resources and to assisting others in their learning** (through counselling and coaching) seemed a healthy stance.

Humanistic education

Rogers (1969) has been an influence on many management developers in the UK, and his passionate advocacy of a **'person-centred'** approach provided important philosophical underpinnings for SML.

Holistic education

It seems self-evident to me that managers are not disembodied brains (see also Mant, 1977): they exist in physical bodies, they feel (even if they pretend they do not), they value and believe in particular ideals (even though it is not always apparent). Schutz (1979) is one of many writers who have promoted a **holistic perspective** on learning. His holistic studies MA at Antioch University in San Francisco was one of a number of American programmes I was able to experience at first hand when working in the USA in the late 1970s.

Self-development

Self-development methods and ideas flourished in the late 1970s. The idea of managers managing their own development through starting with their **own needs** has proved very effective. However 'self-development' has tended to become a catch-all term to include almost anything that is not traditional learning. Some of the proponents of self-development also started to see the need to consider the **context** within which the person was learning (usually their organization). Hence the idea of developing 'learning organizations' came more to the fore.

Work-based management development

These are the methods one can use to assist managerial learning **without managers leaving their place of work**. Coaching, the use of work assignments, job rotation, and apprenticeship are examples of such unglamorous (but often highly valuable) methods. My experience of consulting in various organizations indicated that these approaches could be the most cost-effective learning modes for much managerial learning (see Mumford, 1980, for further discussion of this topic).

OTHER INFLUENCES ON SELF-MANAGED LEARNING

As well as influences from learning approaches, SML has benefited from:

1. Developments in **psychotherapy**, which have provided new ideas on how people change (for example, neuro-linguistic programming – see Bandler and Grinder, 1979)
2. Research on the **nature of management** (for example, Stewart, 1982), which indicates that managing is not a neat subject discipline that can be taught in compartmentalized, standardized chunks
3. Research on **brain functioning**, which shows up the different contributions that the left and right hemispheres of the brain contribute to our ways of thinking (see Mintzberg, 1984)
4. Ideas from philosophy about the **nature of knowledge and of reality** (Bateson, 1973 and Watzlawick, 1978 were specific influences); the notion that 'reality' cannot sensibly be conceptualized as a concrete entity outside of ourselves is a central tenet of SML: managers create their own reality, and teachers and trainers have to respond to that
5. **Eastern philosophy**, particularly Taoism, has provided a subtle and powerful antidote to narrow Westernized modes of thought; this is especially so in relation to the idea that one can work in a **both/and** rather than an **either/or** mode: I shall comment specifically on this in the next section.

BOTH/AND OR EITHER/OR?

In organizing SML to get the benefits of the different strands outlined above, I was guided by the notion that we could work in a both/and rather than either/or mode: we did not need to choose between apparent opposites, since many things that are supposed to be opposites are not. Let me pick out one writer (amongst many) who has categorized management education programmes on an either/or basis, and indicate how his reasoning is unhelpful.

Handy (1975) identified what he claimed were the polar opposites in management education – instrumentalism and existentialism, and argued that management teachers had to choose between these two schools. He described the **instrumental** school as believing that education was **subject-oriented**: that one teaches things to people; that the success of a course is judged on the basis of the person's contribution to society or to an organization; that reasoning and learning are deductive (practice follows theory); that entry to courses is on the basis of organizational sponsorships only. The **existential** position he described as concentrating on the individual (and his or her freedom) not on the group. The view of reasoning and learning held by this school, he said, was **inductivist** (theory emerges from experience). He stated that teachers in this camp disliked assessment and talked instead of allowing feedback. They also preferred to take people onto a course on the basis of personal choice rather than organizational sponsorship.

Handy (1975) argued that it was not possible to 'ride two horses at once' (p. 61), and that all management teachers had to choose one or the other position. The evidence I have gathered from my own research (Cunningham, 1984) indicates that effective management teachers or trainers do not conform to Handy's theory. The people in my research talked very much in terms of working with **both poles at the same time**. Everyone was, for instance, in some way interested in the development of the person and in the person's contribution to society, their organization or their area of work. The notion that a management teacher *has* to choose to help **either** the person **or** society (and cannot do both) is nonsensical. For one thing, the notion that 'organizations' and 'society' are objects which can exist separately from persons is difficult to sustain; secondly, (and conversely) it presupposes that managers can manage **outside a social context**.

To quote the case of one course in which I have been involved (the MBA at Roffey Park Management College):

1. We recruit individuals as self-sponsored *and* as organizationally sponsored.
2. We take assessment seriously, and pass or fail decisions are faced

not as a necessary nuisance but as an important judgemental process to be set *alongside* the less judgemental feedback mode.

3. We value people who are independent *and* interdependent. The course can work only if people *both* consider themselves and work on their own problems *and* consider others and work with them on their problems.

4. The course demands that a person be involved in a *learning community,* as well as pursuing *individual* and *small group* work.

5. Course members use subject-based knowledge *and* they use their personally-created knowledge. Theory and practice are continually counterposed in ways which transcend simplistic deductive–inductive modes.

I have indicated here the notion of a holistic integration of poles, but I recognize that there are 'management teachers' who operate according to one or other of Handy's opposites. I have come across messy, self-centred existentialist programmes which have degenerated into chaotic disasters. The history of much of the 1960s–1970s radical and humanistic education movement showed that many programmes collapsed because of this unbalanced mode of operating (see Swidler, 1979; Rogers, 1983; Leonard, 1979; Deal, 1975).

Equally degenerate instrumental programmes have tended to survive because of a combination of authoritarian control mechanisms, the exclusiveness and secretiveness of staff, and the investment by course members in pretending that their course is satisfactory (otherwise it would undermine their qualification, and if they have learned the hidden curriculum of instrumentalism they would not want to put their careers at risk).

What I have expressed above is my own interpretation, based on my experience of a number of institutions. However, in my research, people time and again expressed their rejection of narrow instrumentalism; they criticized the lack of involvement of such programmes with the lives of course members; the wastefulness of fixed curricula; the lack of effectiveness of standardized taught courses.

SELF-MANAGED LEARNING IN CONTEXT

I want now to put some flesh on the bare bones presented so far. Self-managed learning programmes have been operating in organizations as well as in a college context. I shall focus on the Post Graduate Diploma in Management (by SML) which has run since 1980 at North East London Polytechnic. Discussion of its inception is contained elsewhere (see Cunningham, 1981). I shall indicate here incidents an observer would actually see or hear, and follow each of these with an explanation of why they would observe such episodes; I hope that this will provide a better insight into the course than a purely abstract discussion.

Observed

New course members arrive on a Friday evening in October for the opening of the Diploma at a residential weekend. They join with existing (second-year) course members and do some fairly standard 'getting to know each other' exercises, along with sessions to find out more about the course. So far, this looks very similar to many other management courses. However, as the weekend goes on, differences become apparent. The residential weekend has been organized by a planning group consisting of second-year course members plus two staff. This group steers the weekend, but staff, whilst actively involved in particular sessions, are not controlling what goes on. On Saturday a session is devoted to helping first-year course members form into 'sets'; the sets are groups of five or six course members along with a staff member and a second-year course member (who together act as co-set advisers). The session is disorganized and sometimes chaotic as people try to find a sensible basis with which to group themselves. Eventually they do, and the sets settle down to their first meeting of many they will have over the two years.

On Saturday, all first- and second-year course members and staff gather together for a **community meeting**. This meeting discusses and decides upon course issues. It is chaired by a course member, and whilst staff join in on discussions they have only a minority voice in the proceedings. The community meeting decides on who shall be on the planning group for the next residential weekend. It also decides which workshops and other events shall take place before the next residential weekend, which is in the next term.

Explanation

1. SML is not necessarily an individual activity. Managing one's own learning includes **involving oneself in the learning of others**.

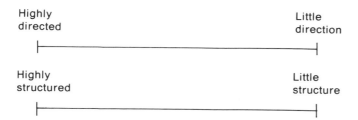

Figure 8.1 The issue of structuring

2. SML events are sometimes quite tightly structured. The difference between SML and other modes is **where the structure** comes from. In most college or university run courses, tutors lay down the structure: in SML the structure comes from collective agreement involving course members and staff.

    This issue of structuring is important. Just because course members control their own learning it does not make the course unstructured. 'Structure' and 'direction' (or control) are two separate variables, and courses can be more of less structured and more or less directed by staff; this can be shown as in Figure 8.1.

    A course can, for instance, be highly directed with little structure. This fits certain T-group or encounter group modes where staff dictate a low structure format and do not permit group members to develop more structure. Most so-called 'taught courses' have high direction and high structure: staff impose both content and timetabling (structuring). Certain self-development groups come into the low structure/low direction category: the trainer adopts a low profile on content and structure. The SML mode is unusual in providing a great deal of structure within a framework which has little staff direction over course content. In Figure 8.1 I am suggesting that a total lack of structure is not possible: an unstructured course is a logical nonsense since to have a course is to provide a structure of some kind, even if it is only to arrange a time when people meet together.

3. The community meeting is a key event as it demonstrates the notion of a self-managing community operating to make collective decisions about the course. All course members are able to be directly involved in decisions about what goes on, though the

community meeting delegates specific tasks to groups (such as the residential planning group).

4. Sets are important in providing **support groups** besides meeting other needs. Each set is assisted in its operations by the presence of the co-set advisers. Second-year course members who want to develop their skills in this area have found it valuable to apprentice themselves to a staff member in order to work with a first-year set. The set also gets the benefit of the presence of someone who has been through the first year.

Observed

After the first residential, John, a manager in a construction company, is at home in the evening working on what he should put into his programme of study. He knows he has to write a contract which he has to present to his set for approval. Some aspects of this contract seem much easier to write than others; he has had no problem in covering his past experience, and he has had a reasonable shot at describing his strengths and weaknesses (helped by diagnostic material provided by the college). However, working out learning goals is proving less easy; he knows he wants to advance within his own company, but specifying a balance of objectives is not simple. He decides to take a rough draft of what he has written to his next set meeting in order to get the feedback and comments of others.

Explanation

Paul Tillich called the fatal pedagogical error, 'To throw answers like stones at the heads of those who have not yet asked the questions' (in Brown, 1971). Managing involves asking questions and formulating problems **before** looking for answers and solutions. So for managers to manage their own learning they need first to formulate the questions: the problems.

I define a 'problem' as existing when we cannot go from where we are to where we would like to be simply by action. If I want to know something about company procedures, and these are written in a company manual, I can simply go and look it up; that is no problem. However, if I currently feel unassertive and lacking in confidence (and

I want to be assertive and self-confident) I may well have a problem. It is probably not at all clear how I can move from my current to my desired state. In the Post Graduate Diploma course managers are advised that they may find it helpful to address themselves to five questions:

1. **Where have I been**? – What are my past experiences?
2. **Where am I now** – What strengths and weaknesses do I have? What is the current situation that I am in?
3. **Where do I want to get to?** – What goals/targets/objectives do I want to set for myself?
4. **How will I get there**? – What programme of study should I design to achieve my goals?
5. **How will I know if I've arrived?** – What criteria can I apply to assess my learning?

Most people find this sequence helpful in assisting them to formulate and choose their problems. I say 'choose' because any problem is a choice. If one decides to accept the situation and does not wish to change then there are no problems. It is only when a person **chooses** to change that problems become identifiable. The situation can be shown diagrammatically as in Figure 8.2. This indicates the link with the five questions outlined above.

In Figure 8.2 the person has the problem of going from *A* to *B*. The position is chosen on the basis of the person's values and beliefs: it is not an externally defined objective reality. My stance then is to reject what I often hear from trainers and lecturers. 'That manager says he wants to learn *X*, but that is not the real problem. What he really needs is *Y*'. The arrogance of such statements is in part based on a notion that 'real problems' exist out there in the world, detached from people; I regard this as an unacceptable standpoint. I may disagree with the goals a manager has set, but that is just my view against his or hers. I believe that I have the right to challenge and question a learner, and in the process they may change their formulation of the problem. However, in SML courses the staff do not have the right to impose *any* goals on learners, no matter how subtly they may wish to do it.

I have argued here for the principle of learners setting their own goals; however there are also practical reasons why this is important. The research evidence on managerial learning is quite conclusive in

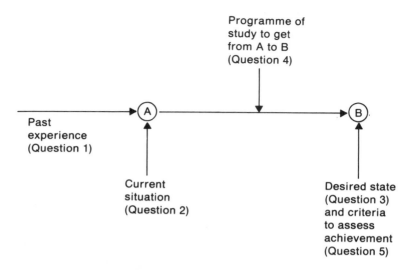

Figure 8.2   The problem of going from A to B

supporting the notion that learning is enhanced if managers consciously **set their own goals**. Kolb and Boyatzis (1984) quote a number
of studies which demonstrate remarkable improvements in learning
and performance when managers were given the chance to set their
own goals, and such changes tend to be independent of how difficult
the goals are that people set for themselves.

Observed

John has returned from the set meeting where his draft contract has
been discussed. His proposals have been analyzed in detail, and many
of his ideas have been exposed, under questioning, as being ill-thought
out. He had been a bit annoyed at the time, as he felt he had put a lot
of effort into his draft contract. However, now that he can re-read his
proposals he realizes that they were not as solid as he had thought.
Just saying that he wanted to 'learn about management finance' and
to 'improve interpersonal skills' clearly was not specific enough. He
decided to talk to his boss, because part of the reason he had put in
'improve interpersonal skills' was on the basis of feedback at his last
appraisal interview. He now realized that he needed to be clearer
about what his boss actually meant by this.

Explanation

1. Sets are often at their most supportive when they confront indivi-
    duals about what they **are or are not doing**. This is a good example
    of how SML transcends the narrowness of Handy's opposites of
    instrumentalism and existentialism. Woolly non-judgemental
    feedback ('I like what you've done') is as inappropriate as des-
    tructive judgemental assessment ('You'll never make a good
    manager'). Supportive confronting involves supporting the
    person as a person and valuing their worth as a human being,
    whilst commenting, positively and negatively, on what they do.
    This can be expressed simply as:
    *   support **being** (that is, the person)
    *   confront **doing** (that is, what they do).
2. Part of helping people to manage their own learning is assisting
    them to specify the precise problems which they wish to tackle. In
    order to get **good answers**, one needs first **good questions**.
3. It is valuable if managers can build into their learning contracts
    evidence they gain from colleagues, bosses, subordinates and
    others at work. However, our experience is that much of this
    evidence is too vague. We have encouraged managers to go and
    seek out good feedback, so that they can have a better basis on
    which to decide what to learn. Sometimes set members (staff or
    course members) have gone to a person's place of work to assist in
    this information gathering, especially if the boss or work collea-
    gues get built into the contract as sources of learning.

Observed

Jane has had her contract agreed by her set at the end of the first term,
and she now finds she has to start to put her plans into operation. She
decides that her desire to learn about basic elements of marketing can
best be met by attending a module on this topic, which is already
provided on the Diploma in Management Studies. The module is one
evening a week for one term. She has been given study leave for one
day a week by her employers, so she comes into the college to use the
library in the morning, prior to going to her set meeting in the
afternoon. She feels she has a problem in running meetings, and looks
for books in the library on this topic. However, she comes across an

entry in the catalogue of a video tape on the subject. She signs out the tape and views it in one of the soundproof booths provided in the library.

Later in the term she decides to pluck up courage and tackle her fear of computers. She arranges a meeting with a tutor, and he shows her how to operate the microcomputers on open access in the computer room. She realizes how valuable it has been for her to have discussed her concerns about computers in the set, as her colleagues were not only able to reassure her about using the equipment, but also helped her to clarify the kind of questions she needed to put to the tutor. She finds that the tutor occasionally gets over-enthusiastic about pushing her into the broader aspects of computer use, but because she is clear about what she wants she is able to steer him back to her own needs.

Explanation

1. A person managing his or her own learning can choose a **variety of ways to learn** what he or she wants to learn.
2. **Back-up learning resources** are important, though many are ill-designed for easy access by managers. Libraries are often organized to suit librarians, and it can be a problem getting the flexibility and responsiveness needed for SML work. The use of learning resources in SML programmes is unlike their use in so-called open and distance learning; much of the latter is not very 'open' at all, being predefined packages which give little or no choice to managers – they are like Tillich's stones being thrown at the heads of managers who have not formulated the questions (and are not going to be allowed to). It is a Henry Ford approach to learning. ('You can have any course you like, so long as it's this one')
3. Tutors may also not be ideally responsive. However, part of the skill of managing one's own learning is to **manage experts**; the experts do have things to offer, and it is short-sighted of managers to ignore this. Managers are, though, rightly suspicious of experts who wish to push their own field of interest too much. To quote Greenberg's First Law of Experts: 'You don't ask a barber if you need a haircut' (Peers and Bennett, 1981). However, if you decide for yourself that you need a haircut, a barber can be useful.

Observed

Jim, a senior manager in local government, meets his tutor from college. They sit down in Jim's office and go through a time diary Jim has kept for the last two weeks. As they analyse his activities, Jim realizes how much time he has been devoting to unproductive work. He appreciates now why his staff have complained about the amount of time he is out of the office or otherwise not available to them. He discusses with his tutor ways in which he could reorganize his time to fit more closely with his priorities.

After they have been through the time diary, they discuss how Jim processes paper (since this is another problem he has decided to tackle). Jim calls in his secretary, so that the three of them can consider how to change the filing system.

Explanation

1. SML can be about learning both high-level abstract theory and 'nitty-gritty' practical skills
2. Learning can take place at work, in college (or anywhere)
3. Course members choose one staff member (not the set adviser) to act as a 'specialist tutor' to assist them with specific learning which needs expert help; ideally, the specialist tutor works with the learner over the two years, although in practice people often switch tutors as their interests or requirements change. This special relationship does not preclude the course member from using other tutors on an occasional basis.

Observed

It is a sunny July Saturday afternoon and this is the third residential weekend of the year. Course members can be observed around the building and outside it. Eight people are struggling with a computer-based business game: some are from the public sector, and they are finding the commercial aspects of the game difficult to handle. Ten people are in a seminar on industrial relations negotiations run by one of the tutors. Tom, Jenny and Tim are busy in the computer room, each working on his or her own specific work problems. Tim has been testing out some proposals his employers are about to implement, and he finds a serious flaw in their calculations. He subsequently reports this to his organization, and they save a seven-figure sum by redoing their sums along the lines that Tim suggests.

Arthur sits under a tree in the grounds reading a book on operations research, and every so often he glances at a group of nine people on the lawn who are painting and drawing. They are in a session on integrating left-brain and right-brain working. Later on, he observes them all lying down listening to a guided fantasy, and he wonders whether he should not have joined that group rather than choosing to work on his own.

Meanwhile, in a darkened room in the main building, a group of seven is watching the film, **The Balance Sheet Barrier**, oblivious of the sunshine outside. Along the corridor Tony, Mike and Sue are using video equipment to practise their counselling skills. Janet, who is on the course, but is also a management tutor in a college, is assisting them, as she runs counselling training courses in her own college.

Down by the lake, well away from the main building, Simon and Carol sit on a bench. Simon is crying: his father died a few day ago; he does not feel up to going into any of the planned activities, and Carol, who is in his set, has agreed to sit with him for the afternoon. Simon is confused because his dominant feeling is one of anger, not sadness, at his father's death. Carol knows that Simon's relationship with his father has been fraught, as it has come up in the set discussions, and she tries to help Simon make sense of his feelings. Eventually, they wander slowly back from the lake.

It is now late afternoon and a Tai Ji group is about to start on the lawn, led by one of the tutors. Tim and Jenny leave their computers to join it, along with Simon and Carol. Mike and Sue emerge from their video session to take part, and Arthur decides to take a break from his book to do some relaxing meditative movement. At the last residential he had labelled Tai Ji 'too freaky and way-out', but having given it a try he has become convinced of its value.

Inside the building, a session on theorizing is being held, and people do various exercises to assist them in being more effective at developing theory from their experiences. In one exercise, course members form into small sub-groups. One person (the problem owner) talks about a problem whilst the others write on cards the concepts used by the person as he or she talks. Together they arrange the cards in a 'concept map' in order to help the problem owner to **model the problem**. The problem owner is then assisted in elucidating the hypotheses with which he or she is working, so that concepts, models and hypotheses can be linked together as theory.

Explanation

1. Residential weekends provide a range of options to cover what course members request. Sometimes people spend time outside formally organized sessions: this is part of **managing one's own learning**.
2. The activities exemplify the **holistic orientation** of the programme; most people are pleasantly surprised at how valuable it is to attend to their learning needs as whole persons: they find they change intellectually, emotionally, physically, socially and sometimes spiritually. All of this is relevant to management.
3. Course members **learn from each other**. The course provides a network which allows people to meet others with matching interests and concerns; it also facilitates mutual support in times of personal difficulty.

    This networking often continues after the formal ending of the course. There are facilities for ex-course members to meet up and be in contact with each other. One set which went through the programme 1980–2 continued to meet of its own volition until 1990.
4. The style of the residential course is in keeping with a both/and orientation: people work hard and they have fun; they are active and passive; they engage in rational and non-rational activity; they plan rigorously and they respond to serendipitous whims.

I like to feel that the SML approach is genuinely scientific in the sense that Bateson (1973) has supported; that is, that one counterposes theory and existing knowledge with experience, and tests each against the other. I agree with Sirag (1979) that 'the future of physics rests in the hands of those who have an equal toleration for mathematical rigor and free-wheeling fantasy' (p. 18). A similar statement could be made about management.

Observed

The two-year course is coming to its end for Mike's set, and they are dealing with assessment, in order to decide on who gets the Diploma

and who does not. Mike has already presented various essays and
reports to the set, and these have been discussed. He is now at the set
meeting at which they are looking at the totality of his work. He first
shows a video tape where he is counselling someone, and after that he
gives his reasons why he thinks this has satisfied the criteria in his
contract on this subject. Other course members and the staff member
(set adviser) question him on this, and eventually they agree he has
met the required standard. Mike then distributes copies of assessments carried out by his boss and his subordinates on aspects of his
performance at work. In discussion it seems that there is doubt on
some aspects of these, particularly as to whether Mike has met all his
previously contracted criteria. The set agrees that they cannot make a
decision on this information, and the task of going to Mike's company to talk to his boss and his subordinates is delegated to two set
members. After this discussion, Mike's specialist tutor joins the set,
and he reports on Mike's work in the areas of finance and economics.
The set quiz him on his report, and eventually agree with Mike and
the tutor that the required criteria have been met. The set then
consider Mike's other (written) work which they have already seen.
They agree that if the two set members seeing Mike's boss and
subordinates get the required information, they can proceed at the
next set meeting to decide on a pass.

Explanation

It is central to SML that the learner manages the assessment process
in conjunction with **relevant others**. In the context of this college
course 'relevant others' means at the very least other set members and
the specialist tutor. In Mike's case above, the person's boss and
subordinates were also involved. At no time are judgements imposed
externally on the learner: the assessment process matches the initial
contracting process in being a **collaborative negotiation**. I have discussed elsewhere other aspects of assessment (see Cunningham, 1983).

CONCLUSION

I have commented on some aspects of one SML course. The course
has had hundreds of managers through it, and it has been carefully

evaluated by outside researchers. On the basis of such evaluations I and my colleagues have developed in-organization SML programmes for younger managers in British Airways; for personnel managers in the BBC; for middle managers in Shell; and for managers in two different health service regions. We also launched an SML MBA in January 1990 run by Roffey Park Management College in conjunction with the University of Sussex. These programmes work with the same basic principles, though designs vary to suit differing needs.

I have not discussed the staff role here as I have commented on this elsewhere (see Cunningham, 1984); however, I see this as the crucial determinant of the success or otherwise of SML programmes. Working in this kind of way relies heavily on staff competence, not just in face-to-face activity, such as in sets, but in the **design and managing of programmes**. If this approach to learning is to expand, the development of people who can staff such courses is going to be the most important factor.

REFERENCES

Bandler, R. and Grinder, J. (1979) *Frogs into Princes* (Moab, Utah: Real People Press).

Bateson, G. (1973) *Steps to an Ecology of Mind*, (London: Paladin).

Brown, G. L. (1971) *Human Teaching for Human Learning*, (New York: Viking).

Casey, D. and Pearce, D. (1977) *More than Management Development: Action Learning at G.E.C.*, (Aldershot: Gower).

Cunningham, I. (1981) 'Self Managed Learning and Independent Study', in Boydell, T. and Pedler, M. (eds), *Management Self Development: Concepts and Practices*, (Aldershot: Gower).

Cunningham, I. (1983) 'Assessment and Experiential Learning' in Boot, R. and Reynolds, M. (eds), *Learning and Experience in Formal Education*, Manchester Monograph, (University of Manchester).

Cunningham, I. (1984) 'Teaching Styles in Learner Centred Management Development Programmes', Ph.D. thesis (University of Lancaster).

Deal, T. E. (1975) 'An Organizational Explanation of the Failure of Alternative Secondary Schools', *Educational Researcher*, 4(4), pp. 10–16.

Handy, C. B. (1975) 'The Contrasting Philosophies of Management Education', *Management Education and Development*, 6(2), (August) pp. 56–62.

Harrison, R. (1974) 'Developing Autonomy, Initiative and Risk-Taking through laboratory design', in Adams, J. D. (ed.) *New Technologies in O.D.*, (La Jolla: University Associates).

Heron, J. (1977) *Dimensions of Facilitator Style* (British Postgraduate Medical Federation).

Kolb, D. A. and Boyatzis, R. E. (1984) 'Goal Setting and Self Directed Behaviour Change', in Kolb, D. A., Rubin, I. M. and McIntyre, J. M. (eds), *Organizational Psychology: Readings on Human Behaviour in Organizations* (Englewood Cliffs, N.J.: Prentice-Hall).

Leonard, G. (1979) 'Frontiers in Education: Past and Present', in *A.H.P. Newsletter* (May) pp. 5–6.

Mant, A. (1977) *The Rise and Fall of the British Manager* (London: McGraw-Hill).

Mintzberg, H. (1984) 'Planning on the left side and managing on the right', in Kolb, D. A., Rubin, I. M. and McIntyre, J. M. (eds), *Organizational Psychology: Readings on Human Behavior and Organizations* (Englewood Cliffs, N.J.: Prentice-Hall).

Mumford, A. (1980) *Making Experience Pay* (London: McGraw-Hill).

Peers, J. and Bennett, G. (1981) *1001 Logical Laws* (London: Hamlyn).

Rogers, C. R. (1969) *Freedom to Learn* (Columbus, Ohio, Charles E. Merrill).

Rogers, C. R. (1983) *Freedom to Learn for the Eighties* (Columbus, Ohio: Charles E. Merrill).

Schutz, W. (1979) *Profound Simplicity* (London: Turnstone).

Sirag, S. P. (1979) 'Physics Education', *A.H.P. Newsletter* (May) pp. 17–18.

Stewart, R. (1982) *Choices for the Manager* (London: McGraw-Hill).

Swidler, A. (1979) *Organisation without Authority* (Cambridge, Mass.: Harvard University Press).

Watzlawick, P. (1978) *The Language of Change* (London: Basic Books).

9

New ways of learning

Don Binsted

This chapter examines some important new ways of learning which are beginning to contribute to management development (MD). They stem from ideas of open learning, distance learning and new educational technology. Definitions will be attempted, and some of the new technologies will be described in general terms. No attempt will be made to provide a catalogue of what is available, nor to deal with the technical aspects of hardware, but further reading will be suggested. The present situation will be outlined, and some possible future developments suggested: the aim of the chapter is to illuminate the position for those who may need to make decisions in this area.

OPEN AND DISTANCE LEARNING; ARE THEY THE SAME

There is some confusion about the meaning of the terms 'open' and 'distance'. Should the Open University more correctly be called the Distance University? Is the absence of entry qualification the only criterion of 'openness'?

Sorting out the confusion

One way of sorting out the confusion is to consider the 'openness' and 'distance' as two independent properties, so that four different types of programme can be recognized: those which are open, or distance,

155

or both, or neither (for example, traditional taught courses fall into the 'neither' category). A computer-based instruction programme may be distance but not open. The following definitions clarify the situation.

Distance learning

- Involves **physical separation of the tutor and the learner** (the word 'tutor' is used to identify trainers, teachers, coaches, authors, etc.)
- Involves the use of **at least one form of media** (print, video, computer output, etc.)
- In general, is suitable for a **solo learner** (although it may also be used with advantage in small groups)
- Needs a **delivery system**
- Works anywhere provided any **hardware** required is available.

Open learning

Open learning involves learners having

- Choice about **learning goals** they wish to pursue
- Choice about **sequence**, or **depth**, of learning
- Choice about learning **process** and level of **involvement**
- **Unrestricted access** (no educational preconditions).

Dimensions of openness and distance

Since most examples of open and/or distance learning do not meet the conditions of complete 'openness' or 'distance' it is useful to consider these as dimensions: the dimensions of 'distance' would appear to involve the extent of learner's face-to-face interaction with the tutor (see Figure 9.1).

Examples of learning situations at the extremes are, for 'not-distance', a traditional residential management development workshop; for 'distance' a self-development workbook (e.g., Pedler *et al* 1978) or workbook plus passive video (the Henley module on Accounting for

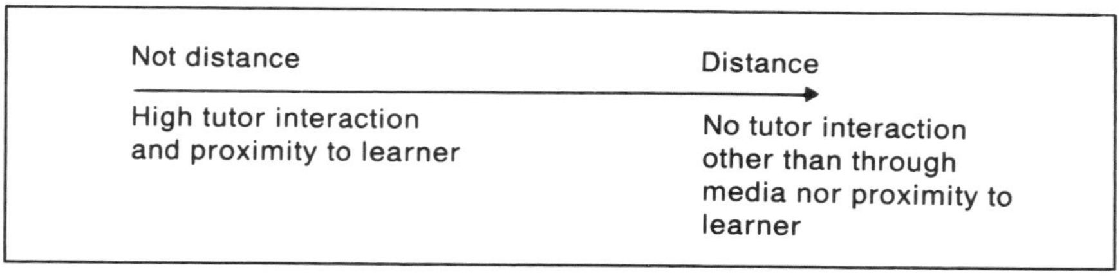

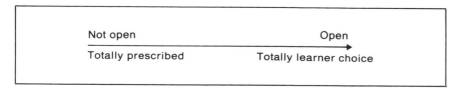

Figure 9.1 The 'distance' dimension

Figure 9.2 The 'open' dimension

Managers). The Open University Business School programme on International Marketing contains elements that are at both ends of the dimension. The broadcast or taped video programmes and workbooks are fully distance, whereas the residential weekend is specifically described as enabling learners to test out their own ideas, and to learn from others, in ways which simply are not possible 'at a distance'.

The dimension of 'openness' would appear to involve the extent to which the learner's activity is prescribed, compared with exerting choice (see Figure 9.2).

Examples of the extremes are: 'no-openness', a standard taught course; high 'openness', the programme developed at the North East London Polytechnic based on self-managed learning (SML) sets (Binsted and Hodgson, 1984; see also Chapter 8 above).

If these two dimensions are put together they suggest a model or map on which a particular programme can be plotted (see Figure 9.3).

In an investigation for the MSC the programmes and packages then found (January 1984) were mostly in the 'distance-not-open' quadrant (see Binstead and Hodgson, 1984). Some were in the 'open-and-

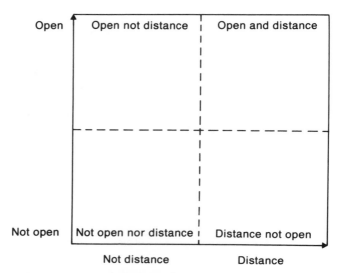

Figure 9.3   The 'open' and 'distance' model

distance' quadrant whilst others were really resources for tutors to use with a learner group and were neither 'open' nor 'distance'.

THE NEW TECHNOLOGY FOR LEARNING

Some would say that the new technology becoming available to tutors offers new ways of delivering 'distance' learning; others would suggest that a more constructive way of approaching the situation is to talk about **facilitating** learning at a distance. There could be some relationship here between how 'open' the learning could be: there is nothing inherent in any technology which predisposes it to be open or not. Development work in the Centre for the Study of Management Learning (CSML) at the University of Lancaster has attempted to create programmes which are both 'open' and 'distance'.

Some technology is well established in the fields of management development (like the use of workbooks), while some is still at the experimental stage. Technology for distance learning (as distinct from technology in the classroom), creates and delivers the materials and processes which **facilitate learning**. There are a variety of levels of technology now available to the management developer at a distance.

Print

Print will be in the form of **study units** or **workbooks** (e.g., various MBA programmes and the Open Business School, Henley, or Cranfield programmes). These may include text, graphics and photographs. The advent of word processors and desk top publishing (DTP) has greatly helped the economic production of text.

Linear or passive video

Either **broadcast** (Open Business School) or on **video cassette**, included in the Henley, Cranfield, Open University programmes, and in the TVI programmes at Aston (these latter are based on videoed lectures of very high quality). The enormous advantage of video is the ability to show dramatized or documentary interactions and situations, and to create very rapidly a context for case studies and exercises. New technology in video production (like the camcorda) makes it easier for trainers to shoot video, or professionals to produce more sophisticated programmes. Delivery systems (video cassette recorders and TV/monitors) are well established and are available in increasing numbers in the home. Video disc technology offers higher levels of interactivity, but is rarely found in the home.

Computer output

Computer output will be in the form of **text and graphics and limited sound**. This may be via mainframe terminals (as at work stations) or on single or networked micros. Micros are also increasingly to be found in the home. Educational packages to run on computers (courseware) are now available in the management area, and utilize a variety of educational designs. The big advantage of computer-based learning is its **interactivity**.

Interactive video (IV)

IV produces **computer-generated text and graphics**, together with **sound and video sequences**. In general the more sophisticated (costly) the hardware, the higher the quality of the graphics, although I personally find that complex graphics are best avoided when video is available. A rostrum camera will produce a far better result than the construction of complex graphics. Most modern IV systems have a 'genloc' capability which superimposes text or graphics on video. Two video sources are available (tape or video disc), but there are several standards of each. In general the video source, the microprocessor, the monitor and the interface which links them together form a unique system and packages will run only on one system: for example, the easy to use 'Take 2' system comprises a Sony video 8-tape VCR, a Sony monitor and a BBC master computer. (See note 1)

The benefits of video tape versus video disc systems is an area of lively debate. There is little doubt that video disc offers significant technical advantage for delivery particularly for the presentation of still frames (55 000 per disc); videotape has an advantage for in-house production of non-generic courseware, or for the early stages of development and testing of programmes for wide use which might then be based on a disc system.

IV +

IV + is the name given to an enhanced form of **interactive video** developed at CSML. As part of a five-year research project investigating the use of interactive video in management development, it became evident that for open learning to take place learners using the programme needed to interact with each other. This was purely a question of **educational design**: for example, to develop learners' interpersonal skills, it is necessary for them to practice and get feedback to achieve essential **discovery learning**. This is achieved by writing programmes for a pair of learners and incorporating a camera into the system; thus in addition to prerecorded video sequences, live video of learners' behaviour is an integral part of the programme. This can be achieved only with a tape system and 'Take 2' is the only IV system which currently allows this, an innovation which won the National Award for Innovation in Education and Training Technology in 1988. The system is shown diagramatically in Figure 9.4, where CBL stands for Computer Based Learning.

Computer mediated communication (CMC) systems

These are computer networking systems which can be used for educational purposes. Typical applications to learning are:

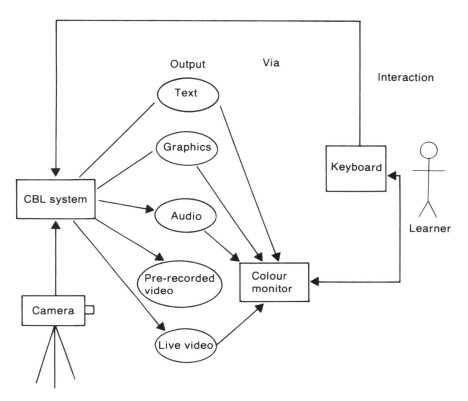

Figure 9.4   An interactive system

- The **storage and retrieval of textual learning material** by learners **anywhere on the network**.
- The use of communications software for **learning dialogues** between learner and learner, learner and tutor, or tutor and tutor.

This technology opens up a wide variety of distance learning opportunities which are being researched at CSML (McConnell and Hodgson, 1990). The technology allows for great openness since learners may search for suitable material, contribute their own, and enter into on-line discussion and conferencing; this can be done by logging on or off as the learner has opportunity. CMC systems provide for a **social dimension of learning** 'at a distance', for further details see the 1989 University of Lancaster study report (Hodgson *et al*, 1989).

Compact disc systems

As more advanced technologies become available, their application for MD will need to be researched. One such is Compact Disc Interactive (CD-I). This is a system based on compact disc technology which will store and deliver audio, images, video, graphics and data; this will be world standard, irrespective of TV standard and make of player (see Chatterton, 1990). Another new development based on compact disc technology (CD-Rom) is Digital Video Interactive (DVI). This system (developed by Intel and linked with IBM) will produce full-screen, full-motion video, text, dynamic graphics, still frames and multi-track audio. This system has developed a method of compressing and decompressing digital data, and has been developed for the training and education market. I would add one word of caution. In our research into IV +, we were not technology-led: our innovative programmes stemmed from the consideration of the **educational requirements to facilitate learning**; we then could specify what the technology should be able to deliver, and this included both the specification of hardware and software capabilities.

Authoring languages and systems

Such systems are an important element of new technology; in theory, they enable a tutor to programme a system for computer-based or interactive video learning. In practice, there is a considerable difference between a very easy to use *system* like 'Take 2' (which offers the tutor a comprehensive menu of options and gently interrogates him or her), and the more complex *languages*, which have to be learned, but *may* offer more options for the designer, if they can be utilized.

New technology has the potential of greatly extending the range of options for creating distance learning. Some types of technology may be essential to certain forms of learning at a distance (e.g., IV + for interpersonal skill development), and may allow learning which has not been possible at a distance before. The use of packages involving artificial intelligence (AI) will bring in a new range of interaction for the learner who can interrogate the programme as (s)he feels appropriate.

Bates (1984) gives extensive coverage of the role of technology in distance education, based mostly on the unique and extensive research and experience of the Open University.

PROGRAMMES AND PACKAGES

Two sorts of open and distance learning material are currently available, and they tend to differ in a number of respects.

Programmes

Programmes are **integrated learning activities** which form a **complete course of study** using some distance learning format (e.g., programmes of around 100 hours' study time). Examples are the Open Business School, Henley, and Cranfield modules. These are similar in a number of respects; they use a multi-media approach of workbooks, passive videos and audio cassettes, and the programmes are held together with course maps, course calendars, and a number of back-up documents for reference. The Open Business School models contain marked assignments, and assessment is an optional choice for the learner. Such programmes are clearly designed for solo learners, although the Henley publicity does stress the option of using the material in small groups. Opportunities are also provided for face-to-face or telephone tutoring, and in the Open Business School programmes, students are expected to attend a residential weekend and tutorials. Another form of programme found in the research for the MSC already referred to (Binsted and Hodgson, 1984) is where organizations had produced their own material internally. In these cases much less emphasis seems to have been given to tutor support; the designs of the programmes seem to reflect fairly strongly the values of the organizations which originate them. One intention of those made in educational institutions is clearly to produce generic material of wide appeal to as many people as possible, and considerable attention has been given to marketing these programmes.

Computer-based and interactive video packages

Such packages are in general of short duration (1–4 hours) and generally have a **limited but specific learning goal**. They may be modules linked together. The packages are either **generic** (which have a wide appeal in any situation), or **specific** to a particular work situation and organization. These latter have particular advantages because they can reflect **real problems in real situations** which the learner can readily identify with. This applies above all when there is a video element (passive or interactive) which can show organization people doing organizational tasks in the context of their own organization.

Packages exist which cover a very wide range of learning objectives:

- **Profile generating packages** which help the manager to identify strengths and weaknesses (See note 2)
- **Business games** (See note 3)
- A package involving some AI on **calculating income tax** (See note 4)
- Packages in a variety of **skill areas** such as time management (See note 5)
- **Research packages** from CSML covering problem-solving skills, interpersonal skills, attitude change, management of change, team-building and tutoring skills (Binsted, 1988).

Mention has already been made that the technology does not of itself prescribe the degree of openness of a package. Some of the early packages relied on programme learning designs, complete with multi-choice questions, remedial loops, etc. This led to a belief that this was a result of using computers, and resulted in closed designs. Since some of the early authoring systems locked the author into these designs, this became a self-fulfilling prophecy, but more recent work has shown this to be false (Topham, 1987).

It has been found that the educational design of some high-tech packages can be improved by the addition of **printed text and workbooks**; rules have been drawn up to decide when this is appropriate (Binsted, 1988b).

INFRASTRUCTURE FOR LEARNING

Although the educational design and use of technology is of vital importance, so is the **infrastructure in which the material is used**

(Hodgson, 1989). Take one example of a stand-alone programme designed for solo learners which requires little or no tutor support, and containing only self-assessment activities. Assume that such a programme was not computer-based, and involved a significant amount of study time to complete: it is easy to imagine the difficulty a busy manager would find in getting the programme to the top of his priority list. The practical manifestation might well be an inability actually to start, or to progress very far when started, and effectively to drop out of the programme. Complete lack of infrastructure might thus be a dominant factor, regardless of the quality of the materials or media used. Conversely, a defined infrastructure – including such things as a course calendar, assignment deadlines, tutorial dates, and completion dates ready for exams – might provide just the trigger for giving the work higher priority. It would appear that in some instances infrastructure may influence the degree of openness experienced by the learner; in any event, it appears to be of the greatest importance to consider materials design and delivery, and infrastructure as equally important aspects of open and distance learning. **Design of infrastructure** is thus of great importance: for example, a short stand-alone interactive video package which has a high fascination value may need one infrastructure, whereas a long programme involving dense text in print may need quite another. Research has illuminated the way in which learners interact with distance learning programmes (Mann, 1987).

The location of the **delivery point** may be critical. This will depend on technology – e.g., whether the learning station is a terminal of a mainframe computer at a work station, or in a special location as a learning resource, or on a home micro. Having made the point about the importance of infrastructure, the **design of materials** also plays a part: the fascination factor of good interactive video, or the avoidance of dense text without graphics, or the use of commentators on video, who 'jolly you along' (Henley) thus all appear to be important.

There are a number of options for **providing infrastructure**. It can come from:

1. The **producing and/or delivering organization** (e.g., Open Business School)
2. The organization in which the **learner works** (self-help groups, site supervisors, etc.)

3.   The **learner** (setting deadlines, targets, making study plans, etc.).

Whether the reader is interested in producing, delivering or buying-in programmes, the message in this section is 'consider infrastructure as much as materials design and delivery'.

NEW WAYS OF LEARNING AND MANAGEMENT DEVELOPMENT

There is a growing discussion about the 'fit' between open and distance learning and MD. There are two elements to be considered: **access** to programmes and packages (which is predominantly the 'distance' dimension), and **suitability** (which is predominantly the 'openness' dimension).

Access

On the question of access, a facility where managers can learn **at times and paces to suit themselves** is a very attractive one, and seems to fit the life-style of the manager who may have to work irregular hours, travel extensively, etc. This is particularly so if the place of study is either at the desk or at home, but raises the question as to whether the learner is going to do this in his or her own time. This certainly seems to be an assumption that some organizations work on, and they therefore rightly claim a saving in cost against conventional methods of development and training. The advantage of 'doing it in the comfort of one's own home' can, of course, have negative connotations for some (what about the wife, kids, dog, etc.?).

Suitability

The suitability aspect recognizes that managers are most frequently mature experienced people who may not be excited by formal study methods, being predominantly people of action. They may be heavily orientated against attending long courses of study, and favour learning from experience, and inevitably look for the practical relevance of learning to their work situation. They may, therefore, be attracted by the use of video, micro-computers and other distance learning media, or the flexibility and choice offered in open programmes or packages.

Overall, there seems to be some sort of fit between learning which is both open and distance and management people; whether this potential is finally fully realized will become apparent as new developments are both created and researched.

THE FACTORS AFFECTING GROWTH OF OPEN AND DISTANCE LEARNING

There are a number of factors which have affected the growth of open and distance learning for management development. These factors can be summarized as follows:

The MSC Open Tech Programme of 1983–4

Some 20 projects were operational in the management and supervisory field in this programme; this represented a total development funding of £7 million, and there is no doubt that this was the single largest intervention in the management field, and without this money it is very difficult to see how many (if any) of these projects would have been operational. There is little doubt that this massive intervention by the MSC was of considerable historic importance; many people were involved in producing the programmes who had never been involved in such activity before.

Educational institutions

A number of educational institutions who specialize in the management field have either entered or plan to enter the field of distance learning; they have a high reputation and subject experts available. The Open University started up the Open Business School, and with Henley, Cranfield, Strathclyde and Warwick developed some of the first programmes.

New technology

Developments of hardware continue; software houses in the educational and training field are producing high-grade management courseware. Some of these groups also offer consultancy, design and training services.

Authoring systems or languages

Such materials (particularly authoring systems) allow training staff to programme micros or interactive video systems with little or no previous knowledge of programming or computers; this enables companies to develop their own sophisticated materials. It does not, of course, solve the problem of designing the material in the first place, which is the key to the quality of all distance learning programmes but it enables sophisticated designs to be transferred to interactive video systems.

TV production companies

The TV companies clearly see the possibility of making and selling high-quality video material into this new market.

Being left-behind

Most management development people are aware of these developments, and are increasingly coming under the influence of marketing activities from providers. The potential is clear, but views about what to do first are anything but clear. The need to do something, however, is pressing, and many organizations have now 'got their feet wet' and produced pilot projects.

RECENT AND POTENTIAL FUTURE DEVELOPMENTS

Small group interactions

There is an increasing use of **small groups of learners**. In many instances the assumption implied in design is that the learner is going to spend most of the time working solo with the materials. This may indeed be a pressing reason for engaging in distance learning in the first place, since the learner may be isolated in some way; however, the use of small groups opens up a number of possibilities. Limited experimentation indicates, for instance, that people using computer-based learning packages seem to learn much more when working in groups of two or three, although this extends the time of interaction. A group of two or three people working through a longer-duration programme (like a Henley programme) may provide infrastructure and support for each other on a self-help basis. The IV + technology allows packages to be designed for a pair of learners to interact; CMC allows for a group of geographically separate learners to interact with each other.

Self-management provision

Essentially, this means providing data bases, menus and choices, so that the learner is free to **select** exactly what she/he wants, and equally **miss out** exactly what she/he wants. This can be linked with self-diagnostic activities where learners can measure their **current levels of competence** in a particular area.

'Openness' in design

An emphasis on design which results in **'openness'** for the learner.

Deeper learning levels

Extension into the **affective learning** area and the deeper levels of **cognitive learning**.

'Off-the-shelf' materials

Self-directed groups inside organizations who have a wide variety of open and distance learning materials available 'off-the-shelf' **to use at any time**.

Hardware developments

New hardware, particularly based on **compact disc technology**.

Authoring languages and systems

More **powerful and user friendly** authoring languages and systems.

VCR/micro provision

Increased availability of VCRs and powerful micros for home-based learning.

AI/expert systems

Utilization of artificial intelligent (AI) and expert systems.

Satellite and cable links

Use of Prestel, cable television, satellite links, etc.

Collaborative expertise

More collaboration between a number of groups or individuals with **different expertise**, since inherently the whole operation of producing distance learning requires a great deal of skill not normally to be found in one person or one part of an organization, or even in one organization as a whole.

DILEMMAS FOR THE TRAINER AND MANAGEMENT DEVELOPER

The problems of deciding where to start for trainers or MD people are legion:

- What **level of technology** to go for – DVI, CD-I interactive video (disc- or tape-based), printed text, passive video, CMC or just computer-based?
- What **hardware** (if any) – which will in many cases fix the authoring language and the courseware that can be brought-in?
- Should one buy-in **generic** material, get it **'customerized'**; make one's own, or get someone else to do it?
- Which **areas of training** to go for – and who will the **learners** be?
- How should we negotiate **realistic budgets** for hardware, software and courseware and design and piloting?

To get started within an organization there are a number of steps which I personally believe are essential:

1. Treat the introduction of open and distance learning as an **organization development** (OD) problem; think out a change strategy based on a client-centred approach.
2. Find out what is available by contact with **producers** and **hardware manufacturers** (exhibitions, promotion meetings, trailer videos), or look for a suitable index.

3. Put as much thought into the **infrastructure** to support learning as into the design or selection of material and media themselves.
4. Evaluate a **pilot project**, using cheap in-house facilities (e.g., for an IV programme, a home made-video) and test the design out on 'real' learners **before** spending big money.
5. Ensure as far as possible that the **first pilot succeeds**.

Whether the trainer goes to workshops or conferences, hires a consultant, buys-in purpose-made courseware or generic material or starts on a DIY basis, the process is likely to involve **discovery learning**: from observation and conversation in the management field, a significant number of trainers and MD people are still pondering what to do.

CONCLUSION

The use of open and distance learning in the management field is being driven by a number of forces, as already noted. How it works out in the end remains to be seen, but I have a growing conviction that one of the key factors will be the **educational quality** of the programmes or packages which become available. Even more important is that the amount of research being done is still quite small; the market could be enormous: Henley in their early publicity quoted a figure of 80 per cent of British managers never having had any formal training. Open and distance learning may possibly divert people from the traditional form of management training and development into open and distance learning activities; many providers of management education and training have already got that message and are producing distance learning materials. The other more exciting possiblity however, is, that these methods may attract many more people to continue their development in a way which is suddenly much more acceptable to them than the traditional means of education or training; this may also be because the cost enables them to engage in activities which would otherwise be closed to them. If this is the case, and the Henley figure is correct, there is the possibility of accessing a market which is four times the size of the current one. The situation may therefore be that rather than substituting one form of training or education for another, people will engage in development which they would not otherwise have undertaken: this could be the difference between development and no development, and if that is the case we could make a significant improvement to the UK's management capability in the next few years.

My personal fear, however, is that if the quality of the materials – or of the infrastructure in which they are offered – is not good enough, or in line with what managers need, then the whole effort will become discredited, as so many previous ideas have become discredited in the management field. The necessary research programmes to allow high-quality material to be produced and intelligently used thus needs to continue; it is also important to realize that heavy marketing could well raise expectations far above reality, which again will surely be a way to discredit the whole operation. I am in general, however, optimistic that the considerable and exciting potential already visible will be converted into new practice.

NOTES

1. 'Take 2' interactive video system developed by Ivan Berg; obtainable from Quadrant Network, GT Associates, High Humbleton House, Wooler, Northumberland BE71 6SU.
2. Accura Human Factors advanced technology group (1985).
3. The Entrepreneur April Computing Executive Ltd, Chestnut Far, Tarvin Road, Frodsham, Cheshire WA6 6XN.
4. The Business Adviser, Taxation Systems Software, Sheffield (1987).
5. Maxim Training Systems, 6 Marlborough Place, Brighton, Sussex BN1 1UB.

REFERENCES

Bates, A. W. (ed.) (1985) *The Role of Technology in Distance Education* (London : Croom Helm).

Binsted, D. S. (1988a) 'Towards a Theory of Design for Interactive Video Programmes', *Interactive Learning International*, 4(3).

Binsted, D. S. (1988b), 'Text, Talking Heads or Live Video? Media Choice in Interactive Video', *Interactive Learning International*, 4(3).

Chatterton, P. (1990) 'Back to the Future of CD-I', *Training Technology* (January–February).

Hodgson, V. (1989) 'Open Learning and Technology-based Learning Materials', *Distance Education*, 10(1).

Hodgson, V., Lewis, R. and McConnell, D. (1989) 'Information Technology-based Open Learning – A Study Report' (University of Lancaster).

Mann, S. (1987) 'The effective design and delivery of open and distance learning for management education : A study of two open and distance learning packages for management education' (MSC/CSML).

McConnell, D. and Hodgson, V. (1990) 'Computer Mediated Communication Systems', *Management Education and Development*, 21(1).

Pedler, M. J., Burgoyne, J. G. and Boydell, T. H. (1978) *A Manager's Guide to Self Development* (London : McGraw-Hill).

Topham, P. (1989) 'The concept of "openness" in relation to computer based learning environments and management education', *Interactive Learning International*, vol. 5, pp. 151–163.

SOURCES OF FURTHER INFORMATION

1. Centre for the Study of Management Learning
    School of Management
    University of Lancaster
    Lancaster
    Tel: 0524 65201 ext. 4013
2. Henley Distance Learning Ltd
    Greenlands
    Henley on Thames
    Oxon RG9 3AU
    Tel: 0491 571552
3. The Management Development Programme
    Aston Business School
    Aston University
    Birmingham B4 7DU
    Tel. 021 359 3611 ext. 5002
4. National Interactive Video Centre
    24 Stephenson Way
    London NW1 2HD
    Tel. 071 387 2233
5. The Open University
    The Open Business School
    Walton Hall
    Bletchley
    Milton Keynes MK7 6AA
    Tel. 0908 274066 ext. 5870
6. Training, Enterprise and Education Division
    Department of Employment
    Moorfoot
    Sheffield S1 4PQ
    Tel. 0742 704996

10

Development work and the learning spiral

John Morris

BRINGING WORK AND LEARNING TOGETHER

What did you learn at school? How did you learn it? Could you teach what you have learned to others? These are formidable questions. Your answers might be: 'I learned a set of subjects which I've mostly forgotten'; 'I learned by being taught and from studying'; 'I don't think I could teach all that, but then I'm not a teacher'; followed by, 'Anyway, it was all a long time ago'.

But suppose the same questions were applied to the **work you are now doing**: What have you learned from doing your job? How did you learn it? Could you teach what you have learned to others? Are these questions any less formidable?

The experience of learning from doing your work is more recent, so you could probably go into far more detail in your answers; but you may still find that you are inclined to answer the last question with 'It's not my job to teach'. And yet, in the constantly changing and demanding world of management, it would be enormously valuable if experienced managers were able to help others to learn what they themselves have learned. Maybe that help would not take the form of 'teaching' in the traditional sense: whatever the label we find most comfortable – such as 'adviser', 'mentor', 'tutor' or 'coach' – we will be referring to the ability to enable others to improve their knowledge, their skill, or whatever else it is that they want to improve.

Many of us would like to do this, but find ourselves in difficulty: **work seems to drive out an awareness of learning**. While we were at school, or taking part in a training course, we knew that we were supposed to be learning. But at work the learning seems to happen without our knowing it. And yet we know that in many ways this is the very best kind of learning – that is why we often claim that 'learning from experience' or 'learning by doing' are the keystones of all real learning.

The problem seems to be this. How can one clearly distinguish 'work' from 'learning', and yet find ways of bringing them together skilfully and deliberately in a **self-managed flow of learning from experience?** In helping managers to tackle this problem, various models of learning styles have been immensely useful. Probably the best known approach is still that of David Kolb (Kolb *et al.*, 1979). This takes the form of four phases, each phase neatly contrasting with another in an elegant cross-formation. If you want to see your preferred style of learning, you complete a simple questionnaire and see yourself clearly represented on the model. You can then compare yourself with other people, of different ages, sexes, occupations and so on.

The four phases are given rather jaw-breaking names, but these can be quickly understood. 'Abstract conceptualization' is the process of **thinking about one's experience**; 'active experimentation' is the **application** of the **results of one's thinking**; 'concrete experience' is the emotional impact of being **actually involved in a new situation**; and 'reflective observation' is the process of **conscious reflection** on what has been **perceived** and **experienced**. The four phases also include contrasting aspects of the learning process: involvement and detachment, action and reflection.

Good models are for focusing our attention on something that interests us, not for covering everything in their domain. It is a tribute to Kolb's model that it has fostered variants – some would say improvements. It has also attracted sharp criticism: in my view, another tribute. I came to the model rather late, from a background in social and developmental psychology. My appetite had been sated with the rich fare of psychological research into learning processes (in fact, it had given me acute indigestion). Human learning turns out, as you can imagine, to be a fantastically complex affair, made even more complex because our **study of learning** is itself a **process of learning** – or, rather, a complicated hierarchical network of processes. When rich food fails to satisfy, something simple and salty is refreshing, and may prove far more nourishing. For me, the Kolb model met this need. His later work in developing the model shows how soundly based it is.

But I also found the Honey and Mumford model (1986) very attractive, especially in working with busy managers in short events. The words describing the phases were simpler than Kolb's, though they were turned into **types of managerial behaviour** rather than phases of learning. 'Activist', 'theorist', 'pragmatist', 'reflector': everyone can readily recognize these, and I found the questionnaire meatier than Kolb's. Add to all this a users' club in which members pool their scores and experiences of working with the approach, and we have a learning model which takes its own lessons seriously.

A further model of learning, in the form of personal development, was developed by Bert Juch (1983). Juch locates his learning model in a rich context of other studies, drawn from many fields. For good measure, he embeds his research investigation in a personal history, showing how he came to develop the model and what his experiences have been with it.

I have found these models illuminating and useful, but have also found it helpful to use another, which is close to them in its structure, but is more 'organizational' in its focus. Organizations are systems for getting work done, by dividing it up (usually very efficiently) and then putting it together again (notably less efficiently). The learning model that I have been using links directly to an **organization for doing work**.

Just a word or two on why I call the model a 'spiral' (Figure 10.1). I join with Juch here, it is really a preference for an open metaphor, rather than a closed one, like 'cycle' or 'style'. Juch talks of 'whirling cycles within a lifelong spiral' (p. 24): I find it useful to think of turnings in a spiral rather than sharp discontinuous levels of learning. But I cannot deny, from frequently repeated experience, that some of the turns can be very abrupt!

From Figure 10.1 it can be seen that at the bottom is the earthy activity of **'doing'** (that most flexible of terms), grounded in a **situation**. Above it are the classic managerial activities of **planning**, **monitoring**, and **reviewing**, and above that **forming** a purpose. If I had to find an extended phrase to include these phases of learning, it would be something like this: Learning from trying to express a *purpose* in action within a situation: *planning* being the shaping of an appropriate action, *monitoring* being the control of action as it occurs, and *review-*

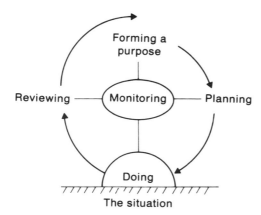

Figure 10.1 The learning spiral approach

ing being the comparison of the action with the purpose. The model has the virtue of being easily transposed from the individual to the group level, and to the organizational level. Since I am interested in linking individual, group and organizational levels of learning, it has been useful to have a model that seems to move so readily from individual to organization.

Another useful aspect of the model is that it enables one to see very clearly an unfortunate side-effect of the conventional form of organization. I call it 'splitting the learning' (see Figure 10.2). This obviously happens because of the manifold advantages of the division of labour, as against the organizational advantage of singleness of over-all purpose (survival, for example, or growth). But when we look at the implications of the division of work for the continuity of learning, it is clear that the devices used within organizations for turning purposes into action may not be those that occur in individuals when strongly-felt purpose is expressed in action. By and large, conventional organizations replace **strong feeling**, which is the individual link between purpose and action, with **tight control**. This produces one of the most depressing effects of this kind of organization – a splitting of commitment that results from a splitting of purpose from performance. I have called this 'the motivation gap' and have conservatively placed it below the managerial level of planning, monitoring and review in Figure 10.3. But many groups of managers I have worked with suggest that the motivation gap is often above that level, so that one

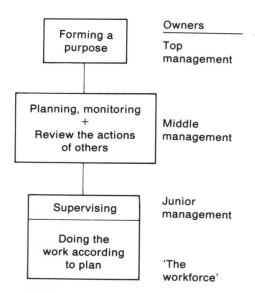

Figure 10.2   Splitting the learning

commonly finds a highly motivated Board of directors signalling their purposes wildly but ineffectively to a distinctly unmoved group of executives (see Figure 10.3).

There seems to be a powerful and attractive way of getting purpose and performance close together again: it is the direct action approach (see Figure 10.4). The purpose is embodied in a **leader**, rather than a mere owner, or director; the leader, full of the energy that flows from purpose, makes direct contact with those who take action, cutting across the managerial layers, and especially those with a concern for planning and review. One finds this commonly enough in small, entrepreneurial businesses, and in 'real-time management', celebrated for its hair-trigger response to emergencies.

Unfortunately, the by-passing of planning and review can have dire effect on many kinds of action. New products and services may take years to gestate, and will never appear if direct action rules. Routine performances may need to be carefully assembled and rehearsed, but will be ignored or under-valued by direct action. Direct action is splendid when it works, and often disastrous when it does not: it is all or nothing, and it certainly has no time for fostering learning, for

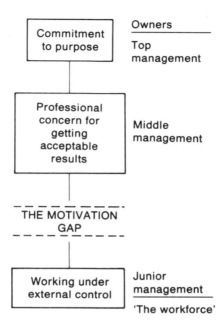

Figure 10.3   Splitting the commitment

enabling it to become conscious and reflective. Such qualities are seen as pernicious, as the forerunners of 'paralysis by analysis'.

Is it possible, then, to find other ways of countering the fragmentation that is all too common in the conventional organization, with its disastrous effects on an energetic flow of learning? Can we combine work and the whole spiral of learning? Clearly, to do so effectively requires an unconventional organization, one in which **purpose can infuse performance without loss of planning and review**. One way in which this purpose can be achieved is in the deliberately small world of a development programme, in which learning comes from project work – not project 'exercises' or project 'recommendations' but real **development work**, in which needs are met and there are changes for the better.

In a development programme, based on live projects, the energy that flows from purpose needs to be shaped into coherent activity through a process of continuous planning, monitoring and review. Instead of these 'managerial' activities being operated through a formal procedure of decision and control, the people who are engaged

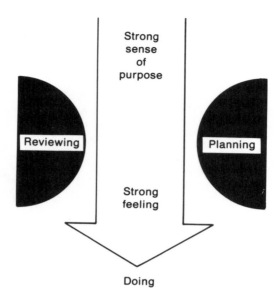

Figure 10.4   The direct-action approach

in the operational work of the project are able to relate their experience to the guiding purpose, which is very much **in themselves**. If we still wish to use the invidious term 'control' (invidious only when it comes to controlling people) we could say that a project is a **continuing experience of self-control** in the light of a **guiding and energizing purpose**. This stands in the sharpest possible contrast to the conventional organization, in which the work done by the 'workforce' is based on the distant and often inscrutable purposes of owners and investors, mediated by complex and often contradictory control procedures.

The development programmes I wish to comment on now have been part of the work of the Development Consortium, which is an innovative venture in management development, hived off from Manchester Business School in 1982 with the aid of the Foundation for Management Development. It is independent and self-funding, existing to foster initiatives in action learning and other forms of development work that seek to bring work and learning into the same set of activities. Unlike the usual management centre, it does not have a fixed staff, apart from the two managing partners and administrative support. It works wherever possible with practising managers as learning consultants and advisers. If other staff are needed, they are brought in for a specific programme. The basic unit of work is a **development programme**, usually consisting of several linked projects.

We often think of a 'consortium' as an ad hoc association of several substantial businesses coming together to manage an important project. The Development Consortium is a more informal association, bringing together individuals and teams rather than institutions, in development programmes of many kinds. These have included corporate strategy workshops with a major public corporation, senior development workshops for a leading textile firm, action learning programmes with the Co-operative Wholesale Society, participation in the design and staffing of the Senior Management Development Programme of the water industry, action research in new work options for mid-career managers, and a linked series of action learning programmes for the Manchester Social Services Department.

What do all these diverse activities have in common? They all take the form of **development activities**, rather than educational programmes or training courses. They all struggle to identify complex issues of real concern to the managers taking part, and they are all closely associated with managerial work, rather than being uncoupled from it. There is one other thing that these activities have in common. They all follow through the **whole learning spiral**, often through several turns. They relate purposes to performance, planning to review. They question purposes in the light of experience, rather than force experience (or reports of it) to conform to fixed purposes. They recognize that an effective development activity must find its own strong purpose, since it is exposed to so many sources of disturbance that lack of purpose will swiftly lead to its dissolution.

But any further search for common factors in diverse activities would probably be mistaken. One great value of development activities is that particular issues can be addressed in all their uniqueness. What might prove useful, however, is to note some of the experiences that seem pertinent to getting the learning spiral to work. The experiences are not pointed enough to be called 'lessons', and they are not solidly enough based to be claimed as 'evidence'. But they may indicate questions for later consideration.

DEVELOPMENT CULTURE AND DOMINANT CULTURE

Development projects bring two cultures closely together; these are the **dominant** culture and the **development** culture. The dominant culture is the set of values and ways of doing things that predominate in the organization, the tone usually being set by the central group of top management (or, in owner-managed enterprises, the owner). In a successful organization, the dominant culture will usually have strong developmental aspects, but these have to fit in to many other day-to-day requirements and pressures (see Chapter 6 above). The development project, on the other hand, has a licence to establish a development culture – and certainly a practical necessity to do so, if it is to be effective in achieving its task. Much of the literature dealing with developmental failures reveals situations in which the two cultures came into collision and, in the short run at least, the dominant culture won.

In the activities of the Development Consortium, the two cultures are brought together from the beginning, because a steering group is invariably part of the programme design. The steering group contains senior line managers from the organization or organizations taking part in the programme; they are members of the dominant culture, faced with the challenge of enabling the two cultures to work together to mutual advantage. The development culture knows all about mutuality: thrives on it, in fact. Not so the dominant culture. Most dominant cultures are greatly concerned with the maintenance of the **existing pattern of authority**, often exercised through a clearly-defined line of command. The task of balancing the two cultures provides a powerful learning experience for members of the steering group, and a continuing insight into the challenges each poses to the other.

COMING TO TERMS WITH TRIBES

Of course, there are far more than two cultures living within the organization; there are also the powerful **sub-cultures of the main business activities**: marketing, sales, production, distribution, finance, accounting, technical services, personnel. Many of these sub-cultures have been lovingly nurtured by professional education and training. Some of the professions provide traditions, career paths, rewards (and punishments) of great power and long standing; they cut across the dominant culture of the business, often providing opportunities for development, and sometimes unintentionally producing inertia, confusion and cynicism.

It does not seem too fanciful to see these sub-cultures as the sustaining elements in organizational tribes, and whenever I have discussed this notion with groups of managers, they have accepted it readily (particularly where other tribes are concerned). Indeed, in many an organization, the tribes and their mutual antipathy are taken for granted: a fact of life. Yet the experience of working with 'multi-tribal' project teams suggests that tribes are to some extent conventional metaphors, rather than all-powerful realities. Tribal loyalties may quickly be contained when a demanding and engrossing task is in hand.

Successful businesses seem to be able to bring the tribes together in a durable confederation, with the larger commitment of securing the success of the business as a whole. In a sense, the whole business becomes an effective blend of tribal loyalties and corporate commitment, like a small nation.

HUNGER FOR UNDERSTANDING OF STRATEGY

Managers who are working on projects quickly find themselves looking beyond their usual boundaries. Partly this is because development projects are chosen to widen their perspectives, and are invariably successful in achieving this; but it seems also to be a matter of getting a sense of how the organization as a whole is moving, and perhaps a hope that this will provide a set of useful guidelines for one's daily work, and a reasonably clear context for the project work. There is also a sense in which 'strategy' becomes a synonym for 'the overall purpose of the business'. Development work encourages questioning, and questioning sooner or later becomes a questioning of **purpose**: 'What are we doing this for anyway?'; 'How does this fit in with the other activities going on?' As the questions becomes wider, one can see them as expressing a real hunger for an understanding of the overbranching purposes of the organization.

The sheer sense of urgency that project work engenders – or perhaps it is rather a sharpened sense of organizational opportunities

– leads to confrontations which are focused on the feasibility of current organizational stances. In one of our programmes, managers in a project set accused top managers of leaving a 'strategic vacuum' within the business; when this was discussed, the top managers argued that the 'vacuum' was one of the many signs of the intractability of an old, highly ramified business with structural abysses a century old. The question for them was: How do we slowly form a strategy that can gain the commitment of all the varied interest groups sharing the business? Within the heightened consciousness of the project set, fresh from disturbing extrapolations of future business threats, this 'slow but sure' approach seemed unacceptably complacent.

It is characteristic of development work that it encourages these issues to be raised, and perhaps coped with; and it reminds us that the hunger for an understanding of strategy is part of the deeper need to couple performance with a durable sense of purpose: performances, however efficient, are not self-sustaining, especially when one begins to question them. At this point, the issue of **leadership** arises.

LEADERSHIP

There seem to be many kinds of leader. One well-known political figure was reputed to have said: 'I don't understand all this fuss about leadership. You just tell people what to do and they do it!' Another kind of leader would see this as domination, acceptable only in emergencies, and even then building up a formidable weight of resentment and subversion.

My own experience in project teams brings out a familiar insight: leadership flows from **demonstrable commitment to purpose**, which releases energies that focus attention. For those who share the purpose, this kind of free-flowing energy is attractive: the person imbued with purpose becomes a readily identifiable focus, an embodiment of what needs to be done. Because a project team is a kind of small world, capable of following through the whole learning spiral (usually several turns of it) in a manageable timescale, the presence of leadership is usually easily recognizable. Because the purpose is so clear and readily available, all members of a project team commonly find occasion to act as leaders, according to skill, sensitivity and circumstance.

KEEPING IT SIMPLE

In a major programme in the public sector, a visiting speaker from an entrepreneurial business made a great impact with his succinct and salty list of Do's and Don'ts for successful management. One of the best received of these was 'Keep it simple, stupid!'

We can understand why senior managers from an uncomfortably visible part of the embattled public sector should hunger and thirst after simplicity. All the more when the relevant Department of State complicates life for these managers by imposing its own notions of simplicity on their planning and operations. Yet it seems clear that success in most activities depends on holding the essentials of the business in mind (and at heart) as a set of vital priorities: 'as complex as you must, as simple as you can' emerges as a lesson from work in development projects, where it seems at times that almost everything is relevant to the project work, yet pressures of time and resource impose severe limits.

LEARNING FROM BEST CURRENT PRACTICE

Reg Revans (1983) identified a common weakness of senior managers which can seriously inhibit their capacity to learn. He noted that they eagerly accepted the influence of top managers who are undeniably successful, but they failed to appreciate that they might have something to learn from their colleagues, and from those who were lower down the organizational hierarchy. 'Best current practice' can be found in many places and at many levels, and it is vital for the manager not to be blinkered by the achievements of his seniors, or to become parochial in his or her choice of practices to emulate. By consciously adopting a broader perspective, the manager becomes able to learn from failures as well as from successes, and from a whole host of contacts, irrespective of formal status.

It is interesting from this point of view to look at the lessons drawn from two influential studies of best current business practice: the McKinsey study of American firms *In Search of Excellence* (Peters and Waterman, 1982), and the British study *The Winning Streak* (Goldsmith and Clutterbuck, 1984). Despite some interesting differences between the two, successful companies emerged as those with a

strong, distinctive culture, represented by the top management. They were firmly based in products and services in which they had a widely recognized competence, and which the managers knew how to manage. And they all had a distinctive ability to do a number of simple things well. But many of the simple things pulled in different directions and had to be skilfully balanced.

From the descriptions given in both books, it is clear that successful companies have dominant cultures with a strong and continuing thrust towards development – particularly to do things **better than others**. They succeed in countering their own tendencies to fragmentation by a great variety of devices: early fostering of general managers; high visibility of top managers and their priorities; internal promotion; continuing attempts to work with their members on the basis of mutual advantage; strong emphasis on informal communication, semi-autonomous business units, and careers open to the available talent.

One might wonder what semi-autonomous business units are doing in a list of ways of countering fragmentation: it is the **fragmentation of learning and commitment** that is of concern here, and small business units, with a close association of purpose and performance within the working group, come very close to providing a natural flow of learning from business experience. Many of these ways of countering fragmentation are open only to top management, and not the whole of top management at that. In order to effect the kinds of changes in structures and systems that many of the successful companies display, one would need a substantial mandate for reorganization. But this is only because we are seeking a solution to fragmentation on an organizational scale. If we reduce the scale, it is possible to see possibilities for bringing the key phases of the learning spiral energetically together on *any* scale of human activity. For example, the release of energies and creativity in those who choose to leave formal employment in order to start their own business is striking, yet commonplace. And within the organization, the current emphasis on self-development programmes enables individuals to look carefully at their own jobs in order to find opportunities for 'negotiated change' in line with their under-used skills and interests. It is perhaps not surprising that many of these programmes focus on the same issues as sophisticated studies of corporate strategy: identifying one's strengths and weaknesses in relation to external opportunities and threats; mobilizing one's resources; setting priorities; and developing the capability of continuous learning from experience.

It seems to me, then, that all the ways of countering the deep-seated drive to organizational fragmentation link up with one key theme. The task is to turn as much work as possible into **development work**, without seriously unbalancing the organization and wasting resources. It is worth recalling at this point, that we have not been arguing for the 'direct action' approach, though that has an intuitive appeal to most of us, with its sense of energy and commitment. The whole argument has been for opportunities for us to move purposefully through the **whole learning spiral**, with our own purposes providing the energies.

The learning spiral, seen as a whole, gives due place to planning and monitoring and review – all of them highly conscious, deliberate, responsible activities. The planning of development work must take into account its effect on other work; if this is not picked up in the planning phase of the learning spiral, it should be evident at the monitoring or review phases. Those development activities that incur avoidable costs or unbalance the system of which they are a part need be carefully checked against their initial purpose. Was the purpose over-ambitious, or naive? Since the purpose itself is part of a set of wider purposes, it can itself become the **focus of learning**. In fact, we all too often take our purposes for granted, and doggedly keep them uncritically fixed, while we continually fail to produce the performances that would adequately express them, or achieve them. If we are committed to continuing learning, we need to keep our purposes **under continuing review**. In this way, as we change and the world changes around us, we can relate them to more comprehensive and coherent purposes: a sure sign of maturity. I know that it can sound rather odd and confusing to talk about 'learning to learn'. But we can easily recognize that one of our purposes can be to **manage our own learning**: to become aware of how we are currently learning, and to find ways of improving it. If we do not manage ourselves, we will find no lack of other people willing and eager to manage us, to their own advantage.

Not all development work has to be cast in the form of a project (though there is nothing to stop us seeing our own learning activities as personal projects: it sharpens the mind). Most enterprises, however enterprising, use the term 'project' rather sparingly, to describe major initiatives or 'one-offs'. And yet every really successful organization is full to bursting with development work, because people have become members of a culture which places great emphasis on doing things well, and then doing them better.

To return to the theme of my chapter: if we want to get the learning spiral to work, we must treat it consistently as a **development spiral** focusing on the endless opportunities for development work – from the smallest improvement in working practices or product quality to the most cosmic 'great society' that our collective imaginations and skills can devise. In development work, small or large, the divided activities of work and learning, purpose and performance, long separated by conventional forms of organization, come together in a continuing process of **changing for the better**.

REFERENCES

Goldsmith, W. and Clutterbuck, D. (1984) *The Winning Streak* (London: Weidenfeld & Nicolson).

Honey, P. and Mumford, A. (1986) *The Manual of Learning Styles*, 2nd edn (London: Honey).

Juch, A. H. (1983) *Personal Development* (Chichester: John Wiley).

Kolb, D. A. *et al.* (1979) *Organizational Psychology*, 3rd edn (Englewood Cliffs, N.J.: Prentice-Hall).

Peters, T. J. and Waterman, R. H. (1982) *In Search of Excellence* (New York: Harper & Row).

Revans, R. W. (1983) *The ABC of Action Learning*, 2nd edn (Bromley: Chartwell-Bratt).

PART IV
MANAGEMENT DEVELOPMENT
IN ACTION

11

An in-house senior managers' programme for organizational change

Bruce Nixon

We live in exciting times: changes are taking place which would have been inconceivable only a few years ago; rising expectations and the forces of necessity are compelling us to learn and find fresh solutions both globally and in the workplace (Naisbitt and Aburdene, 1985). Demographic changes are giving new urgency to the need to make better use of women, black people, young people, older people and the disabled. People expect to be treated with respect and are less willing to tolerate the old, relatively oppressive ways of managing that many of us have grown up with. More people expect their work to be **qualitatively connected to the rest of their lives**; they believe that work should be, and can be, fulfilling, exciting and fun and that there should be excellent opportunities for development and self-expression.

Organizations which meet these expectations are likely to be the ones which survive and prosper in the 1990s; they will attract and inspire the best people and learn how to release their energies and intiative in achieving corporate goals. Only in this way will organizations respond to the unpredictable changes and upheaval which lie ahead.

I believe that this situation requires a new style of leadership (Simmons, 1989) which is more **empowering and supportive**. Key elements of this are likely to be:

- Holding out an **inspiring vision**, based on values and beliefs, which appeals to people at every level
- Inviting others to **contribute their own exciting vision**
- Creating a **climate** in which everyone will offer their full energy, vision and talents
- Becoming a **leader of leaders**, not followers; releasing individual initiative
- Learning to **welcome change and upheaval**, and encouraging others to do so
- Making fresh, accurate responses to **each new situation**
- Creating an **environment** where there is praise, encouragement, support and challenge, instead of criticism and blame
- Seeing the **whole situation** and deciding to see to it that everything goes well
- Giving up the pretence that the leader knows best and always knows what to do; instead, admitting that **we are all apprentices**, constantly learning how to do the job well
- Giving up blaming and complaining, and instead taking responsibility for **deciding and acting**

I do not believe this is merely an enlightened way of managing: it is fast becoming an economic necessity.

This situation, if I have diagnosed it correctly, presents people in management training and development with an enormous opportunity. To rise to the occasion we need to see ourselves as **leaders of organizational change and development**; it will not be enough to continue traditional management training and development with its emphasis on teaching knowledge and skill. Instead, we shall need to create learning situations in which managers can work on the actual opportunities and problems they face in their own jobs. This requires an approach which puts managers in charge of their own learning by providing a flexible but rigorous structure and a supportive but challenging atmosphere.

The following case study describes an attempt to provide such an approach; to bring out and support the managers' desire for change and for new ways of managing people; to help them translate their vision into reality. The work described was started in 1986 and since then many more programmes like it have been run in Sun Alliance and still continue. The author is now working as an independent consultant and finding widespread interest both in a new leadership style and in new approaches to management development (MD) which focus on planning and implementing change and put managers in charge of their own learning. At first they find it strange, and it needs to be carefully presented to them. Once they start to experience it there is no looking back. They say it is exactly what they want.

CASE STUDY SYNOPSIS

Most programmes for senior managers are either run in business schools or management colleges or largely employ external resources. What is unusual about this case study is that it describes a successful programme designed and run **in-company**. It is based on the philosophy that the trainers and the participating managers collectively have all the resources they need. It is a 'nuts-and-bolts account which will interest other trainers who want to initiate something similar in their own organizations.

Two training managers (Richard Allen and Bruce Nixon) took the initiative to start a senior management development programme; they overcame the resistance to such an initiative; they pilot-tested the concept with six 'sympathetic' senior managers who later helped sell the new programme to twelve colleagues. We shall see the lessons they learnt from this pilot programme: how, in their experience, a programme for senior managers needs to differ from one for middle management. The programme is now helping to change the way that managers in the Sun Alliance Insurance Group manage.

The study describes how the participants were recruited, and what the selection criteria were; the organizational issues that had to be confronted as part of the long-term strategy for organization development (OD) in Sun Alliance are set out. The study also gives specific details of the objectives and structure of this twelve-month programme, and the issues and needs that emerged in the pre-course briefing meetings. It describes the design philosophy, and how the first workshop was designed; how we overcame our own fears in conducting the programme, what actually happened, and how that compared with our expectations. We also quote from the reactions of the delegates themselves.

BACKGROUND HISTORY

The need for management development for senior managers (i.e., those at the level below top management) had been widely recognized in the company; external programmes had been used for a time, however, this approach had largely ceased, mainly because it was difficult to establish what benefits managers (and hence the organization) gained. The feedback received typically showed difficulty in applying any learning back in the workplace. We had developed a range of in-company programmes for junior and middle managers; we were also doing a great deal of work with management teams. In all of this in-company work our approach was to help managers develop themselves by tackling the key business and organizational issues confronting them (Allen and Nixon, 1986). However, some key issues could be resolved only by senior and top managers; their role in strategic management and in creating an organizational climate in which people would give their best was crucial. Yet hitherto they had seldom been directly involved in management development programmes. Earlier proposals for the development of senior managers had not met with success (for reasons about which we will speculate later, reasons connected with some of the key issues facing the organization). Despite this, we knew from our contacts that there would be extensive support for a programme amongst senior managers themselves. So we decided to take the initiative. We invited six managers to a small-scale pilot programme; with their help and support we learnt a great deal about how to design and run a programme for senior managers (our previous experience had mainly been in work with junior and middle management). We incorporated what we learned from the pilot in the more ambitious programme.

After many years of working with managers at middle levels and talking with senior and top managers we had considerable information about the **needs** and **key issues** of the organization. In their view, the key areas where **improvement** was needed were:

- strategic management
- the management of change
- the leadership and motivation of large numbers of people
- gaining commitment to common purpose and agreed strategies
- creating effective teamwork and trust

- creating a climate in which people will give all they are capable of and which encourages them to develop themselves
- articulating values and beliefs as a basis for strategy.

From talking with managers, it was apparent that some of the difficulties that **got in the way** of these improvements were:

- competitiveness
- inter-divisional rivalries
- a tendency to 'trash', blame and criticize rather than to take intiatives and to support one ๑nother
- lack of trust or openness
- unwillingness to acknowledge development needs in case this was seen as weakness
- a tendency to over-control
- fear and feelings of personal inadequacy ('who am I to change things?').

Managers in other organizations and industries will no doubt recognize most or all of these, as they are common difficulties. (It must be added that this is not how people behave most of the time; they are usually responses to very stressful or difficult situations.) Some of these were the very issues which had frustrated earlier attempts to initiate a programme. So we knew that we should be 'taking on' these issues in trying to start and successfully complete a new programme.

The Senior Management Development Programme would be a major further step in a long-term strategy to tackle these issues; if we chose the participants well they would be respected people who would be widely influential, and many of them would move into top management over a period of time. If the first programme was successful, many more could take place and thus, over a long period, the programme could be extremely influential. We believed it would help considerably in bringing about beneficial changes in the way the Group was managed. It was a very exciting opportunity.

SELECTING THE DELEGATES

We knew from the pilot programme that the selection of delegates would be critical. We wanted twelve participants representative of all the key trading and service divisions of the Group; we knew from experience that there would be varying degrees of support from top management. Therefore we approached most participants direct and made it clear to them that it would be their responsibility to secure approval to attend; the delegates supported this approach as the most appropriate way of quickly and easily securing approval. We were open about our **specification for delegates**; they should be:

- determined to achieve excellence
- open: about themselves, their needs and difficulties, and to what others have to offer
- keen to learn and develop
- willing to share what they have to offer
- willing to be supportive: both encouraging and prepared to tackle difficult issues
- prepared to be rigorous in tackling important issues
- already successful in a key senior role, and likely to progress further
- committed to see the programme through regardless of changes in their job.

We approached people who we thought met this specification, people with whom we already had a friendly working relationship and most of whom knew about the work we had been doing with middle managers and supported our approach. In some cases, we asked them who they would find it exciting to work with on a programme like this, and we followed up these suggestions. One or two declined our invitations but we soon had twelve would-be participants. Our thinking was to work with people who were 'ready' and would carry back to their job and their colleagues what they had gained. We were not at this stage aiming to 'take on' people who were reluctant or resistant to change.

It may help at this point to define what we mean by 'senior managers': the managers were at the level below top management and typically in charge of substantial parts of major service functions or major business sectors (e.g., the Chief Accountant; the Overseas Division Manager in charge of all services; the Manager, Computer Services; the Manager, Linked Life and Unit Trust Business Area; the Commercial Business Manager; the Deputy Investment Manager).

Many have since been appointed to the Boards of the newly formed companies within the Group.

PITFALLS TO AVOID

We wanted to avoid the pitfalls of traditional management training. In our experience, these are:

1. Insufficient research before designing programmes to find out what individual managers **really need and want**
2. No steps taken to **build relationships with the managers** before the programme
3. Not enough emphasis placed on building the trust and the safety to talk about **what really matters** and the **real difficulties** people have
4. Emphasis upon knowledge and skill rather than helping managers bring about real changes in their **work**, and continuing changes in their **attitudes** and **behaviour**
5. **Individual** and **organizational goals** not properly set, and not enough time devoted to planning, and planning the support for acting
6. Insufficient attention to **individual needs**, and participation may be low because of a high participant–tutor ratio, rigid course design and lack of opportunity for managers to take responsibility for their own learning.
7. Content is regarded as **too theoretical**, and **not relevant**
8. Contrived situations used as vehicles for learning rather than the living reality of the **participants' own work**
9. Insufficient **organizational support** for participants, on return to the job, to apply what they have learned.

We were determined to avoid all of these pitfalls by talking to each participant about his own goals and needs, building relationships, developing trust, focussing on his work and the changes he wanted to make, creating a **long-term learning structure** that would support change, build in support and give responsibility for personal learning.

PROGRAMME DESIGN

Lessons learned from the pilot programme

What would be different about working with senior managers, as compared with middle managers (Nixon, 1985)? Some differences would be obvious: the focus would be broader and more long-term; on strategy rather than operations; and it may well be harder to develop an atmosphere in which people would be really open about their needs and difficulties – at least, that was our irrational fear. (Why is it that we see senior people as more inhibited and somehow less human?) Among the lessons we learnt from the 'pilot' programmes were that:

- full representation of all the key **trading and service divisions** was extremely important to senior managers
- **selection** was vital: one or two people with severe difficulties in trusting others or difficulties with our design philosophy could impede the progress of others
- more structure was expected by senior managers, but the right balance between **structure** and **flexibility** was crucial
- talks and handouts had to be very polished and confidently delivered; hence more time for **preparation** was needed
- unlike middle managers, the senior managers did not initially take to the idea of learning to counsel each other and preferred **private consultations** with tutors
- nevertheless, they would welcome the formation of **support-groups** which would meet between the formal events of the programme
- it was important to keep the pace brisk, to be flexible and responsive and to be decisive (and right!) in making **changes** to the programme
- we should progress from strategy to managerial skills and issues, and finally offer the opportunity to deal with key personal issues, only when enough **trust and safety** had been established
- senior managers often have expectations of a structured and largely didactic design; therefore the design should be thoroughly explained *before* each delegate decided to attend; for this reason we decided to hold a 'pre-day' fully to explain our approach

- they wanted practical help and guidance on **real back-at-work issues**, and very little theory
- despite our fears, we were **fully capable of running the programme ourselves** and had a great deal to offer at all levels – knowledge, skills and attitudes
- the managers wanted, and expected, us to **stand up and express our views** – not to be cautious or 'hold back'.

Principles of design

The principles on which the programme design was based were as follows:

1. The subject matter of the programme would be the **stategies of the participants**, and whatever plans, actions, skills, attitudes and issues needed to be worked on to implement them.
2. There would be no **contrived exercises** (e.g., simulations, role-plays, case studies or games).
3. Learning would be largely by planning, acting, reviewing and reflecting – and (most important) **learning** from each other.
4. On the basis that there would be twelve well-informed participants from a wide variety of disciplines, we decided **not to invite in any expert speakers in advance**; we would discuss the need with them during the first workshop and subsequent briefings. We also decided not to invite top management to participate as speakers, on the basis that these senior managers had good access to top management back in the job. In making this decision we did calculate the disadvantage of not having their active support; however, we judged that the results would speak louder than anything else.
5. Tutors would give short talks on key issues that might not otherwise be addressed and provide suitable videos, papers, articles and books; some inputs would be on tools and techniques. We would also 'speak out' on major issues, say things that we thought needed to be said. Otherwise, our role would largely be to offer appropriate **structures and methods**, to lead sessions or small groups, and to coach and counsel.
6. Delegates would work in a variety of forums; in the plenary group; in support groups; in topic or interest groups; in pairs; in

private consultations with tutors; or on their own. Three tutors would be provided. The **individual and distinct needs** of each participant could thus easily be provided for.

7. The programme would be a **twelve-month experience** on the basis, first, that such delegates are concerned with longer-term change and strategy and, secondly, that significant learning requires a sufficiently long period for planning, acting, reviewing, reflecting and trying again.

In many ways the approach was similar to that adopted with middle managers (Nixon, 1985). The most significant differences were:

- **Three workshops over a twelve-month period** as opposed to two over four–six months
- The emphasis on **long-term change and strategy**
- The relative caution that we expected about learning to **counsel each other** or deal with **key personal issues** other than in private consultations with tutors
- that a programme at this level could have a **profound influence** on the way in which managers in the Group manage.

PROGRAMME STRUCTURE

The structure of the programme is shown in Figure 11.1. The purpose of the 'pre-day' was thoroughly to explain the underlying design and the principles, and to get real commitment to the programme before 'signing on'. We wanted delegates to be *sure* beforehand. We were considerably helped by two delegates from the 'pilot' programme who gave a frank account of their experiences and the benefits they had gained, as well as the difficulties they had encountered. We chose two people who were respected, well known and would be frank about their experiences.

The individual briefing meetings were designed to enable the tutors to build relationships with the delegates; to help the delegates think clearly about their needs, and how they would use the programme; and, finally, to enable the tutors to collect information about the needs of delegates and their key issues so that they could design each workshop appropriately.

Pre-day	June 1986
Individual briefings	August–September 1986
Design work	September 1986
Workshop 1	October 1986
Implementation	
Support groups meet	
Individual briefings	
Design work	
Workshop 2	February 1987
Implementation	
Support groups meet	
Individual briefings	
Design work	
Workshop 3	June 1987
Review of design	

Figure 11.1   Programme structure

To:
- Explore the changes taking place in the UK, and global environment (economic, technological, social . . .) relevant to Sun Alliance
- Build a vision of how Sun Alliance and your part of it needs to respond
- Decide how you and your team need to contribute
- Develop career strategies and plans which you will implement
- Identify the key issues you need to resolve, and changes you need to make in order to achieve your goals
- Further develop any crucial skills
- Build a cross-divisional support network for achieving excellence

Figure 11.2   Programme objectives

Each workshop would be of about three-and-a-half days' duration. Between each workshop delegates would implement their plans, and it was our hope and expectation that they would meet each other in small 'support groups' to give each other help and encouragement in implementing their strategies. This has happened. The objectives of the programme and an outline of each workshop are shown in Figures 11.2 and 11.3 respectively.

Workshop 1   Developing a strategy for excellence
- Scenarios: scanning the business environment
- Making Sun Alliance No. 1 – what that means
- Creating a vision for my sector
- Objectives, strategies, plans
- Key issues for me

Workshop 2   Leadership in Sun Alliance
- Review progress since previous workshop: successes, new developments, difficulties
- Key issues to emerge
- Leadership in Sun Alliance
- Developing really effective teams
- Managing change
- Other key issues or topics
- Update and further develop plans

Workshop 3   Consolidating success
- Further review of progress
- Further work on key issues or skills
- Developing people and creating the environment and support for people to achieve excellence
- Further plans
- Review of whole programme

Figure 11.3   The three workshops

This was the programme which we presented to twelve potential participants in June 1986. Eleven ultimately emerged as firm participants and we started the briefings at the end of the summer.

THE KEY ISSUES FOR THE PARTICIPANTS

From the briefing meetings the three tutors gained a clear picture of the key issues facing each delegate, his views on the best ways of using his time in the first workshop and the 'pay-off' that would result if the workshop fully met his requirements. With the flexible structure and the high tutor–delegate ratio it would be perfectly possible to meet these needs and expectations.

A number of common issues emerged:

- Creating a **shared vision of the future** to which all are committed

By the end of this workshop you will have:

1. **Built a clear vision** of the way ahead for Sun Alliance, for you and your part of the organisation – fully consistent with you, your values and your beliefs
2. **Explored** and shared ideas about **the major changes** taking place in the UK and the rest of the world
3. Developed **clear objectives, strategies and plans** you will implement
4. **Identified** the **key issues** you need to deal with now **and** the **changes** you need to make
5. Identified and started to develop any **skills and knowledge** you need to achieve your objectives
6. Built **a support group** for yourself

Figure 11.4   Objectives of workshop 1

Day 1   (Starting mid-afternoon)
S1   Welcome and introduction
S2   Introduction
S3   In Search of Excellence (video)
Day 2
S4   Creating vision and strategy
S5   Scanning the environment – major trends
S6   Implications: for you and your team; key issues to be resolved
S7   The key to it all: you
Day 3
S8   Identifying and planning key changes
S9   Work on key issues and changes
Day 4
S9   Further work on key issues and changes
S10   Commitments: plans to implement strategies and arrangements for support groups
S11   Review

Note:
*S = Session

Figure 11.5   Programme for workshop 1

- Dealing with **change** in a **relaxed, flexible** and **optimistic** way
- Coping with **increasing pace and pressures**
- Getting things done without **bruising people** (others or oneself)
- Creating an **environment** in which people can achieve all they are capable of

- Building **trust, support** and **cooperation**
- Using our own creativity and skill in a **positive** way.

Reassuringly, these issues were similar to those identified by the three trainers prior to initiating the programme. On the basis of these needs the first workshop was designed, as shown in Figures 11.4 and 11.5.

WHAT HAPPENED IN PRACTICE – THE FIRST WORKSHOP

In practice, the first workshop far exceeded our expectations. In a relatively short paper it would be inappropriate to describe the workshop in detail; we will instead comment on some of the factors which seem to have been crucial to its success:

1. The introductions were absolutely crucial in creating a **climate of openness and trust**. So often introductions are a superficial ritual; we devoted some three hours to this session, and the questions each participant addressed were extremely carefully thought out:

    - Your name
    - Where you are from – brief history
    - Three things it is important for us to know about you (that aren't obvious)
    - Current important issues for you as a manager – opportunities or difficulties
    - Something you are proud of about yourself
    - Aims for the programme and for this workshop.

    Before the introductions took place participants paired up to work through what they would say. Their chosen partner stood beside them whilst they introduced themselves. The tutors started by introducing themselves in an attempt to set a standard of openness; this was commented on by the delegates as having been **crucial in setting the tone**.
2. The use of the video 'In Search of Excellence' was useful (at least to some), in that it raised a wide range of managerial issues and in a sense 'legitimized' being **visionary**.
3. All the major sessions were introduced by tutors who gave short

inputs on the key issues involved; they said the things that were hard to say, and thus perhaps made it easier for others to say things that might otherwise have seemed too risky – e.g, encouraging them to talk about how it really is at their level, the difficulties they face as men and how they **really feel**.

4. The session on 'Creating Vision and Strategy' was also crucial. We stressed that their strategy should be based on a vision that was rooted in **personal values and beliefs**; that this was how to create a strategy to which they and their team would be fully committed. We stressed that the vision should be **complete** – not just of their sector of the business but of the Group as a whole, and that it should include their personal life, otherwise it would not be integrated. We encouraged them to use pictures, symbols and music – not just words – to describe their vision. Some of the work on vision and strategy was done individually and some in syndicate; but perhaps the most crucial part was at the beginning when we encouraged each of them to choose a 'friend', who would listen and give encouragement whilst he talked about his vision. As in the introductions, the senior managers were being introduced to the power of being listened to (without noticing it). This was followed by a plenary session in which everyone shared their vision. The atmosphere was emotional and 'electric'.

5. Another key feature was the use of **feedback**. So much of the time organizational life is about criticism, 'trashing' and complaining (whether face-to-face or behind one's back) rather than taking positive initiatives. What would it be like in an environment where people were given appreciation and friendly advice instead? We decided to show people what it would be like. Session 7 (Day 2) was an opportunity for people, first, to celebrate their own successes, achievements and qualities and, secondly, to receive from others, both sincere appreciation and friendly advice. Most people found the first part extremely difficult and yet **a full appreciation of oneself** is so crucial to achieving excellence. The managers were learning to do amongst themselves the very things that would pay dividends in their own teams back on the job.

6. It was important to work **one-to-one** with the managers and to encourage free expression of thought and feeling. Several managers had very strong feelings about issues, both personal and work-based, and they could see clearly that these affected

their performance. Working on these feelings enabled them to make clear decisions about what they needed to do.

7. The formation of **'support groups'** was crucial. Their formation was encouraged during the first workshop; the process began with the choice of a 'friend' during the introductions. Each pair then chose another pair to form a support group which regularly met for the rest of the workshop. We encouraged these support groups to meet after the workshops – and they did.

8. Finally, the **support the three tutors gave each other** was vital. We were trying to confront some of the rigid patterns of the organization (Nixon, 1986); doing this requires confidence and courage: you can easily lose your confidence, even think you are the 'lunatic who has 'got it all wrong'. Yet the situation **requires** you to do it, and managers want you to do it. If you open up the issue it makes a huge difference, as others then feel safe enough to follow and speak freely too. If you do not, nothing changes and the opportunity is lost; you have played safe when the task required you to take the risk. It is stressful and at times frightening; it requires the support of your colleagues to encourage you to keep doing it, to say to you 'Yes, you've got it right' or, even, 'Go further!'. The feedback we received from the pilot programme confirmed this: this is what the managers expect you to do – to 'stand tall' and state clearly what you believe.

Why do we feel able to say that the first workshop 'far exceeded our expectations'? Surely it was too soon to evaluate the programme after one workshop? Indeed it was. But the comments of the delegates were astonishing, and their vision of how they wanted the organization to be was inspiring. Their diagnosis and their vision was almost exactly the same as our own. This was very exciting and encouraging to us. We quote part of a summary of the common features of their visions in Figure 11.6; their strategies were based on these visions of the future. In Figure 11.7, we quote some of the comment on the workshop.

WHAT HAD HAPPENED THREE MONTHS LATER?

At the end of January 1987 before designing the second workshop, we contacted the participants to find out how they had been getting on.

Human environment – belief in people

- Good leadership – top management in front
- Freedom and encouragement
- Dealing with conflict openly – not shirking it
- Tolerant and patient
- Good supportive place to work
- Working towards a common purpose
- Cooperation – energy directed outwards – not in competition or holding on to power
- Not bureaucratic
- Not perfection – allowing mistakes
- Valuing ourselves and each other

Posture towards change

- Quick to respond
- Innovative
- Correct definition of the business
- Hopeful and optimistic
- Good strategic planning

Figure 11.6   The vision of Sun Alliance

- A different way of life
- I've appreciated how much better I could be
- Nicely flexible – able to get out of it what was necessary
- Learnt to appreciate my strengths
- If only the office was like this we'd get a lot more done
- Tremendous supportive atmosphere from the first day
- One thing: I came battered and bruised. It has restored my self-confidence. Everyone has similar problems.

Figure 11.7   What participants appreciated

All the managers had met, typically off-site at a hotel, at least once in their 'support' groups, and reported that these meetings were highly productive. Apart from the support this provided in achieving their goals, there were other benefits: managers of service functions were building (much needed) closer relationships with their 'customers' (managers of trading units); trading unit managers were getting expert help; some of the barriers mentioned earlier were being broken down; certain key issues for the Group to tackle were emerging in these meetings which they wanted to work on in the second workshop; the managers were clearly excited about the whole development.

What were the individual managers doing differently? Most reported **significant changes in how they were managing**:

- 'I am pacing myself better; I have learnt to say "No" and to be "selfish" when I need to be; I am keeping better contact with people; I am feeling better about myself'.
- 'I have been very active with seniors and colleagues in developing the strategic corporate plan. I have made progress in getting the support of colleagues'.
- 'I am enjoying the job more. I am looking forward to changes with enthusiasm'.
- 'I have come back with a very positive attitude. I have always been fairly emotional. I've accepted it. I have tried to be more conscious of my impact on others'.
- 'John and I are more open with each other'.
- 'Things have gone very well. There is a better understanding amongst the team. Interpersonal relationships have developed in the right direction. We have moved forward in the right direction. We are performing up to best expectations. There is a good chance we shall evolve the correct philosophy from here – not yet completed but it is easy to envisage. The task for 1987 is to move on this process of evolution and implementation'.
- 'What am I doing differently? I am working at breaking down the barriers and misunderstandings. I am generating a team spirit. . . It is very much appreciated. I found it difficult'.
- 'I am very keen to motivate people properly and get the best out of them. I am breaking down the office "aura" and people do speak up more. I am developing a different way of working – different from what people are conditioned to. Progress so far is encouraging'.
- 'I have thought deeply about what I really should be involved in; what others should be involved in. I have sorted the structure and processes out. I have sorted my role out'.

THE SECOND WORKSHOP

The second workshop was conceived and designed to build on these successes, and also to help the participants continue their development and tackle any further blocks or obstacles. There was a real fear (both amongst the delegates and the tutor team) that the second workshop could not live up to the heights and standards achieved in Workshop 1; these fears proved unfounded judging by the end-of-workshop plans and comments of the participants. Most explicitly stated that Workshop 2 had been of even more use than Workshop 1.

So how did we build on the successes of Workshop 1? Again it is not possible or appropriate to describe the workshop in detail (the outline design is shown in Figure 11.3), but several factors were crucial to the continued success:

1. We again created a climate of openness and trust through detailed **'re-introductions** covering both successes and difficulties since Workshop 1 and current thoughts on how to use Workshop 2. As in Workshop 1, these introductions took three hours to prepare and complete (longer again than we anticipated) and were enormously valued by everyone.
2. We introduced the concept of 'Influencing through a Network' and identifying key people with whom to **build links**; this proved very useful to many. So often managers devote an inordinate amount of energy to getting things done only through the very formal channels and not using their 'friends' in the business. Most participants included better use of their network in their end-of-workshop plans.
3. For Day 3 we offered a range of sessions to enable participants to tackle their own priorities (as they had emerged during Days 1 and 2) and we included space for **private thinking and planning**. Having three tutors allowed the flexibility for the following structure to emerge:

   Plenary session
   To explain the proposal structure for the day and to enable people to choose options
   Options 1
   Presentations; managing stress; team-building; personal thinking time

Personal counselling sessions

One-to-one sessions or personal thinking time. The timetable provided for two 45-minute personal counselling sessions with a tutor or another participant – one before and one after lunch

Options 2

Counselling skills; influencing; managing a secretary; personal thinking time

Support groups

To compare the functioning of the support groups in the workshop with that of 'back at work' teams

4. The option groups provided a 'bonus' in mixing up the support groups; it gave everyone the additional opportunity further to develop their links with the whole group, and thus their **personal networks**. This was a specific request which emerged from Workshop 1.

5. We encouraged the participants to see the benefits of, and make full use of, all the resources and expertise available to them, and **overcome the fear of asking for help**. This is emerging as a key factor in the whole process – it is very often difficult for senior people (particularly men) to ask for help. It may show 'I have a weakness' or 'something I am not fully in control of'. The logic then goes something like: 'To be a Senior Manager you shouldn't have to ask for help or even feel as if you need it – if you do have any weaknesses you hide them away so that no one can see or suspect'. As we in the UK are slowly discovering, this thinking is fundamentally backward: people are very perceptive; they can see when senior managers are having difficulties and are in need of help. It does not help anyone to try and disguise this, or pretend it is not so. We are slowly creating an environment through the programme where people are **taking charge of their own learning**; asking for help and gradually dealing with more fundamental issues (e.g., getting a better balance between work and home life; dealing with feelings such as resentments or anger and other personal issues affecting work).

6. Again we provided a strong push to produce **concrete strategies** and **action plans** to be shared with the whole group. The commitment and excitement generated by doing this provided crucial support to the participants and increased the probability that they would successfully implement them.

THE THIRD WORKSHOP

Once more, we went out to talk to the participants to find out what they wanted in the third workshop. The enthusiasm of the extremely busy senior managers to return for Workshop 3 was overwhelming and their encouragement to the tutors was to 'tell us all you know and don't edit your thinking' – quite a different situation from the caution shown at the start. From the comments we received the main attraction and stimulation was to return to a safe, open environment with space and time to think with friends who would be straight but supportive.

The design that we developed differed from the original intention (as shown in Figure 11.3) and included: celebrating successes; taking responsibility for leadership in the Group; why leaders need to counsel, be counselled and teach others to counsel and then, as in Workshop 2 a day for options (influencing, running meetings, dealing with difficult people, delegation, etc). Again, the managers took charge of attending the sessions to suit themselves which included having personal time to think. Many had periods of 1:1 time with each other.

EFFECT OF THE PROGRAMME ON THE BUSINESS

In truth, we do not know. We have not systematically asked, nor are we likely to. In the world of business, managers are impatient of research. They are pragmatic: if it helps, they want more of it; if it does not, they stop it. In this respect it is significant that by 1989 seven programmes had been held and two more were planned for 1990. We now realize it is a very **long-term initiative** whose benefits will take years to have their full effect and to be evaluated. The best indications we had at the end of the second programme were the final comments of the participants.

- 'I now find myself once again firmly in touch with my personal philosophy and more importantly, confident and excited by what we can all achieve within the Group. Words somehow seem inadequate – a breath of fresh air, a common-sense revolution, of great significance to us all for the future – all these things and much more'.

- 'As a result of this programme, the integration of the two companies [Sun Alliance and Phoenix] has been made easier and less painful. For this alone . . . the . . . Group owes a considerable debt'.
- '[The] management development function . . is already changing the culture within the Group'.
- 'I've enjoyed these three sessions a tremendous amount and am very different as a result. I'm more confident and am carrying through the changes very much into my working life. It's continuing as well. Some courses you forget everything in six months, but with these sessions, they're remembered and it impacts all aspects of managing a team . . . This will change the attitudes of Group management and really make Sun Alliance No. 1'.
- 'This has been the best experience of my working life . . . I find it difficult to describe what I have got out of it but . . . I have been inspired, encouraged and supported. This has given me the confidence to make it happen for me, my patch and my Group. I am positive the benefit will be lasting and . . . when I recall [the] event . . . I will gain strength'.

Another interesting indication was that the participants asked us to arrange a fourth workshop twelve months after the third – something we never anticipated. As the reputation of the programme spread, demand for places on future programmes grew.

CONCLUSION

Reflecting on the experience, our principal conclusion is how much we underestimated ourselves. We used to see ourselves as 'professionals'. What a limiting and disabling view that is! If we see ourselves as **leaders**, and we are prepared to give a few years to the task, we are quite capable of helping to bring about enormous changes in the way managers in an organization lead. We can do this by creating conditions which will release the vision, optimism, creativity and energy of managers themselves. It involves us in taking risks and dealing with fear of failure; it involves working through one's friends to get things done, not ignoring the formal structure of an organization but recognizing that change comes about through **mutual support, cooperation** and **friendship**.

NOTE

1. Bruce Nixon, now an independent consultant, acknowledges with gratitude the considerable help and encouragement he received from Richard Allen (then Home Division Training Manager) and Don Hole (who succeeded to that position) in conceiving, designing and implementing this programme. Richard is now an independent consultant and Don now works with Equitable Life.

REFERENCES

Allen, R. and Nixon, B. (1986) 'Effective In-House Management Development : Challenging Tradition', *Industrial and Commercial Training* (July–August).

Naisbitt, J. and Aburdene, P. (1985) *Re-inventing the Corporation —Transforming Your Job and Your Company for the New Information Society* (London : Book Club Associates).

Nixon, B. (1985) 'Some Effective Ways of Working With Managers', *Industrial and Commercial Training* (July–August).

Nixon, B. (1986) 'Power and Patterns in People and Organisations', *Management Education and Development*, 17(4)(Winter).

Simmons, M. (1989) 'Creating a New Men's Leadership', *Industrial and Commercial Training* (September–October).

12

Action learning – a questioning approach*

Jean Lawrence

Learning and progress accrue only when there is *something* to learn from, and the something, the stuff of learning and progress, is any completed action (Peters and Waterman, 1982, p. 134).

There isn't a logical difference between how American and Japanese managers think about decision making but the weight of experience in decision making can be very different. The Japanese tap into their experience to inform their understanding. They regard their day-to-day corporate experience as a learning lab from which they may acquire wisdom. (Pascale and Athos, 1981, p. 112).

McKinsey and Co., with whom all the writers above were associated at the time these notes were written, are not known for their enthusiasm for action learning. But their statements express truths, gleaned from their own experience, about the approach we are to explore.

Reg Revans has been working with managers in action learning since his days in the coal mines in the early 1960s. But there was a long gap in UK activities while he worked in other countries, and no one here caught up with his thoughts, until a group of us began to work with him (as a 'set', in action learning terms) to promote this 'new approach to management education' here in 1971. Revans had in 1968 developed the Belgian programme as the first action learning based

*I am grateful to my partner John Morris for the suggestion that I write in a questioning way about the questioning approach! – and for much else over the years!

214

programme of management development (see Revans, 1971). Action learning is relevant to all the issues of the day – and many of the day after! – but here we are concentrating on its application to Management Development.

Out of our experience together we formed ALP (Action Learning Projects) International and, after about a year of 'talking about action' in our meetings and seminars we were fortunate to be able to take action[1], developing a management development programme for GEC. This programme, the first in the UK, is fully described in *More Than Management Development* (Casey and Pearce, 1977), mainly by GEC managers. I remember that the 'crunch' in the process of contracting for the programme (some eight months later) came at the Reform Club – and at that time I, a woman, had to enter via the basement! I believe we *all* learned from that – a good many changes were made!

Since then, action learning has spread round the country and almost every management education institution claims to be doing it somewhere in the mix of their activities. Some other organizations have also developed ways of working with the ideas. It seems to be 'done' in a wide variety of ways, some of which are described in *Action Learning in Practice* (Pedler, 1983) by practitioners. I want in this chapter to use some of my own experience of management development programmes over the years to try to discuss some of the questions I am often asked. I remember that as I went through that original set experience in our group of ten, meeting once a month or so, I had as many sceptical questions as I now hear from others – and still new ones occur to me.

Questioning – **more and more discriminating questioning** – is at the heart of action learning. The reciprocal process in a set is not feasible in a book but let us move now to some more or less discriminating questions and try out the approach as best we can.

'ISN'T ACTION LEARNING JUST "LEARNING BY DOING"?'

It is learning by doing – but not **'just'** learning by doing. We learn by doing from the cradle onwards: in action learning, we go further by making arrangements, often very simple arrangements, to **enhance the opportunities to learn from our experiences**, and to **speed up the process**.

The arrangements create a structure within which people can explore their own experience and that of a few like-minded others, as they move cautiously further and further into new and challenging activities.

The small basic structure is a 'set' – a group of five or six people who work to test and question each other until each is much clearer about what he wants to do, and why. Each member knows that after he has taken his next step it will all be re-examined with him in order to learn from that particular event and to plan, with him, the next possibilities. After the discussion he will, by himself, choose the next step – and the work of the set will proceed in this way until the set disbands. The support given by the set provides quite a different picture from the 'learning by doing' concept, which is often used in relation to infant and junior learning. Here the child tries something, fails, tries something else and proceeds to success in this way, supported mainly by the teacher. In management the work that is pursued in action learning is important and failures can be tolerated only marginally. The support of the other members of the set minimizes the possibility of serious failure, and tests plans for 'trials' so thoroughly that even minor failure is unlikely. The support comes mainly from the set, not from the 'teacher'.

So in this 'set process' step-by-step analysis is undertaken and each move is brought into consciousness by reviewing it and exploring its significance. Day-to-day events are exposed and understood in their own right, but also as part of the rather lengthy process of **getting change to happen**. In its turn, this interpretation and digestion of the small events week by week can be understood by each individual as part of the progress he and the others are making in their learning. Perhaps even more individually and deeply, the experiences can be consciously accepted as part of the **person's own growth**. Each can 'reorganize his own experience' as Revans has it or 'reframe his problems' as Braddick and Casey (1981) suggest. Individual behaviour can be observed in the group; gradually as the set matures, insight can be gained into the way each member behaves in back-home situations, and into values and attitudes which have a vital influence on effective management.

When changes in behaviour occur and are noticed by a member of the set, others can provide support with their own recollection of his or her previous ways of behaving. There is then agreed evidence of **personal learning** – and encouragement to hold on to the change.

Learning is by no means confined to the sets. In the part of the organization in which the set member works, many managers may begin to take a new view of the task – and also, perhaps, of the way to tackle a problem of this kind. A client (later a managing director) in a senior management exchange programme wrote that he had benefited both from the work he had done with the visiting participant and from his contacts with his own staff member working in another company: 'This company has undoubtedly benefited enormously at all levels at which [the visiting participant] has had contact and where the concept of action learning is understood. I for one would welcome further involvement in what I believe to be the most practical and useful Management Training Programme that I have had the good fortune to be involved with'.[2]

'ACTION LEARNING SEEMS TO HAVE A LANGUAGE OF ITS OWN'

'P & Q', 'problems and puzzles', 'clients', 'sets' and 'set advisers'. They come from Revans's writings. **P & Q** and **puzzles and problems** refer to a basic distinction of great importance in action learning. 'P' is programmed learning, available knowledge. 'Q' is questioning where there is no certain answer – question flows from question and more than one response can be accepted as sensible. One of our difficulties in tackling some of the intractable economic social and political problems that beset us may be in part that while our education system is more and more full of 'P', our lives are more and more full of huge issues susceptible only to the processes of 'Q'.

Puzzles have a solution, however difficult it may be to find – we will all agree with it when it is presented. **Problems** – and **opportunities** – are the stuff of action learning. We can work on them in a variety of ways and come to many different conclusions, all open to discussion and disagreement.

These concepts can be used when we face any dilemma – how much P & Q? – Is it a puzzle or a problem? In this chapter I shall be talking only about action learning in management development, but it is relevant to all kinds of problems – on the shopfloor, in hospital wards, in communities – and work in these areas in the UK and across the world has been described elsewhere (Revans, 1980; Pedler, 1983).

I should like to quote here an example of the relation between P & Q in management. If my problem is to find a way to create some activities to improve the public relations of the water industry, I can ask many experts about public relations techniques, analyze the cost, look at how it is done in other industries, nationalized and private, and in other organizations – gather as much 'P' as I can (and incidentally a good many new questions). But no book will help me to see how to persuade X (a senior manager) what should be done, nor reassure me that it is indeed X who should be persuaded first, nor whether to write a report, nor why I find it difficult to decide to call that particular meeting together – which, on the face of it, looks eminently sensible. Nor, indeed, will the book define the odds on my losing my hoped-for promotion if I do stir up the wrong kind of interest in high places on the issue. Problems of this kind involve uncertainty and the questioning process in the sets gradually ensures that a wide variety of directions are carefully explored, leaving, at each stage, the project champion (see below) to make his own decisions, justify them and then live with them.

Much has been written about **sets** (Revans, 1983, pp. 50–4).[3] I have said something about the process in responding to the previous question, and will say more in the comparison with consultancy later on. For me **action learning** has three essential characteristics – the participants work on **real work** (not exercises or cases); they learn from each other by a **questioning process** (not from teachers); and they carry through the work to **implementation** (not just to a report or analysis, recommendation and planning).

The logical outcome is a structure in which a few people work together on one or more real tasks until they have made a **visible contribution to progressing their problems**, and have themselves **inevitably changed** in the process. Their work has included their **recognition** of these changes, and their **derivation**. We call these structures 'sets'.

Project champion is the name I have given to a set member who is working on a particular task and is learning from it. 'Championing' is described in Peters and Waterman, (1982, pp. 208–9). The task he is working on has many of the characteristics of other projects, but in addition there is a continuous effort to make the learning explicit.

Clients are the **problem owners**: They are the people who, at this moment, want an answer. Clients will pose the problem, and will be available to hear progress and to support the implementation as they agree a way forward with the project champions. They remain responsible for what occurs, but will be greatly influenced as the project champion develops his investigation, his hypotheses and experiments, and then asks the clients' agreement on a plan of action.

Nominators or sponsors select the participants for the programme and usually play a part in selecting the problems to be worked on.

The **set adviser** is the person who helps a set to work well, and is interested in promoting the achievements (and in particular, the **learning**) of the members of the set. This role has been described in a number of articles by practitioners (Casey and Pearce, 1977; Harris's and Pedler's chapters in Pedler, 1983)[4], and the work of the set adviser is referred to later in this chapter. Set advisers can be, and often are, consultants or trainers, but other managers can fulfil the role, especially if they themselves have participated in an action learning programme.

The **programme** provides an 'envelope' in which all this can occur legitimately, and provides added learning opportunities through coordination of meetings and interaction of sets. The arrangements may also help participants to enter more quickly into learning and to take back with them into their 'normal' lives what has occurred, with minimum attrition; the 're-entry problem' in the form familiar to course organizers is virtually unknown. The form of the programme should reflect a clear understanding of the agreed objectives, and is discussed fully in a later section.

'IT ALL SOUNDS VERY OPEN-ENDED'

How do we know what we are becoming involved in? Isn't is a political hot potato? It is open-ended, but we can manage the process. We can agree carefully what we are trying to do, and for whom. We can be clear about our priorities – for example, are we focusing on developing individual managers for later promotion, or on changing the culture of the organization? Are we developing a level of management in their present jobs, or reorganising a department in the face of a change in its environment? Often we are concerned with more than one objective. Several goals will be achieved in the programme –

managers will develop and changes will occur in the organization – and work will be done on the specific agreed tasks. But it helps if those who are setting it up are clear at the outset about the **balance of aims**.

We can reduce the uncertainties still further. We can foresee some of the likely outcomes of the programme; in general, we can predict who will be affected and how we will try to meet the objectives we have set ourselves. Additional beneficial results, which we could not predict, may occur, as they did in the GEC programme.[5] Admittedly we cannot foresee with any clarity the outcome of the tasks the participants take on – as we cannot when we tackle real problems in our own jobs; this difficulty is inherent in the kind of problems we have chosen to tackle. Authority for action, however, always remains with the client. The participant will always be no more than transient in his commitment to that work – unless arrangements are changed towards the end (and, in my experience, that would be very unusual). His task is to learn how to get action to happen where he has no direct authority but strong commitment as a project champion. In 'own-job' projects he has direct authority derived from his 'normal' client, his boss. But he will probably designate part of his work, probably new work, as the focus for attention, and agree this with his boss and his colleagues. He may risk trying out new ways of working in this designated area and will be scrutinizing, with the set, each step as he takes it.

Clarity of agreement about the nature of the task to be worked on, how it is to be evaluated, and what resources are available, are all necessary at the beginning – but even more important is the recognition that these matters are likely to be **renegotiated as the work progresses**. Unlike 'filleted projects', found in some training courses, real work will take a path that cannot be forecast with confidence; the definition of the task may change as more information is made available. The subsequent renegotiation often includes a change in the focus on a particular manager as the 'client' for the work being done – the 'owner' of the problem. As the problem is explained and symptoms are identified which lead to diagnosis of the 'real' problem (itself perhaps a temporary diagnosis) all may agree that the **ownership has in fact changed**, and a new 'client' is named.

Politically this can be a 'hot potato', if there is a lack of confidence that change will be accepted if it is promoted from below. It is necessary that top people – those whose decisions can encourage or forestall most important changes in the policies or shape of their organizations – believe that **things will change**, with their agreement, as a result of the programme. Often this does mean the exercise of political skills by those who, within the organization, are introducing action learning. The process of introduction, in itself, may provide considerable learning for the organization and, unavoidably, for those who introduce it. As in all developments, **timing** is important; often as the likely results are understood the chief executive will take the lead.

Even then, a lot of preliminary work may be needed to help senior managers to appreciate that what is being embarked upon is not just another training course where the manager's 'knowledge in the head' will grow. The manager returning from such a course may have very little effect on the work of the organization. Signing a cheque and putting forward a name, however carefully selected, is not enough to promote learning, and the changes in the organization, which are inevitable if learning has taken place.

So, yes, action learning does require top management commitment to organization learning – and therefore change – and if this seems like a 'hot potato', there should perhaps be a number of ways of cooling it! But it is *not* a charter for chaos. The meat of the programme is all that occurs after this top management commitment is obtained. Those involved can be trusted to work on it with no more hiccups and difficulties than are involved in any change process. Probably there will be less difficulty here because so much attention and analysis is focused on these particular changes, in order that maximum learning is achieved.

'WHERE DOES ACTION LEARNING MAKE ITS BEST CONTRIBUTION?'

Does its whole success rely on the choice of 'problem'? Its most valuable contribution is to increase general management skills at all levels: not to make an accountant technically more competent at manipulating data, for example, but to help him to influence others from his expert base. Action learning will tackle how he can get his ideas across; let him see the value of his role more clearly, lower the fences round his department; indicate better ways to make his data useful to his peers, his staff and his boss, and help him to recognize that it is valid to work on unclear human organization problems using as much skill and care as he usually spends on reaching his technically correct answers.

This can be achieved for every manager at every level. One managing director said he had not realized he could give attention *of the same kind*, to personnel matters and the way people behave, as to his business problems of marketing, finance, etc. till he met action learning, in a lecture by Revans. As a result he got his entire management staff working in mixed groups on his business problems and monitoring their learning.

Action learning is not useful for increasing technical competence, nor for increasing knowledge about management. Talking *about* management, gaining new knowledge that the manager may need (or thinks he may need) can be done in a thousand ways more effectively than through action learning. It is useful only if the need is for more **effective managerial action**.

In business schools and colleges a great deal is done to improve knowledge, techniques and particularly analytical skills. I recall that after Manchester and London Business schools had been running for five years the Owen report (BIM, 1971) said that while they were very effective in teaching these skills, they did little to help their students work with people, or with the implementation of decisions. It was difficult to see, at the time, how they could, but that was the nudge I needed to pursue action learning with vigour: I got in touch with Revans.

At Manchester, I was building on experience already gained through a growing commitment to use projects (a huge variety within the species) in our programmes; joint development activities were a feature from 1971 and 'stretched' courses with projects woven into the programmes began in 1972. The first 'stretched' courses provided group project work for operational managers in manufacturing units other than their own. Twenty days' work was spread over four months. (The organization had originally asked for a three-week management course.) Action learning including a full phase of implementation has proved difficult to integrate into a business school or college except in lengthy qualification programmes (e.g., MBA part-time programmes). Several institutions in the UK and one in Ireland offer those long programmes based on action learning using real problems in organizations centrally in their work.

If the special contribution is in the area of general management and we are to learn by taking action, then we need 'whole business' problems or as near to that as we can find. Since we are not involved in passing on or applying known answers, the **choice of problem**[6] is vital to success. Often a list of problems can be generated with ease; it seems that the better the organization the greater the number of **real problems** that are on their agenda. We need to select problems that will stretch the participants we have in mind; these will often be the ones which would normally be on the desks one level above. They must certainly be inter-departmental, not already studied and reported many times, and be of appropriate size for the length of programme. The most difficult criterion to handle concerns the obvious requirement – **reality**. If it is real, how can it fit into the pattern of a programme? If it is implementable – a feature of a real problem – how does that relate to urgency? If we want something done – to make a contribution to this problem – can we wait six months starting next March or May, perhaps?

One way of working at these issues, and ensuring the connection between the reality of the work that is to be done and the central concerns of the organisation, is to work through a steering group. Garratt's programme manager[7] may be an alternative; here he is a designated member of the steering group often called 'programme coordinator'. Line managers concerned with getting things to happen join with developers, and perhaps external consultants, to take responsibility for the form of the programme. They select the participants, and the 'projects' and ensure that a 'client' is identified for each, sometimes a member of the steering group. The first part of their work ends with one-page descriptions of projects written by clients and a list of participants ready to enter a programme whose broad design they have agreed.

The distribution of problems to individuals or groups can be done in a variety of ways. In many programmes, the clients present the problems publicly to all the participants and all the other clients, the tutors and training staff. Usually more problems are presented than are required so that real choices are available. In the consortium programme, after the presentations, the sets go away by themselves to discuss the possible projects and come up with their individual choices. (They had already developed criteria for choice, which included not working in their own company and working in an area of management with which they were not familiar.)

If participants can choose the task they will work on and with whom they will work we can expect high motivation to work and learn. Some say, though, that this is not like real life. My experience is that quite often participants can choose their own projects and sometimes their sets. For group projects, they may be able to form their own group. More frequently, groups and sets are formed by the steering group. In GEC, each participant was allocated his project and his set by the central management development manager. In more recent programmes, much more choice has been made available to participants.

In a complex programme where there are many groups or sets the process of choice can be fairly chaotic and should in my view be encouraged to be lengthy. The explanation of choices, the criteria on which they are based and the stresses that are generated are (or can be) an important part of the learning process. It is the first occasion in the programme where participants have to **live with the results of their choices**. That will occur on many occasions later, but perhaps at no point with such immediate and clear results for the participants themselves. Later in the programme a review of the choices made can provide useful personal learning, not least about organizational pressures and culture.

As the set work begins, the role of the steering group changes to monitoring the progress of the programme, being visibly interested in the **results** of both the project tasks and the learning, but not judgmental about the way each project task is being achieved – that is the job of the client and the set, with the help of the set adviser. An important role of the steering group is to 'hold the ring' and to manage effects in the organization which may be inimical to the continuation of a series of programmes.

Examples of potentially damaging effects have included demanding too much time from top managers too soon, over-burdening a single department with reports and change proposals, or giving working papers to interested staff without due clearance. After the start the steering group will be supporting particularly the credibility of implementation, ensuring that their colleagues (above and below them as well as at their own level) do actually expect that changes will result from the programme. This may later include informally helping clients to get items onto the agendas of influential meetings. A strong factor in enabling programmes to continue is that acceptable changes are made, especially those benefits top management **did not expect to occur**. This seems to be true even when other objectives (e.g., manager development) are important, often more important.

Steering groups for programmes change their roles after a few programmes. They may be thought to be a good forum for working on wide management development issues, putting organization strategy and development together, or they may take responsibility for other particular groups (e.g., graduate intake) and reconsider with their new joint experience, appropriate methods of development for them; or they may say, 'this is fine for those top-level managers, what about those one level down?' and work step by step towards a full role in management development.

'HOW CAN WE ARRANGE EXCHANGE PROGRAMMES?'

We have heard of exchange programmes where senior people go to work in other organizations. How is all this arranged? Like porcupines making love – with difficulty! Many current top managers have experienced a period of secondment, an opportunity to work in another industry, country, organization or role, and all seem to look back on it as a highly developmental period. A manager moving to a new job has a short but exciting learning period and often in retrospect recognizes the struggles as having been highly developmental. The trick is to give more people these opportunities without disrupting current performance in the sending or receiving organizations: gone are the days when someone, whether good, useful or promotable, could be 'spared' for an extended period; or when someone with few skills in the work could be accommodated and take the place of a hard-pressed good performer, in order to learn. Job swops, secondment and job rotation are even more difficult in the current climate and although they may be feasible for junior managers usually cannot be contemplated at relatively senior levels.

But there *are* real problems to be tackled, issues to be explored, in every organization at every level. The more managers are hard pressed by change and cost-cutting, the more there are opportunities for special effort to be applied to important one-off problems. If the work is real, it has to be done somehow. So projects or tasks can be tackled in a special way and managers can learn from that experience, bring-

ing with them to the task the advantage of good managerial experience. In addition, **project exchanges** do not have the same difficulties
as job swops – the effect of ignorance of the precise field of action is
limited. Indeed the project champion often stimulates a new view of
the problem precisely because of this ignorance. If it is thought that a
consultant from outside, or the line managers in their normal roles,
can get to a better solution and get the change made more easily and
quickly, surely this should be carefully considered; then the only
remaining issues are who learns from the process, and how are
managers to be developed here?

Some time will be required from the current managers working as
resources in the area of the project, but that will be essential, anyway,
if the work is to get done at all. The kind of work required of them
may well be different. For example, they may be involved in initial
information giving, then authorizing, and arranging resources for
implementation. In other circumstances they will perhaps be managing the data-gathering, doing the analysis, developing alternative strategies and scenarios, and planning and monitoring the implementation. The 'project champion' participant is likely to take on these
activities; as the project progresses he will be authorized to do so. He
may need more junior people to help him – they would have been
equally necessary in other circumstances.

There are, then, few difficulties in finding problems or in expecting
results in terms of changes and managerial learning. The difficulties
arise from the lack of inter-organization communication channels and
the problems of getting like-minded companies and institutions to
take decisions together, matching their participants and dovetailing
their requirements in terms of time. There is a role here for an
established organization to provide an 'exchange' of information on
needs and opportunities at this high level, and to play a part in
managing such a network of programmes. The Consortium Programme (sometimes referred to as the Rolling Programme) in 1975–8
met this need, providing a top-level exchange programme which
involved nine UK organizations. It failed to continue after three years
because it could not extend its base to involve enough organizations
so that very high-level participants would be available regularly for
each programme. At that time, none of the organizations involved
would contemplate basing the programme in an institution, particularly a business school, believing (rightly in my view) that it would be

emasculated by institution pressures. A steering group of the participating companies organized the programme in hotels and conference centres, and I provided a focus for communication at Manchester Business School.

I was somewhat anxious about letting go the central administration, fearing dilution of the sharp-edged and seemingly risky activities we were involved in; I feared pressures to make it too tidy and simple so that the learning opportunities provided by the uncertainties of tackling real problems (not filleted ones) would be diminished: I had seen too many projects made progressively simpler to fit course, staff and institutional requirements. Staff enjoy preparing projects and learn enormously in the process – often, quite unintentionally, at the expense of the learning of those they mean to teach; managers too are often concerned about the acceptable risks within their own organizations; administrators like things to happen in a regular convenient pattern and prefer not to have to adapt too frequently to the demands of real life. Things have changed in the decade since then. As understanding of how to manage this kind of programme has increased, the anxieties have faded; the risk of promoting and administering a network of programmes of this kind from an institutional base should surely now be taken.

In the current climate, more and more institutions are recognizing that work is the best base for learning, and that managers learn best by managing difficult situations (taking on new jobs, starting new ventures, changing organizations are examples in many managers' experience). A catalytic organization promoting a partnership between those who wish to speed the change towards learning while working, and those who represent the vast army of organizations in which managers work, would provide a way of helping the porcupines to be productive. We still need an aphrodisiac in British management learning – maybe just an encouraging arrangement would do!

'ARE THERE GROUP PROJECTS IN ACTION LEARNING'

The Belgian programme was based on individual project work. More recently I have heard of group project work in this connection – is that really action learning? Yes, for me it can be. These programmes *can* meet my basic criteria – real projects, learning from each other and implementation. But because the set work is different it is more difficult to hold the programme at a high level of learning and thus the tutor-set advisor role is even more demanding. Implementation, though achievable, is often less focused; participants learn in their groups from the activity while in the programme but often a few (not often the whole group) continue to be marginally involved after returning full-time to their jobs.

Set work in group project programmes differs considerably from set work in individual programmes. The group itself is not a set, though its members probably come from a wide variety of backgrounds – and should, in my view, always be working on 'new' work. The individuals in the group are working towards a single objective and exploring their part in progressing the work. This kind of group is in danger of becoming only a good and useful taskforce, so **learning** has to be a clear and important **objective**: unless they define their individual roles very clearly, the pressure the group can put on each individual, and he can put on himself, is not of the same order as that in the individual or paired project set. When the group works well, the work and learning are brought together by a process of critical examination of what is being done and an exposure of the difficulties; members of the group question each other from their own experiences.

There is a qualitative difference, however, between this kind of questioning and the questioning of an individual who is **entirely responsible and at risk** in his own project. The individual needs the questioning of other members of the set who will not share the direct responsibility for what happens on that project, but reciprocally need his help for their work. To get the benefit of these **open confronting questions** born of an equal need for help, we experimented in group project work with putting two (or perhaps three) project groups together for a day to work in a set. In these sets, time was allocated so that one group would question the other about their project, and then reciprocate. The original groups had been formed of people who had no recent experience in the area of their group project. When this joint set meeting occurred, fairly expert people in the field of the project from the other group were able to question those who were struggling to find effective ways of progressing their unfamiliar work. Some of those asking these questions from their expert positions would also be involved in the implementation of the project work at a much later stage; this enhanced the benefits of the cross-group questioning. The sets were huge but the participants seemed to be able to cope with that by working as a team in their own groups, asking questions of the other group. We also created mixed groups towards the end of a group programme to share their experiences of the learning processes in the groups. These experiments will be repeated.

Inter-group meetings are akin to the meetings with other programmes (in Belgium and Sweden) arranged in the Belgian, GEC and Consortium programmes. The level of commitment in sets and in action learning programmes creates difficulty in sharing, especially early in the programmes. It takes a very mature group to attend as much to the outside world as to the inside. More work needs to be done to experiment with increasing the learning group to group, set to set, and programme to programme. Much of the learning in one set on one project (or, say, five projects) is at present lost to others. Perhaps more use of delegates or representatives may help?

'WHAT FORMS OF PROGRAMMES ARE APPROPRIATE?'

Is it true that top management programmes are always full-time exchanges? Are other forms appropriate only to other levels? No, there are other versions for top managers and many variants to meet different needs at different levels. It is true that a full-time exchange programme, probably running over six months, must involve a number of different organizations in making a high investment in the development of single members of their workforces, so it will be likely that participants will be limited to very senior influential managers. In the UK these programmes have involved managers likely to be appointed to company, division or group boards, and in many cases this has happened. So we can expect this form to be used only at top level. But the reverse is not true; very senior managers can be developed in programmes with a different design, particularly if the objectives are different (e.g., the priority objective is team-building in a Board).

The form of a programme is very much dependent upon the purposes being addressed. There is an enormous range of choice. Action learning is well placed to meet three objectives (a) management development; (b) organization change and development and (c) task achievement. Tasks will be tackled and some progress will be made whatever choices are made about the form. The main influence will come from the priority given to one or other of the first two objectives, management development or organization development (OD), though both will no doubt occur to some extent. Numbers involved and the level of investment in money, time and support facilities, may also play a part.

Decisions about the form will include whether other organizations should be involved, or the programme should be entirely domestic, and how limited within the domestic world; whether work should be taken on individually, or whether there would be more benefit to be gained by working in a group. Managers may be challenged to work in an area of management of which they are ignorant, or on a familiar task, and there may be good reasons for them to work part-time.

Often a priority for organization change may influence form in the direction of own-organization, part-time and perhaps group work, while a strong need for manager development suggests perhaps individual work, several organizations, exchange and full-time. But many variants are possible to fit many different organizations' needs. Sorting out these issues and gaining commitment to the form can be a fairly lengthy process. Some examples are given in Table 12.1.

The GEC programme (1) was full-time but not an exchange programme though there were some exchanges between companies in the group. It also included a number of other variants of both organisation and task.[8] In GEC, managers were 'one below eye-level' because Sir Arnold Weinstock regarded his 100 or so managing directors as 'eye-level' – they had face-to-face contact with him. So it was a senior programme involving high-level projects worth six months' full-time work.

The Consortium programme (2)[9] was also full-time but involved 'exchange' projects; its aim was to develop top-level managers. It required a considerable investment in time and money and participating companies regarded it as an alternative to, say, Harvard.

The Social Services programmes (3) was devised to develop managers at a particular level but also to increase mutual understanding of the work of the various departments and functions. The large manufacturing company (4) wanted to raise the competence of its managers in project management in one department and to share some understanding, knowledge and skill from one specialist area in the department to another. Similarly, an eight-month part-time pro-

Table 12.1 Choosing the form of management development programmes in action learning

Example	Organization		Task		Time
	One or several	Own or exchange	Group or individual	Own or other	
(1) GEC	One group several companies and customers	Both	Individual or pairs	Both	P/T F/T
(2) Consortium (or Rolling) Prog.	Several	Exchange	Individual	Other	F/T
(3) Social Services	One	Own	Group	Other	P/T
(4) Large Mnfg Co.	One Dept.	Own	Group	Other	P/T
(5) Water Industry	One (10 regions)	Own	Group	Other	P/T
(6) Large Retail Org.	One	Own	Individual	Other	P/T
(7) Small Family Trpt Co.	One	Own	Individual	Other	P/T
(8) Manag. Action Group	Several	Own	Individual	Own	P/T
(9) Africa (Planning only)	Several	Own	Individual	Own	P/T
Quality Circle	One	Own	Group	Own	P/T

gramme in the water industry (5) was intended to develop 24 individual managers in each programme, as well as to increase the common appreciation, across the regions, of what went on in the water industry. This programme included two taught modules – they were in fact the starting point for the programme and the project work was built round and through them.

In the large retail organisations (6) some gaps at the top were foreseen and development of selected senior individuals was regarded as urgent. The complexity of the organization, its long history and current reorganization indicated an internal programme. The need to develop a few very senior managers suggested individual projects. In the small transport company (7) the whole management team needed development both as individual managers and as a group. The new managing director, a family member and an MBA, felt over-trained compared to his managers, and wanted them to gain some understanding of the whole system of the small company and to develop towards board roles.

The Management Action Group (8)[10] was director and managing director level, each manager working in his own company and meeting for a day every five or six weeks. After an introductory week, the programme, in this case, consisted only of the set, and a series of set meetings. The set met consistently for seven years and survived a number of job changes or promotions among the set members. The members continued to come because they found the thought-provoking day away fruitful – and worth the cost.

The result of the analysis is the same for the action planning in the African planning programme (9) which involved twenty or more managers from different African countries each time. But as explained in the penultimate section in this chapter there can be no implementation within the African programme.

The final example, for interest in the comparisons, is quality circles. As can be seen from Table 12.1, the form differs strikingly from the other programmes. This may be appropriate. As I see it, quality circles are a very low-risk form of action learning related to everyday work, and the priorities in the objectives are likely to be different.

Whatever the form of the programme, it goes through a similar process from introductory work and identification of the projects to investigation and analysis, testing the arguments and ideas. At around the mid-point there is usually a pause and a very stringent evaluation of the proposals before moving further into action. The second half is concerned with experimenting and implementation, review and disengagement, and later reviews.

In the single long-running set at director level (8), each member went through this cycle many times as he defined for himself new tasks and projects. A new task usually overlaps with the last one, which is by then perhaps in the early stages of implementation.

'DO YOU NEED OUTSIDE STAFF IN THE GROUPS/SETS?'

Why can we not do it ourselves? I am not sure you always do need outsiders, except at the beginning; but even those whose training and professional interest is in how people work together, and how groups work (or fail to work) find it quite difficult to be one of a working group which is making its way of working explicit and open to examination and interpretation. I have found this to be true for myself when working with social workers, psychologists, development managers and trainers. An outsider (who, essentially, is not involved in all the processes leading up to each participant facing this new experience which is to be real and evaluated) can work without the level of anxiety, discomfort, and defensiveness present in the others. He or she can help members of the set towards the **open, communicative, risk-taking, thoughtful, caring, imaginative, reflective behaviour** which is needed. Then there is a chance that the realities of working relationships, the members' area of ignorance and the many constraints on action, can be exposed and accepted, and the difficulties overcome. Not that the outsider is free from anxiety. But this kind of anxiety – about starting a familiar process with new people – is well recognized and can be managed, so it is not likely to impede the work. It is important that someone has as his priority the way the set is developing as a **challenging supportive working unit**, while others have quite different priorities in these early stages. They may be more concerned with finding a way of **surviving in the set**, understanding what is expected of them, dealing with doubts about the value of the experience just beginning, wondering why they were nominated for it, and sorting out why the outsider is not teaching or leading in the conventional sense, says very little, and does not 'keep order' in the set.

The outsider, the set adviser, is not the same as other members of the set, but need not be from outside the organization. A supervisor or colleague may feel confident to fulfil the role though he or she will have additional difficulties in dealing with the set's expectation based on their own past experience; an internal trainer or manager from another department or function or company in the group will have fewer difficulties on that score. This arrangement has often proved successful especially after the first programme. Preliminary work on understanding the role (both intellectually and emotionally) is of course necessary. Nothing can replace the experience of being a set member, as a starting point. Working in a set alongside someone experienced in helping sets to start and to work well is one way to gain further experience; another is to work with a set alone but alongside a more experienced person working in another set. Then a discussion of each meeting can take the form of a review of the role and how it was taken up in each set. It is usual, in my experience, gradually to transfer the work to internal staff in the later programmes even if external experienced staff are used at first.

Once work has started, the set adviser will re-examine with the set his usefulness on a number of occasions (though not at every meeting!) and may withdraw as the programme progresses. The difficulties of implementation are frequently under-rated and the set may well need the help of a set adviser for at least part of this process. There is often a role in helping to legitimize micro-politics at this stage. Often the set adviser has more varied (but recognizably secondhand) experience of organizations, their structures, culture, power systems, than members of the set and may be able to help by providing frameworks for analysis. This may be less appropriate in mixed sets where there must already be considerable experience of organizations. Even today, there is less written about implementation than analysis and the function of helping the set members to generalize their experiences may be especially valuable.

It is possible, particularly at this later stage, that the balance between attention to task completion and making learning explicit can move too far away from learning in the absence of a set adviser. This phenomenon varies from set to set, and pressure from the client system is usually part of the reason for over-concentration on the task at the expense of monitoring the learning. The task can **drive out learning**, as it so often does in ordinary managerial life.

'IS ACTION LEARNING SUITABLE ONLY FOR THOSE ABOUT TO BE PROMOTED?'

We are involved in developing managers to be more competent in their own jobs – there's little chance of promotion at the moment. Would Action Learning help? Yes. Action learning is an enormously flexible approach in terms of the needs it can meet, as long as the need is not met just by familiarity with techniques or a 'programmed learning' approach.

The design of the programme and the choices made about the form it will take (see Table 12.1) will be highly influenced by the need to **develop people in their own jobs**. This does not necessarily mean an individual project/own-job/own-organization/part-time programme. There may be a strong case for 'team-building' where group projects or exchanges within a department are indicated. This was the situation in a Social Services programme: there was a strong need to understand others' jobs and roles. Group projects where there was no recent specialist experience in the group featured in the programme; a side-effect was a much increased understanding of the **difficulties and constraints in top jobs** previously seen as remote – names had been known but not persons; and responsibilities, far from the sharp end, were little understood. The top people were enormously impressed by the unusual initiatives taken by those further down the system and appreciated their own previous neglect of these resources within the organization. Nothing changed in terms of promotion, but there was an identifiable change in the way those in the **organization worked together**.

'ISN'T ACTION LEARNING JUST "CONSULTANCY"?'

No. In consultancy, the consultant's learning is incidental to the task in hand, and the client should be alert to ensure that it never takes priority over task completion and client organization learning. In many assignments organizational learning is likely to be in the form of acquiring digested expertise from the consultant (very near to 'P'). The consultant appears as an expert in the field in which he or she is to work and has often been asked to help because his 'P' in that situation is higher than that of the internal managers. Good consultants work hard to reduce the organization's dependence on them (and spend less energy than most of their colleagues on preparing the ground for the next – and continuing – jobs), but their own learning is not part of the design. At the worst, the experience can be likened to an excellent oft-repeated lecture, and at the best, as in 'teaching', the edge of the subject is explored mutually and the excitement of learning is shared, but unevenly. The client's learning, both in quantity and rate, is highly influenced by the consultant, as it is by the teacher.

In action learning, the **excitement of learning is built in from the beginning**, both in the set and in the client organization. There, perhaps only after the very early stages, the deep exploratory questions a good manager asks generate the excitement of shared insights and learning. The stuff of the set is this questioning and the excitement is now inevitable as the challenge of the exploration is pursued. The participant who, in the parallel situation, is the consultant, has to struggle with his perennially questioning colleagues who will explore every argument or idea he puts forward knowing he has no expertise with which to blind them. They do not assume that he is right or likely to be right; they know they are uncertain in their own work and need this examination process to give them confidence but have high trust that with the help of the set he *will* get it right. When he returns to his client organization again he is subject to questions and exploration for they too are sceptical and cannot completely rely on his expertise. Once again back in the set, he will be supported in whatever difficulties he has with the client system – 'it's the same for all of us in our different ways, we are all struggling' – and given the confidence, with ideas thoroughly re-examined, to go back and continue. 'Comrades in adversity' indeed, as Revans put it (1982). As he survives this process he no longer fears dealing with peers who have expertise he does not have, but values their contribution. Nor does he doubt his ability to influence work where he has no formal authority.

'HOW DOES ACTION LEARNING END?'

The participant cannot implement it completely, can he? In earlier project work aimed at the development of learning within courses, the implementation phase hardly existed. The project would typically end with a report and recommendation to the client – often a teacher, standing in! The process of getting an organization to accept not only the recommendations but actually to **make the changes** challenges the project champion and the other members of the set. The project champion has done the work in developing the ideas, but has a limited time in which to see the implementation begin and to make sure it is progressing well when he leaves. He has to foresee the real difficulties he will encounter and cope with determination with those he does not foresee. The recognition of political pressure and the need to work with the power system is often a revelation to people who have worked only within a function. They may have seen the structure in which they work encouraging sniping across the boundaries, without any obvious opportunity to use the real relations between groups within the organization to achieve important progress. Now they can find new ways of influencing change.

It seems that it is hard for participants as they approach the end of a programme to see how to disengage from their project work. The idea that implementation has occurred is difficult to accept when they know that a final report has not been written, (they have already decided that will not help), that the final memos have not been sent, that the person they think should be appointed is not actually in place. It seems helpful to suggest that implementation has occurred when the participant leaves the organization in which he has been working on his project, or leaves the project work itself, in such a state that the work is more likely to progress than to cease. The reverse is frequently true in organizational life – change processes can easily be killed off. If the project champion is no longer there to hold the boundary and the change relies on him, organization forces can collude to stop it; the organism rejects the foreign implant and rapidly reverts to normal. However, if the project champion in an action learning programme has done his job well, he will have arranged that enough powerful people in the system are involved in the work on the project with him, so that his disappearance is hardly noticed and the energy remains with the powerful group, and they or one of their number becomes the project champion. The powerful group ensures that the work is unlikely to be able to be scrapped by organization forces of rejection, lethargy or resistance to change: the organism itself is mutating and the 'external' influence becomes irrelevant.

The programme does not end there. Usually the sets review their work a few weeks before they are due to return to their normal jobs or to leave the programme. This review provides an opportunity to look back at the experience and to work at the process of disengagement from the project work. They can also face up to re-engagement in a normal managerial role full-time and wonder what will change, and for how long. Often career planning features in this discussion. Differences as they experience them, between the person who entered the programme and the one who now leaves, are identified and evaluated.

Later reviews (perhaps one month, and then six months, after they return) also give programmed opportunities to see the direction of changes in the light of their experiences, and to support those for whom the direction is not always seen as entirely positive.

'HOW CAN ACTION LEARNING FIT INTO TRAINING PROGRAMMES AND COURSES?'

On the face of if, it can't! It is not possible at one and the same time to say, 'Within this programme of x weeks, we are teaching you management, you are receivers, we are givers, we will arrange for you to go through some clearly defined exercises. Each of them can be evaluated in terms of performance of the giver and the ability of the receiver to respond in a predicted way by performing well-defined tasks'. And also to say 'We are here to help you to interpret your intentions and your actions within a programme bounded only by time, place and agreement on a task – an objective for work over an extended period, maybe six months.'

Nevertheless, as Revans has so often said, 'P' is also necessary. It is possible (though difficult) to combine 'project experience' 'work experience', 'projects', etc. with a taught course. The combination of such disparate activities carries the danger that the programmed activity drives out the unsure, unplannable leaps into reality. The integration of the project work into the programme, so that it does not stand alone as an 'add on' or 'something other' is difficult *and* essential. It will always be second best to promoting an action learning programme on a base of previously understood and well integrated 'P' (e.g., if new graduate intake are taught *about* management, perhaps two or three years later an action learning programme can build on this early knowledge and experience). The programme can then be based wholly on the performance of real work and carried right through to implementation and review.

Where the attempt is made to combine action learning with taught modules, much of the real work has to be done in the design stage. This is true of all programmes involving experiential work; it is difficult to achieve integration within the staff group so that staff in taught sessions and those in experiential work (where they are not the same people) all feel a responsibility for the success of the total programme. Time will be allocated so that they will have worked together sufficiently to appreciate the way the whole programme will develop and where the 'joints' may at first creak. Also they will have noted how in management games or perhaps structured behavioural exercises, the excitement of highly programmed and carefully arranged sessions (arranged not least in order to provide excitement) can compete (and usually win) in gaining the temporary allegiance of learners.

Less programmed work, with its intrinsic excitement but apparent lack of shape and defined ends, cannot survive alongside the short-term demands of clear deadlines in a business game. Given space and careful introduction, and clever timing of sessions within a programme, commitment to real project work is easily gained and grows with increasing understanding of the realities in which the learners are involved. Then the energy and excitement knows no bounds. In many institutions this is the way that real project and eventual action learning work may be introduced. It usually means dismantling a programme so that it is spread over a period of perhaps six months (or in degree programmes, an academic year) with the whole group meeting for an introductory period, other residential phases, and a review period just before the 'end' of the programme. In this way work done in organizations can begin at the beginning of the programme, be supported by all the 'course' work and 'end' as the results of the work are embedded in the organization when the programme ends. That it grows and does not wither as courses are repeated requires high skills (political as well as professional) on the part of the 'introducers'. It can so easily become a routine problem: 'the part of the course that is seen as difficult'; 'it's a bit of a nuisance to set up'; 'perhaps we can simplify it this time'; and thus you can lose most of the learning.

Staffing such a programme seems to present minor practical difficulties. Often, here, groups will work on a single project. The groups can be left to tackle the work without help; but often the intention is to facilitate their work and raise their level of awareness of the learning opportunities presented. 'Tutors', used to tutoring exercises, business games and teaching in formal sessions, perhaps on the same programme, find it difficult to justify being 'out' for a day with a group where the group is doing the work and does not need direction. The tutor is being asked to be a set adviser and the last thing he will have the opportunity to do will be to tutor; perhaps he will say very little in the day, but what is said at that one moment may have great value. Often in practice, tutors find other priorities take them away and groups are 'visited' less frequently than might seem useful. One group recently reported 'our thanks also to our "tutor" – they call it distance learning, I believe!'

'ARE THERE HEAVY REQUIREMENTS FOR SKILLED RESOURCES?'

This is a difficult question. Taught courses are perhaps being regarded as the norm, and measurement of the resources used in them is frequently controversial. Senior courses might perhaps be nine or ten weeks long; planning them is not very demanding on resources once a pattern has been set, though very high on resources the first time through. Running such a course might require a director (perhaps half-time), a 'teacher' each day on average, and quite demanding administration backup.

For an action learning programme of similar calibre there is more work each time at the planning stage, though first time round it would certainly not require more resources than the taught course. When the programme runs, administrative backup is markedly less, but of a high order – remarkably adaptive, for instance. Participants' meetings are short and infrequent, and residence is hardly a feature. Participants are not usually away from home and do not need 'looking after'. Few materials are circulated or prepared, and most of those which are needed are provided by the participating organizations. Academic or trainer resources are required on a much higher staff–student ratio, say 1–6 rather than 1½–30, but – for far fewer days. The requirement will vary considerably with the design but perhaps it will be fifteen to twenty – instead of sixty days; and normally there is no need for a separate extra course director. The 'programme manager' may well be a manager in the organizations concerned, a member of the steering group and has usually worked on the development of the programme. Some specialist help may or may not be required for (say) five days overall. In many programmes, particularly after the first time, set advisers are drawn from a wider field than just academics or trainers.

So from the academic-administrative side for a group of thirty there may be little difference in resources in man-days. A taught programme can increase its intake above this figure with very little more staff time, and perhaps little loss of value – though many would question this. In action learning more people means more sets of five or six people and each set needs a member of staff (academic or manager) for some days – perhaps fifteen to twenty. Increased numbers may also provide enhanced learning opportunities, because more groups can learn by sharing their work on the projects, and be stimulated by the set work in other sets. Administration may be slightly strained by the increased comings and goings. An individual project programme of this size needs more setting up and more administration while thirty projects are running.

The main difficulty in embarking on such programmes, for the academics, trainers and administrative people (apart from any role change), is that the **patterns of work** are so different from those required for the normal course offered by an institution. Booking whole days and three-day meetings, often off the premises, for a number of staff (possibly coinciding) may interrupt the academics' other plans and not fit with terms or avoid rush periods on other courses, etc. So the demands may seem greater than they are, and are often said to be so. Course or programme prices must be realistic so that those involved feel equally rewarded – institutionally or perso-nally – not for the number of words said but for their **personal involvement in the work.**

Client organization staff are much more involved in an action learning programme. The participant will typically be working on his job part-time and on his project part-time (perhaps one day per week) for about six months. His colleagues in his department, division, or company may be involved with his work. Someone senior, probably a chief executive, will have become involved at the beginning of the programme discussions to ensure that change action is expected and accommodated.

Development managers become **partners** (with line managers and perhaps outside help) in the 'design' of the programme, and take the **risks** involved. But they and their staff working in the programme in any way will be unable to deny that they have learned themselves, and most feel that, first time round at least, it is an important developmental experience, so the resources in the organization are enhanced and strengthened. Many clients and colleagues associated with the programme have made similar statements. But it must be recognized that the process of (joint) development of the programme does use resources and tests the reality of the commitment to management development and this form of organisation change.

'HOW DO LEARNERS RATE ACTION LEARNING?'

Most of the popular training approaches are low on risk and high on consumer satisfaction. How does action learning rate? It is much more difficult to get an immediate standing ovation! We have all heard the lecture which consists of little more than a series of anecdotes; many of them humorous, received enthusiastically – some of the jokes are memorable. In action learning we are asking good competent managers to face difficult problems which may be well outside their normal competence, perhaps in another organization, with the spotlight on them, and often they will believe that their future careers will be much affected by their performance. We offer them nothing more than each other and expect an act of faith.

By the end of the programme, we can hope for enthusiasm. They will be aware of what they have learned, and may have seen changes in behaviour in themselves and others. They may have achieved a task and seen a change (probably four or five changes) of some importance begin to take shape, and know they had considerable influence – for they will have followed closely the work of all the others in the set. They will have taken high risks on entering the programme, and have felt themselves at risk many times as the work progressed, and they will have survived in good order. A very few leave the programmes part-way through and a few emerge unmoved and unscathed, as reported by one participant in the GEC programme.[11] There must be

similar experiences on taught programmes, though physical withdrawal (as opposed to mental or emotional withdrawal) occurs
equally seldom and leaving unscathed is not always highly visible.

The risk for trainers and developers is higher in starting out in
action learning. Most trainers enter a programme not having worked
with a set and they convince their management on the basis of theory
(Revans) and 'it seems to have worked there' – and often they seek the
help of an experienced ally. Fortunately, most people (though not all)
are aware what they are taking on and prepare the ground carefully,
getting help as they need it, and sometimes very early in the process.
The steps to be taken have been carefully outlined in an 'action
manual'.[12] The idea seems so simple: put a few people together, get
them to take on a task or tasks, and let them get on with it. But most
institutions have too many rules and procedures, too many sensitivi-
ties about authority and too much vagueness about their own
purposes and their expectations of others, to find that comfortable. So
it is complex – to give a degree of authority, to let loose an open mind
on a problem not in his own backyard, and to work to get his mind
more open, his behaviour more innovative, does involve risk. The
rewards can be huge, an encouragement to moves in these directions
in the culture of the organization, as well as achievement of changes in
each single problem area; and more competent managers using more
imagination and strategic thinking, more easily able to get things done
once decisions are taken, and more able to make good actionable
decisions. Consumer satisfaction is not usually a problem at all. Most
programmes are repeated (e.g., seven of the nine in Table 12.1) where
there is still a need. The difficulty, in 'market' terms, is in maintaining
the integrity of the product so that learning remains equally as
important as task.

'ARE ACTION PLANNING AND ACTION LEARNING DIFFERENT?'

*Why is the action planning done at the end of our courses not action
learning?* The last time I had this question I was talking to a colleague
who works in action learning about the work I had been doing in
Africa. At the Centre there, technically well qualified senior managers
come for five or eleven week courses in general management. They
all come from developing countries, almost all from Africa. They

work in groups of five or six throughout the programme, meeting for one period each day, so they know each other's country, organization, job and personality quite well towards the end. We then convert the groups from integrated task groups working on exercises and assignments in the programme to sets ready to work on action planning.

Each member of the set presents a real problem (not a puzzle – these should have been dealt with in options) he is particularly concerned about. Reflecting on the work he has done on the programme, he now wishes to prepare a plan to progress it. The set works in the normal way for (say) one-and-a-half hours on each problem and after his session the member goes away to sum up his new ideas. These are re-presented and examined in the set, and each member takes a last look at the revised version of the action plan in the same way just before the members leave the programme. All the work is done in the sets, the same groups in which they have worked together for many hours throughout the course. The work seems valuable and is regarded as an extremely useful part of the programme. The staff have now incorporated this process in all their programmes.

But this action planning in the set cannot, because of a geographical spread of thousands of miles, be concerned with **implementation**. There is a hope that 'things will happen' and support by letter, telex and telephone is available from the Centre and from set colleagues, but the invaluable working through implementation step by step with the support, analysis and evaluation of the set cannot be experienced. As they leave, we wonder about the future course of action actually to be pursued by that manager who has to tackle keeping a secure boundary round his research centre, with squatters seeking life-giving water from his water source; or that other who must tackle the nepotism from above him which ensures that one of his four divisional managers who does not perform (or even arrive for work very regularly) cannot be moved – and the set's analysis here was extremely imaginative! Or the one whose responsibility is to provide the government with the income from the farmers on his coffee project but who knows that the money is demanded from the farmers by the 'patriots' or 'terrorists', on the border, on pain of death – and he is equally at risk if his own demands are too harsh! Managerial problems take on a new dimension, and the lack of support during early implementation stages, a new importance.

Action learning requires this testing of the pious hopes and case study solutions arrived at in the early stages of the sets. However well done, however discriminating the questions and the analysis, we know that the really significant challenges will occur **as we move to change things**: vested interests will be threatened, someone's *amour propre* upset, the dominant power culture will react, and the resulting processes have to be carefully managed. Powerful people will have to be convinced of the value of the plan, persuaded to cooperate, or be overpowered by the carefully selected band of allies the project champion has collected together.

In many sets, it is in this area that most insights are gained – not necessarily mind-blowing revelations, but a growing understanding of how the power system works (and how it can be worked with) to achieve change. One's own immediate structure and the system within which it is embedded often seem quite invincible, but others in the set can, by careful persistent and sympathetic questioning, identify chinks and open up new pathways. Checking assumptions and testing boundaries can have surprising results. Unfortunately, little of this valuable questioning, persuading and risking is available within the supportive environment of a programme that does not include implementation.

THOUGHTS ON ENDING

As I have struggled to write this chapter responding to questions remembered over the years, such clarity and insights as I have experienced have come (as they always seem to) in two different ways. Sometimes we see a simple new way to look at something – an incremental eye-opener – which helps learning. Members of a set have called these the 'nuggets in the gravel', others say they take home from each set meeting one or two ideas they can apply next week. At other times the simple nudge of a question occurring as one responds to another can change the way we see ourselves and be a permanent, unrepeatable eye-opener! Questions always lead to more questions: and perhaps more discriminating questions! It seems unlikely we will be able to make progress on the vast organizational problems in businesses, governments, and society without developing the skills of asking and responding to more and more discriminating questions. It is certain that we will not find in any book an answer on how to distribute food to the starving; how to enable computers to arrange to do the heavy, dangerous and repetitive work without causing hardship to people; how to ensure that we give adequate health care to all new-born babies; or how to house even our present population.

NOTES

1. Revans, R. W. (1971) pp. 54–5: a distinction underlined in the often ignored Chapter on the theory of action learning.
2. Letter to author re Consortium programme, from John Bird, then Chief Executive, Private Systems Business, Cable and Wireless Ltd (14 October 1976).
3. Many others refer to the processes in sets, often while discussing the set advisor role (e.g., Casey, 1976, adapted in Pedler, 1983, pp. 205–16).
4. Also my early personal exploration (Casey and Pearce, 1977, pp. 96–7).
5. Mike Bett, then Personnel Director, GEC, wrote of the need for improved communications 'probably the most important lesson those involved have learned' (Casey and Pearce, 1977) and specific actions were taken.
6. In Revans (1982) Chapter 31, he writes of choice of Projects, Clients and Fellows (participants), and I see he uses a 'questioning approach' to start the chapter!
7. Garratt's Chapter 2, especially pp. 32–3, in Pedler (1983).
8. A list of the projects and the way they were tackled is given in Appendix III (pp. 139–44), the variants discussed (pp. 19–20) and summarized to nominators (pp. 132–3) (Casey and Pearce, 1977).
9. 'The Self Developing Manager', a description of the Consortium programme printed by Cable and Wireless, a participating company, to help recruit other organizations (available from International Foundation for Action Learning, c/o 26 Harcombe Road, London N16 OSA).
10. The 'Management Action Group' was originally spawned by the Management Action Programme, sponsored by the MSC and operated by EMAS Ltd.
11. David Carr's Chapter 7 in Casey and Pearce (1977).
12. Appendix 1, 'Getting Started – an Action Manual', in Pedler (1983).

REFERENCES

Braddick, W. and Casey, D. (1981) 'Developing the Forgotten Army: Learning and the Top Manager', *Management Education and Development*, 12(3), pp. 169–80.
Casey, D. (1976) 'The Emerging Role of the Set Adviser in Action Learning Programmes', *Journal of European Training*, 5(3).
Casey, D. and Pearce, D. (1977) *More than Management Development: Action Learning at GEC* (Aldershot: Gower).
Owen Report (1971) *Business School Programmes, The Requirements of British Manufacturing Industry* (London: BIM).

Pascale, R. T. and Athos, A. G. (1981) *The Art of Japanese Management,* Simon and Schuster.

Pedler, M. (ed.) (1983) *Action Learning in Practice* (Aldershot: Gower).

Peters, T. J. and Waterman, R. H. (1982) *In Search of Excellence* (New York: Harper & Row).

Revans, R. W. (1971) *Developing Effective Managers – A New Approach to Management Education* (New York: Praeger) (includes a full report of the Belgian Programme).

Revans, R. W. (1980) *Action Learning, New Techniques for Management* (London: Blond & Briggs).

Revans, R. W. (1983) *The ABC of Action Learning,* 2nd edn (Bromley: Chartwell Bratt).

Revans, R. W. (1982) *Origins & Growth of Action Learning* (Bromley: Chartwell Bratt).

GUIDANCE TO READING ON ACTION LEARNING

For basic ideas and practice in the UK: Casey and Pearce (1977); Pedler (1983); Revans (1983).

For a comprehensive guide to thinking about wider applications of the principles, with examples of practice worldwide: Revans (1982) and (1983).

13

Learning design for effective executive programmes

Jim Butler

Since 1975, much has been written, if not practised, about the most effective ways of training and developing managers – particularly experienced people: those who have already had, if not basic management training, then some practical exposure to managing.

There have been so many persuasive arguments to suggest that although many adults working in business organizations need formal management training (and this usually refers to the technical areas of management – i.e., marketing, finance, business planning, etc.), the most significant learning can come only from **doing the job** – that is, running a project, function or business unit and being held accountable for doing so. Experiential learning, it seems, can be only defined within the domain of the work-place – learning by doing is the only way. Few of us who have worked in management development for a number of years would doubt that the work-place is the only really legitimate arena for applying managerial expertise; it may, however, not be the best place to learn all the skills (or certain of them) that have to be learned, particularly skills in developing new **behavioural competences** for 'experienced' individuals, and the action skills required for implementing business strategies and bringing about organization change.

This point is particularly pertinent to able young middle managers who may already be operating at an acceptable level of competency

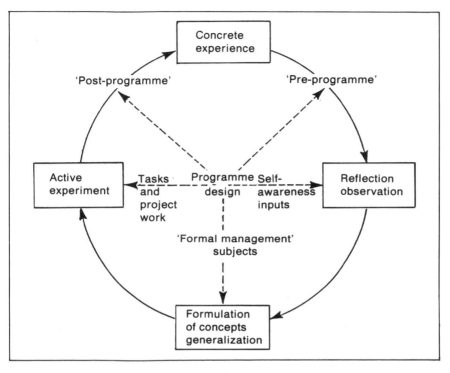

Figure 13.1   The learning design for executive participants

within their own function or discipline and who have been identified as managers with potential to effect improvements in their company's performance and to fill key senior positions in the future. Such managers have already learned 'by doing' and have 'concrete' (in the sense of Kolb, 1976, see Figure 13.1) in-company experience but are required to go on learning and to acquire new and perhaps 'better' experiences in order to progress their careers and take their companies forward. In a very real sense managers with in-company service bring 'concrete' experience with them when attending off-the-job executive programmes. They have already had hard experience in 'live' business environments and their early days on a formal programme (whatever subjects are being taught at the time) are likely to provide the opportunity for reflection and observation. These 'cognitive additions' can add real value to experiences on the programme itself, especially when accompanied by experimentation (and off-the-job venues provide

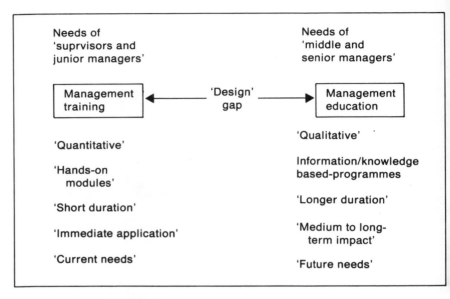

Needs of
'suprvisors and
junior managers'

Needs of
'middle and
senior managers'

Management training ← 'Design' gap → Management education

'Quantitative'

'Qualitative'

'Hands-on modules'

Information/knowledge based-programmes

'Short duration'

'Longer duration'

'Immediate application'

'Medium to long-term impact'

'Current needs'

'Future needs'

Figure 13.2   The conventional design dichotomy

'protection' for experiments). The cycle to learning can be assisted, if not perfected, on a formal programme for any one individual by the effects of timely tutorial interventions and the availability of peer group support.

The principal proposition of this chapter is that although I would certainly not deny the importance of practical experience, my work (and that of many others) shows that so-called 'work experiences' are not the prime source of all (and perhaps the most significant) experiential learning for managers. A great deal can be learned (in addition to abstract concepts and generalizations about management) on formal programmes, especially if the design of such events takes into account the existing level of experience, knowledge and skill of participants and treats it as a **potential barrier** to certain modes of new learning as well as a **possible foundation** for further development. Such design must move away from the conventional dichotomy (see Figures 13.2 and 13.3) that separates management **training** from management **education,** and move toward a much more dynamic perspective that recognizes that in practice management training and education overlap, and that learning events should be designed to ensure

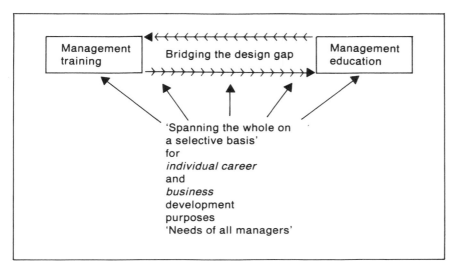

Figure 13.3   Dynamic perspective for managing change (skill and organization)

that the learning process links and combines theory with practice, knowledge with skill, and insight with action thereby enabling individuals to make **transformational learning leaps** as well as **incremental learning steps** (see Honey and Mumford, 1989).

What follows is a description of two very different formal programmes, within which there are design features that provide unique learning opportunities for international senior and middle managers, run at BAT Industries residential Group Management Centre, Chelwood Vachery in Sussex.

MANAGEMENT DEVELOPMENT PROGRAMMES (MDPs)

The MDPs run at Chelwood are industry-specific general management programmes. They cover the main business interests that make up BAT Industries Group Plc – tobacco and financial services. The current programmes are for functional managers (in Marketing, Finance, Production, etc.), with potential for development as general managers or senior functional heads. The principal aims of the programme are to enhance the delegates' understanding of how management functions and disciplines are integrated to meet current and future business needs of 'whole businesses', and to assist them develop effective learning strategies and tactics for self- and career development purposes.

The first of these aims is addressed by a design feature that comprises three main stages. The first is a **preparatory assignment** which takes place in the delegates' own company: note that they are not referred to as 'participants' or 'programme members': they are nominated rather than sent to Chelwood programmes, and arrive with a real sense of representing their company.

The Chelwood part of the programme lasts two–three weeks and represents the second stage, the fulcrum of the whole programme, followed by the third stage, **re-entry and debriefing**, when delegates return to their companies. A fourth and unscheduled stage is the all-important **continuity of learning and development phase**, which of course depends on the success of that which has gone before, as well as the business environment to which the delgate returns.

Twenty-five–thirty delegates for the MDP arrive at Chelwood from all parts of the globe (sometimes as many as twenty different nationalities are represented) with high expectations derived from both the accolade of being selected and the reputation of the programme passed on by colleagues (i.e., Chelwood's worldwide alumni). Programme tutorial staff are much influenced by the notion of 'The only man who is educated is the man who has learned how to learn . . . how to adapt and change' (Rogers, 1969), and they aim to fulfil not only these expectations but also to help maximize the accompanying 'readiness to learn' by encouraging **proactivity and self-development** from the very start.

The design of the programme affords the opportunity for delegates to gain some depth of knowledge in the principal management disciplines, while at the same time promoting a breadth of understanding of the management task of running business organizations. It is my belief, after running many international general development programmes, that some managers demonstrate a predisposition to learning in an integrated way (perhaps another indicator of general management potential and quite as reliable as current performance appraisal and assessment centre test results). This propensity can be supported and developed, but management subject speakers, however competent in their own specialism, find it extremely difficult to teach in an integrated fashion.

The initiative to develop management teachers and teaching materials for integration at IMI Geneva (1986) (now IMD in Lausanne) under the leadership of Director Juan Rada is welcomed, but has yet to reveal exactly how management subjects can be taught in an integrated frame. We know from experience that some managers can (and do) learn in an integrated way, and that we should perhaps therefore direct our efforts in management education to designs that facilitate the self-learning process.

Self-development within the MDP design

To facilitate the integration of the MDP sessions further and to address the second main aim of the programme, delegates are introduced early on to the notion of self-development and are reminded of their own responsibilities for identifying and making the most of different learning opportunities that are likely to arise during the programme. This process is initiated by the formation of a number of **learning teams**, each consisting of six or seven delegates (this learning teams concept is much influenced by the work of Reg Revans and his disciples of action learning). A member of the resident tutorial staff is assigned to each team to advise and support them throughout the programme.

What now follows is a detailed description of five sessions designed to help delegates generate **self-awareness information** that will enhance their understanding of **existing behavioural identity**: as an individual (personality), as a learner (learning style), as a team player (role preferences), as a manager of others (management style), and as a professional careerist (in the sense of making career choices). The whole self-awareness process comprises a series of sessions that make up 'a course within a course' and is called Managing Your Own Learning and Development (MYOLD).

MYOLD – part I: personal learning objectives (first day of the programme)

The first session in teams provides an opportunity for delegates to get to know one another while working on a real and valuable task.

Delegates are asked by the team tutor to 'scan' the programme contents, make a note of those subjects that are likely to be most important, and to describe briefly for themselves what they hope to learn. As readers will know, it can be difficult to determine one's own learning needs, especially when faced with the daunting prospect of surviving a two- to three-week programme. Many real needs may be suppressed either consciously or sub-consciously because they are 'painful' to remember; individuals who have been criticized for their mistakes or inabilities will have 'learned' how to avoid exposing their learning difficulties to others, and will almost certainly prefer to 'learn in secret'. The objectives noted by delegates at this stage are usually sketchy, but a great deal of significance is placed on the discussion that arises – on concerns as well as expectations. The notes produced form working guidelines for delegates' own use during the programme, and indeed a useful basis for **review and action planning** at the end.

Health and learning

At this early stage of the programme, delegates are also offered a voluntary 'Keepwell' course (devised and led by Dudley Cooper, Senior Fellow in Corporate Health and Director, Prospective Health Unit, City University, London). This course consists of a brief assessment of health and physical fitness status, followed by a presentation where delegates are able to compare their individual performance against health risk analysis. An exercise course capable of adaptation to all age and fitness levels is explained and delegates are encouraged to follow the course during their free time. An interim fitness assessment is carried out mid-way through the course to encourage and motivate, and another assessment is carried out at the end of the course. This demonstrates the significant improvements which can be made even during a three-week programme, and seeks to encourage delegates to continue with an exercise routine when they leave Chelwood. Originally designed as a counter to the enforced physical inactivity experienced during lectures and syndicate sessions and to the effects of the social side of the programme, the 'Keepwell' course is now perceived as contributing rather more to the wellbeing of delegates than had previously been envisaged. Consistently positive feedback from delegates and high levels of participation indicate that managers are not only well aware of the health risks associated with their lifestyles, but also enjoy the enhanced feelings of wellbeing which can derive from participation in a relatively modest exercise routine.

Frequent comments made about more positive attitudes to themselves, improved sleeping habits and better powers of concentration strongly support the contention that this must be conducive to more effective learning; the design of the 'Keepwell' programme also reinforces the Chelwood 'message' that individuals have a responsibility for their own development and focuses their attention on a **behavioural model of health**, rather than on the traditional medical model.

After the introduction to the 'Keepwell' course and the first session on MYOLD, the programme continues with more formal management subjects of business and political environment, information technology and strategic planning, and delegates tend to take up the stance of pupil-student waiting to be taught. They are shaken by the second input on MYOLD timed for the mid-point of the first week: this session is designed to promote **self-awareness on personality differences** and **learning style preferences**.

MYOLD part II: individual learning styles (mid-week, first week)

A number of questionnaires and inventories are used including the Pentagon version of Saville and Holdsworth's Occupational Personality Questionnaire (OPQ) and Honey and Mumford's (1986) Learning Styles Questionnaire (LSQ). The questionnaires can be completed in 60–90 minutes, and are self-marked; questionnaires are completed in learning teams but interpretation and discussion of the results take place in plenary.

Interpretation is handled in a very descriptive non-evaluative way, with the speaker using an example of the residential tutorial staff's individual profiles to make points on differences. This usually works very well, with the delegates feeling that there is no obligation for them to share their own profiles in general session at this stage, but simply to observe differences and to understand what the indicators are purporting to say about themselves and others. The results of OPQ are related to an 'optimistic' model of personality make-up and personality development at work; the model does not ignore or deny that 'fixed' innate traits exist, but stresses that they are only part of an individual's overall personality and in work situations and assuming optimum development of other 'developable' traits and behaviours, probably become less significant over time.

In the context of managing one's own performance or behaviour at work, personality traits are treated as a 'knowable' characteristic for an individual, and therefore an important part of 'information about self'. Once raised to an accessible level of consciousness, personality becomes part of one's own self-awareness and can lead to **proactive strategies** in making changes and taking advantage of different learning opportunities. LSQ results are also examined in plenary, again in a descriptive manner; general norm and BAT Industries managers' worldwide norms tables are used and explained. Delegates are then issued with Honey and Mumford's work booklet *Using Your Learning Styles* (1986) and encouraged to read it thoroughly before the next MYOLD session.

Before Part III MYOLD input, delegates have completed more than a third of the programme, working through formal subjects including three days of Finance in the latter part of the first week and a day of 'Effective Marketing Management' early in the second. By this time they have usually established rapport with colleagues and tutors, particularly in their learning teams (some meet informally between sessions) and are more ready to discuss and share their feelings about their assumptions and preferences on learning effectively. Some are already raising questions of 'best fit' regarding their own learning preferences, the design of the programme and subject tutors' teaching style.

The raving activist (albeit we do not seem to have many among our delegates) begins to wonder whether he should have come on the programme at all – too much lecturing, too much reading and not enough time for 'action'; whereas the strong reflector is questioning the merits of the frequent syndicate discussion in different subject areas, and the lack of time to complete exercises satisfactorily. We have found that the reflectors and theorists do in fact seem to prefer the lecture-room sessions with clear conceptual visual aids and the methodical working through of formulae and data.

The pragmatist (and they seem predominant on MDPs) has a different 'carp' – he is concerned with the practical value of MYOLD as we have developed it thus far: 'When are we going to get the chance to practise and try out some of the suggestions in *Using Your Own Learning Styles*?', he asks. These reactions are fairly common at this stage of the programme and are a reasonable sample of the more extreme cases of 'complaint', 'observation' and 'concern' raised at the beginning of Part III.

Very rarely do delegates cast doubt on the validity of the OPQ and LSQ results (and we have now had 300 + managers from all parts of the world participating). No cultural difficulties have arisen save on interpreting some of the colloquial phrases used for certain questions in the questionnaires. Indeed, the majority express the view that they believe the OPQ and LSQ profiles have reported accurately and fairly. (The notion of 'fairly' derives from what many believe to be good and bad profiles; however hard tutors try to explain that the trait description of these instruments are not value-loaded, delegates still attach their own values to the results, usually with reference to certain 'managerial types' who they know and believe to be successful).

MYOLD part III: effective team working

The aim of this session is to enhance delegates' understanding of their own team role preference when working with others. Belbin's Self Perception Inventory (SPI), a much simplified and shortened version of the battery of instruments (now incorporated in his computerized package 'Interplace') he used in his earlier work (1981) has proved to be a reliable indicator of team role preferences. I was involved in some of Belbin's work some years ago, and underwent the full battery of psychometric and psychological tests. My primary team role preference was strong Resource Investigator; the SPI version reliably renders the same propensity on a test–re-test basis. Delegates using this instrument acknowledge its usefulness in providing self-awareness on their psychological positioning and stances when working with others. The instrument is easily self-marked, and has strong face validity for the user.

The results of the SPI are discussed in relation to management team effectiveness, and delegates are reminded that they have been placed in learning teams using the 'usual criteria' of professional discipline, with the additional criteria of national and industry group company differences, but without reference to any personality difference. (In the business world, management teams are brought together or emerge because of their professional and functional expertise; rarely are such teams selected and 'balanced' according to personality or psychological dispositions; we therefore resist the temptation of selecting teams according to team role preference inventory results.) It is also explained that they will, later in the programme, be asked to work in the same teams on a live business project.

MYOLD part IV: managerial styles

Managerial styles are treated as another part of 'knowable' data, and self-awareness is promoted by using managerial style questionnaires based on the original research of David McClelland (McClelland *et al*, 1976).[1] This also is an extremely 'user friendly' instrument in the three parts we offer. Part 1 is a subordinate version of the respondent questionnaire and this is sent to delegates before they leave their company with a request to choose a 'trustworthy' subordinate to fill out the questions related to how he or she perceives the management style of the delegate. Part 2 is the respondent questionnaire and is filled out by the delegate manager himself or herself. The results are compared and interpreted by using the third part, a short but comprehensive profile–interpretive booklet.

Dominant managerial styles are described on six descriptive dimensions: Coercive, Authoritative, Affiliative, Democratic, Pacesetting and Coaching. There is of course no 'right' style for all managers in every situation; each style has different affects in varying circumstances. The interpretive notes are fully descriptive, with guidance and suggestions for practice and application. The whole package provides the delegates with a tangible piece of information on themselves and has good face validity.

Two – three weeks is just about long enough for delegates to get to know one another sufficiently to give some, albeit qualified, feedback on their own perceptions of the validity of MSQ profiles in describing their fellow delegates: remember that delegates work together on syndicate tasks in all formal subject areas as well as completing a business project together, and tend to reveal how they are likely to respond to subordinates, especially when deadlines for completion are looming large and someone believes it necessary 'to take charge'.

MYOLD part V: career and self-development (early in the third week)

This MYOLD input is just prior to the commencement of the project work, which takes much of the final three or four days of the programme. This input is concerned with individuals' perception of their past work experience, and how they might 'choose' to progress their careers further. The whole emphasis of the MYOLD thread through the programme thus far has been to help individuals become more competent in both identifying and realizing learning opportunities that will help them improve their **current performance**; the emphasis now shifts to the medium–longer-term consideration of **career development**. It would appear that most delegates attending the MDP have not given very much thought to their career since joining their company – at least, not in the sense of actively thinking through what **realistic options there are for meeting their own aspirations**. Although some managers on our programmes have definitely demonstrated a very proactive stance to their own career development, others seem relatively passive and prepared to rely on their companies', succession planning systems. I have no evidence that BAT Industries Group's operating managers differ markedly in their attitudes to careers from other business organisations's managers.

An instrument developed from Schein's Career Anchors questionnaire (1978) is introduced here to generate self-awareness data on **occupational identity, aspirations** and **career choices**; the questionnaire is a self-marking inventory that takes about thirty minutes to answer, but rather longer to interpret. Initial interpretation of results takes place in plenary, but this can be of only general assistance to most delegates as they come from different national as well as organizational cultures and there are therefore obvious variations in perception of what is (and is not) possible for them as individuals. It is recognized that a single session on career development can never be complete, and delegates are left with many questions to address and seek answers to for themselves. The very nature of self-development in the context of looking at one's own career is that it is a **continuing process**, and that individuals need to consider all factors – family and personal circumstances as well as work and vocational opportunities.

The session ends on a positive note with the distribution of Dave Francis's excellent little work book *Managing Your Own Career*

(1985). This handout provides delegates with a really tangible aid to helping them think further about their own achievements, personal circumstances and career aspirations beyond the programme and into the foreseeable future.

Live business projects : active experimentation (last four days of the programme)

The grand finale to the formal subjects on the programme is the completion of live business projects. Projects are introduced early in the programme and dedicated sessions are then scheduled at intervals over the duration of the entire three weeks. The last two days are usually devoted almost entirely to completing projects **Learning teams** (having worked together on MYOLD inputs for the last two-and-a-half weeks) become **project teams** and are presented with terms of reference on substantial business projects. The sponsors of projects are senior managers from BAT Industries Group companies, and will already have worked with Chelwood tutors in putting together the principal issues to be addressed in project briefs. The sponsors understand fully the aims and objectives of the MDP in using their projects as a learning vehicle for delegates, but nonetheless are primarily interested in answers to their problems.

Chelwood tutorial staff are careful not to involve sponsors in the possible and potential 'learning' benefits for delegates as this would confuse roles and possibly detract from the realism of the projects themselves; it is our experience that if delegates on programmes are presented with projects and told that they are real, alive and owned by business managers really looking for answers and solutions then it is imperative that this is so, and is seen to be so.

Managers on training programmes are discernibly perceptive when it comes to recognizing what is 'real' and what is contrived; if they are asked to work on a case study or syndicate task, they usually oblige in the knowledge that it may well render some interesting learning for them. With a live project, however, they become as much involved with the sponsor and his perceptions and views about the problems as they do with actual data. In this sense they are highly sensitized to the concerns of people involved in the exercise and if it is really a 'real' project, the sponsor also had better be really interested in the outcome, otherwise delegates are liable to play a very different game.

Many of the projects are personally owned by sponsors who may be just about to launch a new venture for their company, or present a business project plan to their Board for investment capital purposes. Occasionally the sponsors have already launched or presented their projects and are looking for confirmation or refutation of certain strategies and tactics. Provided, however, that the actual situation and state of the venture is explained fully in the project brief at the very outset to delegates, this does not detract from the importance and realism of the exercise.

Project teams are supported by **project advisers**, whose role it is to ensure that the teams organize themselves effectively and involve all their members. At this stage of the proceedings, the teams are reminded that they were put together at the beginning of the programmes using the 'usual critiera' for management teams where selection (or, perhaps more often, emergence) of a management team is based on some functional or professional expertise. An added criterion for the learning team formulation was used, that of nationality and industry–company sector, rendering **balance and spread** in the teams on at least **three significant dimensions**.

Tutors encourage the teams to reflect and share again the information they have on team roles generated during MYOLD Part III, and to consider their **role preferences** in the context of organizing themselves to complete the project. This way, the team role data are treated in a practial rather than an academic mode and delegates can really test out their preferences. Revelations come for those genuinely moving across professional boundaries: for example, an accountant in one of the groups working through the marketing data understood for the first time the difference between a profitable segment of a market and overall profitability across total market share. Similarly, a marketing man in the same team really learned why accountants 'get all steamed up' about slow stock-turns with financial resources tied up in working capital, by actually having to work through the client company's accounts and identify the elements that influenced the declining return on trading assets.

Learning continues, I believe, right up to the presentations to sponsors at the end of the programme, as delegates are usually totally absorbed in their team's performance. They usually share the task of giving the presentation, but to explain the details of their final reports revert to their own disciplines supported by colleagues who have also contributed to the 'whole analysis' and formulation of the recommendations. Live business projects create energy and excitement in a way not possible with 'case material' and case studies, exposing the project team to organization, business politics and data owned by the sponsoring company. Vested interests and power relationships are very difficult to simulate in case studies but virtually impossible to eradicate from live projects, even if the script writers have tried to do so. Business projects form an important part of the MDP, and provide a challenging, rewarding and insightful learning experience for delegates in their learning–project teams.

MYOLD part VI: preparing and presenting action plans (more 'reflection in action' penultimate session)

The penultimate session is concerned with **action planning** in readiness for disengagement from the MDP and returning to the 'real world' of the delegates' working environment. Continuing in their learning–project teams, delegates exchange views on the most salient features of the programme for themselves, and how they plan to **progress important areas of new learning** 'back at the ranch'. Tutors work with the groups in providing an outline checklist to help delegates focus their attention, and make reference to their notes on personal learning objectives, prepared on the first day of the programme.

The important thing about this session is that individuals support one another in working through **practical ways of implementing change** and/or **improving some area of their expertise** back in their own company environment. One person in the group is asked to summarize his own principal action points, together with those of his team colleagues, for presentation in plenary to the whole group at the end of the programme. This **programme exit planning exercise** ensures that delegates remain active in their recall of important subjects covered ('important' to each individual) to the very end of formal proceedings.

Presentations are usually a mixture of serious points for action tempered with humorous (though rarely facetious) comments on the performance of certain team members during the three-week MDP. This session is right at the very end of the programme and after completing project work, delegates are feeling more than a little fatigued. Humour should not be taken as a sign of casual and uncaring behaviour in this context. It often indicates 'tension release' and reveals real concern for certain areas of difficulty, areas that may have occupied an individual or the whole group for some time but have almost certainly rendered new learning experiences.

It is difficult for many managers openly to articulate and admit to progress **at the time it happens**; there is often a 'distancing' of overt recognition by both the recipient (the individual or individuals benefiting) and other participants (colleagues who may have positively contributed to improvements and also learned from the experience themselves). A joke or funny story as an account of the experience becomes a safety valve for 'pent-up' anxieties and genuinely-felt embarrassment either for the story-teller or his colleagues involved in the plot, depending of course upon his or their prediction of audience response and assessment.

On one programme, for example, the spokesman for team A, in explaining benefits which may accrue to one or two participants or perhaps the whole team, told a story about how an exchange between a tutor and one of their group had led to confusion in their team over the understanding and application of a financial performance indicator 'Return of Net Trading Assets' (RONA). The incident was elaborately explained by poking fun, albeit in good taste, at the tutor for seemingly becoming impatient with the person and resorting to the use of some choice North of England adjectives to illustrate the point. The ensuing laughter from team A, and reinforcement from the rest of the audience, indicated that everyone had remembered the incident. The interesting observation from a learning point of view was the individual most affected by the incident acknowledged the value of the support of his colleagues by joining and sharing in the story and overtly claiming ownership of the 'new' and accurate understanding of the term RONA. The exact nature of the interaction in team A just after the exchange between tutor and delegate can only be conjecture, but almost certainly such interactions were supportive of one of their team requiring help, and who knows how may others benefited from the discussion that took place? The work of Reg Revans (1971) has shown that when a genuine peer group is faced with 'uncertainty, threats and sanctions' from not 'knowing', the minds of individuals become concentrated which can lead not only to consensus on common problems but also to managers supporting one another in finding solutions. There was certainly learning for the main actor in this example and for his team – and, indeed, perhaps the whole 'audience' in the plenary session. The novelty of the explanation and detailed account of 'coming to grips with dear old RONA' gave all present in the plenary session the opportunity again to check out their understanding, and at the same time also provided an enabling vehicle with 'protection' and 'safety nets'.

LEARNING TO IMPLEMENT BUSINESS STRATEGIES

A very different design from the MDP described above has proved successful for groups of managers determined to be more effective in formulating their **company's business plans**. In large multinationals like BAT Industries there are bound to be many (perhaps never enough) intelligent people striving to be personally successful whilst at the same time genuinely working hard to keep their company ahead of their competitors. But being intelligent and trying hard is never enough in fiercely competitive and changing business environments.

Conventional management education courses and programmes have always been designed to reduce unintended error and to eradicate hitherto unrecognized ignorance, and of course this must continue to be important in management education, particularly for new entrants to management jobs, and for junior and inexperienced managers: facts and figures, systems and techniques in key areas of production, finance, marketing, sales and distribution and personnel have to be learned. However, such conventional management education is of only partial benefit to the already experienced manager who seems to understand the concepts and techniques of business operations but still frequently demonstrates difficulty in designing and implementing **effective action strategies** to achieve new objectives and change. It is not more learning of an esoteric nature that will help him or her here, but a new experience that first enables him or her to become aware of the absence of certain competences and skills, and secondly the opportunity to practise and perfect some kind of new expertise.

In order to address this issue, the management educator must consult the more dynamic learning spectrum of design mentioned earlier in this chapter (see Figure 13.4); for there is no other area of management where the overlap of management training – education – and therefore the interaction of knowledge and skill, theory and

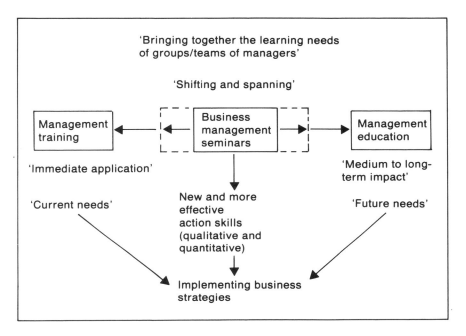

Figure 13.4   The design spectrum perspective

practice, insight and action – is more critical than in implementing new business strategies.

Learning to turn business strategies into operational reality the Business Management Seminar (BMS) – a new design

During 1986 we at the BAT Industries Group Management Centre, in close consultation with senior directors from our operating businesses, decided to experiment with an approach that would attempt to integrate management education and new skills learning for selected teams of managers, whilst at the same time actually 'getting their jobs done more effectively'. Their 'jobs' in this case refer to the implementation of some strategy of medium- to long-term importance in achieving part of their company's business plan. Selection criteria for those taking part was carefully described to our operating businesses so as to ensure we really attracted individuals (together with their teams) of requisite seniority and responsibility for implementing busines strategies.

The new design BMS was offered to BAT Industries operating group companies on a very selective basis with the following aims:

- To strengthen the strategic and general management **competency skills** of key management teams within operating groups–companies.
- To build effective management team cohesion that would render measurable improvements in **implementing** various **managerial strategies** related to business growth and/or change.

Content and tutorial support

The seminar has three principal components (see Figure 13.5), the first of which is a **pre-seminar briefing** session by Chelwood's Director of Studies in the delegates' own company environment lasting approximately half a day, ideally one month before the commencement of the first module at Chelwood. The six days at Chelwood are devoted largely to practical sessions in teams supported by the Strategy Tutor (Maurice Saias from the University of Aix-Marseilles III) and the Organizational Behaviour expert (Chris Argyris from Harvard). There are formal introduction sessions from tutors, but all other sessions are directly focused on the issues and problems concerning each team.

The third principal component is a four-day module follow-up/progress meeting at Chelwood some eight months later, again led by Argyris and Saias. The main objective of this session is to address **practical implementation problems** that may have arisen during the interim period.

The original teams also invite certain of their colleagues to attend this follow-up session (i.e., 'significant others' identified as key players in implementing business strategies). New delegates identified in this way for the second module only are invited to complete the full four days, the first two of which are spent in tutorial sessions with Saias and Argyris to familiarize them with what has gone before. They then join their team colleagues for the remaining two days of this second module.

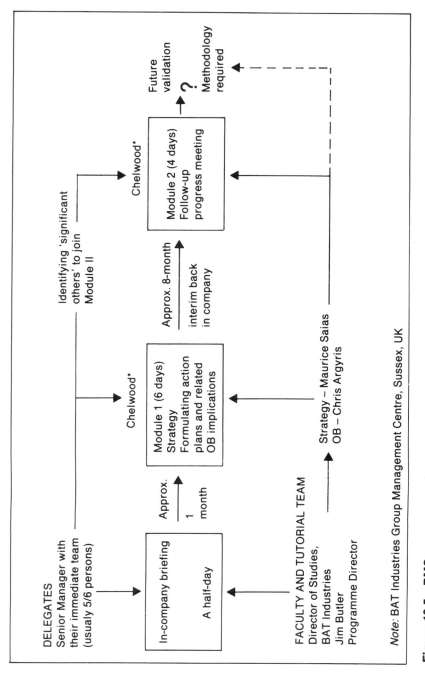

DELEGATES
Senior Manager with their immediate team (usualy 5/6 persons)

In-company briefing

A half-day

Approx. 1 month

Chelwood*

Module 1 (6 days)
Strategy
Formulating action plans and related OB implications

Approx. 8-month interim back in company

Identifying 'significant others' to join Module II

Chelwood*

Module 2 (4 days)
Follow-up progress meeting

Future validation
?
Methodology required

FACULTY AND TUTORIAL TEAM
Director of Studies, BAT Industries
Jim Butler
Programme Director

Strategy – Maurice Saias
OB – Chris Argyris

Note: BAT Industries Group Management Centre, Sussex, UK

Figure 13.5 BMS programme design

Impact of the BMS design – individual and management team learning

By 1990, four years on from the first pilot programme, we have had eight teams participate on the BMS from five very different businesses. The seniority of the team leader has been at an Operating Group/Company Director level, or just below. Our Operating Groups are sizeable businesses in themselves; the subsidiaries of these large operating groups we refer to as Operating Companies, and they trade in many countries throughout the world in businesses as diverse as insurance and tobacco.

Some teams have been led by operating company directors: for example, we have had two operating company Board directors; one was from a manufacturing and merchanting-based business who led his team in looking at their marketing strategy as a crucial part of their five-year business plan; the other was a sales director from an insurance-based business looking at organization and sales–marketing strategies for their immediate planning cycle.

The important similarity of each of the team leaders involved is that they were directly responsible for the implementation of strategies to achieve part of the company's business plan and were collectively accountable (together with their peer group directors) for the **overall company business plan results**. We have some evidence that each of the teams that has participated has subsequently implemented new strategies, the success of which has yet to be fully validated. In the meantime we and our client companies were sufficiently confident of the benefits to schedule two programmes for 1990, each of which sought to attract three to four teams per programme.

Example of new skills learning in the BMS design

The immediate impact of the seminars is clearly visible for each team participating during the first six-day module. The effects on individuals and teams as a whole when real 'breakthroughs' are made are clearly discernible: such breakthroughs often come after the team has become 'stuck on' key issues of strategy formulation, and one or both of the seminar tutors intervenes. For example, the merchanting team looking at marketing strategy during the first module of the BMS had debated the merits of applying a particular technique of competitor analysis, the outcome of which could result in changing their pricing policy. There seemed to be a shared understanding on the technical features of the approach and consensus on the advantages of applying it to the job in hand, and yet a marked reluctance to commit to implementing the strategy by some (or a majority) of the team. The interesting thing here was that the 'blockage' was obviously not due to ignorance or lack of skill, in the sense of not knowing what technical device(s) were available and how to implement them (indeed, this had been effectively covered by the strategy tutor early in the session), but more to do with the very 'skilful' way that some team members managed the potentially embarrassing and threatening (principally to the architect of the existing pricing policy – i.e., the director and leader of this team) prospect of changing current practice. The high level of skilfulness in avoiding threat and embarrassment (Argyris, 1982, 1985) was resulting in the maintenance of existing governing values and assumptions, and was not only a block to learning **new ways of solving strategic problems** at hand, but was also a block to learning **new human interaction skills** that reduce potential embarrassment to individuals personally and threats to organizational norms.

Those team managers 'covering up', in this example did so very competently (i.e., it was difficult to detect the cover up and certainly almost impossible to discuss it in the group, hence the need for the tutors to intervene). The team members, in other words, were skilful in protecting their boss from an embarrassment that they attributed to him (without any articulation or testing of such embarrassment), because he was the orginal 'perpetrator' of the current pricing policy and, as a member of the team later explained, had been overheard on many occasions confirming his commitment to it.

Concern, surprise, perhaps even shock could be used to describe what these same managers experienced when they for the first time **illustrated** and then **tested** by open **enquiry** this **attribution**, and found that the director was anything but embarrassed or hurt by the suggestion that they should consider fundamental change, especially over pricing policy! His lack of awareness of 'cover up' tactics was not due to any personal inability to recognize what may appear obvious to the reader, but because of the high-level skills his colleagues were applying and sharing in their inferences.

This was just one example of one team making a real breakthrough into what Chris Argyris (1982) has called 'double loop learning' (see

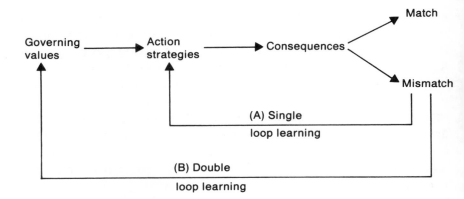

(A) The 'single loop' reinforces action strategies that produce behaviours that are characterized by control, face-saving and self-fulfilling tactics (à la Argyris, 1982 Model I, Theory in Use) and can lead to miscommunication and escalating errors.

(B) The 'double loop' approach challenges the status quo and can lead to new action strategies and behaviours that are characterized by seeking and testing valid information, encouraging enquiry and free choice (à la Argyris, 1982 Model II, Theory in Use) thereby reducing self-fulfilling, self-sealing processes and error escalation.

Figure 13.6   Double loop and single loop learning

Figure 13.6), moving from a predominantly status quo defensive–control stance of operating to a more open exploratory mode of performance by **challenging the governing variables** of how things are 'normally' understood. Permitting free and informed choice on real options, gaining real commitment which leads to action strategies that are subject to **enquiry** and **testing** will thus subsequently result in the implementation of more effective **problem-solving**.

Beyond the seminar: implementing strategies back in the company environment

Certain progress was made by each of the participating teams during the interim between BMS modules and, of course, this was discussed and further advanced in the follow-up progress meeting. What we have not yet been able to do is to validate the effects of the new learning after the completion of the two modules and, indeed, test whether or not the new learning 'sticks' over time for **individuals**: individuals who may well have contributed to the success of the current strategies under consideration but who later perhaps leave, move on, are promoted from the original groups, but nevertheless remain significant players in the business as a whole.

We are committed to ascertaining the effect of this new learning and how the original recipient is able positively to affect others with whom they work in their company environment: for, as already mentioned above, this may well be an example of certain types of skill learning that can best be learned (or be learned only), off-the-job, but the relevance of such learning can be validated only by practising managers doing real jobs, implementing real strategies and bringing about real change in their business environments.

CONCLUSION

As I have attempted to argue above, with some practical illustrations and examples, not all of what has to be learned by managers can be learned on-the-job in the workplace. There are certain areas of theory and practice, insight and action, that are critical to managers in developing new behavioural competences and managing and changing their business organizations, and these perhaps can be learned *only* on formal programmes, away from their normal place of employment. If it is necessary for organizations to change drastically to meet the challenge of today's environment, and if in one way such changes as listed by Peters (1988) (most of which require radically new behaviour on the part of managers) are to be achieved via formal training programmes, then an immediate paradox arises: 'the programme' is necessary only because the required behaviours are not a normal outcome of existing practice and procedures, otherwise there would be no need to develop them in programmes and seminars. Yet if they are not a normal part of organizational procedure, managers may sense a disjuncture between programme content and everyday organizational life, and be cynical about programme exhortation and resist change.

The problem is thus not that experienced managers cannot learn, or that they resist learning on formal programmes, but that they have learnt too much and too well already: they have 'learnt the ropes' and these lessons about how their organization works may obstruct their openness to **further learning** – further learning that will almost certainly be more important to survival and success in the future than existing ways of doing things.

Although there may initially be conflict between a value being advocated in formal training and the structure and culture of the 'learner's' organization, it is essential to help the learner persist with this 'new experience'; within the normal workplace it is of course hardly possible for an individual to persist in such circumstances: it would take not only exceptional courage and energy but in some businesses a strong propensity to commit professional suicide. A formal programme can, however, effect learning design that provides 'legitimacy' and 'protection' for the practice of new actions. We now have evidence that these new and more effective actions/behaviours can be transferred to the workplace provided that the programme **design** encompasses groups of managers that share part of the same organization culture, as with the example of our BMS above and/or extend beyond the programme (both pre- and post-programme **links**), as with the other example in this chapter, the MYOLD course within the BAT Industries Management Development Programme.

I have argued elsewhere (see Butler, 1988) that the able manager selected for the appropriate programme at the right time in his career can experience an immeasurable boost to improving his individual performance. In the light of new personal experience, I would add that business organizations can also benefit considerably from the initial investment of selecting and nominating their experienced middle and senior managers for executive programmes: provided the design of such programmes addresses 'learning issues' for individuals and their organizations and moves them beyond **insight** (many conventional education events provide this) and towards **new strategies for improvement and change**.

NOTE

1.   Quesionnaires published by McBer & Co. (Boston, Mass.).

REFERENCES

Argyris, C. (1982) *Reasoning Learning and Action: Individual/Organization* (London, New York: Jossey Bass).

Argyris, C. (1985) *Strategy Change and Defensive Routines* (New York: Ballinger–Harper & Row).

Belbin, R. M. (1981) *Management Teams: Why they succeed or fail* (London : Heinemann).

Butler, J. E. (1988) 'Learning More Effectively on a General Management Programme', *ICT*, 20(4) (July–August).

Francis, D. (1985) *Managing Your Own Career* (London: Fontana).

Honey, P. and Mumford, A. (1986) *The Manual of Learning Styles* (London: Honey).

Honey, P. and Mumford, A. (1989) *Manual of Learning Opportunities* (London: Honey).

Honey, P. and Mumford, A. (1986) *Using Your Learning Styles* (London: Honey).

IMI (Geneva) (1986) *Report of the Commission of the Year 2000: Integration of Management Education* (Geneva: IMI) pp. 9–13.

Kolb, D. (1976) 'Management and the Learning Process', *California Management Review* 18(3) pp. 21–31.

McClelland, D. C. and Burnham, D. H. (1976) 'Power is the Great Motivation', *Harvard Business Review*, 54(2).

Peters, T. (1988) *Thriving on Chaos – Handbook of Management Revolution* (London: Macmillan).

Revans, R. (1971) *Developing Effective Managers* (London: Longman).

Rogers, C. R. (1969) *Freedom to Learn* (Colombus, Ohio: Charles E. Merrill).

Saville, and Holdsworth, (various years) Publications including the full range of the OPQ instrument, developed in conjunction with over 50 organizations in the UK and Europe (Esher, Surrey).

Schein, E. H. (1978) *Career Dynamics* (Reading, Mass.: Addison Wesley).

FURTHER READING

Argyris, C. (1987) 'A Leadership Dilemma: "Skilled Incompetence" ', *Business Economics Review* (Summer) (University of Wales).

Argyris, C., Putnam, R. and McLaren Smith, D. (1987) *Action Science* (San Francisco, London: Jossey Bass).

Boyatzis, R. E. (1982) *The Competent Manager* (London: John Wiley).

Butler, J. E. (1990) 'Beyond Project-Based Learning for Senior Managers and Their Teams', *Journal of Management Development*, special issues, 9(4), 'The Executive Learner'

Casey, D. (1976) 'The Emerging Role of the Set Adviser in Action Learning Programmes', *Journal of European Training*, 5(3).

Janis, I. L. (1972) *Victims of Group Think* (Boston, Mass.: Houghton Mifflin).

Mumford, A. (1980) *Making Experience Pay* (London: McGraw-Hill).

Mumford, A. (1988) *Developing Top Managers* (London: Gower).

Pedler, M., Burgoyne, J. and Boydell, T. (1988) *Applying Self-Development in Organisations* (London: Prentice-Hall) esp. Parts I and II.

Prospect Centre (1988) *Strategies and People* (Kingston: Prospect Centre).

Rogers, J. (1971) *Adult Learning* (London: Penguin).

Salaman, G. (1986) *Working* (London: Ellis Horwood/Tavistock).

Scheffler, I. (1985) *Of Human Potential: An essay in the philosophy of education, human nature and value* (London: Routledge and Kegan Paul) esp. Ch. 1, pp. 10–40, 76–7.

Schon, D. A. (1983) *The Reflective Practitioner: How Professionals Think in Action* (London: Temple Smith) esp. Ch. 8, pp. 236–66.

Smith, R. M. (1983) *Applied Theory for Adults* (Milton Keynes: Open University Press).

14

Using the outdoors

John Teire

In recent years a growing number of companies have been making use of the outdoors as part of their management training and development; they are finding that courses with projects based on physical activities present their delegates with a challenging variety of managerial situations which cannot be matched in the lecture room. Those taking part soon realize that they are learning quickly and directly from their own experiences: the outdoor projects demand qualities of leadership, teamwork and managerial skill, and when combined with review and discussion are a powerful training medium; the lessons learnt can soon be applied back in the workplace.

Yet, to be effective as a training method, the outdoors must be used appropriately. The activities themselves – be it climbing, canoeing or any other – are a **means to an end**: they need to be linked with theory, discussion and review to make the most of them.

Course design is also important, and depends upon the **training objectives**. What are you setting out to achieve? How does it relate to other company development activities? How will you follow it up in the workplace? As a way of answering some of these questions and sharing information on the use of the outdoors, this chapter is written as a case study on the development and running of such a course for a particular company. It covers the background, the course itself from a participant's point of view, and subsequent follow-up in the company.

THE BACKGROUND

Like many others the company is experiencing changes in markets, technology and traditional ways of doing things. Product life cycles are shortening and there is a need for greater flexibility. Not surprisingly, this has had an effect on the people and on their training and development needs. The company has evolved a management training programme to cope with these changing times. This has aimed at broadening management understanding, increasing the awareness of working with and managing others, and developing specific skills and knowledge for the industry. After a while it became clear that the managers who received a grounding from the programme were now ready and eager for a next step which would take their learning further. With this in mind, the training manager and I sat down together to explore the possibilities.

THE OBJECTIVES

The next step for us had two main objectives. The first was to build on previous courses, particularly in the area of taking **personal responsibility** in management, and understanding and working effectively **with other people**; the second was to look at the process of **change**, and how individual managers were coping with it. It was also our objective that any further development activity should be a participative one, and should give delegates a practical and relevant challenge from which they could learn.

The many ideas we generated just did not fit together into a neat jigsaw puzzle; they kept moving around as we tried to get hold of them. But we realized after a while that this was just the same in any company: it is impossible to have a complete and unchanging picture of what is going on. We found that we had ended up with a set of concepts which we felt were important and which we wanted to build into a week's programme. To do this, we needed a basic structure and a range of activities which would highlight the concepts in an experiential way and show how they were inter-related. At this stage we had more or less decided on a residential week somewhere off-site.

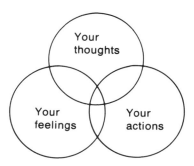

Figure 14.1 Relationship between a manager's thoughts, feelings and actions

THE DESIGN

One of the first concepts we wished to make use of was the relationships between a manager's **thoughts, feelings** and **actions**, as shown in Figure 14.1.

Many training courses concentrate on the delegate's thoughts by presenting a series of concepts and ideas; a few (but not many) take into account the manager's feelings and deal with personal motivation and attitudes; a growing number are looking at 'action' by using outdoor projects and physical skills. We wanted to bring these together in a more balanced way which would also show how all three **influence each other**. This was particularly important for helping the manager understand his own **reactions**: one of the problems which many of us have in managing is **ourselves** – our set patterns of behaviour, our fixed ideas and our conditioned feelings about things.

We needed activities which would be unusual for the delegate and would challenge the elements of thoughts, feelings and actions; through the challenge he might see and understand his own reactions better. We decided to make use of outdoor projects incorporating sailing, canoeing, rock climbing, horse-riding, orienteering and trekking. But the outdoors itself was not the only objective. We also decided to use the 'great indoors', and to learn from how one planned and reviewed the projects. Many of these would challenge the manager's preconceived ideas of what he could and could not do, as well as allowing him to see how his feelings affected his actions. We all

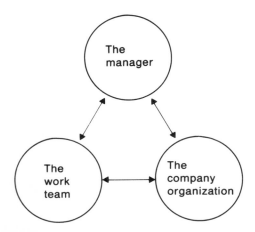

Figure 14.2   Interdependence with work team and organization

have unused potential: often unused because of the **unnecessary constraints which we impose upon ourselves**.

Another concept we wished to use was the **the interdependence** that the individual manager has with both his work team and the company organisation (see Figure 14.2). So many times these are taken in isolation from each other, and the ways in which the needs of each is related are not seen at all. This is particularly so when we add the third of the concepts, that of the **task** and the **process**, where the 'task' is what we are doing, and the process is how we are going about it, often with little awareness. Both of these concepts, we felt, were important for understanding and working effectively with other people.

Any increase in the manager's awareness of these would not be a bad thing! It occurred to us that the most direct way for those taking part in the programme to learn about them would be for them to have some responsibility for the **organization of the week's structure** as well as for the **daily tasks of living together**. Within the limits set by the resources available, the delegates could have the task of designing part of the week's programme and balancing and coordinating the many different (and often conflicting) needs; this would include planning the week's menu and buying and cooking the food each day: the course would have a budget to do this.

It was important for us that the delegates be given a choice in what they **did** and in the **roles** that they took. This meant that although there were many activities and projects available, no one delegate would have to do them all, and different delegates would have done different things during the week. Some of these were group activities, some were for the individual, and some involved everybody. By giving the delegates a range of tasks and activities from which they could learn but also giving them some responsibility for organizing and managing themselves, we hoped to create a realistic and challenging environment.

So, as a basic structure, we decided on a residential course of six days' duration with twleve to fifteen delegates at a training centre in North Wales; the choice of place was important but only in how it fitted in with what we wished to achieve. Taken together, we thought, these would give ample opportunity to explore the last of our concepts, that of managerial **responsibility**: in so many cases, we can see when things are going wrong, but we are not prepared to do anything about it **ourselves**; it is easier to blame someone or something else, than to take a little risk and have a go ourselves.

THE EXPERIENCE

The theory has already been stated. But what actually happened? The personal account which follows is by Dave, a participant in the programme, reflecting his own experiences. Right at the beginning he had decided to keep a diary of the events, and extracts from this are given here.

Before the residential part of the programme a meeting was held at the company for the training manager and me to introduce it to the delegates and to start them off; we explained the thinking behind it, the range of possible activities and the need to do something about food for the week! They held a second meeting by themselves two weeks later.

Although twelve delegates shared the week, and took part in many common tasks, there was also opportunity for individuals to select options relevant to their own needs. Most days there were two to four groups doing different projects and coming together to take stock, review and reorganize as necessary. To put the diary into context, bear in mind that the Monday morning was set aside for detailed planning and organization of the week (started a number of weeks earlier at the two meetings on the company site), Thursday was a full day's project outdoors on the hills which involved everybody, and Friday evening was reserved for some creative entertainment. The rest of the time was organized by the delegates.

DAVE'S DIARY

This first meeting is held to discuss what the course is about and what is likely to happen. We make little progress. It has a debilitating effect on my responsibility cells, at the same time stimulating my mouth cells. During the meeting I make a number of promises to myself. These are:

1. that I will keep a diary
2. that I will not put myself in a position where I could be elected as the MD and
3. that I will try to practise the art of **responding** rather than **reacting** to situations.

The meeting goes on and we talk about food (my subject!). There is an overwhelming apathy about this. I quote 'Don't bother, beans is fine'. This strikes at my very parts. I offer to be quartermaster (my mouth again). Again there is overwhelming apathy, but an acceptance upon my threat of withdrawal. Things begin to look up as the meeting continues. Stan asks, 'who wants to go sailing?' This sounds more like it. We provisionally organize a sailing party. After more talk we agree to meet again in two weeks.

A very different atmosphere at this second meeting; lots of talk. I had circulated a menu and a shopping list but there is no response from anyone except Bob who says 'why can't we have fresh meat?' Despite the three commandments I react, and instantly wish that I had not. Not as easy as it sounds, this responding thing. Suspicion is rife that the whole course is a big 'con' and that any arrangements we make will be reversed and we will be told to 'get out of that'. I begin to believe this. It all sounds too good to be true. I receive lots of help and enthusiasm from people outside the course who do not see the black cloud. Maybe there isn't one.

I think of some activity and prejudge it, for example canoeing, there's no way I am going in a canoe. Conversely I think of an activity which I would enjoy and my imagination pictures me climbing impossible cliffs or canoeing in fast flowing mountain streams. I must admit I feel somewhat frustrated at not having a finite situation to unravel, and problems to overcome. Others are in a similar frame of mind but are prepared to tackle the situation as it happens.

After our second meeting the suspicion deepens. Why don't the garage know anything about the hire cars we shall need to get us there? Why are the catering people delaying our order? Why is there such a large queue at Tesco?

Sunday

The sun shines. We arrive in good order and, first of all, pick the best beds. A touch of remembrance of thirty years ago at school. John and George do not arrive although the others do. Is it all a con? We eat, we lock up the centre and we go to the pub like schoolgirls whooping. We say we don't care. I think that we do. We get back and they still haven't arrived. What next I wonder. Then they do arrive. There is lots of duvet stuffing, pillows, laughter and silliness. Did we know that they would come? Of course we did. The very idea!

Monday

We have an 'unstructured breakfast' and it is a huge success. Brian has been doing an imitation of a Kamikaze pig all night. He and I will not last the distance, I swear. There will be an unexplained accident . . .

When the range of projects is announced I feel dread at the thought of undertaking some of them and a thrill of excitement towards others. This is crunch time. Do I go for what I feel I would get something from, or wait and see what the majority split is?

I choose the latter and then realize that this group appears to have forgotten all the advantages of group discussion. I become aware that there are definite sub-groups, those prepared to go along with the majority without any input, and those anxious to get on with it. I try to respond to the situation but find I cannot find anything to respond to. This task is more difficult than I thought. As I look out of the window I can see a man over the wharf from me. He stands, building a fire in an old ship ventilator in the autumn sun. It is Monday, 10.30 a.m. I do not envy people but I might envy him. I expect that he thinks that 'process' is what you do to peas. I think that he is right.

I lose interest in the proceedings but, noticing that others are the same, I decide to make a suggestion. This time a pen lands in my lap with a voice saying 'get on with it, Dave'. I feel relief. At last I can do something useful.

Once (at the board) things move. Suggestions are constructive and the situation assumes one of order. People air their views and a programme materializes. It is evident that some are unable, or unwilling, to make decisions. It also appears that certain activities are under discussion, but the less appealing ones such as cooking and washing up are not mentioned . . . Perhaps they think these will go away if ignored. A separate chart is drawn up for each day and individuals enter their requirements under specific projects. This saves a lot of argument and debate and I feel that I have achieved something.

The afternoon's project of problem-solving based on orienteering is a chance to achieve some concrete objective. Everyone is involved, in small groups, and we need to give attention to target setting, communications, and dealing with limited information. We also have to judge the capabilities of each team member.

The exercise benefits everyone. My colleagues take it in turns to direct and we progress at a cracking pace. Mistakes are made and assumptions prove incorrect, but overall we all feel a sense of achievement.

We get back having correctly completed the task. One group, considered to be expert, comes in one hour after everyone else. Until they arrive we all have a laugh at their expense. When they arrive, w⌐ say nothing, and mumble about 'having to go round the course anti-clockwise is difficult'. We are two-faced and charitable. We return and have a good meal. It occurs to me that it is the same ones who are charitable who also say that the meal is good. I cannot unravel that.

The evening discussion is very similar to the morning session. However, the division of the larger body into the smaller sub-groups is an interesting exercise. We divide ourselves into discussion groups to review the events of the day. I bend the resolutions that I had made and change groups three times. Does this mean that I am trying for selection rather than being selected? Some of this is gratifying, but not all. I think this only applies to me. I do not care. Yes I do. Why? I end up with three people I know and like. Fine. The different groups separate and we talk and laugh.

I feel happier in this closer environment, but nevertheless, I am finding difficulty **coming to terms** with some of the statements being made. After some time it becomes apparent that the group need help, but can I offer the kind of help that would be constructive and would the group benefit? I decide to soft pedal, concentrate on two members and then to meet the obstacle on my own ground at a more opportune moment. This works and a **relationship** is beginning to form, to which I can offer a useful **contribution**. It is getting late. The door opens and Ken comes in in his pyjamas saying, 'what's all the noise?' He says he can especially hear my voice. If only he knew that two hours earlier I would have apologised. I say 'hard luck, mate' and I am ashamed later. But at that moment I can justify what I say as a response. I ought to make efforts in this direction, but suspect I will not.

We go to bed, giggle at the snores leaking from next door and fall asleep. Brian and his pig gain the benefit of divine intervention. He lives till morning.

Tuesday

Sailing today. I am up alone at 6.30 a.m. and listen to the shipping forecast. They say 'Irish Sea, gale force 9 is expected soon. Good'. Bad, it is cancelled. First thoughts, let us go quickly, we are all packed up for the day. Too late. We have breakfast and then meet to replan. I find myself trying to establish a **consensus** and then remember my promises. I stop and observe.

We are doing better. Peole are making an attempt to **listen**. How are we managing this **change of plan**? Some **adapt** easily, others are stuck. Is this a time to respond? No, not now. Peter is doing fine. Do not cramp his style. We do not need two leaders. Good stuff, this self management, when we do it well.

I take on the **challenge** of a canoeing project with a team of four. Do what you are unsure of, said the tutor. It is better for your learning. Well, here goes. What an eventful day it turns out to be. There is no handholding with this one. In at the deep end, so to speak. We are given three possible projects with information on weather conditions, tide times and a guide to the progress we could make if we work well together. None of us has had any canoeing experience before. We set to and sort out our objectives for the day and select a project which we feel will give us a challenge.

During the day my ideas about canoeing are turned around. How **fixed opinions** can get in the way. Watch out for this. I find that I can do much more than I would have dreamt. We have lots of **problems to overcome as a team**, and spend as much time on dry land, **discussing and deciding**, as we do in the water. My problem person from last night is in the team, and I make a special effort; it works.

A pity we miscalculate the falling tide and can only get back to the centre by carrying the canoes through the wood. We do look silly.

My return is met with a headache. A belaboured cook is panicking over supplies. I **respond** easily and fix it. Am I improving? I take time to write to the kids. There is lots they do not know about me (and the reverse). Will I live long enough? Wish my dad had. I write to Joan; warm feelings. Good.

Another good meal. Did I misjudge the feelings and capabilities of my colleagues? How could I have found out? That is something else to ponder on.

After dinner we discuss the day in our small groups and I find that my fears of the impression I give are well founded; I think this is my major task; to take a 'step back', to be **aware** of its effect.

We go to bed and I find that I am also a Kamikaze pig. Am I on the start of a **learning curve**?

Wednesday

A sound night's sleep and I awake feeling refreshed. Will my legs work when I swing them out of bed? They do. Relief and I get as far as the showers to wake up the rest of my body. The breakfast group has been up already, and smells of bacon and eggs come drifting up the stairs. At breakfast there is much talk about yesterday's activities. I hear a lot from the group that went rockclimbing. This is my project for today. I listen and take it in, being aware of forming ideas which would only cause problems. What comes across clearly is the extent to which people become **involved** in their projects and how this **practical approach** sorts the theory out and brings us face to face with our own **abilities**. The tutors seem to be there for **guidance**, **safety** and **advice** when **necessary**, but most of the time we are having to sort ourselves out. What things have I **avoided in the past**? More importantly, what things am I **avoiding in the present**?

Rock climbing today. What a surprise – we all enjoy it. A different team and different personalities to contend with. And different skills to take into consideration. Paul is 17 stone, and with his positive attitude is turning out to be the star of the course. He causes us to slow down and pay attention to each other. Do I ignore others at work? How am I to know? Am I learning to stand back a little more, instead of rushing in? Our day is one of working closely together, while pushing through fears which come from our minds. I see similar fears getting in my way at work. Are they in my mind? Must investigate further when I return. One incident in particular strikes me. On one section of our climb, Brian sits down and refuses to go on. We spend twenty minutes with him, giving support. With no effect. It is only on our way back that he says he needed a kick up the backside to move him. Remember not to be stuck with just one style of dealing with people. **Be adaptable**. Also, we can learn from **what we do not do** as well as from **what we do**.

In the evening we review the day's projects and then change the groups around to discuss the 'entertainment' for Friday evening. I catch myself falling into the lead. Before bed a small group do some relaxation exercises. Not for me. I go to bed very tired and try to learn my monologues for Friday evening, but never get beyond 'Now Pa, who had . . .', because I fall asleep.

Thursday

Today is our all-day project for everyone. We wake and I just know that the preparation of the packed lunches will be left to John and myself. How wrong I am. All hands set to. There is no 'organisation', but everything is completed swiftly and effectively.

There has been a build-up to Thursday as the highlight of the week. As a result there is considerable **enthusiasm**, and judging by the alacrity with which we leave the centre, everyone is **determined** that we are going to do our utmost to **succeed**. But to succeed in what?

We set out separately in the discussion groups used in the evenings. Good. Our group follows the rules and enjoys a self-righteous feeling. Soon, Bob becomes impatient with John's map reading but we get on well and arrive at the first rendezvous point with another group and everything is going well. Bob asks us to **monitor** the way in which he interrupts people. We do so in style.

We manage to rearrange the groups quickly as required for the task, and I launch a brief sermon on 'no competition'. I just do it and enjoy it, but as I seem to be banging on, I shut myself up. Everybody is **confident**. We pick up more gear and flog on back up the hill. John cannot manage going up hills. Smoking? I carry his bag and try not to feel smug and I believe I may need similar help later. From then on I carry double packs to **assess capability**.

Wales is like a documentary; it shows all the best bits. Super, I fall in a bog! I'm very wet and I imagine the rest of the group thinking 'go on, make a joke out of that!' I do; it is not always easy. At lunchtime we meet up with the other group and all are happy. It is only when the majority of people are formed up that I realise one is missing.

Leaving the others, I retrace my steps to find a member of the team sitting at the bottom of the hill. He has severe muscle cramp and does not have enough strength to climb the hill. After some discussion I carry him piggy-back taking care to put him down before we come into view of the others, to save embarrassment. Neither of us speaks but words are unnecessary. Then I go back for his kit. This is another of those instances that the memory retains for the rest of your life. Words are inadequate to describe how I feel. Perhaps I am too sensitive.

Later, during the 'rescue', **tempers fray** and we manage in a totally **unco-ordinated** way. Wetness dampens the spirits and puts people **under pressure**. The heavy pack reminds me that I am **coping**. I realise that my pressure is not knowing whether I can manage, and I try not to be boastful when I can. We arrive back with some steam left and our original group are so **elated** we decide to walk back. We enjoy it, but wonder what effect our behaviour has on the others. I hope they understand. We all arrive back and everybody is happy again. It **worked well**.

There is more panic in the kitchen, over milk this time. Steve does a Dave and fixes it. Is the pleasure it gave me the same for others when I do it? I hope so.

At the evening **review** we come back to our **disorganisation** at the 'rescue'. It is bad news. On reflection, if I had not been determined not to take on the 'MD' role and overpower the situation, things may well have been different. I conclude that this was neither an honourable objective or a very sensible one. It must have contributed.

There is a certain contentment to be found in letting things happen all around you, and spending time **observing** while the *now* spirals into chaos. But during **reflection** the contentment fades away. Worse still, we cannot relive this afternoon.

Friday

I wake up with yesterday in my mind. How our **understanding** of a situation can change when we stand back! For me, yesterday was all about groups working together, and the **responsibility** each of us has. I can see it going on at work amongst the different departments, and how we blame each other instead of doing something about it. There is a lot to learn here.

Sailing today, rearranged from Tuesday because of the weather. Stan is a man transformed. We are due to be out for the morning only and the others are expecting us back at the centre for lunch.

Yet at lunchtime when the question is asked 'Do you want to carry on?', we live the biggest lie of the week. In the afternoon, discussions are planned to finalise the evening's entertainment. Steve and I have put together a couple of sketches, but these need rehearsal and polish; also, we have not **consulted** any of the other groups. If we stay at sea, these **discussions cannot take place**. We debate as a group, and come to the conclusion that we will stay at sea but inform the centre via ship to shore radio. What have we done? We are enjoying ourselves, the evening's entertainment has taken second place and perhaps the other groups will put something together without us. More to the point, we have **avoided the responsibility of involvement** and **put our own interests before that of the others**.

The sailing is of great value and brings out qualities in people which had never suspected. We see each other in a new light and are amazed at what we achieve in a short space of time. It is not until we approach the centre in the evening that unspoken thoughts of apprehension are apparent. In the centre we narrate our day's experiences, carefully avoiding the evening's entertainment. There is a disgruntled atmosphere and I am aware of **annoyance** about our absence during the afternoon.

The evening meal is superb. The cooks have put in a terrific effort. The organisation as well as the quality cannot be overlooked. I think that if a small number can organise themselves, why are larger numbers incapable of the same?

The evening approaches and I can see that everyone is conscious of not having **fulfilled the suggestions** put forward earlier in the week. As groups chat, most people are hoping that by **ignoring the situation** it will go away. However, as we know deep down, there is **no avoiding the inevitable**.

Someone has a few direct words with Stan about how the sailing trip, which started at the first meeting many weeks ago, has had an effect on this evening. Stan is quiet and thoughtful. This leads me to offer him the monologue I had prepared. We go into another room and Stan in very **nervous** but **willing to have a go**. He does and it is magic. He is very good and I am pleased afterwards when he thanks me. This changes the mood and the 'entertainment' gets under way. I do a hastily put together sketch with some others about the week; we play some games and enjoy the general air of relaxation which develops. I regret that I am the first to crash out. I do not want to break up the party but I go limp from my head downwards. Good sleep.

Others have the stamina to stay on into the early hours discussing many matters of a personal nature which have come to them during the week. There is a good **feeling of togetherness**.

Saturday

Everyone is busy cleaning, scrubbing and getting everything ship-shape. The remarkable thing is that **none** of the activities is **pre-planned**. We all know **what wants doing** and, when one job is finished people look to see **what else is required**. This is what it is all about – **working as a team**.

When the work is complete, group photographs are taken, we say our goodbyes and offer thanks before leaving. Each of us is deep in thought as we travel many miles without talking, each remembering the week as each wants to remember it.

REFLECTIONS

On the journey back, the training manager and I had many thoughts buzzing around. Had it worked? Did we get the right balance? Had the delegates seen the underlying reasons? What will be the effect in the coming weeks? One thing we were sure of – it had been a full and rich week with many experiences for the delegates to learn from.

By the time we arrived back, we had talked ourselves into a few early conclusions. First, we were surprised and pleased that the delegates had taken to self-catering and had produced such a high standard of cooking; giving them the **responsibility** for this had been the right thing. Secondly, the decision to leave the **choice** of projects to the delegates had been right. We had not wanted to force them into anything, or to organise the week for them. Giving them this responsibility had thrown up many valuable **organisational** problems. Thirdly, not seeing the outdoors as the main reason for being there but making use of it as an aid to learning. Finally, on the overall structure of the week, we felt that we might have achieved a better balance by restricting certain activities to particular days. Surprisingly for us, the conclusions from the delegates were that we should not change anything. The point they made was that **to learn**, they had **to struggle, make mistakes, create their own problems**, and **enjoy their own successes**. If only, they said, they had **believed** at the time that we really were giving them the opportunity which we said we were! However, these are my thoughts. What about Dave's?

'My first reflections after the week were about how we all anticipated problems and assumed that these would be created by interference from the outside. This turned out to be completely unfounded. Most of our problems were self-generated! Far worse than the real thing. How much of the time are we doing this?

'Of my **longer-term reflections**, one thing has become very significant. This is about the three promises I made. The first was to keep a diary – which I did. The second was not to get elected MD. This proved to be particularly **selfish** during those times when I could have **contributed more**. I tended to listen and watch. A **balance** between the two is **more desirable**.

'Promise number three, to **respond** rather than **react**, proved difficult. However, with practice, this has become easier and has had a **significant effect** on those around me **at work**.'

SOME TIME LATER

Since the course which Dave wrote about, we have brought together delegates from a number of courses to share views and experiences. The structure of this day was for the participants to work in small groups and then to present summaries of their discussions with flip charts. These fell naturally into the three areas of before the course, during the course, and after the course, and the charts (Figures 14.3, 14.4 and 14.5) give the main points of general interest which emerged.

One thing which struck me about them was the absence of the activities which the delegates were taking part in on their courses. Many people who are considering a course which makes use of the outdoors have a natural concern that it should be relevant to the manager's job and to the company. Often, they have difficulty in appreciating the link between, say, an orienteering or a sailing activity, and the day to day problems back in the company. Here, the delegates have **concentrated on the learning** which has **come from the activities**, rather than on **the activities themselves**, which indicates that it is the resultant learning which is important and relevant.

The flip charts here are like most flip charts produced by syndicate groups for presentations to other delegates. They give the essence of their discussions, and the presenters fill them out with examples. Perhaps you could use your own experience of similar situations to see the meanings behind the words.

IN ADDITION

In addition to the components which emerged about the course and about the value which people found it to have afterwards, the review day itself was well received. The delegates said that it acted as a refresher and gave them further insights from each others' experiences back at work. From this meeting and from a questionnaire we sent out, a few observations about using the outdoors came into my own mind.

Why the outdoors?

Potentially we can learn from all situations, so what is the particular value of the outdoors for management training? Three things emerge.

<u>BEFORE THE COURSE</u>

<u>FOR OURSELVES AS INDIVIDUALS</u>
* WE HAD A MIX OF FEELINGS AMONGST US ABOUT THE COURSE.

* THERE WAS ANXIETY ABOUT THE UNKNOWN, WHAT CHALLENGES WOULD
  THERE BE? WOULD I BE ABLE TO COPE? WHAT ROLE SHOULD I TAKE?

* THERE WAS EXCITEMENT ABOUT THE OPPORTUNITIES IN STORE, WE WANTED
  TO MAKE THE MOST OF THEM.

<u>OUR PRECONCEPTIONS OF THE COURSE</u>
* THESE VARIED FROM PERSON TO PERSON.
* SOME OF US WERE SUSPICIOUS AND THOUGHT WE WOULD BE 'SET UP'
  DURING THE WEEK.
* SOME OF US SAW IT AS A 'PRACTICAL' FOLLOW-ON FROM THE PREVIOUS
  COURSE.
* OTHERS WERE ANTICIPATING INTERPERSONAL, LOGISTICAL AND
  ORGANISATIONAL PROBLEMS TO DEAL WITH.

<u>AS A GROUP</u>
* WE FOUND THE PRE-COURSE PLANNING MEETINGS WE HELD
  OURSELVES TO BE VERY VALUABLE.

* IT WAS NOTICEABLE HOW WELL WE ALL GELLED TOGETHER
  — GROUP EMPATHY.
* THERE WAS A FEELING OF WANTING TO 'GET IT RIGHT' AND
  MAKE IT WORK.

Figure 14.3   Summary chart: Before the course

<u>DURING THE COURSE</u>

<u>MOTIVATION</u>
* THERE WAS A HIGH MOTIVATION BY INDIVIDUALS TO 'HAVE A GO' AND
  ACCEPT CHALLENGES.
* INDIVIDUALS AVOIDED THOSE ACTIVITIES WHICH THEY CONSIDERED TO BE
  TOO HIGH A PERSONAL RISK.
* THERE WAS AN UNSELFISH, SUPPORTIVE ATTITUDE. AMONGST ALL THE
  DELEGATES.

<u>LEADERSHIP</u>
* WE WERE HOPING FOR 'LEADERSHIP' TO EMERGE.
* THROUGH THE WEEK WE SAW EACH OTHER IN VARIED AND CHANGING
  ROLES WHICH WE HAD TO MANAGE.

* INDIVIDUALS WERE ADAPTABLE IN THE DIFFERENT ROLES THEY TOOK....

* .... AND THERE WAS A NATURAL AND SOMETIMES SURPRISING
  SELECTION OF LEADERS AND FOLLOWERS IN DIFFERENT
  SITUATIONS AT DIFFERENT TIMES.

<u>TEAMWORK</u>
* AS THE WEEK PROGRESSED WE BUILT UP TRUST AND SUPPORT WITH
  EACH OTHER.
* THIS LED TO GOOD TEAMWORK AND MORE WILLINGNESS BY
  INDIVIDUALS TO HAVE A GO.

<u>.OTHER THINGS OF VALUE</u>
* OUR REVIEWS AND DISCUSSIONS BEFORE AND AFTER THE ACTIVITIES.

* THE WIDE CHOICE OF ACTIVITIES WE HAD.
* HAVING TIME AND SPACE TO ONESELF PERIODICALLY - RESPECTING
  THIS NEED IN OTHERS.
* LEARNING TO RECOGNISE OUR LIMITS.

Figure 14.4   Summary chart: During the course

AFTER THE COURSE

(A NUMBER OF MONTHS BACK AT WORK)

FOR OURSELVES AS INDIVIDUALS

* IT HAS CLARIFIED AND REINFORCED THE PREVIOUS COURSES.

* THERE IS AN INCREASE IN OUR SELF-CONFIDENCE.

* WE HAVE A BETTER UNDERSTANDING OF OUR OWN ABILITIES.

* IT SHOWS THAT A POSITIVE ATTITUDE CAN LEAD TO SUCCESS.

* OUR MANAGEMENT OF TASKS AND DECISION MAKING IS IMPROVED.

FOR OUR RELATIONSHIPS

* WE HAVE MORE UNDERSTANDING OF, AND PATIENCE WITH, OTHERS

* THERE IS AN IMPROVEMENT IN THE METHODS AND ABILITIES OF MANAGING OTHER PEOPLE.

* WE NOW BRING SITUATIONS OUT INTO THE OPEN TO RESOLVE THEM.

* WE HAVE AN INCREASED AWARENESS OF THE RELATIONSHIPS IN A TEAM (INCLUDING THE FAMILY AT HOME)

FOR THE COMPANY

* DIFFICULT PROBLEMS ARE NOW TACKLED AS A ·RESULT

* THE SHARED EXPERIENCES AND COMMON LANGUAGE ARE LEADING TO BETTER COMMUNICATIONS.

* IT IS POSSIBLE TO SEE HOW A COMPANY STRUCTURE CAN AFFECT PEOPLE'S BEHAVIOUR.

* THERE IS A REALISATION THAT WE, THE PEOPLE, ARE THE COMPANY.

RESERVATIONS

* SOME PEOPLE MAY 'MISS THE POINT' OF IT ALL

* OTHERS MAY TREAT IT AS A HOLIDAY.

* THE OUTDOOR ACTIVITIES MAY NOT SUIT CERTAIN TYPES.

Figure 14.5   Summary chart: After the course

Firstly, it is realistic. The problems, decisions and experiences are not hypothetical. Secondly, it is a challenge to our conditioned ways of thinking and seeing. The unusual circumstances (for most of us) can shake us out of our ruts and cause us to see things more clearly. And thirdly, it involves our actions and our feelings, as well as our thinking apparatus (which often only gets in the way). The **learning** is not *about* the outdoor activities. **It is about ourselves**, individually and in teams, and about how we **react** in these **different circumstances**.

What is your purpose?

The design of a course like this depends upon your reason for doing it. Is it **teambuilding**, do you want to improve an existing team, or perhaps gell a new project group? Is it **individual development**, drawing out the potential of the manager and giving him understanding and confidence? Is it **organizational understanding**, seeing how people can learn to work together effectively? Or is it for the **improvement of relationships** amongst departments; for **developing leadership skills**; for **understanding change**? **Knowing your purpose is important** for knowing how to design your course at the beginning. Each of these objectives is possible, but the way in which the activities should be used will vary. The activities are not an end in themselves, but are a means to an end (or even a means to a beginning!).

Where does it fit?

The purpose and design of a course also depends upon your other training and development programmes. Is it a first off for the delegates? Does it follow on from another course? Does it lead in to another phase?

The course described here was designed to build on previous courses which develop **awareness**, **understanding** and **skills of managing** and **working with others**. It was because of this that we gave the delegates **responsibility** for their course and their learning. For other situations, the initial design could well be different. In this case the participants seemed to take up the **opportunity** readily.

Keeping a perspective

Lastly, keep it in perspective and do not get carried away with the physical activities alone. Although we have made use of the outdoors here, we have also made use of other things for learning too. There were the **pre-course meetings**, the **self-catering**, the **indoor activities**, the **delegates' time alone**, the many **one-to-one talks**, the **group discussions** and the timely **reviews**.

All of this certainly does not mean that everything ran like clockwork on the courses. You may remember from Dave's diary that at many times just the opposite was the case. But really this does not matter. The purpose is not to '**get it right**'. Again, I should like to leave the last words to Dave.

'Life is not long enough to keep retracing the path and discussing where we should have gone. **The experience of going is the real lesson** . . . Perhaps the greatest gift is the ability to stand away and view yourself and the situation from the outside. Being self-critical achieves little on its own. Changing the criticisms into actions is satisfying and reaps its own rewards.'

FURTHER READING

Bank, J. (1984) *Outdoor Development For Managers* (Aldershot: Gower). Bank discusses the what and how of OMD as well as presenting a number of company case studies and an outline of the work of many of the providers.

Beeby, M. and Rathborn, S. (1984) 'Outdoor Management Development : Choices About use', *Management Education and Development*, Vol. 15, Part 3.

Creswick, C. and Williams, R. (1979) *Using The Outdoors For Management Development and Teambuilding* (FDITB) – is one of the earliest reviews. They discuss the range of applications and explain the progression during a typical course.

Honey, P. and Wobley, R. (1986) Learning from Outdoor Activities.

Mossman, A. (1985) *Personnel Training Bulletin* (Tapes) Issues 21 and 22 (January/February), Didasko, Huntingdon, Cambs. – talks to providers and users of Outdoor Management Development

Mossman, A. 'Ways of Using the Outdoors For Manager and Management Development' *Management Education and Development*, Vol 14, no 3, pp. 182–96 – differentiates between manager and management development in the outdoors and describes the differences between the management training and self development approaches. This paper concludes with a fairly comprehensive bibliography of good and bad reports on OMD.

**PART V
ISSUES IN MANAGEMENT
DEVELOPMENT**

15

The cultural contexts

Bob Garratt

'When I hear anyone talk of Culture, I reach for my revolver'. Such strong sentiments are not restricted to Goering alone: many of the managers I meet in the course of my work have similar feelings, but these are changing and for the better. They are coming, sometimes grudgingly, to the realization that 'culture' is an area of growing importance: it seems to be what links organization strategy and structure, through vision and energies, with the values and behaviours of the people comprising the business and delivering its targets.

This chapter is a distillation of my recent work. In it I have tried to do two things: first, to tease out the meaning of the word 'culture' in the very different contexts of the (specialist) department: the organization, and the international environment, and then the management of the total concept. Second, to stress that most of the tools needed to measure and manage the cultural dimensions are already easily available and ready to be applied to the increasing range of 'cultural' problems. What is needed is a conscious effort on the part of the managers to **give priority to managing them**.

I shall define 'culture' as 'the way we do things around here': it is a combination of the values, behaviours and history of an organization which define (often tightly) the limits to thought and behaviour in the organization. New entrants hit it when they do what they think is right in their job, only to find others saying 'Oh no, we don't do things like that round here!' (See Chapter 6 above). Such a simple definition

299

gives too uniform a flavour to the subject; it hides the complexities of different levels of culture and their interactions in and between organizations. However, it is a good start when working with directors and managers.

The idea that culture can be **designed, directed**, and **managed** is so seductive that managers can get quite excited and energized to 'do something about our culture'; being typically action-fixated, they will then demand to start the change process. This often causes problems for management developers who are as ill-informed and ill-equipped in this area as their managers. Both need training and development since culture is literally, central to creating and maintaining an effective organization. I hope that this chapter gives some clues to the ideas and processes that can be used.

A CULTURAL HEALTH WARNING

'Culture' has become a particularly fashionable issue with directors since it was legitimized, initially through *In Search of Excellence*, (Peters and Waterman, 1982), The possibility of integrating the three 'hard' areas of business (systems, strategy, and structure) with the three 'soft' areas (staff, skills and style) via shared values, has made possible the discussion of culture and values at the top level of organizations in a way that has not been possible for twenty years or more. But 'culture' is in danger of losing its meaning if those who are so eagerly embracing it use it in too profligate and ambiguous a way. Moreover, many new converts see culture as the new cure-all which it patently is not. If it can be said to be anything at present it is the thin film of lubrication which enables people to **work together within their organization structure** for **common ends**. This notion of culture helping alignment and attunement in an organization is central to understanding it.

Most companies with which I have worked see culture as a unitary thing; I initially annoy them by saying that it is a series of different things at different hierarchical levels of an organisation – and that directors need to handle each level differently. However, there are strong stereotypes about the unitary nature of culture which can lead an organization to some very basic problems of profitability. For example, it is accepted in most multinational businesses that I have interviewed that their company culture must – and should – transcend national and all other cultures. Such a notion of culture is implicit in the planning of most executive directors and in their subsequent behaviour; yet the results regularly contradict their assumptions and behaviour. They ask 'how can the same sort of people with the same sort of education in the same sort of job in our global organizational structure, do such different things?' The question is usually set emotionally in terms of frustration, anger, and despair, often because the questioner is aware of the varying levels of profitability and complexity that will be needed to manage what is being uncovered.

This is typical of the problems many companies face in trying to direct the international cultural dimensions of their business. It is not a particularly British characteristic; there is evidence to show that US and Japanese corporations have considerably more problems in coping with international cross-cultural aspects than, for example, North Europeans and Overseas Chinese (See March, 1980). It would be a mistake, however, to think that managing cultures is a problem only for organizations who have to trade across national boundaries. The **internal organizational culture** is being seen as of increasing importance as companies face up to radical and structural change. Coming to grips with the internal dimension alone is enough for most managers, but few have this luxury nowadays. Increasingly managers, particularly top managers, have to cope simultaneously with both the internal and international dimensions. How they cope with this is of great interest.

My experience of working with companies across cultural boundaries has been that the problems are often felt but then hidden, rather than exposed and managed. The reasons for this are complex but amongst them is an awareness that to confront them would force a radical change in the Board's ability to think about the multicultural dimensions of their work; this, in turn, would force reconsideration of their **present allocation of time** – and this is often treated as sacrosanct 'because we are busy enough already'.

This is true but, as an Institute of Directors report (1990) shows, most directors are untrained for directing, and so tend to focus their use of time on the operations cycle of work and learning (where they have trained and been comfortable) rather than on the strategic cycle in which such 'soft' subjects as culture lurk. It is patently most effective to start any re-evaluation of the role of culture in management with the Board. That this is not always possible is accepted, and very useful pilot projects can be started and measured without Board involvement; however, they need to be built into the overall organizational learning process or such projects may be seen as setting up alternative power bases within the business and will be resisted by the Board, demeaning culture in the process.

The subtleties and differences of thinking about the cultural dimensions needed will rapidly show up a lack of knowledge and skills in many directors; such lacunae are difficult for any individual at Board level to talk about so progress is rarely made – unless there is team commitment to do so. This is usually not the case, and so the issue is hidden again, whilst the already inadequate corporate culture is brought to bear once again on a problem which has regularly proved intractable. Yet the Board knows that doing 'more of' or 'less of' the same thing will not change the problem. How can they **re-frame the cultural issue** so that it is resolvable within their own resources?

SETTING THE CONTEXT

My experience has been that the very act of saying that it is legitimate to talk of cultural difference at Board level, and get people used to so doing, is sufficient to allow the re-framing of the problem so that constructive change can happen. There are often audible sighs of relief around the table when some basic vocabulary, concepts, and measures are introduced to help define and explore the area of 'culture'. Often the analogy of 'it felt like a boil being lanced' is used. I have learned to curb my didactic tendencies on such occasions and to work from the Board's existing positions on one fundamental issue – **difference**, and how to value it. Around the table it is usually easy to get agreement that there are physical, social, and psychological differences between those present; it is then not difficult to get agreement that the reason this particular group is charged with giving direction to the organization is that they represent the synthesis of the various specialized functions needed for the organization to sustain and develop itself. As such, they must subscribe (albeit subconsciously) to the idea that such amalgamation allows for **synergy** amongst them – that the individual inputs give an output that is **quantitatively and qualitatively better** than the simple sum of the inputs.

Such statements are usually met with acclamation: 'So why then', I ask, 'do you as a Board who obviously value the differences between you, behave in a way that tries to eliminate rather than celebrate and use the differences in your operating units and with customers?' This is the time when some resentment can erupt. Then a dispassionate review of strategic-problems – business and people strategy – will usually gain support for my plea to develop thinking and procedures in the cultural context. It is at this point that a start can be made on coming to grips with the paradox that the more an organization tries to impose a unitary 'corporate' culture on its disparate parts, the more the differences becomes magnified and difficult to manage. If this does not work, then a quick study of the main reasons for corporate collapse (Argenti, 1976) – too many people of the same sex, age, education, and nationality at the top, with too little authentic information about the changing environment, and few managerial information systems – usually makes the case adequately for 'sufficient diversity' of personalities and cultures (see Ashby, 1956).

SOME WORKING DEFINITIONS

With line managers, I use at first the notion of 'culture' being 'how we do things around here', and get them to give examples of how they ran into this organization's culture when they joined it; this elicits great passion and merriment and helps make the profound point that unless people are psychologically 'included' in their workgroups and the organization then they can never be seen as 'competent' in it, no matter how well qualified. As we get into the deeper comments coming from this, we can take a deeper look at culture itself.

The word 'culture' is loaded with ambiguity and complexity. For the sake of this chapter I will use a single definition:

an historically transmitted pattern of meanings embodied in symbols, a system of inherited conceptions expressed in symbolic forms by means of which men communicate, perpetuate, and develop their knowledge about and attitudes towards life. . . man is an animal suspended in webs of signification he himself has spun. I take culture to be those webs, and the analysis of it to be therefore not an experimental science in search of law but an interpretive one in search of meaning (Geertz, 1973).

But I do not say that initially in the Boardroom. The cultural divide would be too great!

There is significance in the vocabulary that any operating group uses and the above quotation is so far outside that used by business or organizations that it invites initial hostility and rejection – made manifest in such comments as 'stupidly academic', 'psuedo-science', 'soft', etc. In that form, it has no significance for the Board. This does not diminish its conceptual value, but it does make it indigestible when presented in unadulterated form. That is why it is important to use the 'empathetic' approach of starting from where the line managers are, and **using their experience to create the higher concepts** – the move to the 're-framing cycle' (Watzlawich *et al.*, 1974) of learning which allows them to explore recurrent organizational problems by using a cultural perspective to re-frame the problem. This is necessary to gain Board awareness of the 'webs of signification' which they have spun themselves. An awareness of the organization's symbols – logo, predominant colours, furniture and furnishings, equipment, etc. – and the ways in which a new entrant becomes 'included' (Smith, 1986), often through subconscious behaviour and semantic modification created by the existing staff, is crucial in opening up the cultural dimensions so that organizations may develop constructively.

Present perceptions, behaviours and values can be measured by such processes as the Handy Organizational Culture Questionnaire (Handy, 1985), the Organizational Climate Survey, and Neuro-Linguistic Programming. In so doing, a veritable maze of dead ends and diversions can be constructed; it is not my intention to do so, and I have to contain myself from following those seductive idiosyncracies and differences found in organizations, and use them only in those dinner party conversations where one can add the tag 'not many people know this'. What concerns me much more in my consultancy role is to get the Board to find and focus on those aspects of the cultures within which they work that affect and determine the **effectiveness** and **efficiency** of their organization.

A WORKING VOCABULARY

To do this it is necessary to try and give more definition to our use of the word 'culture'. In a small working group, 'culture' can be taken to refer to national characteristics, political beliefs, organizational style, individual attitudes, historical progression, and the fine arts. Little wonder that confusion can reign even between those who work together each day! I have developed my own categorization of 'cultures' which I use when working with an organization. This involves four levels of cultural differentiation:

Micro-culture	relates to the world of the **functional specialists**, and **workgroups**
Mini-culture	relates specifically to the **organization** and its **social structures** (a sociological notion), otherwise known as the 'corporate culture'
Macro-culture	relates to the wider, **national multiracial and international contexts** (an anthropological notion)
Meta-culture	relates to the transcending of mini- micro- and macro-cultures by those **giving direction** to the organization (i.e., the management of the other three levels of culture – an integrative notion).

How do these very different levels of culture work in practice in an organization?

'**Micro-culture**' is usually the best understood as it is the most personal; it is where we spend our daily lives. This is the most basic (some would even say 'tribal') level of culture (see Chapter 10 above): it is where you are accepted or rejected as an individual. Because of this there are often complex 'rites of passage' for acceptance, usually involving you in proving yourself through some emotional and/or physical test. If inclusion happens, then all is well; if not, the individual becomes a social isolate. This can happen at all levels of an organization and in my experience is very common in the senior and top management positions. It is rarely managed well in organizations and yet, if not managed, can create massive problems as the mini-culture is the foundation on which all the others are built. Mini-culture is measurable by a wide range of group and team psychometric tests.

'**Mini-culture**' is the level commonly known as 'corporate culture'; it encompasses the social composition and history of specific departments and divisions within the corporate whole. How they started, who was involved, and for what reasons, are key indicators of microcultures. Who holds power now, and what values do they espouse – raw divide-and-rule power, or stability and continuity, or professionals coming together to run high-quality projects, or very personalized activities nearer to a group of high-powered colleagues? What is the prevailing 'party political' flavour? Are there strong religious tendences at Board level, or are there particular ethnic characteristics which predominate? These are typical of the types of questions which reflect the mini-cultural aspects I would want mapped and debated. To this can then be added some of the more management-orientated mini-cultural analyses. What is the organizational culture? Which stage of the product lifecycle have the various units reached? Which functional specialism is dominant in which parts of the company? In process terms, it is usually much easier to begin mapping in the technical areas and work towards the 'softer', less appreciated, aspects rather than vice-versa. The Board then starts from what it knows, and can ease itself into the more difficult areas. These are measurable by, for example, Handy's Organizational Culture Questionnaire.

Interest in the mini-culture or 'corporate' culture is growing as top managers take more interest in strategy and find the complexities of implementing their strategic ideas need more than just instructions to the operational people. A picture of the future, a way of getting there, and a way of getting aligned to get there, are all needed and I shall say more about this at the end of the chapter.

'**Macro-culture**' analysis and mapping is a more difficult step to take in the move towards an organization's understanding and management of culture. Most Boards accept that there are the mini- and micro-cultural aspects to the process of managing, even if they would prefer not to express it in that way. They are usually more comfortable with terms like 'Managing the human side of enterprise', 'Motivating and maintaining morale', or 'Proving that people matter around here'. However, they do understand that their organization operates in a wider political, multiracial, and international context. This is characteristically much more unpredictable and disruptive and much more difficult to manage. Macro-culture can be measured on such dimensions as Hofstede's cross-cultural maps. (Hofstede, 1980).

Managers are unlikely to grace this domain with the term, 'political science' or 'anthropology', but these are the areas into which they are moving. Considering the narrow educational backgrounds most managers have it is hardly surprising that they have difficulty coming to grips with macro-culture; but come to grips with it is what they will need to do – a troubled US manager working for a British multinational in Hong Kong facing a problematic Taiwanese member of staff is not so unusual a problem nowadays. Neither is negotiating across a table on behalf of an international consortium with backing from a range of overseas financiers whilst facing your opposite number who, in turn, represents a newly industrialized country's minority government being backed by the World Bank for a new infrastructural project. It is no good in these circumstances insisting that there can be only one culture around here, and that is our corporate one; it just will not wash. Acceptance that the game has risen by at least one plane, and that the roles of all players become much nearer to that of diplomat–negotiator and international troubleshooter is the only way out. This requires training and development, if only to ensure the clearing of diaries of operational impedimenta to get seriously into the management of the macro-cultural role.

I have argued elsewhere about the characteristics of Boards (Garratt, 1987), of their tendency to keep their eyes and hands on daily operations, rather than on policy and strategy, because this is how they have behaved over a long period; and of their rarely being able to retrain to cope with the less tangible world of macro-culture which they are expected to inhabit when they join a Board. Ideally, there is a strong case to be made for directors being properly inducted and trained in the **art of directing** – of managing the boundaries between their inherently controllable organizations and the inherently uncontrollable and unpredictable world outside. Because this is rarely done, it is hardly surprizing that most directors show signs of great stress when asked to attend to such environmental monitoring, analysis, and prediction. They usually take the comfortable route and return unofficially to their old job whilst keeping the perks of their elevated job title. For the organization such behaviour is disastrous, as the external boundaries are not manned, and so it loses touch with the outside world.

In an ideal world, directors would add to their range of disciplines political science, anthropology and design as key tools in their directoral kitbag. But as these are not only not offered by the business schools, but are actively rebuffed by them, some quick and dirty methods are needed to help transform current problems into useful practice.

Macro-culture is for me about the broader national and international contexts in which the organization operates. It can be regional, but is typically national – and, increasingly, international – in scope. It encompasses the issue of nationality, religion, politics, language, and combinations of these which Boards find often opposed to their organization's micro-culture – and its assumed primacy when the micro- and macro-cultures are in opposition.

CHARACTERISTICS OF META-CULTURAL MANAGERS

It is the act of rising above the three levels of culture and **re-framing them to make good business and organizational sense** that is required of the meta-cultural manager. It is here that the wheat of the effective strategic manager is sorted from the chaff. Managers with only a 'binary' thinking style (either something is good, or else it is bad; it is either right, or it must be wrong) cannot cope with the macro-cultural level of complexity. They are comfortable with single cultures once they know how to manage the deviances from them, but find the management of the continuous differences and disruptions involved with macro-culture unacceptable to their binary style. When the macro-cultural factors combine on an n-dimensional matrix, who is to say what is right and wrong? There is no simple choice, no time to get totally accurate information, and each choice made will affect all the others in ways that are not always predictable. Moreover, the whole picture is liable to disruption from other people apparently way beyond their control. When these other people are significantly different from their Board's culture and powerbase – northerners against southerners, westerners against easterners but, worst of all, foreigners against us – then trouble will follow. This is the point where the meta-culture can be brought into play for the benefit of organizational effectiveness: unfortunately, it rarely is.

'Meta-culture' is for me the synthesis of the organization's mini-culture and the environment's macro-culture into a workable whole which transcends the cultural aspects of both; it is not a permanent and binding notion, rather a way of understanding and valuing the differences and making the most from them – a **design** notion which gives both parties common meaning and common objectives for a period of time. To achieve this requires styles of thinking and learning amongst the directors which are far removed from the binary stance. A combination of the ability to value differences, and to use the energies of apparently opposing forces to your own creative ends, has to be the target for the Board – the design and management of their meta-culture. But, again, the skills needed are in short supply in management and management education. The use of opposed forces to achieve creative ends is very much the province of the designer; valuing differences whilst seeking common grounds on which to build is the province of the statesman–diplomat. Neither are commonly found on executive Boards, and yet the future of business through the exchange of learning, know-how, and technology would seem to involve more and more the crossing of national cultural boundaries in a manner sympathetic to those boundaries.

It would seem that significant reconsideration needs to be given to the **selection processes** for a Board. If what I am finding is transferable, then it will be necessary to select those who can tolerate ambiguity, cope with uncertainty, think creatively, determine policy, manage cultural boundaries, implement strategy, and delegate effectively. As many of these are 'right-brain' functions (see Wonder, 1984), outside the usual managerial areas of logic and certainty, careful selection must be made on the potential for such skills and not as a reward for previous good performance in 'left-brain' functions. It seems normal for Boards to reward long-term left-brainers by asking them to join the Board; that they are usually incapable of coping with the right-brain functions necessary for their new role is rarely addressed. The consequences in organizational effectiveness are often profound and lead over time to corporate collapse. In many of the less effective and efficient organizations I think that we are now seeing the consequences of twenty or thirty years of 'brainless' thinking by their Boards and top managers. This seems to be particularly so when the organizations have been run entirely by engineers and/or accountants.

This sits in uncomfortable contrast to the idea that in future it will be necessary for organizations to invest in, rigorously codify, legally protect, and then actively diffuse to the customers their products or services. Behind this lies the idea that learning is central to business survival and growth; the notion that for an organization to survive its **rates of learning** has to be equal to – or greater than – the **rate of change** in its environment and is a key to creating a healthy organization.

Most businesses are not organized to create a climate of learning and a culture which celebrates and uses learning as a key organizational output. Yet people learn – or, in an unhealthy organization, fail to learn – all the time they are working. A key question for me is: How well does the Board appreciate and encourage this? If not, they are on the road to corporate collapse. If so, then they need to review their corporate strategy, people strategy, vision, values, and cultures to reinforce the ability of their organizations to learn and turn this into product or service.

There are some very human problems here which reflect back particularly on macro-culture. A company engaged in, for example, research and development, will have substantial investment in assets which are largely uncodified or semi-codified (i.e., it will be in the heads and hands of its researchers rather than neatly compiled in instructions manuals). It will transfer this to its customers through turning its learning into goods and services to sell. However, around the world customers insist increasingly that they manufacture their own goods. What they wish to do is to buy the **essential investment in learning** that goes into those goods – the 'intellectual property rights' – through licensing or joint-ventures. This creates problems of ownership and access to its learning for the originating company; and the essence of those problems are mini- and macro-cultural.

For example, many newly industrialized countries and Third World countries have governments who insist that they buy 'the best' from the Western world: 'the best' is usually translated by both sides as 'state-of-the-art'. There are ethical questions here about whether, for example, to sell the latest 'glass cockpit, fly-by-wire' airliner to a country which does not have many basic electronic landing aids. There are also commercial questions: if you do so, you will in some way be 'giving away your carefully won commercial secrets'. This has gone as far, in my experience, for defence companies to discuss seriously building into their product (with proper warning) a small explosive device which would trigger if the customer tried to investigate the key component.

Culturally speaking, this is the antithesis of the (often unspoken) aspiration of the customer who is hoping to be at the leading edge of his field by emulating the leaders. A joint-venture of a French and Arab company on a high-tech product led to cross-cultural misunderstandings of a high order. The French thought they were basically selling on an existing technology and helping the Arabs to manufacture it well; the Arabs thought that by joint-venturing they would get into the inner research secrets of a company they aspired to overtake. Both were puzzled, then angered, when their aspirations were not met. Both became angry when each accused the other of cheating on the joint-venture contract. In the end the project broke down with great organizational and personal bitterness on both sides.

This brings me back to the need to be very clear, particularly at the macro-cultural level, of the roles of people in, across, and above, the national cultural levels. One needs to build these into **job descriptions inside the organization**, and **contracts between organizations** in the initial stages. Then, as the work matures, the top managers need to create a working climate which can cope with the creative ambiguity of both having structure, yet also the flexibility to deal with the many differing personalities and cultures involved. This is often referred to as having the strategic skills to create a 'loose/tight fit'.

NECESSARY ROLES

When John Stopford and I started looking into these issues in 1978, we produced a list (Garratt and Stopford, 1980) of the different types of manager who seemed to be operating at the macro-cultural level.

Ambassadors	senior general staff of peripatetic missions outside the organization
Diplomatic technicians	senior functional specialists on visits or short-term secondments
Expatriate residents	medium- to long-term-stay career-builders living abroad
Home country nationals	indigenous local managers of national or multi national companies
Third country nationals	managers in international organizations who are neither from the headquarters nor the local country
Home country hosts	managers who receive guests, and foreign clients and ease them into the local social and business environment.

This list is neither exhaustive nor exclusive and managers can hold a combination of these roles; it was an attempt to help define the **strategic boundary** managers and **operational boundary** managers. To be explicit, the Board are the strategic boundary managers – monitoring the external environment, analyzing and predicting, disruptions from that environment, and trying to give the 'business brain' a good chance of being able to **design** the future rather than simply **react** to it.

Tension does arise from conflicts between the mini- and micro-, and the macro-cultures. The mini-culture is trying to maximize its internal return and tends to discount macro-cultural considerations as outside its remit. Its members are right on the last point; this is where the top managers need to take up their **meta-cultural** role. Boisot (1987) has shown that the amount of time needed to design a project from the macro-cultural viewpoint is relatively large; this can rarely be done before or during the tendering process so it often needs be done immediately afterwards. There is some evidence that if you can be seen to be operating in full an ambassadorial, meta-cultural role, there are ways in which the personal contacts established mean that you may never have to go to tender at all.

THE ROLE OF MANAGEMENT DEVELOPERS IN DEVELOPING CULTURE

Those who are essentially trainers will find the lack of material in the cultural area deeply frustrating. Currently culture is not an easily trainable area; it is more an area for **developers** – who can work with managers from where they are, relate this to a vision of the future, and the necessary business targets, and find an appropriate process for developing themselves and their work whilst also ensuring the redundancy of the developer on the way. This is easily said, but most developers do not have easy access to their directors or line managers affecting 'culture' at any of the four boundaries mentioned above. Yet they are often more sensitive to the problems and possibilities of effectively managing culture than their top management. The question is 'How to connect?' Part of the answer is potentially painful, in that it involves emotional and financial risks: specifically, successful developers who have made a major impact on helping develop an appropriate range of cultures for their organization have put themselves forward to become a member of one or more senior management

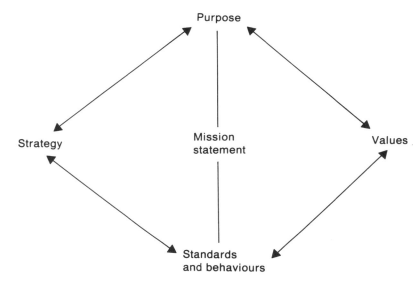

Figure 15.1   The Campbell and Devine sense of mission model

teams creating and managing strategic change in their organization. They take on what is effectively a line responsibility for delivering the organizational culture and climate which delivers the business results whilst making the best use of the individuals involved. This can feel quite daunting at the start. But, as I have said before, the tools to measure where the organization is on each dimension are available; they allow top managers to know where they are starting from with their people strategy, and this, in turn, allows them to see how they are progressing as later measures are taken.

The research of Campbell and Devine (1990) gives a useful model (see Figure 15.1). They have been investigating aspects of mission statements and see the need to develop a model which links an orientation to the future – **purpose** – with a way of implementing these – **strategy** and **values** – whilst valuing and rewarding the past and present – **standards** and **behaviours**. They argue that all of these are made manifest and coherent through the mission statement. To a greater extent I agree with the tenor of their research. I argue that management developers need be as conversant with business and people strategies as they are with behaviour and purpose; I feel that this is the challenge for management developers in the 1990s – to be

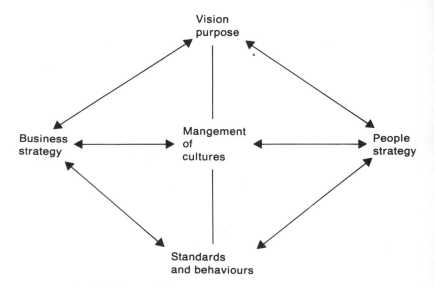

Figure 15.2   The pivotal role of the management of culture

able to work on the same terms as their strategic managers and be able to develop them in all the key areas: individual, team, organization, and inter-organization. The only point on which I would argue with the Campbell and Devine model is that I think that the pivotal position is not held by the mission statement but by the **management of cultures** (see Figure 15.2). This is what both bonds and energizes the organization; it creates the climate in which people can cooperate for specific ends. I commend the management of cultures as a key challenge for management developers and directors over the next decade. Handled constructively, it should make a beneficial difference to their effectiveness and efficiency; handled badly,it it will lead, in an increasingly multicultural world, to corporate collapse.

A CASE STUDY OF CHANGE AND CULTURE (To preserve anonymity this is a conflation of my work with various clients)

A financial services group was keen on expanding overseas, specifically in the Far East. When asked to advise them on the business and people strategy I made myself fairly unpopular by insisting that before we rushed off to 'become more international', as was their wish, we established first where we were. Given that information, it should be much easier to know how to get where we wanted. Coordinates are essential on what can otherwise be seen by top management as a 'soft' issue, and therefore of secondary importance. Once my point was accepted we set off to measure what we could in a brief time. We undertook an organizational climate survey through a sample using a diagonal slice of people in the organization. This looked at the **actual** and **ideal** perceptions of such issues as standards; responsibility; conformity; non-financial rewards; financial rewards; organizational clarity; warmth and support; and leadership. Analyses of the responses, using parametric and non-parametric statistics, exploratory workshops built around the anonymous verbatim responses, and neurolinguistic programming techniques, teased out the organizational issues, values, reward systems, 'webs of signification', and organizational myths and folklore from which we could start the process of creating the new mini- and macro-cultures.

When the information was received along with the business strategy it became clear that, however strong the wish of the directors to expand abroad, there were some fundamental business and people issues in the UK – particularly of vision and clashing cultures – which needed to be tackled if the expansion overseas was to be built on solid foundations. These were achieved through workshops and in-company action learning programmes for the top teams to get them into their directing roles, and to create a 'performance and behaviour-based appraisal system' which became a key to creating the 'new' consistent culture they wished to grow across all levels of their business. This went surprisingly well, and took some two years – cultural change happens in years not months: in well-established cultures it can take a decade to change fully – before it was felt to be working. The Far East market was growing rapidly and their preferred merger target was still interested.

We are now moving into the more complex directoral and managerial task of trying to cross macro- (national) cultural boundaries whilst maintaining a consistent mini- (organisational) culture. We started by working with key groups who will have to learn how to work together if the new business is to have any hope of success. This involved personal psychometric testing, the Handy Organizational Climate Survey, as well as further organizational climate surveying on both sides. This led on to an introduction to the area of macro-cultural analysis, using such work as Hofstede's cross-cultural maps of major trading nations. This was first to make it legitimate amongst the managers to debate cross-cultural issues, to learn to value and celebrate national differences, then to find ways of working which played to the strengths of both. (To say 'both' is too simplistic – there are some fifteen nationalities already involved in a relatively small group.) The analysis has given a quite different dimension to the work of many of the managers and has helped managing across macro- and micro-cultural boundaries in a way which is acknowledged would never have happened if each business had fought to get control, then imposed their culture on the other.

As business faces up to a future that involves the **constant** crossing of cultural boundaries, it will be essential for managers and management developers to prepare themselves for what is going to be one of the most exciting challenges to their skills.

REFERENCES

Argenti, J. (1976) *Corporate Collapse: Causes and Symptoms* (New York: McGraw-Hill).
Ashby, W. R. (1956) 'Self-Regulation and Requisite Variety', *Introduction to Cybernetics* (London: John Wiley).
Boisot, M. (1987) *Information and Organisations: The Manager as Anthropologist* (London: Fontana).
Campbell, A. and Devine, M. (1990) *A Sense of Mission* (London: Economist Publications).
Garratt, R. (1987) *The Learning Organisation* (London: Fontana).
Garratt, R. (1990) *Creating a Learning Organisation: A Guide to Leadership, Learning and Development* (Cambridge: Director Books).
Garratt, R. and Stopford, J. (1980) *Breaking Down Barriers: Practice and Priorities in International Management Education* (Aldershot: Gower).
Geertz, C. (1973) *Interpretation of Cultures* (New York: Basic Books).
Handy, C. (1985) *The Gods of Management* (London: Pan).
Hofstede, G. (1980) *Culture's Consequences* (Beverly Hills, Cal.: Sage).
Institute of Directors Report (1990) 'Professional Development of and for the Board' (London: Institute of Directors).
March, R. M. (1980) 'Manpower and Control Issues', in Garratt, R. and Stopford, J., *Breaking Down Barriers: Practice and Priorities in International Management Education* (Aldershot: Gower).
Peters, T. and Waterman, R. (1982) *In Search of Excellence* (New York: Harper & Row).

Smith, P. (1986) 'The Stages of a Manager's Job', in Hammond, V. (ed.), *Research in Management* (London: Frances Pinter).

Watzlawick, P., Weakland, J., and Fisch, R. (1974) *Problem Formulation and Problem Resolution* (New York: W. W. Norton).

Wonder, J. (1984) Whole Brain Thinking (New York: Morrow).

16

Management development and organization development

Graham M. Robinson

In my introduction to this chapter in the second edition of this *Handbook,* I described it as reflecting the experiences of twenty years of working in the fields of organization and management development. During that period the conviction had grown that the distinction between effective organization development and effective management development is artificial to the point of irrelevance. The distinction had significance only in considerations of **relative ineffectiveness**. Both types of development are dependent upon the closeness of their association with clearly developed, articulated and sustained organizational strategies, to which the members of the organization – including the organization and management developers – are deeply committed. Both are dependent upon a process of thorough situational analysis, diagnosis and appropriate action; both are dependent upon the skills, competence and credibility of the practitioner on the one hand, and upon the confidence, commitment and sense of ownership of the client manager or group on the other.

In the interim, there have been a number of significant shifts in thinking on the subject of management education and development in the UK. The publication of the Handy and Constable reports meant that a whole new generation of politicians and members of various British management bodies developed a belief that management development was important and that something should be done about it.

Unfortunately, there does not appear to be a high degree of consensus as to what that 'something' should be: thus, we have those who are deeply committed to the concept of an accredited, chartered manager, with a basic qualification that is somehow different from a DMS but not quite an MBA, while others are anxious to identify a set of core competences, mastery of which will equip the manager with the necessary skills, knowledge and, of course, competence to tackle any of the problems that global competition, European restructuring, Japanese technical wizardry and Soviet technology can throw at him or her.

In all of this, the role of organization development has come to occupy more and more of a back seat. This is a pity because, in the view of the author at least, unless all of this development of managerial talent is harnessed to the achievement of the **real strategic business aims of the organization** to which that manager belongs, it is likely to prove a wasted investment (at least for the organization that foots the bill). The absence of the organization development perspective from the debate is a tragedy, but not altogether surprising since, as Ralph Kilmann comments in his book *Managing Beyond the Quick Fix* (1989). 'The field of organization development, as it first emerged in the 1950s, was envisaged as offering methods for systemwide change that would significantly improve the function of entire organizations. For the most part, however, this majestic vision has been lost and forgotten.' However, the fact that organization development has not managed to live up to its earlier aspirations does not mean that it is, therefore, irrelevant. On the contrary, it is probably more vital than ever, from a highly pragmatic perspective: 'Today, however, as many organisations are coming to realize that 'future shock' is upon them, the need for fundamental, systemwide changes is being voiced more and more frequently. Now entire organizations must be transformed into market-driven, innovative, and adaptive systems if they are to survive and prosper in the highly competitive, global environment of the next decades. Given this situation, there is an urgent need to rejuvenate the theory and practice of organization development – to apply programmes for systemwide change'.

The focus of this chapter is on the orientation of the client manager towards the contribution of the specialist or practitioner. It is argued that this orientation has often been more positive (and, as a result, more effective), in the case of management development than with many of those initiatives which were pursued under an organization development banner. There is seen to have been a greater sense of identification with the norms and values of management development than with those of organization development (although the latter have had a significant influence on the former). Organization development, it is argued, has tended to import values to the client organization which owe more to the application of scientific discipline to management practice as a result of the business school revolution of the 1960s, than they do to the strategies and values of the client organizations seeking support in the face of major uncertainty and rapid change. As a result there has been a tendency, in Europe at least, for organization development to be an externally 'owned' process, identified with particular practitioners, academics and consultants, rather than as a process **vital to the internal functioning of the organization itself**. While, to a lesser degree, the same has been true of management development, leading towards a 'flavour of the month' trend, there has been a much closer sense of management identification with the concepts of management development, even if only in the negative sense of saying 'we ought to do more of this'.

The success, in the 1980s, of those writers who pursued the holy grail of 'excellence' has served to give emphasis to the importance of common values and strategy to successful organizational performance. But like the writers on organization development before them, the product champions of excellence have come under fire from those who are managing the realities of a run-down printing works rather than managing the supercompany on behalf of superboss with a superteam. Rosabeth Moss Kanter (1989) senses a 'growing weariness with hearing one more heroic story that simply does not match the mundane issues that managers struggle with every day, the hard choices that they must make . . . They are noticing that when everyone aspires to capital-E Excellence, it only makes the competition tougher it does not guarantee business success'.

The chapter concludes by referring to a study which suggests that many European corporations (private and public sector) are weak in both strategy and common values. If these findings hold true, it is argued, management development should be taking a lead with groups of client managers in forcing the clarification of organizational strategies and values. In so doing, the emergent values may well not match with those underlying organization development as described in the literature. However, the irony is that the genuine and lasting development of the client organizations that the practitioners seek may be achieved only as a result of such a process – which is **political, confrontational** and **pro-active** rather than scientific, consultative and advisory.

BACKGROUND TO CURRENT MANAGEMENT ATTITUDES

Management development is often perceived as 'an attempt to increase managerial effectiveness through planned and deliberate learning processes.' (see Chapter 1). Client managers have tended to have fairly clear views about management development within their organizations, and they have usually had few problems in making a distinction between their perceptions of management 'development' on the one hand and management 'training' on the other. While the latter has been perceived as a process necessary to the acquisition of specific management skills (such as budgetary development and control), management development tends to be viewed as a broadening, educational process by means of which the individual is initiated, shaped or fitted to the attitudes, values, rites and rituals of successively higher levels within the organization. As such, management development may or may not encompass formal training, and it may be self-managed (many organizations attach especially high value to processes of management self-development, even to the extent of welcoming back the prodigal manager who, having resigned 'to gain experience in another environment', now returns to the fold with renewed vigour, while others stress the value of a broad base of experience, but reward 'loyalty and long service' which automatically places limits upon the opportunities available for such broadening).

To an extent, then, client managers will relate management training to a process by means of which the individual acquires the skills associated with a **specific management job or level**; they will tend to regard management development as having much more to do with career development and **progression up the organizational ladder.** This difference in perception tends to be thrown into much sharper relief in organizations where responsibility for management training is assigned to the training function, while management development is assigned as a personnel responsibility; this distinction is further reinforced where there is, (real or perceived), competition between the two functions over which is accountable for what, and as to which has the more senior status. Whatever the situation in a specific organization, there would appear to be a general consensus among client managers that both management training and development are a 'good thing' and that their organization probably has not done, or is not doing, enough in these areas.

The views of client managers towards organization development are quite different. For a start, it tends to be less immediately meaningful to managers outside the personnel and training functions themselves. In response to an illustration or example of a piece of organization development work, client managers will tend to respond with a reference to the name of a particular consultant or academic who 'once did some work with the company along those lines', rather than indicate any familiarity with, or expectations of, organization developments *per se*. As a result, organization development tends to be known in terms of what particular practitioners do, rather than as a process or discipline with which managers are naturally familiar.

An interesting phenomenon among human resource specialists is the use of the initial letters 'OD' in discussions relating to organization development processes and practice. Unlike other management specialisms developed over the past twenty years, the initials do not appear to have been picked up by client managers themselves. Thus, while it would be quite unremarkable to hear an experienced line manager make reference to O & M (organization and methods), OR (operations research) or to DP (data processing), the letters OD roll rarely off the tongues of the same individuals. Similarly, personnel and training people rarely, if ever, make reference to MD or MT to refer to the areas of activity mentioned earlier in this chapter. Since 1986, a new set of initials has been presented to the world by training and personnel specialists with considerably more impact upon their line management colleagues than was the case with OD. Thus, it is not uncommon to hear managers referring to their commitment to a process of 'HRD' – Human Resource Development – even if they do not have too clear an idea of what it is; this means that it is almost certainly 'a good thing'.

This use of the label OD and its association with specialisms such as OR may provide a clue to one of the significant areas of difference between management development and organization development, and this difference relates to management's sense of **identification** with and **ownership** of the two processes. In the 1960s, operations research was perceived as having a particularly significant contribution to make to the resolution of highly complex management problems in conditions of high uncertainty and risk. It had already made dramatic contributions in the military field during the Second World War, when inter-disciplinary teams of scientists had applied the scientific method to the analysis, modelling and resolution of previously intractable problems. At about the same time in the 1960s, a number of reports were circulating in the USA which were highly critical of current business school practice. Such practice was, at that time, highly dependent upon 'crude, non-rigorous, highly specific descriptions of particular businesses. There was little if any generalization across many businesses to formulate a set of general principles that could apply to many situations' (Mitroff and Kilmann, 1984). The successful application of scientific method to the resolution of complex management problems offered by OR people contrasted strongly with the perceived inadequacies of the business schools. The latter, argued Mitroff and Kilmann, over reacted, consciously trying to emulate the academic departments that had spawned the successful scientists and technologists. They 'hired' newly accredited PhDs from prestigious universities who had been trained in the so-called 'pure' (i.e., untainted by practical application) sciences and academically respectable disciplines (e.g., computer science, economics, industrial engineering, mathematics, political science, psychology, sociology). As a result, the academic respectability of the business schools went up enormously.

The expectations that organizations had of the scientists in the OR teams, both in the university departments and in 'user' organizations in the private and public sectors, were extremely high and many successes were scored (for example, the development of critical path analysis and PERT). Not unnaturally, therefore, the suggestion was made that the success of the natural scientists should be capable of being emulated by the behavioural scientists. Initially, this emulation took the form of the development of Human Factors Group within the OR teams (in the UK within the British Iron and Steel Research Association (BISRA), and the National Coal Board, for example) and direct consultancy provided by the universities and research institutes, such as Birkbeck College and the Tavistock Institute. In the USA, specialist behavioural science teams sprang up at the interface between business and academic institutions to examine the specific contribution that the behavioural sciences might make to the development of these organizations and, thus, organization development, OD, was born.

There was a fundamental difference in the antecedents of management development and organization development. Management development was always a process 'owned' by the organization itself; it may not have been done particularly well, but the manager within the organization could identify with it as a process that had specific meaning for him, within the context of the norms and values of the organization by which he was employed. Organization development, on the other hand, was more specialized, more specific (and, in aspiration at least, more scientific), it tended to be the domain of the business school and the research institutes rather than incorporated into the organization itself. Although not writing specifically about organization development, Mitroff and Kilmann provide a possible insight as to why the values and concepts of organization development have rarely been incorporated into the organizations that it was meant to be serving: 'A PhD straight out of graduate school who had never in his or her life even been near a real business organization, could teach, write, and do research on business and management. While they thus achieved greater prestige in their own network, they increasingly lost touch with the business community and the world at large. Intentionally or unintentionally, they shut out from the halls of academia the very reality they were supposedly in the business of studying'.

The Mitroff and Kilmann argument may tend towards the extreme and, as noted above, they are not referring to organization development as such but to the relationship between the business schools and business in general. It does, however, provide a backdrop for the image of the organization development practitioner as 'outsider'. The practitioners themselves have tended to prefer this role – as facilitator and change agent, as consultant and catalyst, as opposed to that of integrated participant in the hurly-burly of the organizations which they have aspired to develop.

With the dramatic economic changes of the 1980s, the increase in uncertainty at all organizational levels and reduction in confidence in the ability of Cartesian logic to produce the right answers to the complex problems of organizational and business life, there has been a good deal of questioning of the contributions offered by all the specialisms which developed so rapidly and with such promise in the 1960s. Line managers tend to be suspicious of operations research, other than in those areas of complexity where it has an established track record (vehicle scheduling, stock control and reordering, life cycle forecasting, etc.); it tends to be perceived as 'esoteric, backroom stuff', highly mathematical and largely beyond the comprehension of the managers whom it is there to serve. O & M, on the other hand, has lost some of the gloss that it had in the 1960s, not least because its emphasis on rationalism leads to a natural (though not always fair) association with rationalization which in turns means 'putting the squeeze on my department'. Organization development has suffered in its turn from its identification with outsiders to the organization. Its emphasis on humanist values had a rough ride in organizations forced by economic necessity to experience the massive employee shake-outs of the late 1970s, early 1980s and which have returned at the beginning of the 1990's. At the same time there is a much greater awareness of the limitations to the skills that managers have at their disposal to enable them to tackle the challenges that the new circumstances present. Therefore, of these four specialisms (OR, O & M, OD and Management and Development) more is probably expected of the latter than of the others. As a manager, it is I who am looking for help in raising my capability to deliver against frightening levels of demand and expectation. It is I who need that support in order to maximize my chances of survival. It is my head on the block. I am apt in these circumstances to ask very forcibly the question 'what's in it for me?' By and large, the answer is more likely to be sought from the management developer than from the other specialists with less personally perceived concerns.

ORGANISATIONAL DEVELOPMENT FRAMEWORKS

Before pursuing the theme of similarities and differences between organization development and management development further, it will be helpful to be clear about the particular frameworks within which organization development has endeavoured to operate. (The word 'frameworks' is used rather than 'definition' or 'frame of reference' because the field has become too imprecise, in the view of this writer at least, for any one of the many attempts at definition to be entirely adequate). Bennis (1969) described organization development as 'a response to change, a complex educational strategy intended to change the beliefs, attitudes, values and structure of organisations so that they can better adapt to new technologies, markets, and challenges, and the dizzying rate of change itself'. (Such a description places organization development at the apex of the organizational pyramid.) It is strategic, it is concerned with values and it is concerned with structure. If organization development interventions are to be effective in terms of Bennis's description, then they must be made with the full participation and commitment of top management. Beckhard (1969) wrote:

> In an organization development effort, the top management of the system has a personal investment in the programme and its outcomes. They actively participate in the management of the effort. This does not mean that they must participate in the same activities as the others, but it does mean that they must have both knowledge and commitment to the goals of the programme and must actively support the methods used to achieve the goals.

Perhaps less elegantly but with a shrewd eye for the realities of organizational life, Reddin (1977) wrote: 'When change agents tell me that they plan to attempt a change from the bottom up, I remind them of the military dictum that the penalty for mutiny is death'.

But is this insistence on top management involvement realistic? In the current climate such involvement is usually the result of massive (and usually externally induced) change, such as merger, take-over or bottom-line crisis (the Burton Group, Rover, British Airways, ICL all provide examples where such involvement has been the springboard for organization development type interventions). But in the majority of organizations, the demands of running the operation in a difficult, but not necessarily catastrophic, environment may make the demand for such involvement unrealistic. Bennis himself goes on to suggest that his description of organization development may be to provide 'an abstract and perhaps, useless, definition.' In order to clarify his position, therefore, he goes on to provide four examples of organization development in practice:

1. Team development
2. Inter-group conflict resolution
3. Confrontation meetings
4. Feedback

Each of these examples is concerned with 'process' issues having an impact on the effectiveness achieved by particular work groups, either internally or at the interface between groups. Each is also concerned with the intervention of a third party 'change agent' or facilitator. Margerison (1978), writing nine years after Bennis, picks upon this latter point to suggest a simpler framework for organization development than that of the earlier writers: 'The term "organization development" . . . means the skills and methods used by people to facilitate organizational improvement'. While Margerison's description may reflect what organization development has often become (and may provide an explanation as to why client managers have a hard time in recognizing the term 'organization development' at all), it has lost two key elements of the Bennis and Beckhard requirements. The first of these is **strategy** and the second is **top-level commitment.** While their aspirations may have been too high (reflecting Mitroff and Kilmann's concern about business schools' distance from organizational realities), Margerison's description opens the door to the cynical comment that organization development is what organization developers do when it is successful; when it is not, it is what the client manager did and, therefore, is not organization development.

A useful framework probably lies somewhere between the two and needs to include a reference to the areas of knowledge, the particular skills and methods the organization developer would characteristically employ. Margulies and Raia (1972) go a long way towards meeting this requirement when they state that 'organization development borrows from a number of disciplines, including Anthropology, Sociology, Psychology and Economics. It generally involves the use of concepts and data from the behavioural sciences to attempt to facilitate the process of planned change'. The toolbag is specified with the references to the disciplines upon which organization development practitioners draw, and the stress upon planned change goes some way to meet Bennis's emphasis upon organization development as a strategic activity (though it would not be argued here that a strategy and a plan are one and the same thing). Margulies and Raia go on to write that:

'Organization development is essentially a systems approach to the total set of functional and interpersonal role relationships in organizations. An organization can be viewed as a system of coordinated human activities, a complex whole consisting of a number of interacting and interrelated elements or subsystems. A change in any one part will have an impact on one or more of the other parts ... organization development itself can be viewed as a system of three related elements – values, process and technology.'

They then provide examples of what these three elements might comprise. These examples are summarised here.'

Values

1. Providing opportunities for people to function as **human beings** rather than as resources in the productive process
2. Providing opportunities for each organization member, as well as for the organization itself, to develop to **full potential**
3. Seeking to increase the effectiveness of the organization in terms of all its **goals**
4. Attempting to create an environment in which it is possible to find **exciting and challenging work**
5. Providing opportunities for people in organizations to influence the way in which they **relate** to work, the organization, and the environment
6. Treating each human being as a person with a complex set of needs, **all of which are important** in his work and in his life.

Process

1. Data gathering
2. Organization diagnosis
3. Action intervention

Technology

1. New ways of organizational learning
2. New ways of coping

3.   New ways of problem solving.

The set of values provided by Margulies and Raia are essentially
humanist in orientation. This provides another clue to the externaliza-
tion of organization development from the organizations within
which it is practised. The values as listed are desirable to most people,
but the experience of organizational life in the 1980s and 1990s has
done little to suggest that these values are shared within the organizations themselves. More difficult still, because organizational members
can identify with them at an individual level, they are easily espoused
by the organization in formalized expressions of its values ('Our
greatest asset is our people and their unswerving commitment to
Company goals'). But, to paraphrase Argyris and Schon (1974) and
Argyis (1976) the values in use are demonstrably different: 'Despite
the best endeavours of Senior Management the economic pressures
have meant that we have had to release five hundred valued members
of the work force.' The experience of organizational members during
the 1980s has thus tended to be at odds with the stated values of
organizational, functionalist or pragmatic values concerned with
being clear about terms and conditions of staff (or, increasingly, sub-
contractors), priorities and budgets for equipment, finance and time.
These values place emphasis upon **effective and efficient delivery** and
customer care, as opposed to the more general values of **human potential** and **employee satisfaction**.
   This is not to disagree with those who argue that it is possible to
have both sets of values represented (and, hopefully, shared) within
the organization, but to suggest that the emphasis placed by organization development practitioners upon humanist values puts them in a
frame of reference that is essentially external to that of their client
organizations. In the 1970s, as the pressures of impending recession
increasingly made themselves felt, the discussion was frequently to be
heard as to whether the organization developer should remain professional and independent of the politics and in-fighting within organizations (in which individual and corporate survival were becoming
dominant themes) or whether they should regard themselves as part of
the process and be there in the thick of it. In the 1990s and beyond, it
can no longer be a matter for debate – the value position of the
practitioner will have to be made clear.
   Galbraith (1977) did not start from the same, humanist, standpoint

that characterizes the writers referred to so far. He was, however, very much in tune with the systems orientation espoused by Margulies and Raia and placed great emphasis upon the importance of strategy, in common with Bennis. But perhaps the most significant difference in style in Galbraith's work from the work of those alluded to previously was in the sense that he wrote for the manager who **owned** the problem rather than for the organization development practitioner who **analysed** it. Indeed, he referred to **organization design** as the key issue and not to organization development:

> 'Organization design is conceived to be a decision process to bring about a coherence between the goals or purposes for which the organization exists, the patterns of division of labour and interunit coordination and the people who do the work. The notion of strategic choice suggests that there are choices of goals and purposes, choices of different organizing modes, choices of processes for integrating individuals into the organization, and finally, a choice as to whether goals, organizations, individuals or some combination of them should be changed in order to adapt to changes in the environment. Organization design is concerned with maintaining the coherence of these choices over time.'

These choices are fundamental and confront the manager with increasing frequency.

Writing some time later, Galbraith (1983) developed his systems orientation further to indicate that organizations 'consist of structure, processes that cut the structural lines like budgeting, planning teams, and so on, reward systems like promotions and compensation, and finally, people practices like selection and development'. This approach is considerably more in harmony with the prevailing, functionalist orientation that is characteristic of the 1980s and 1990s management style, than is the humanist approach characteristic of Bennis, Margulies, Raia etc. His emphasis upon the notion of choice and, in particular, **strategic choice**, would also find favour with Mitroff and Kilmann who berate the business schools and their academic antecedents for their post-1960s emphasis upon training students to tackle exercises rather than to solve problems.

'It is vital as a culture that we come to appreciate that there is a vast difference between structured-bounded exercises and unstructured-unbounded problems...In a phrase we have bred a nation of certainty-junkies. We have trained the members of our culture to expect a daily dosage of highly structured-bounded exercises. The difficulty is that the problems of organizations and society have become highly unstructured and unbounded.'

Mitroff and Kilmann's reference to 'certainty-junkies' will strike a chord in the hearts of management trainers who are asked so frequently to 'dispense with the theoretical stuff and give us some techniques'. All too often the expectation seems to be that provided one has the analytical ability to take a problem apart and break it down into its constituent parts, it will be possible to examine it logically and resolve it with precision. Unfortunately, the resolution of organizational and managerial problems tends to be less about elegance and simplicity and a great deal more about subtlety, ambiguity and choices.

'TELL ME SOME GOOD NEWS FOR A CHANGE'

In the 1930s the sale of comics (escapist 'penny dreadfuls') skyrocketed. The same period saw the rise of Hollywood and the Busby Berkeley musicals. Both had as much to do with the harsh realities of an economically depressed industrial society as the 'Fame' musicals had to do with youth unemployment in the 1980s. Both situations required a catharsis, a discharge from the unremitting gloom of the dole queue and the company insolvency stories. It is not surprising then, that the studies of excellence and success from the McKinsey Group (Peters and Waterman, 1982 and Deal and Kennedy, 1982) and others (Goldsmith and Clutterbuck, 1984, and Kanter 1984) have proved to be so successful. The intention is not to suggest that these works are to management in the 1980s, what the penny dreadfuls and Hollywood were to the unemployed of the 1930s; there are, however, certain parallels. Peters and Waterman leave the reader with a warm feeling for the anecdotes of successful organizations awash with style, shared values and champions; they do not, unfortunately, leave that same reader with any prescription for action if that reader happens to be the manager of an organization which is manifestly unsuccessful or in a declining industry (a serious omission which Peters has endeavoured to rectify with *Thriving on Chaos*, 1987).

Nevertheless, The McKinsey 'Seven-S' model offered by Peters and Waterman has some close affinity with the systems model offered by Galbraith:

- strategy
- structure
- systems
- staff
- skills
- shared values
- style.

The elements of the McKinsey model are very similar to Galbraith's (for 'people' in Galbraith, read 'staff and skills' in Peters and Waterman, for 'systems', read 'processes', for 'part of shared values', read 'rewards', and add 'style'). Both emphasize the importance of **strategy** as a cornerstone in fostering corporate success. But Peters and Waterman make no reference to organization development as such, though they do refer to one or two practitioners by name (including Bennis). Writing for an audience of managers, the concepts, values, (even the name) of organization development, do not enter the pages of the best selling book on management practice in the last decade. Once more, this would appear in keeping with the view of organization development as an externalized process as opposed to an accepted area of effective management practice to be internalized within the organization.

The key to unlocking this situation lies in the strategic focus emphasized by Bennis, reinforced by Galbraith, and central to the McKinsey 'Seven-S' model. Unless the organization development process (and, indeed, the management development process) is closely related to, and in keeping with, the organization's **driving strategy,** it cannot be effective. This may well mean that the practitioner may have to forego the lucrative assignment where the strategy espoused (or used) by the client organization is inconsistent with those humanist values referred to by Margulies and Raia. He will certainly have an obligation to make them explicit, change his values, or play Iago to his client's Othello.

STRATEGY AS THE INTEGRATING THEME

Professor Phillipe de Woot (1984) has sounded a loud cautionary note about the enthusiasm among European managers for the findings of the McKinsey group (and, by implication, for Goldsmith and Clutterbuck in the United Kingdom as well). He points out that the assumption underlying their approach is that most companies are overmanaged in what they refer to as the 'hard Ss' (strategy, structure and systems, see also Chapter 15 above). They have developed these to an extent where the individual manager is reduced to being an administrator of a decision system rather than being required to be a **decision taker**, (and certainly not a risk taker), himself. The writers on corporate excellence concentrate their attentions on reviving interest in the so-called 'soft Ss' (staff, skills, shared values and style) which, one might think, should be regarded as a shot in the arm for the humanist values of organization development. But, argues de Woot, this makes sense only if the underlying assumptions of over-management and over-control are correct. In the European context, he finds little evidence to suggest that they are.

The results of a six-year research programme headed by de Woot suggest that very few European organizations practise the basics of strategic management which are a prerequisite for corporate success, regardless of whether the management emphasis is hard, soft, or balanced. An organization committed to these basics would demonstrate that commitment through elements such as clarity over corporate goals, systematic management development at all levels, and a range of sophisticated decision-support processes and systems. In the absence of these, he argues, to jump upon the *In Search of Excellence* bandwaggon may be meaningless or downright dangerous for an organization lacking in professionalism and 'tightness' (clear operating procedures, control systems, levels of authority, etc.). Such 'tightness' needs to exist not only at the centre, but throughout all of its operating units; no large company can be truly innovative, and entrepreneurial (let alone intrapreneurial) if it has not developed a highly professional base for its total operation. He warns against interpreting this professionalism too narrowly, stating that 'tightness' based only on financial controls is totally inadequate since it gives the headquarters no ability to provide strategic direction and to communicate fruitfully with its offshoots.

Such is the state of apparent backwardness in Europe that de Woot found:

1. that a number of top managers did not believe in defining clear objectives, and making them explicit throughout the company. 'I am not the Pope', he quotes one as saying: such companies, he reports, suffer from 'Shakespearean' intrigue and instability
2. that top management frequently fails to set a strong lead
3. and that employees 'are often slaves to external social values, rather than to the organization's culture'.

Once more, the critical finger is pointed at the negative consequences of adherence to values that are external to the organization itself, whether these external values are those of society at large, or those of the academic community, as claimed by Mitroff and Kilmann, or those humanist values claimed to be at the heart of organization development by Margulies and Raia.

In the absence of a clearly expressed strategic framework and an associated and consistent organizational value system to which their contribution can relate, organization and management developers alike are likely to share a common experience of floundering around in a sea of apparently random (at best feudal) managerial behaviour. In such an environment, development, whether organizational, managerial, group, or individual employee-based (as with HRD), is likely to be characterized by a series of fits and starts and sudden changes of direction resulting from the importation of new techniques having all the characteristics of the flavour of the month. If de Woot is correct – and experience would suggest that at least he is on the right track – it is clear that the thrust of both management development and organizational development in Europe should be towards the specification, clarification and communication of **organizational strategies and values.** In order to be effective in this role, the developers have to **earn the right** to contribute; they have not always been particularly successful in so doing – not simply, as Mitroff and Kilmann argue, because they have used inappropriate models imported from inappropriate cultural and value sets, but because they have not had the corporate 'clout' to be heard. Perhaps the two things go together.

ON THE HORNS OF A DILEMMA

To summarize, for organization development interventions to be effective they must be consistent with, and contribute to, the strategies and values of the organizations within which the intervention is made. However, it has been suggested that most European organizations pay scant attention to managing strategically, preferring to adopt a more reactive, 'seat of the pants' approach. This unsystematic approach creates a vacuum which is filled by the importation of values and quasi-strategies from outside the organization – for example, from government statements, from business schools, from external change agents or from internal specialist functions, such as personnel or training. But because these are imported values and do not form part of a 'tight' whole, they are fragmented and essentially ephemeral. Beckhard's response to this situation, presumably, would be to argue that this is precisely why organizational development interventions should be made only with the involvement of top management; unfortunately, experience suggests that the internal specialists rarely carry the corporate 'clout' to make effective interventions at that top management level. Therefore, when the need for such an intervention is recognized, it is more often than not assigned to an external adviser who owns another set of values . . . and the process is perpetuated. The resolution of the problem must lie **within the organization itself**, and a resolution is essential to corporate survival, for the non-European competition does not appear to share this problem to anything like the same degree. 'If we do not create a managerial revolution,' warns de Woot, 'we will wake up one bright morning and discover that . . . we have become underdeveloped and colonized. By then it will be too late.'

It is interesting to note that similar concerns are expressed among management developers. For example, Critchley and Casey (in Chapter 22) argue against the conventional approach to team management development, a view which would suggest that before a management group can seriously address such issues as strategy formulation or the determination of key tasks, it is first necessary for them to build a degree of **openness and trust**. Critchely and Casey argue that, on the contrary:

'High levels of openness and trust are only rarely needed, and management groups get most of their work done very well without them, preferring for safety and comfort to remain relatively closed, and, covertly at least, distrustful. To ask such groups to make a major cultural shift, to take such big risks with each other as to be fully open and trusting, requires some mighty cogent justification ... if their purpose is to be of real value to their clients ... they should start by encouraging their clients to clarify the role and purpose of the management group in question, to identify the nature of the tasks which they need to address as a group – complex puzzles or real problems, and then to consider the appropriate modes of working, and the skills and processes that go with them. When we have reached this stage, most of us have the skills and technologies to provide what is needed. What is often left out is the diagnostic work which gets us to that stage.'

CONCLUSION: RESOLVING THE DILEMMA

If management development is effective it will result in positive organization development, with 'effectiveness' being measured in terms of enhanced organizational capability. It has been asserted in the earlier part of this chapter that management development is more generally recognized by in-company management as a 'good thing' than is organization development. This is because highly stretched managers can usually identify a potential personal benefit to themselves from an effective management development process; this benefit may not necessarily be obtained directly. 'My boss should go on this programme' is a statement not unfamiliar to the management trainer.

It was also asserted that expectations of management development programmes, with some notable exceptions, tend not to be very high. However, the very fact that management development as a potentially 'good thing' is a commonly shared value in organizations gives the management developer a significant 'leg-up'. It is eminently sensible for the management developer to ask the question of senior management: 'Management development for what?' Indeed if the question is not being asked, then the organization ought to be seriously questioning the value of having management developers anyway. The answers to the question should lead, step by step to a clarification of the role and purpose of the management group. This is the investment in the diagnostic process argued for strongly by Margulies and Raia, and so frequently neglected in practice, as has been observed by Critchley and Casey.

Presented with the results of the diagnosis, the next step needs to be placed firmly in the hands of the management group itself, and that is a questioning of the **group's contribution to the achievement of overall organizational strategy, aims and objectives**. If the answer is not apparent, then, either the group has misjudged its role and purpose, or the strategy, aims and objectives are unclear. Whatever the reason for the situation in any specific instance, the group, which owns the problem, should push and push hard for its **resolution**. In this, the members of the group must be supported and encouraged by the management developer; he cannot afford to sit on a professional fence, for, if he does, he will have earned the comparatively low expectations so often expressed by line managers. If, on the other hand, he does get involved in the uncomfortable process of questioning and reappraisal that will result, he will have made a significant contribution to a genuine process of organizational development. Such a process will not of necessity incorporate the humanist values espoused by writers such as Margulies and Raia; it may even bring about the management revolution felt by de Woot to be so vital for European economic survival. Some practitioners who go down this road will no doubt wish that they had heeded Reddin's warning that 'the penalty for mutiny is death'. But whatever the outcome for the management developer, going through the process should make a significant contribution to the two things that all the writers referred to in this chapter seem to be agreed upon, and that is that genuine organization development is contingent upon the espousal of clearly formulated and communicated **strategies** on the one hand, and internally developed shared **values** on the other. When this is achieved, the similarities and differences between management development and organizational development will be meaningless, because we shall be talking about one and the same thing.

REFERENCES

Argyris, C. (1976) *Increasing Leadership Effectiveness* (New York: John Wiley).
Argyris, C. and Schon, D. A. (1974) *Theory in Practice: Increasing Professional Effectiveness* (San Francisco: Josey-Bass).
Beckhard, R. (1969) *Organization Development: Strategies and Models* (Reading, Mass.: Addison-Wesley).
Bennis, W. (1969) *Organization Development: its Nature, Origins and Prospects* (Reading, Mass.: Addison-Wesley).
Deal, T. E. and Kennedy, A. (1982) *Corporate Cultures: Rites and Rituals of Corporate Life* (Reading, Mass.: Addison-Wesley).
Galbraith, J. R. (1977) *Organizational Design* (Reading, Mass.: Addison-Wesley).
Galbraith, J. R. (1983) 'Strategy and Organization Planning', in *Human Resource Management*, 22(1/2).
Goldsmith, W. and Clutterbuck, D. (1984) *The Winning Streak* (London: Weidanfeld & Nicholson).
Kanter, R. M. (1984) *Change Master* (London: George Allen & Unwin).
Kanter, R. M. (1989) *When Giants Learn to Dance* (London: Simon & Schuster).
Kilmann, R. (1989) *Managing Beyond the Quick Fix* (London: Jossey Bass).
Margerison, C. (1978) *Influencing Organizational Change* (London: IPM).
Margulies, and Raia (1972) *Organization Development: Values, Process and Technology* (New York: McGraw-Hill).
Mitroff, I. and Kilmann, R. (1984) *Corporate Tragedies* (New York: Praeger).
Peters, T. (1987) *Thriving on Chaos* (New York: Alfred Knopf).
Peters, T. and Waterman, R. (1982) *In Search of Excellence* (New York: Harper & Row).
Reddin, W. J. (1977) 'Confessions of an Organizational Change Agent', *Group and Organization Studies* (March) (International Authors BV).
de Woot, P. (1984) 'Le Management Stratégie des Groupes Industriels', *Economics* (Paris) quoted by C. Lorenz, *Financial Times* (London) (26 November).

17

Handling cultural diversity

David Ashton

The impact of cultural differences on work organizations, their operations and effectiveness, has become a popular subject during the last few years. Some of the reasons for this increased interest may lie in a more general trend which recognizes the importance of 'soft' data as a basis for explanation of differences in the performance of organizations. Interest may also have grown because a number of practitioners have been able to develop approaches which have made progress on real problems associated with cultural differences in work organizations.

In this chapter, we are going to start by defining 'culture' and 'cultural differences', and then look at the key ideas that have been developed in this field since 1975. With these key definitions and concepts in mind, we can then go on to examine the relevance of such approaches to learning in general, and development programmes for managers in particular. We shall consider the impact of the cultural differences both on the determination of appropriate content for development programmes and on its learning styles and strategies. The final part of the chapter will be concerned with a key development benefit which can arise when **cultural differences are present in a development group**.

KEY CONCEPTS AND APPROACHES

In this brief review of relevant concepts it may be best to start with some exclusions. By 'culture', we refer to those **national** differences

Table 17.1   Key dimensions of cultural difference

Country examples: high score	Dimension	Country examples: low score
US Australia Britain Netherlands	Individualism	Pakistan Guatemala Taiwan Indonesia
Japan Germany Mexico Italy	Masculinity	Netherlands Chile France Sweden
Nigeria Malaysia Panama India	Power distance	Israel Denmark New Zealand Britain
Portugal Uruguay Belgium Japan	Uncertainty avoidance	Singapore Denmark Hong Kong Britain

which affect, among other things, the way in which people work together. There has also been a growing interest in work performance arising out of specific differences in **organizational** cultures. However, this latter body of knowledge relates to a very different set of original concepts, and will not be a subject of focus within this chapter.

Perhaps the single most important figure in the development and analysis of cultural difference in organizations has been Gert Hofstede (1980a). While working within a large multinational company, he undertook a study of national differences among large numbers of employees in more than forty countries. His definition of 'culture' is based more on an anthropological approach – he describes this group identity as 'a collective programming of the mind'.

Hofstede analysed his data across all his countries in which he carried out his investigations, and identified **four key dimensions** which provide maximum differentiation between national cultures. Table 17.1 identifies each of these dimensions and gives some examples of individual countries which have extremely high or low scores on these dimensions.

It may be helpful just to say a few words of explanation about each of his dimensions:

- **Individualism** – This reflects the extent to which a society focuses on the importance of the **individual** rather than the **group** within the society
- **Masculinity** – Hofstede has assessed this by looking at the extent to which general roles in a society are allocated along traditional **male/female** lines
- **Power distance** – This covers the extent to which **inequality** is accepted by less powerful people in a society
- **Uncertainty avoidance** – This dimension focuses on the strength of concern about **order and security** in a country.

Hofstede's data enabled him to 'place' countries on these particular dimensions – although it has been difficult to explain, to everyone's satisfaction, the reasons for the positions of particular countries. Careful reflection nevertheless yields some interesting points. On the whole, wealthy countries tend to have a high index score on the individualistic ethic – although there are one or two which, (like Japan), are clearly exceptions. Other countries which have apparently little in common in terms of culture and heritage score highly on one particular dimension. For example Germany, Mexico, Italy and Japan all score highly on the masculinity dimension – in these countries, therefore 'male values' are likely to dominate in their organizations. Hofstede reports some general trends for all countries in two of the dimensions of cultural difference – tolerance of power distance was reducing in all countries, and concern for uncertainty avoidance was increasing in most countries.

The impact of these cultural differences, expressed in these key dimensions, is however, not necessarily so clear cut when we look at the level of the work organization and other factors which support or modify these cultural differences and need to be taken into account. From the point of view of the development programme, it is important to understand different societal approaches to **individual and group learning**, in order to anticipate the likely responses of an individual from a particular society to a new learning experience in his work organization.

André Laurent (1980) identified national differences among individuals' views of their **business organizations**. He found the North American and North European employees tended to take a more instrumental view of business, whereas the Latin countries of Europe took a more 'social' view. Laurent defined the 'instrumental' view as emphasizing the rational organization of tasks – and the manager's role was defined by these tasks and his functional responsibilities. Within this overall view, boss subordinate relationships tended to be seen as impersonal; authority was associated with role or function in the organization. The social view, by contrast, emphasized that the business was a group of people who needed to be managed. The manager's role, therefore, defined by social status and his authority came from personal and functional attributes. In a social organization, subordinates were expected to be loyal and deferential to their bosses – in return for more personal relationships and support.

Little has been published on culture and organizations which directly examines the impact of national differences in development and training. The work of Seddon (1985) is of particular interest here; he identified the dangers of applying a **western organization** development approach to African business organizations. Seddon noted several contrasting assumptions, in two key areas:

- **Approach to development** – In western organizations, the employee takes responsibility for his or her own development. African employees manifest greater dependence in relationships and hence expect all development opportunities to be identified and arranged for them. They also would not wish to lose face by encountering novel, and therefore risky, situations. Neither would they understand the western conception of a conflict between employers' and employees' needs.
- **Tactics of development** – Western learning designs are likely to encounter problems in Africa. African employees require highly structured interventions which do *not* assume openness in relationships.

Seddon argued that the host culture was better regarded as a potential strength, rather than a hurdle to be overcome, and development approaches should take account of this.

In reviewing this work of Hofstede, Laurent and Seddon, two broad conclusions emerge: first, national differences *do* matter, and should be taken into account when constructing development programmes. Secondly, we are only just beginning to understand all the issues and problems of improving our decision-making in this area.

CULTURAL DIFFERENCES AND THE CONTENT OF
DEVELOPMENT PROGRAMMES

Against this background it becomes a matter of practical concern to take account of such differences when designing and running development programmes for multicultural groups.

A first area of concern is the **content** of such programmes. Hofstede (1980b) wrote an article questioning the transferability of American theories. Given that American motivation theory is likely to focus on the **individual** employee, he argued that such an approach would be wrong if straightforwardly transferred into a collectivist society – where it will be more effective to work on the motivation of **groups** of employees. Seddon's (1985) experience in Africa would support this view.

In the design of a multicultural development programme, it is essential to look carefully at each of the principal **subject areas** of the programme, in order to understand the cultural limitations of the concepts and approaches which may be inherent in each. The extremes can be readily spotted – for example, it is unlikely that key economic concepts, and their application to the workings of the national economy, or the main structural characteristics of an industry, will vary from one country to another. At the other extreme, however, it is highly likely that the approaches to employee relations will vary – because of legal and political as well as social and cultural differences – on a country-by-country basis. Between these two extremes lie the rest of the fundamental subject areas of management. We would suggest that it is more than just the human resources field which may be affected by cultural differences.

The following contingency approach may help in the determination of subject content:

1. Identification of a **key concept or framework**
2. Identification of **normal contingency factors** associated with the **application** of that approach
3. The additional consideration of the **impact that national differences** may make upon the **application**.

Here is one example to show how such an approach might be implemented.

Productivity

Productivity is apparently a universal theme and a wide range of applications have been reported on the specific productivity approach known as quality circles. To date, however, the literature has tended to give only individual stories and to develop 'folklore' – that is, subjective and often journalistic accounts of successes and occasional failures. Clearly the quality circles approach was initiated in a specific cultural context; it seems to have been an American idea, but developed within a Japanese group-oriented context. Equally, it is clear that not every national context of employee motivation and productivity improvement is similar to that of the Japanese. Among the contingency factors to be considered, therefore, would be an identification of key characteristics of Japanese attitudes to work organization – this would take account directly of national cultural differences. These differences would then be assessed against the key features of the *other* national cultures, in which the quality circles approach might be applied or recommended.

Finally, if the approach seems to be worth examining in these new cultural contexts, then cultural differences should be part of the **application** discussions – in order to encourage awareness of their likely impact on the effectiveness of quality circles as a productivity 'solution' for the development programme delegates' own work context.

In one sense, the quality circles approach is an easy example to make – since most readers will not be Japanese and, more significantly, they will be very ready to acknowledge the cultural differences of Japan from their own societies. It is the author's experience, however, that almost *all* management and business subject areas and specific techniques should be approached on the contingency basis outlined above, when decisions are made about course content on multicultural development programmes.

CULTURAL DIFFERENCES AND LEARNING METHODS

Management development is an area which has been closely associated with innovation and experiment with learning methods. Many of these innovations have come about because of the apparent inappropriateness of formal, one-way methods (like lecturing) as an effective means for helping experienced managers to learn. But these newer methods have tended to develop in English-speaking developed countries – particularly the USA and Britain. They often involve extensive participation by the management students, including exposure of personal feelings and values, which are not usually shared by working colleagues except in the development context. It will not be surprising, therefore, that some of these methods are initially found difficult by people of other cultures, where the importance of role differences and more formal methods of education and training may be strongly stressed. Indeed, approaches to learning and social interchange may be markedly more restricted and less relaxed in some of the English-speaking countries. Such cultural differences do not rule out the use of these more participative methods in management development, education and training; but they do mean that the manner and timing of the introduction of such methods must be extended where cultural differences among delegate managers are present.

In introductory sessions, it may be important, with a multicultural group, to give everyone the opportunity to contribute – particularly in terms of talking about their own experience and the differences of their own national and business situations. Once these individual views (and some insight into these individual differences) are established, it may be relatively easier for both delegates and trainers to handle the differences and to understand the likely limitations on the contribution of individuals. Such participation by *all* delegates at the beginning of a multicultural programme becomes critical to their effective participation in later stages of the programme. But time *must* be given for all of these individual contributions to be brought out, and it must be done in a non-threatening way. The primary objective is to enable all people to **contribute**, rather than rigorously to test their ideas. Such preparation and initiation is a necessary start for effective learning in a multicultural management group.

There will, of course, be other opportunities to build on cultural differences and their impact on business as a means of learning in a multicultural group. Thus, for example, discussions about the business environment could build around **mapping exercises**, where individuals are given the opportunity to lay out their own 'national maps' which identify the important factors in their own business environment – increasing trade union power, inflation, government controls, or whatever. These 'maps' will explain what is important to enable the effective operation of their organizations in their national context.

There is also some argument for ensuring good opportunities in a multicultural programme for **small group discussions**. These must not, however, be set with such tight time limits that the predominant language group – most often the English-speakers – dominate, because the task must be able to be achieved within great time pressure. Smaller groups do make it much easier for individuals to make a contribution in somewhat uncertain circumstances.

Obviously, having realized the impact of learning methods on cultural differences among delegates, it is particularly important to judge the **pace** of the first few days correctly; trainers must also provide opportunity for individuals of all national backgrounds to make contributions, and for these contributions to be recognized by their peer delegates, as well as accepted by the teaching staff. At that point, cultural differences may become less important – individuals will have a confident and positive base on which to build their participation and response to the range of learning methods which may be involved in the rest of the programme.

CONCLUSIONS

Much of this chapter has been concerned with the differences – and, by implication the difficulties – that cultural diversity may make to effective manager education in effective manager development. It would be wrong, however, to deal with cultural difference primarily in this negative light. Again, from the author's own experience (Ashton, 1984), for mature and successful managers of whatever nationality, comparison of themselves with other (and different) managers is a particularly valuable means of learning. The process of comparison has to begin with 'What I am' or 'What our company or system is'; this is likely to provide a basis of **self-understanding** as a starting point. This can be built on through discussion with other managers who are equally effective in their own circumstances, yet offer remarkable contrasts in the way in which they approach their work, and the goals and priorities which they set.

Practising managers are more often impressed by and learn better from others with effective but different **working models** for their own managerial roles, than they do from textbook theories – and it is right that this should be so. A multicultural group offers such richness because of the diversity of approach and assumptions of the individuals and businesses concerned that, if the communication barriers of inherent cultural differences can be overcome, then the potential plus which comes from the richer and varied bases for comparison can offer a genuine advantage and key additional feature for development and learning in a multicultural context.

Clearly this cannot be achieved quickly; programme designs must take account of lower introductory sessions and of a greater need for all to participate in the initial stages. But if that foundation can be achieved and confidence be given for all to participate, then the richer bases of comparison may provide a more effective and stronger development by the end of a development programme. The insidious assumption may be that the theories and approaches of the trainers, (or of the parent company) provide the most effective universal way of approaching management and business problems in all countries; clearly, this is not true and this form of 'acculturalization' must be resisted: it will be only an ineffective form of 'colonization', which has in the past been detrimental to the effective operation of organizations in different national contexts.

REFERENCES

Ashton, D. (1984), 'Cultural Differences: Implications for Management Development', *Management Education and Development* (Spring).

Hofstede, G. (1980a) *Culture's Consequences* (Beverly Hill, Cal.: Sage).

Hofstede, G. (1980b) 'Motivation. Leadership and Organization: Do American Theories Apply Abroad?', *Organizational Dynamics* (Summer).

Laurent, A. (1980) 'Once a Frenchman always a Frenchman . . .', *International Management* (June).

Seddon, J. W. (1985) 'Issues in Practice – The Education and Development of Overseas Managers', *Management Education and Development* (Spring).

FURTHER READING

Ratiu, I. (editor) (1987) 'Multicultural Management Development', *Special issue Journal of Management Development*, Vol. 6, No. 3.

18

Developing local nationals

John Crosby

The aim of this chapter is to provide the reader with an appreciation, in some detail, of how one multinational company undertakes its management development work. Although many of the processes which will be described apply to UK expatriate and third country national staff, the focus here is primarily upon developing **local nationals** for advancement in their **own companies**.

Broad conclusions, by definition, have no place in opening paragraphs. Similarly it would be inappropriate to ascribe an academic thesis to the work which will be described, as it represents a process which has been developed in a series of practical steps and refined by experience. Nevertheless, if there is a philosophy which can be derived from the company's experience it is that management development activities are fully effective only when they are **integrated with other strategic planning processes** undertaken by a Board and that, within a multinational company, they should rest upon personnel systems which operating companies have developed (within a broad policy framework) to meet their local needs and circumstances. Within the personnel function itself, the management development system requires input and collaboration from most of its sub-functions: effective management development activity is not the sole prerogative of management development specialists.

COMPANY CONTEXT

British-American Tobacco Company Limited (BAT Co.) is a multi-national tobacco business, with over 60 000 employees, and is now part of BAT Industries whose interests also embrace financial services. It is primarily an overseas company with operations in 52 countries; only one of its subsidiary companies is located in the UK. Because of the company's philosophy and also because the substantial home base typical of most other multinationals is absent, it has developed a decentralized and devolved form of management. Thus, in terms of management development (as well as of the personnel function as a whole) companies are expected to be as self-reliant as possible; as already indicated, they have discretion within broad limits to develop their own procedures to reflect operating circumstances and their national culture. In this respect, BAT Co. is the antithesis of some US multinational companies in which, for example, appraisal procedures and personnel records are standardized around the world.

COMPANY VIEWPOINTS ON MANAGEMENT DEVELOPMENT

1. **Planned managerial development** is vital to the success of the business. In a mature and highly competitive industry (without unique patent/protected technology or access to scarce natural resources), the quality of management is a fundamental strategic issue.
2. We recognize that a multinational company has special responsibilities to contribute to the **national economies in which it operates** and that the development of properly trained and experienced staff is one such responsibility.
3. It is our belief that 90 per cent of management development takes place within a manager's **own company and work context**; although home and overseas courses have an important role to play in the process, our philosophy of development is rooted primarily in the identification of potential followed by carefully planned job movement to provide the experience necessary for progressive advancement to senior posts.
4. We expect our operating companies to provide their management

staff with basic training in management techniques and company business knowledge and to develop effective succession planning processes; the head office involvement in these two activities is normally limited to providing specific help (when requested) in developing new **training procedures** and to monitoring planned **succession arrangements** for Board-level and senior specialist posts within the companies.

THE ELEMENTS OF MANAGEMENT DEVELOPMENT

Selection

To begin with the obvious (and therefore a point sometimes over-looked), the ultimate effectiveness of management development activities must be closely linked to the quality of **incoming managerial staff** from graduates – young professionals upwards. We have there-fore agreed with our companies that their recruitment policy should be to recruit candidates for managerial posts whose abilities (or deve-lopable skills) not only match current requirements but also have the potential to meet **future job needs**. In parallel, our companies have adopted a mutually agreed framework for selection: the main ele-ments of this are the use of written job descriptions and specifications, an operating company-wide methodology of interviewing, the train-ing of selectors at all levels in the chosen methodology, the use of group selection techniques when candidates numbers warrant, and the conduct of validation studies to pinpoint cases of success and failure in selection. It is important to stress that, within this framework, companies have discretion to use the forms of job description, inter-viewing techniques, psychological tests, etc. which they feel are most relevant to their local circumstances.

Where requested, training in advanced selection and interviewing skills can be provided by the head office personnel function in the UK, either within the operating company or (as is becoming more typical) on a **regional basis**. A key pre-requirement before any form of person-nel-related training course is offered is that one or more local person-nel management staff must be prepared to continue the work, with reducing help from the centre.

Appraisal

Appraisal is regarded as an integral part of management development
and companies are expected to devise forms of appraisal to suit their
local circumstances. The actual documentation used within companies varies significantly therefore in length and content. Equally, the
style of appraisal discussion will vary from country to country,
depending upon the directness of questioning and comment which is
culturally acceptable. To ensure both a minimum standard and also
that certain key points are covered, the following guideline has been
adopted by companies. It is typical of the form of guidelines which the
head office personnel department discusses and agrees with companies
on all important personnel issues (including employee relations and
remuneration, which are not discussed in this chapter).

Policies

To use the performance appraisal process as a basis for ensuring that
there is full agreement between a manager and his subordinate about
the principal objectives of a job and the tasks to be achieved. It should
serve as the main means for **assessing performance against agreed work
objectives** and for identifying **training and development** needs.

Strategies

. Define principal **objective–goals** to be achieved and the **standards–
means** by which attainment is to be judged
. **Review performance** against the previously-agreed principal
objectives–goals and measures
. Identify training, experience and development needs in the light
of an employee's **current and next likely post**
. Define any **external circumstances** which have helped (or hindered) materially the achievement of agreed objectives
. Record an individual's **career aspirations**, and any features which
could **restrict** his/her promotability
. Provide internal training courses for managers in the techniques
of **appraisal interviewing**.

The need for strategy 5 was learned the hard way some years ago: one

STATUS CODES (Col. 4)   PERSONAL CODES (Next move – Col. 7)

I   — International (Expatriate)   Rt   — Retirement

TCN — Third Country National   Pr   — Promotion

L   — Local National   D   — Development/Company requirement

LN   — Local Non-national   X   — Transfer — indicate destination

C   — Contract   ?   — Not known

JOB TITLE JOB HOLDER	JOB Gp.	JOB HOLDER					REPLACEMENTS	
		Nationality	Status	Born	Current Appt.	Next Move	Code	Name
(1)	(2)	(3)	(4)	(5)	(6)	(7)	(8)	(8a)

Figure 18.1   Organization forecast and succession plans

John Crosby

REPLACEMENT CODES (Col. 8)

P — Planned

E — Emergency

O — Other Candidates

COMPANY:

DEPARTMENT

DATE COMPILED

19	19	19	19	19	19	19	19	19	19	REMARKS
(9)	(10)	(11)	(12)	(13)	(14)	(15)	(16)	(17)	(18)	(19)

Figure 18.1 (cont.)

key employee in an overseas company had been developed progressively for a local Board-level post. When the post was offered, he refused to take it on the grounds that his social and family ties to his provincial town had become such as to make it impossible to accept a promotion which involved a relatively modest geographical transfer!

Succession planning

Although the period may seem unrealistically long, we find in practice that sensible decisions about training, development and job movement of identified candidates of potential for senior posts require something up to a ten-year planning span. Whilst the crystal ball becomes a little hazy towards the end of a projected ten-year period, the **discipline of forecasting** is vital. We have therefore developed with our companies a form for 'Organization Forecast and Succession Planning' (OF&SP) (Figure 18.1). This allows planned promotions, retirements and organization/job changes to be recorded against each managerial post, together with an indication of firm or potential future candidates. Envisaged new posts are also charted.

In parallel, an Individual Career Plan (ICP) document (Figure 18.2) has been introduced to record both biographical and work experience data of identified candidates **and the action which is planned for them**.

The use of both documents (OF&SP and ICP) could become mechanistic were it not underpinned by positive management action. To this end, an agreed set of strategies exists as indicated by the following guideline extract statements.

- Identify and analyze the professional and managerial knowledge and experience content of the key posts which are **critical to business success** (Board, head of function and senior specialist levels).
- Identify the subordinate jobs and experience opportunities available within the operating company (considering also opportunities within the operating group at large with the help of Head Office) which provide **logical progression to the key posts**.
- Identify candidates at all levels within the management structure who have **potential** to meet the requirements of key posts and plan their career progression.

Name	Present Appointment	Date of Present Appointment	19	19	19	19	19	19	19	19	19	Nomal Retirement Date
Nationality	Job Group	J / P										

International Status
Yes/No/Willing to accept if offered
(delete whichever is inappropriate)

Ultimate Estimated Promotability within Company/within
Tobacco Division (delete whichever is inappropriate)

General Manager

Head of Function

Estimated Grade Potential

Date of Birth: Place of Birth:

Marital Status:

Children: Sex: Date of Birth:

Education:

Previous Experience:

Group Service:

Date   Job   Company   Grade

Languages:

Training to Date:

Potential Posts
R = Readiness for Promotion   A = Availability for Promotion

Job Title	Job Group	Location	Overdue		Now		1–3 years		3–5 years		5+ years	
			Readiness		R	A	R	A	R	A	R	A

Training Proposals/Plans:

Development Proposals/Plans:

Action

Special Aspects to be Borne in Mind:

Proposed by Head of Function:
(name and initials) Date:

Recommended by General Manager:
(name and initials) Date:

Figure 18.2 Individual career plan

Once an individual company board has reviewed and agreed its succession plans, head office becomes involved in respect of nominated candidates for local director and major head of function posts. Awareness of, and a concern for, the appropriateness of succession planning for such posts, together with associated proposed development plans for potential candidates, is clearly regarded as a BAT Co. Board concern and the subject is on the agenda of two Board meetings annually. Succession planning is therefore fully integrated into the vital planning processes of the company, and is subject to the same regular examination, detailed scrutiny and commitment as are other key business activities.

Once plans have been agreed, the role of the head office personnel function is to keep under review the development of identified candidates with the companies concerned, to arrange central training courses and programmes where it is impractical to expect these to be run locally, and to facilitate developmental transfers/secondments between operating companies as well as periods of attachment to Head Office when opportunities for relevant experience do not exist or are restricted locally.

Management training and education

Companies undertake managerial and functional training of their staff, using in-company or external national facilities depending upon the size and sophistication of the business and country. Nevertheless, there remains a positive role for the Head Office to organize courses in respect of both functional and general management training and updating. Arrangements include:

1. **Specialized functional courses both in the UK and on a regional basis**. In the personnel field, for example we have developed our own 'Training for Training Managers' course in recognition of the absence of such facilities in many countries. This course, typically of three weeks duration, ranges from the identification of training needs to the writing and handling of tobacco-industry based case studies. Increasingly, it includes use of video facilities.
2. **Functional appreciation courses outside a manager's immediate knowledge area**, such as 'Finance for non-financial managers' and 'Marketing for non-marketing managers'.

3. **General management courses**, arranged by BAT Industries at its Chelwood staff college, the most important of which are:

    (a) **The management training course** designed to acquaint younger managers with basic management skills, including human relations skills, and also with the main features of our industry

    (b) **The management development programme** designed to provide managers with 'management education' in the broad aspects of business and with recent–developing trends and activities which can affect both their own and their companies' future operations

    (c) **The business manager programme** designed for seasoned managers who are candidates for general management positions (or for a major head of function post) at home or overseas; this programme is conducted on a **project** basis

    (d) **The senior management programme** designed on a conference basis to allow general managers and heads of function in major companies to examine strategic issues affecting BAT Industries' interests and also possible developments to its existing policies and practices. (See also Chapter 13)

In any one year it is not uncommon for up to 150 BAT Co. managers to attend Chelwood programmes; the vast majority are local nationals employed in our overseas subsidiaries.

In the human resource field, BAT Co.'s specialized courses not already described include a performance appraisal workshop to assist companies to identify for themselves the appraisal needs appropriate to their situation; an appraisal advisers' training course (designed on programmed learning principles) to equip selected company employees to guide their colleagues in both the interviewing and goal–objectives setting aspects of appraisal; a remuneration practices course which covers job analysis, job evaluation, salary surveys and salary structures.

Assessment centre techniques

We have been experimenting in the UK with the use of assessment centre techniques and have now developed a two-day programme which we call an 'Individual development programme (IDP)'.

Through the use of various exercises and psychological tests, participants have an opportunity to ascertain for themselves what are their present strengths and weaknesses, against the norm of a general manager's post in an operating company, and to re-examine their aspirations. Results of an IDO are communicated in detail to participants and to accountable line managers, and ultimately are fed into the overall succession planning process.

Experimentation has shown that it is not appropriate to extend participation in the programme to managers whose first or working language is not English. However fluent their spoken and written English may appear to be, they are likely to be at a disadvantage when a large amount of complex written material has to be absorbed in a limited time and also when faced with the cut and thrust of group discussion. An equally important point is that observers may well be inhibited in making judgements where they feel (however unspecific their feelings) that demonstrated performance using English language may be below that which an individual could display in a home context.

In the long term, assessment centre techniques will be imparted and commended to operating companies, and it will then be their decision as to whether or not they are appropriate to their local needs and culture.

Staff movement and management development

To help companies expedite the development of staff, the London Head Office has a fundamental role to play in finding suitable development opportunities on a worldwide basis. **Secondments**, to acquire specific knowledge or expertise, are typically of three – twelve months' duration. **Transfers**, which provide developmental experience, are typically of two – three years' duration. Examples of the latter form of movement include a Sri Lankan to Hong Kong, an Indonesian to Sri Lanka, a Malaysian to the UK, a Chilean to Central America and a Mauritian to Zaire.

There is a parallel role to play in identifying managers in overseas companies who may be prepared to accept a long-term international career **outside their own company**. The problems of international staff movement are growing in as much as many countries are imposing ever-more rigorous limitations on the granting of work permits and the remittance of earned income (even when a direct exchange of staff is involved). Equally important, one can no longer assume that the domestic circumstances of managers (or their perceptions of the quality of life in many countries) are such that they would necessarily welcome geographical movement. Nevertheless one still has to try if management development opportunities available within a multinational company are to be optimized for the benefits of both the staff concerned and the organization as a whole.

GENERAL OBSERVATIONS

It is always tempting – but the temptation is to be avoided – to draw conclusions of general application from one company's experience. However, we believe that the following elements have contributed to the success of our management development activities:

1. The **integration of succession planning** with **other planning processes** undertaken by the boards of both BAT Co. and its operating companies. Succession planning is therefore regarded as a key management process rather than as a special domain of the personnel function. As indicated earlier, the subject is on the agenda of two BAT Co. Board meetings annually and is preceded by detailed examination of projected appointments, transfers and development plans by individual directors with the assistance of the personnel function.
2. **Devolved discretion to operating companies**, within mutually agreed guidelines, to develop the format of procedures most appropriate to their company and national context. Effective management development must be the responsibility of line managements and they should be able to feel some 'ownership' of the methodologies involved.
3. The recognition that management development is an **integral (indeed an inextricable) part of the personnel/human resource function overall** as it impinges on most of the function's specialist activities, including those such as the underlying philosophy and design of remuneration policies which have not been discussed in this chapter.

This last element perhaps deserves additional comment. Whilst, for example, management development and training specialists at various levels will be expected to take the lead in identifying training and experience needs and in making proposals on means of meeting management training and education requirements, they must closely relate to (and cooperate with) colleagues responsible for other human resource aspects such as recruitment, manpower planning, appraisal, assessment centre work and remuneration. Put another way, their contribution will be optimized if they are able to take a **generalist** as well as a **specialist** view of situations. Thie philosophy which is implied in this approach to management development is that it is most effectively conducted when all activities which contribute to the recruitment, growth, retention and motivation of staff are considered **collectively**, and **complement** one another.

A FINAL COMMENT

Although hiccups happen inevitably in any management process (such as downturns in identified managers' performance or unexpected illness–turnover which can create the need for highly accelerated development of individuals) – and no management process works as smoothly as implied in the published form – we can claim to have been successful in developing our managers. The proof will be in the bottom line, and in the extent to which we grow and retain our senior management population.

19

Women managers

Judi Marshall

When I first reviewed the literature on women managers. I was surprized to find so many articles asking whether men and women were *really* 'different'; most of the authors were trying to prove that they were not, so that women could be endorsed as suitable management material. In the main, they were able to find data to serve their purposes, for example on leadership behaviour. But this is only part of the story. It is more appropriate to view men and women as 'both the same and different', as sharing fundamental aspects of human existence but approaching them from distinctly different bases and from different social positions. Certainly research shows that women and men can *behave* similarly as leaders, but it also reveals differences in their initial approaches and in how their behaviour is responded to by others (see Bartol, 1978 for a review). Women tend to emphasize **people management** over **task structuring**, whilst men have opposite priorities; women are often inhibited in exercising position power because other people reject or undermine their use of authority, stereotype them in devalued 'female' roles, act dependently towards them, and so on.

As an opening to this chapter I shall argue that we currently need to concentrate on men and women's **differences**, rather than to acclaim their undoubted similarities as a necessary phase in movement towards true 'equal opportunities'. In the remainder, I shall discuss the training and development initiatives currently arising from an identification of women's separate needs.

SIGNIFICANT DIFFERENCES BETWEEN WOMEN AND MEN

There are two interlinked bases for my assertion that women and men
are meaningfully different. The first involves theories of archetypal
patterns, in terms of which women broadly represent a different range
of potential human characteristics from those of men. The second
involves the recognition, to which my work in this area soon lead
(Marshall, 1984), that because of inequalities in social power, men's
characteristics have traditionally been valued more than women's,
and so have shaped organizational life. These frameworks help
identify women's development needs and show why these are currently so important.

Male and female values

Various theoretical frameworks distinguish between male and female
values as two potentially complementary viewpoints on the world
reflecting an archetypal polarity. This is especially clearly expressed in
the Chinese concepts of yang and yin, and has close parallels in
Jungian psychology. Drawing on these sources, the male pole is characterized by self-assertion; separation; control; focused perception;
classifications; rationality and contractual arrangements; and: the
female pole by interdependence; merging; acceptance; awareness
of patterns, wholes and contexts; emotional tone; personalistic
perception. Male and female values are qualities to which both
sexes have access, rather than the exclusive properties of men and
women respectively. But through physical make up, orientation (and,
to a certain extent, social learning), women are grounded in the female
pole and men in the male pole. As managers, women draw, to varying
degrees and in individualistic ways, on a distinct base of values which
distinguishes them from men. Individual development involves
balancing the capabilities of one's grounding with appropriate aspects
of the other perspective. This offers a more flexible array of abilities
than does either set of values alone. But this is to some extent an ideal
picture.

Social power

In its recent history, Western society has emphasized male values, and these have shaped its organizations, cultural norms, language and so on. Female forms are relatively devalued and underdeveloped. This is such a pervasive aspect of our culture that it is unusual to identify ways in which women differ from men without the assumption being made that women are somehow at fault. All too easily, men become the unquestioned norm against which women's behaviour is compared, and any deviations are seen as unusual and therefore to be penalized.

In this chapter, 'differences' are not viewed as 'faults' of either sex; rather, they are aspects of our cultural and gender heritage which can be used either productively and creatively or inappropriately and degeneratively. It cannot be assumed, for example, that what men do in organizations is somehow 'right'; their management styles and career patterns reflect a narrow range of possible options. There are disadvantages of which men themselves are aware. Established ways of working contribute to job stress, and may eventually lead to coronary heart disease; hierarchical forms of organization restrict development opportunities for all but a small group of 'successful' people. (Although there is no room to do so here, it is worth questioning whether we know what men's development needs *really* are.) It is possible, however, in contrast, to over-idealize female values: openness to the environment can have its degenerative forms of being overwhelmed, invaded and dependent.

The social dominance of male values has inhibited the development of complementary, female, alternatives. This is shown culturally by an emphasis on individualism, competition and control, and limited attention to interdependence, collaboration and acceptance. Along with other commentators (for example, Capra, 1982), I see the re-emergence and elaboration of female values as a significant aspect of a current 're-vision' in society, with potential benefits for men and women alike. But unless they are taken seriously, and allowed considerable space for experimentation, they will continue to be constrained by the current pattern of culture. Women's separate development is, then, an essential element in any social evolution, and so is the focus of this chapter.

Women's development needs

Many women now want to join in the world of employment and benefit from the financial rewards, achievements and personal growth it offers. They are joining in a largely male world; in doing so they have conflicting needs. Until recently, equal opportunity initiatives concentrated on gaining acceptance for women, and emphasized their capability to work similarly to, and as well as, men. Moderate success in this direction has been achieved; but the foundations of women's identity as managers are different, as are their experiences of the organizational culture. These issues are now becoming central as they determine the shape of women's approach to work. The analysis of women's current development needs below highlights the difficulties they face as a result of these conflicts, although it is important to remember that these are balanced by many satisfactions and opportunities for achievement which women also value. I shall draw for illustration on my research with middle- to senior-level women managers in the retailing and book publishing industries (Marshall, 1984).

Many women managers are operating from values, assumptions and perspectives which reflect their female grounding, but are not widely represented or accepted in organizational life. This creates conflicts and pressures, and many describe themselves as working in 'hostile environments'. In their everyday work and career prospects, women are continually affected by inequalities in social power, although usually these are in the background rather than the foreground of their experience. These become most apparent when women, placed in one-down positions because of their gender, find that others reject their use of authority power because it contravenes stereotypes of femininity, or they are passed over for promotion despite appropriate qualifications and experience. It is common, for example, for female managers to be mistaken for the secretaries or assistants of male colleagues, to find that their opinions go unheard in meetings, or to be denied development opportunities such as assignments abroad because it is assumed they will not cope. Maintaining their own self-image and confidence, and managing relationships with others thus become high priorities.

As women's characteristics do not correspond to images of 'good' management, they are encouraged to play down their femaleness and to copy male models of behaviour in order to succeed. Many have done this to great effect, and developed capabilities which would otherwise have remained dormant. But this often leads to conflict between their work and personal self-images. Some established managers are currently acutely aware of what they have given up in order to succeed organizationally: they are looking for more female-compatible ways of working. This is particularly reflected in dilemmas about management style and career management. The influence-based, person-oriented management style which many favour is in sharp contrast to the competitive, independent, achievement-oriented model they see around them; it can make them personally vulnerable, prove ineffective in competitive environments, and limit their chances of promotion. The managers I interviewed wanted to blend aspects of several approaches together into a more robust style. Most were hesitant about the choices of 'using their femininity' and 'adopting male tactics' they could immediately identify, as these might not fit their self-image or allow them to build cooperative relationships with others at work.

Some women managers are looking for different ways to the standard, life-long career pattern of fitting employment into their lives; many also want it to serve purposes other than conferring social status. Those I interviewed considered a wide range of factors including intrinsic job challenge, their health, relationships and their sense of personal identity in any decisions they made about work. Female values thus shaped their engagement with employment; some had rejected promotions which threatened these priorities. Being employed was one highly significant role amongst several for them, and they wanted 'to lead a balanced life', but found this difficult.

Research evidence suggests that women bring a different range of viewpoints to management. Gilligan (1982), for example, distinguishes between two moral codes, one used more consistently by men and the other by women. The male moral system views the world in terms of rights and principles, which can be defended and used as the basis for decision-making. The female system perceives life as a network of social relationships, with the individual at its centre. 'Right' and 'wrong' become relative and pragmatic, dependent on the situation. Gilligan concludes that women 'speak in a different voice', a view that is widely held amongst linguistic analysts too (see Spender,

1980). Other authors identify variations in cognitive style; they detach intuition from its associations with emotional guesswork and offer a definition in terms of subjective and contextual awareness which has much to offer management thinking. It is, however, usually difficult for women managers to get their perspectives heard if they differ from established frameworks, and this may eventually undermine their own faith in them.

Despite the strong needs for alternative strategies expressed above, women have few sources on which to draw for fresh ideas. Their traditional roles of housewife and mother have become compromised in the recent moves towards work as a significant role; but at work there are few competent female models to aspire to. Even those women who do survive in organizations without copying dominant styles remain invisible, their learnings and accommodations kept private. Stereotypes of hard, lonely older women managers are so powerful that most of the people I interviewed did not want to stay in management until retirement in case this happened to them. This dearth of role models is partly because female values remain in the background of organizational life and do not impact on its public face. It is also because women have tended not to identify or mix with each other at work. To gain acceptance, particularly at senior levels, they have identified with their male colleagues rather than with other women. Women also therefore need opportunities to share their perspectives, experiences and ways of coping, but without incurring organizational penalties for doing so.

The analysis of needs above reveals five main development priorities for women:

1. Extending their **range of job skills**, especially those of self-expression
2. Enhancing **interpersonal and management skills**, with particular attention to power issues
3. Developing strategies for **being effective in** and **influencing** current organization cultures
4. Reviewing **what they want from employment**
5. Doing all these in ways which allow them to express **female aspects of their identity**.

Shared development needs

This chapter has concentrated on differences, and so has had little to say about the many **development needs** which women share with men. These are particularly in the realm of specific skills or general management training such as MBA programmes. In fact, it is impossible to exclude as potentially relevant any area of training, as long as sufficient attention is paid to the sex of trainees and issues of gender are discussed as relevant: rather, women need to gain access to a wide array of training, on which they are under-represented relative to men, and to see promotion opportunities ahead of them to make their experiences meaningful.

These areas are, however, relatively unproblematic as development opportunities if the woman manager is secure in her own self-image and needs, and is able to appraise and act effectively within the organization culture. If these foundations for organizational identity are in doubt, her engagement with more skill-oriented training is likely to be unclear and possibly half-hearted.

Different approaches to development opportunities

In fact, women's attention to development so far has given priority to issues which men, whose choices about employment are less apparently problematic, might view as 'background'. This contributes to differences between men and women in how they approach development opportunities. From my own experience, and from discussions with other trainers, it seems that women tend to bring their **whole selves**, their full range of life roles, to any activities and want to be changed by their experiences. Men, in contrast, present themselves as **organizational people**, looking for relevance within a particular area of expertise, and doubt whether radical change in adult life is possible. One consequence is that women may need help to integrate learning into the other life areas which it affects. Assertion training, for example, may improve their management skills but create temporary havoc in relationships at home. Trainers will need to be alert to, and prepared to work on, these wider repercussions.

MANAGEMENT DEVELOPMENT PROVISION

There is now a wide range of courses and other development activities directed at women managers. A valuable source on new offerings is *Women and Training News,* produced by The Women and Training Group and part-sponsored by the Department of Employment. The activities covered below are not solely relevant to women, but do directly address their concerns. In some areas such as assertion, men are now showing an interest in training initiated for women; in others, women's training shares a label with men's, but typically takes a different form in practice. It is important to recognize that the patterning of social power which has helped shape women's development needs can also hamper appropriate attention to them; for this reason, training **structures** are as significant as specific course **topics**. These aspects are dealt with separately.

Training structures

Networking

As they become more aware of the world of work, and concerned about their places in it, many women are looking for people of 'their own kind' to mix with. They also often feel cut off from established channels of communication and information-sharing. Various motives have led to a growth in women's networks and associations, some official (like the European Women's Management Development Network), others informal; some with a specified constituency such as women in publishing or computing, and other looser groupings of people who have common perspectives. Broadly-based networks offer members reference points outside their immediate work context, and news on current developments. Informal networks within a company or locality serve other, more supportive, functions as well.

As these activities grow, women are exposed to possible role models as well as friends and contacts. Coaching by mentors higher up in their organizations has been a vital factor in many women managers' success; networking offers more lateral coaching relationships. Some organizations are deliberately creating opportunities on induction programmes for new female recruits to meet established women managers, making such relationships more possible. Advice to trainers and members on creating and fostering networks is also now available.

Women-only groups

Although we are experiencing their re-emergence in society, female values remain fragile and their development tentative. They need protection if they are not to be swamped or overridden by their robust male counterparts. Similarly in their development, women need the comparative safety of working in women-only groups. Here, participants can to a certain extent suspend dominant cultural stereotypes, and explore and compare experiences which either men do not share or which affect them differently. Even patterns of conversation make this more difficult to do in mixed company. Men and their opinions tend to dominate, and either leave women out or assign them to supportive roles. This pattern occurs even in mixed sex discussions of *women's* issues. Men often speak for women with a clarity the latter are reluctant to contradict from their more diffusely formulated ideas. In women-only groups participants can concentrate on understanding and supporting each other, and on finding clear expressions of their own needs, rather than on competing for attention. They are also more able to take risks.

Women-only groups and networks vary across a wide spectrum in terms of their ways of working and the issues they address. Some act as support groups, talking through attitudes, motivations, problems and choices, gaining new perspectives and sharing ways of coping. Some are organized on a company or occupational basis and have a clear objective of professional development. They run seminars on particular management skills, invite guest speakers, and so on; some represent women's viewpoints to their organization or industry. Recent initiatives in assertion and management effectiveness training have done much to establish women-only courses as viable and valuable activities; their number is rapidly increasing, despite debate and some criticism. Amongst other things, this reflects a growing identification amongst women, and in this way too provides new models of possible working practice.

Women-only groups are not, however, appropriate forums for all issues, and for all times. Sometimes conflict within the group is suppressed, and harmony becomes more important than allowing a diversity of views. This may mean that members leave rather than address their issues within the group. Managing conflict is an area that women need currently to work on, both in relationships with men and with each other; many reject men's competitive attitudes as a model, and are looking for alternatives which combine cooperation and self-assertion.

Many men find women-only activities bewildering and threatening, and it is no easy path to introduce them into organizations. Once a group is set up it is not unusual for individual men to make powerful bids to join or to find out what is being discussed. Any group which has the function or desire to report back to the rest of the organization on topics of general relevance must consider how the boundary can be managed in this direction too. These 'safe spaces' then, need, careful management and attention.

Flexibility

A keynote of women's development needs as outlined above is **exploration**. Predetermined course formats are not usually sufficiently flexible to meet this requirement. There is therefore a trend to schedule free time on courses during which members can work individually or in small groups on topics of their choice, using trainers as resources or guides. The diversity that women bring to courses is also accommodated by attention to contracting at the start of the course and as it progresses. Typically, participants are asked to write down three things they **want** from the course, three things which will **stop them achieving** these objectives, and three things they have to offer. These are then displayed publicly. Contracts help participants clarify their expectations, and give trainers an opportunity to state clearly those the course can and may not meet. Contracts can be reviewed part-way through the course to monitor progress; they help increase the course relevance and tailoring, and demonstrate participants' responsibility for their own learning. They are more common on women-only than on other training courses. (Perhaps misguidedly, it is usually assumed that men are a relatively uniform category in terms of training needs and styles.)

Dispersed training

A key need identified above was for women to increase their competence in potentially inhospitable organizational cultures. Once-and-for-all training is seldom the best solution to such issues, but many trainers are forced into this format by tradition, participants' difficulties in getting time away from work, financial constraints, and so on. Some courses do, however, meet at regular intervals for several weeks or months with opportunities for members to test out their new skills in between. This format has been especially successful for some assertion and self-development training.

Self-development groups

Opportunities for maximum flexibility are offered by self-development groups for women. Some examples along these lines already exist. The then Manpower Services Commission funded a significant initiative to set up and evaluate such groups (see Boydell and Hammond, 1985, in *MEAD* special edition). A group meets at regular intervals, with a trainer acting as facilitator. Participants manage their own process, identify their individual and collective needs, and plan and run a programme of activities to address them. The emphasis is on **holistic development** (see Chapter 8 above), covering work in the context of other life areas, and recognizing the interdependence of thinking, feeling and doing. Initial evaluations are that such groups can be highly successful, and support their members in significant work and personal learning. Managing the group's development and decision-making themselves gives participants valuable experience, and also opportunities to experiment with more varied styles and strategies than they use in their own jobs.

Training topics

Assertiveness

The single most significant and important training topic for women so far has been **assertiveness**; this directly addresses their 'inferior' position in terms of social power, and offers ways to reclaim personal and organizational power. Assertion training helps women develop their personal self-confidence and their interpersonal skills, including their ability to express and honour their own perspectives, even when these do not conform to established organizational norms and ways of thinking. Participants are usually concerned to find work styles which reflect their female grounding and reject behaviours they find too aggressive or competitive.

The basic principles of assertion training are: respect for self and others; equality; responsibility for one's own needs; maintaining appropriate boundaries between oneself and others; and choice – including **when** and **whether to be assertive**. Typical exercises involve practising various assertive techniques such as dealing with anger, accepting or giving criticism, and saying 'no'; role-plays of problem situations; explorations of non-verbal behaviour and its implicit messages; and distinguishing between assertive, passive and aggressive behaviour. Dickson (1982) provides a valuable primer.

Some organizations have recognized the benefits of assertion training, and are now offering it widely. Many courses, however, go on outside companies as part of women's development for themselves, but with obvious job implications. Most current courses are for women only, but an increasing number of mixed courses are being introduced. Assertiveness is an essential first rung of management effectiveness training for women; the future is likely to bring more refresher and advanced offerings to consolidate its contribution.

Management effectiveness

Several higher education establishments and training organizations are now also running direct 'management effectiveness' courses for women. Some have a base in business knowledge and skills such as finance and marketing; others cover an established range of skills such as time management, negotiating, stress management and decision-making, but take on a distinctive flavour because their participants are women. In sessions on stress, for example, conflicts between different life roles and the pressures of working in competitive environments usually figure as concerns. These courses generally recognize the importance of participants' identity issues to their approach to work, and include activities to clarify personal needs and build confidence.

Re-defining management skills for women

Once women pay attention to management skills in this way, many established values and assumptions are brought into question. A focus of attention at the moment is the 're-vision' of notions such as leadership, management style and management effectiveness from a more female-compatible perspective. Some tentative models are already emerging from this process, including courses on selected topics identified as key skills for women, such as influencing. More important than guidelines or prescriptions is the freedom women are being offered through some development opportunities to explore for themselves and achieve their own uniquely appropriate blend of **female and male values** from which to operate.

Life planning and career building

Another early training concern amongst women was life planning, and this is still a priority. The basic format of reviewing one's past history, assessing strengths and weaknesses, identifying unfulfilled ambitions, and so forming plans for future development is already well established. Women bring several distinctive concerns to these activities, and their own pattern of life phases; the early thirties are emerging as a critical time for many as they review their career progress and wonder whether to have children. Balancing career with a home life is a continuing focus of attention, becoming especially significant in choices about whether to marry, have children, move, take promotion or change jobs, and how to manage potentially conflicting needs in dual-career families. Whether to interrupt their career at some point is a particularly difficult decision for women; some companies are now offering 'returner schemes' to allow extended leave for parenting, with opportunties for keeping in touch through occasional training or work experience. Although such measures are helpful the dilemmas and practical difficulties remain, and research shows that women who interrupt their careers are likely to be significantly disadvantaged in later working life. Moves to provide more work-based child-care facilities seem to offer more advantages, including career continuity.

For many women, these choices are related to how 'ambitious', in conventional terms, to be. The managers I interviewed had notions of career which drew on a more female base of values; they wanted a sequence of satisfying and challenging jobs, but upward progression was less important to most of them than leading a **balanced life**. They were prepared to become self-employed, change occupation or work part-time in order to meet other goals. Very few could rely on another person for support; any new directions had therefore to be financially viable. Many of the established women managers I meet are using life planning to explore these possible options, often putting their whole lives in the balance at a particular choice point. Some are wondering whether the strain of working in an organization culture they find inhospitable is worth the benefits, and are looking for companies which are more influenced by female values. Whatever their choices, women cannot guarantee that anyone else will shape and manage their careers for them. Many life planning reviews therefore offer highly directed advice on career building; they openly declare that to succeed in organizations, women have to be exceptionally clear about their objectives and persistent in pursuing them. Some women reject these ideas, and point to their own success through more opportunistic progress.

Sexuality

An area which is beginning to receive training attention is sexuality at work. Courses on sexual harassment are becoming available, aimed at a mixed audience of advisers to victims and victims themselves. As women and men more often work together as equals, individuals are more exposed to dilemmas about sexual attraction. Some women are concerned about the management of sexuality in intimate working relationships, and looking for opportunities to explore their feelings and strategies in this area. This may well become an additional topic in assertion or management effectiveness courses.

Men and women as colleagues

The initiatives covered so far have concentrated on building bridges between women and the organizations in which they work; workshops which take 'men and women as colleagues' as their theme offer a more direct opportunity to influence **organizational cultures**. Typically, participants work in both single and mixed sex groups reporting back in full session; attitudes to work, sex role stereotypes, management styles, and so on are not only discussed but put to the test in role plays and problem-solving activities. Training objectives are enhanced understanding of the similarities and differences between women and men, individual learning about one's own attitudes and behaviours, and awareness of how organizational structures and cultures carry and enforce norms and values about gender. When workshops involve several employees from one company, it is hoped that further exploration and development will occur on their return to work.

Such workshops require considerable skills from the trainers involved. Sex differences in power, language, values and emotional expression all figure prominently in the discussions themselves and need careful handling if some participants are not to feel misunderstood or even damaged in the process. But the dialogue such arenas offer is a vital next step to developing women and men's relationships at work, and so, despite its challenges, must be fostered.

CONCLUSION

In this chapter I have charted women's current development needs and training provision; in these terms, we live in times of considerable change. In the USA, where affirmative action legislation is extremely powerful, there is now said to be a backlash against paying separate attention to women. In the UK, too, there are signs that some men resent concentration on women's needs, and are prompted by it to voice more concerns of their own. This is a potentially healthy move if men and women can avoid getting locked into competition for attention and concern. The argument that because one sex suffers disadvantages or difficulties at work, the other cannot legitimately question them, is not very convincing; the main danger is that current power differences and cultural patterns will so shape development activities that women's perspectives will remain muted. To guard against this, we need both **separate development** for women to strengthen their perspective and confidence, and **joint development** through dialogue between women and men.

REFERENCES

Bartol, K. M. (1978) 'The Sex Structuring of Organizations: a Search for Possible Causes', *Academy of Management Review* (October).

Boydell, T. and Hammond, V. (1985) *Management Education and Development (MEAD) Journal*, special edition, 16(2) (Spring) 'Men and Women in Organisations'.

Capra, C. (1982), *The Turning Point: Science, Society and the Rising Culture* (Aldershot: Wildwood House).

Dickson, A. (1982), *A Woman in Your Own Right* (London: Quartet Books).

Gilligan, C. (1982), *In a Different Voice: Psychological Theory and Women's Development* (Cambridge, Mass.: Harvard University Press).

Marshall, J. (1984), *Women Managers: Travellers in a Male World* (Chichester: John Wiley).

Spender, D. (1980) *Man Made Language* (London: Routledge & Kegan Paul).

FURTHER READING

Women and Training News (From Ann Cooke, The Women and Training Group, Hewmar House, 120 London Road, Gloucester, GL1 3PL Tel. 0452 309330).

20

The role of the management trainer

Alun Jones

An increasing number of practising trainers in the UK are beginning to adopt the language of the organization development consultant and are moving into the kind of work that is more to do with directly intervening in the organization than with the traditional activities associated with trainers. Increasingly in the training literature the terms 'intervention' and 'training consultant' are appearing.[1]

The problem is that a large proportion of trainers (and of training) in the UK is still traditional in nature. Few trainers have any training in the behavioural sciences and most are strongly based in the specific technology of their industry. Their basic practical or academic training is concerned with that technology and their 'training in training' has often been grafted on, sometimes at a minimal level. They have learned by experience about training within their particular industries, and this has continually reinforced a specific 'industrial skills' emphasis in their activities and outlook. This is to be compared with the strong assertion by many professional consultants that competent intervention must be based on adequate training in the behavioural sciences (see Bennis, 1969).

Whichever view is taken, it is apparent that, although trainers in the UK as elsewhere are moving into this field of intervention, there is a vast gulf between the majority of trainers and the organizational consultant; this is understandable, as it is clear that they are out of very different stables. Further, although there is a growing body of knowledge and experience about organization development consulting there is yet little systematic work and literature available about training development and training consulting, and what there is gives an impression of being an extrapolation from the world of the behavioural scientist and the OD consultant.

However, a number of research projects (see French and Bell, 1973; Argyris, 1970; Binstead and Stuart, 1979) have begun to chart this relatively new training territory. These studies have started from the traditional activities of trainers and the traditional processes of training and have then begun extrapolating into the fields of organizational intervention which many trainers are exploring. The intention is that this charting will link up with the growing and well-established field of OD.

Some new models and frameworks have been built up which capture and give some conceptual form to the experience being gained. From them, it is becoming apparent that **management trainers themselves have some learning to do**.

LEARNING TO INTERVENE

If trainers are to become more interventionist within organizations, and to make a more direct and significant contribution, then a number of changes are necessary.

Change in the basic 'model'

It has been suggested that much of training in the UK, and the activities of trainers, have been built upon an 'educational' model (see Figure 20.1). The key to such a model is the strong **primary contract** between the trainer and the individual trainee; it is left to the trainee to make a **subsidiary contract** with his or her organization to apply and utilize the new skills (learning) acquired, just as the educational system leaves it largely to individuals to apply their education within society.

Thus a **transfer and application problem** is created by the nature and the methods (and often by the location) of the training. It can be seen from training literature that many trainers and researchers are well aware of the problem and are taking steps to alleviate it (see the

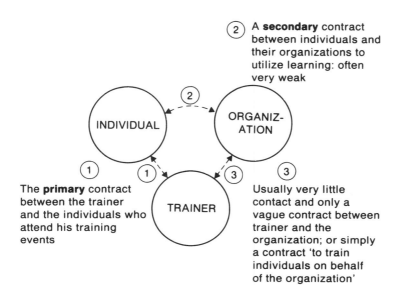

Figure 20.1 The education model

ongoing work by Burgoyne *et al.* at the Centre for Management Learning, Lancaster and by Huczynski and Logan at Glasgow (1986).

The problem can be solved only by **changing the underlying model or assumptions** on which the whole training activity is based. It demands the trainer 'intervening' more **into the organization itself**. He will need to make the primary contract with the organization and not merely 'provide training' on behalf of it – few organizational problems are as simple as that. The contract needs to embrace how the learning is going to be **applied** and **utilized**, and what else has to happen in **support of the training**. Probably more important in this organizational model, the trainer is concerned to arrange a primary contract between the individual trainee and his organization, represented often by the **immediate manager**. The secondary contract is there for the trainer to help bring about the learning that is required as a part of the primary contract. In summary the training (and thus the trainer) takes on more of an organizational emphasis and focus than an educational one (see Figure 20.2).

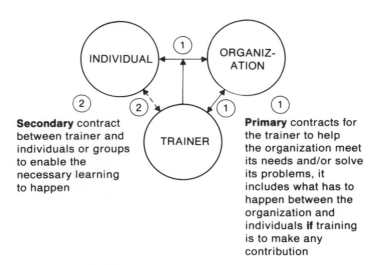

Figure 20.2   An organizational model

Change in the role of training

It follows from a change of model that a change in the **role of training within the organization** will also be required if training is to become more interventionist (see Zender, 1980). A shift thus needs to be made from merely providing skilled manpower to becoming involved in mainstream **organizational processes and problems**. The trainer will help to identify where new learning is required, and where it will contribute; and then help to **cause that learning to happen** in a wide variety of ways – not only by providing a specialist 'teaching' service.

Getting involved in mainstream and vital activities and processes which have a direct effect on the organization's fortunes and performance will have implications for the **status** of the training function, and its **place** within the organization for a change in role is an interactive process between what the organization is willing to accept, and what the trainer is able to provide.

Change in the emphasis of the trainer's activities

To fulfil this more interventionist role there will also need to be a change in the emphasis of the trainer's **activities**. The obvious one is that he will have to operate more in the organization, in departments and in working groups, and less in the training department or training school or room. He will need to put more emphasis on diagnosing the **organizational need** in depth and in translating it into learning requirements. There must be a better balance between activities aimed at acquisition and those aimed at application of skill (i.e., trainers will need to extend the boundary of their learning interest outside the training room); and this will lead to activities more concerned with evaluating **eventual and practical results,** and less with assessing the result of the training sessions. The outcome will be a better balance of activities concerned with the whole learning process within the organization and not mainly with improving the training technology and training expertise within the training department and 'schoolroom.'

Change in skills of trainers

These activities, if they are to be carried out effectively, will demand skills which will be new for very many trainers (MSC, 1979). Some of them may be termed 'intervention skills' but many are a normal part of any systematic training process. In other words, they are skills which many trainers have not been called upon (or allowed) to apply as a part of their normal activity. In other cases they are special skills within the trainer's armoury which the average trainer may not have developed to any significant degree of expertise. Trainers who have established a vital and effective role within their organizations have often achieved this by developing and applying skills which result in more effective intervention and penetration into the organization; these skills they have applied within a clear and consistent training process which most trainers recognize. If this is to be the experience of more trainers, and if training is to make a more effective contribution in more organizations, then two requirements appear to be necessary:

1. For trainers to develop a more **strategic and organizational** view of their training activities; this will include the need for trainers to extend their own boundaries of both time and space
2. For trainers to become more **aware of,** and then to **develop,** the training skills which have greatest effect in **intervening** and **penetrating** usefully in organizations.

The following section attempts to create a framework or taxonomy of training interventions so that individual trainers may identify and learn how to make a more significant and worthwhile contribution to their organization's functioning. The final section suggests some practical applications of the taxonomy.

A BASIC TAXONOMY OF INTERVENTIONS

From studies of the experience of trainers who have been developing a more interventionist role (either from outside or as an integral part of their organization), it is possible to put together a process or cycle which describes the particular activities and skills a trainer can contribute to the organization as he develops a more interventionist stance and role. The activities can be grouped in an eight-point taxonomy under clearly defined areas, although in practice they are neither as neatly grouped nor as chronologically tidy as the list may suggest. They are an extension of the well-known training cycle, to which a number of new and crucial activities have been added.

Helping to diagnose the need (Diagnosing)

This is both broader and deeper than merely identifying the training need, which sometimes degenerates into 'suggesting the training solution' or 'devising the training plan'. It involves activities which help to diagnose precisely what is required and what part training (or learning) can play in bringing about what is required. It deals in **organizational terms and currencies**, and not in training jargon. It is concerned with organizational needs, goals and problems, and not with training activities.

Determining the specific contribution of training (Translating)

This is a key link for the trainer and demands a 'translation' of business and organizational needs and objectives into **learning needs and objectives**; it is probably one of the most vital activities in enabling 'training' to make a real contribution and intervention into the mainstream business. It is an activity many trainers are not often involved in, or skilled at, yet it is one which the trainer misses out at his peril: it is the key activity where the trainer's strategies (if he has any) can be directly linked with current and future **organizational strategies and plans**.

Designing learning strategies and methods (Designing)

The skilled trainer will bring about a great deal of the required learning through his contacts with managers and their staff in helping them diagnose what is required. Nevertheless an important part of his expertise is also to design training programmes, events or situations to **enable learning to happen effectively**; some of this may well need to be achieved away from work in a classroom involving groups of managers and staff. This activity most trainers are well-experienced in, as it is the focus of many training of trainers' courses. However great strides have been made in **designing learning** which trainers need to keep abreast of.

Developing and organizing training resources (Resourcing)

A growing aspect of the trainer's management skills, as opposed to his direct training skills, is his ability to develop all the **resources required by the learning design**. Thus he will use line managers and supervisors quite often to instruct or train, rather than using specialist trainers or instructors. His role in developing managers, supervisors and others to train their own staff involves him in some critical intervention strategies; in this area of activity his ability to influence the allocation of resources will be measured by the resources he can attract. The need to be in the organization's **networks of decision-making** will guide him in maintaining close contact with key managers, especially those in charge of finance.

Bringing about the acquisition of learning (Implementing)

This is separated from the sixth step in the process because it still tends to be the practice for many trainers to concentrate mainly on the acquisition of new skill and knowledge. Separation, although it may seem artificial, may help to emphasize the point that both **acquisition** and **application** are equally necessary in the process. But it depends where the trainer, and his organization, draws his boundary. Traditionally his expertise has been to help people acquire skills in a training environment; he ought to have skills there, but the learning that is required may have to be achieved on-the-job, within the context of the day-to-day organization. The trainer will then have to concentrate his activities in the manager's 'court' and not in the comparative security of the training room.

Enabling the learning to be applied and developed (Enabling)

If much of the learning has been achieved on-the-job then acquisition and application are hopefully achieved together. If, however, training has been brought about in a training situation away from the organization the trainer will need to give a great deal of attention to helping staff apply what they have learned in their job contexts. Many trainers see this as outside their responsibilities; and, unfortunately, many managers would have it so. An important series of activities to do with application and development of learning on-the-job is necessary if the trainer is to achieve more effective intervention and effectiveness in organizational terms. His **contacts** with managers and his own **personal credibility** with them will play an important part in this aspect of his work.

Catalyzing support action (Catalyzing)

Closely linked with this activity in the departments of the organization is the influencing that will almost certainly be necessary to ensure that other things happen within the organization as well as individuals achieving learning. This activity should be one of the results of diagnosing the need effectively, as that should have revealed the need for a **variety of actions and decisions**, as well as training ones. Whether or not the trainer acts as a catalyst or stimulus to see that these other things happen will depend partly on his influencing skills, but many other organizational factors will apply here, including competitiveness and inter-organisational 'politics' and rivalry. One important factor is whether managers will allow the trainer to work **alongside them as a resource**.

Evaluating organizational results (Evaluating)

Most training literature on evaluation concentrates on assessing the training activity in training terms; it is often retrospective. But an effective intervention activity concentrates on evaluating the whole of the strategy against the diagnosed need; often it will involve the managers themselves in evaluating results, assessing what has been learned and applied and what else needs to be activated. In this it is a similar activity to helping them diagnose needs and demands similar skills of data collecting and interpretation. Again, it will be carried out largely inside departments and not in the training room (see Jones, 1981).

These eight categories form a cycle of training interventions which take the trainer more and more outside his traditional boundary of training. Like any cycle it can be **entered** at any point, and so the trainer's ability to use and develop whatever opportunity is offered as a change to initiate an effective training intervention applies at all points of the cycle. Usually the cycle begins as the result of some kind of **stimulus**, either from outside or inside the organization. Sometimes the trainer himself will provide the stimulus to heighten the awareness of a real need; but he will be on dangerous ground if he merely manipulates the organization to want his 'solution'. Logically, wherever the cycle starts, the trainer will get round to helping to diagnose the need appropriately and as comprehensively as possible. So this training intervention process can act as a guide to the trainer to ensure that his activities are progressively interventionist and likely to penetrate the organization for it is **'inside' the organization and its processes** that the trainer needs to contribute if his activities are to become increasingly effective. This can be illustrated in diagrammatic form as in Figure 20.3.

PRACTICAL APPLICATION OF THE TAXONOMY

How can this taxonomy be applied in practice? Trainers involved in management development have found it useful to divide the taxonomy into three parts: developing every opportunity offered and helping to diagnose the need and translating it into what learning is required clearly from the **pre-training activity**; in the vernacular, it has been called 'getting it right'. The next three categories of the taxonomy: designing, resourcing and implementing, are about **planning and doing the training**, whether in the training department itself or

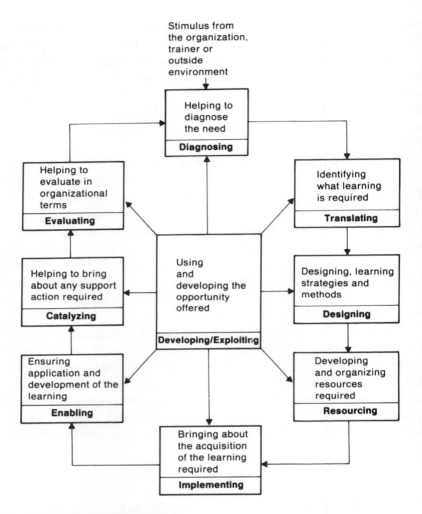

Figure 20.3   The training cycle

inside line-departments. Those three together can be called 'doing it well'. And the last three, enabling, catalyzing and evaluating, together form the **post training activities** which, when carried out effectively, are all about 'making the training stick'. So in practice it is useful to perform this exercise particularly where the management trainer's primary role has been to provide training events and programmes:

'GETTING IT RIGHT'→'DOING IT WELL'→'MAKING IT STICK'

Within these categories there are a number of activities which management trainers can follow in order to help them to be more interventionist, starting from their well established programme providing base. Let us examine them one at a time:

Getting it right

Most experienced trainers will admit that the most challenging task they have is to maintain the relevance of their training programmes in meeting **real organizational needs**. Four activities seem to be key:

1. **Building up networks:** in order to develop and exploit opportunities within the organization the trainer needs to expand his networks of **key managers**. This will enable him to be on the spot (or at least available) when problems arise rather than 'out there' in the training department, busily running programmes which may have lost their cutting-edge of relevance.
2. **Organizational understanding:** he needs to spend much more time understanding the **context of the problem** or the **organizational demand** within which training or learning is required to make a contribution. His understanding of the organizational need will be a key factor in his ability to translate this into a relevant learning objective. It will also be crucial in his designing learning that managers can actually **use and apply**.
3. **Before and after:** he needs to spend more time clarifying with managers what has to be done **after the training programme** both by the learners and their immediate bosses, and by others around them at work. The transfer and application problems need to be tackled before the 'training' happens. This will ensure the programme is seen as a part of a **total and continuous process** and not as an isolated event.
4. **Contracting:** encouraging and 'training' participants to write out contracts about what will be expected to happen on and after the training event and how it will be assessed and measured has been found to be a significant intervention activity. It goes without saying that these contracts need to be the result of enough discussion between participants and their 'bosses' to ensure understand-

ing agreement and commitment. The trainer needs to **influence this essential process**.

Concentration of effort on these 'getting it right' activities will help to ensure the relevance of the training that is going to go on. As a by-product it can also prepare the learners to want to use the training programme or event for their own purposes and to see it as a part of their own **on-going learning process** (i.e., to take more responsibility for managing their own development). As trainers are required more and more to demonstrate the value of their activities to the organization, 'getting it right' is becoming an imperative.

Doing it well

Even in this well-established traditional area of designing and running training, trainer roles are changing. Three rapidly developing aspects of these changes are worth highlighting here:

1. **Learning to learn:** many trainers have moved the emphasis of their training programmes away from their own skills of teaching and leading towards enabling managers to become more conscious of their own ways of learning. The work of Kolb (1984) and Honey and Mumford (1986) has developed techniques for making managers more aware of the **styles** and the **preferences** of their own learning processes (see Chapter 7 above). Developing this awareness within training programmes enables managers to begin to see 'training' as a **resource which they need to manage themselves**, rather than as something a trainer does to them.

2. **Learning to transfer:** a great deal more can be done in most training programmes to encourage and enable managers to apply the learning that they have been achieving. In one way, this is just simply a practical application of the learning cycles mentioned above in that managers within the programme are asked to reflect upon what they have been doing, to come to conclusions about it, and to plan to test it out in their work situations. Instead of leaving action planning to the last session of the programme, it becomes an integral part of the programme: managers collect their actions together as a final summary of their 'strategy for action' when they leave to go back to work, and so the trainer lays

emphasis on application back at work throughout the programme, rather than simply on acquisition of knowledge and skill
while on the programme.

3. **Learning together:** although there are obvious benefits in
    managers learning more about management and about them-
    selves in stranger groups away from their own organization, they
    also need help to **learn together with the managers they have to
    work with.** More and more trainers are designing programmes for
    family groups of managers. Vertical groups, including a variety of
    levels or grades in the organization and multidisciplinary groups
    across departments form the more usual training group; the
    managers who have to **manage together** are thus also enabled to
    learn together. In this way, through dealing with critical masses of
    managers within the same organization sharing similar learning,
    the transfer problem of getting the training **into** the organization
    afterwards is very often overcome (see Chapter 13 above).

Again these developing 'do it well' activites for trainers who are
becoming more interventionist are focused on managers taking responsibility for their own learning, and making it effective in their own
managing situations within the organization.

Making it stick

The trainer who is developing a more interventionist role within his
organization can carry out a number of activities which ensure that
the training he has been organizing sticks. All of these activities look
outward into the organization, and demand the trainer cross the
boundary between his department and the rest of the organization:

1. **Following-up:** if the trainer is going to have any direct influence at
    all over what happens after participants leave his training events
    he must organize **follow-up activities.** Preferably these are done in
    person, but in some cases he may have to resort to the telephone
    or written communications. The follow-up is not concerned with
    helping the participants to learn more about the training event
    they have left; its main focus is **applying the learning within the
    organization.** It is a catalyzing, enabling role where the trainer is

concerned to talk not only to the participant, but to his boss and the people around him. It may mean not only dealing with training problems using training jargon and currency, more likely it will involve talking about the real issues within the departments in which the participants work. More important, getting involved in these kinds of discussions about processes within the organization enables the trainer to see more clearly **other training needs** which managers may have. In this way, it becomes an integral part of the next cycle of 'getting it right'.

2. **Fulfilling contracts:** it is essential that the trainer gets commitment to the participants and their managers reviewing the contracts they made prior to the training event. He can encourage and stimulate this to happen simply by asking for information about the **results** of the discussion about contracts. If he can get involved in these discussions as a part of his follow-up then this obviously puts him in a good position for further influence and intervention. It goes without saying that the trainer must there be talking in the **manager's language** and not in training language. Many trainers are finding the value of sub-contracts between **pairs on the same programme**; this enables managers to experience the process of using **colleagues as training resources**, and not simply looking to the trainer for counsel and help. Where the management development programme is based on one organization or one department this subcontracting clearly lends itself to action learning sets, tackling real problems and issues within the organization.

3. **Evaluating results:** evaluation has been found to be one of the most powerful techniques both for intervening in the organization and for making training stick. Clearly it has to be concerned with the results of the training in organizational terms, and not with how well the training event was conducted. Further, it has to be carried out by participants and their managers and not by the trainer – data is for their use in applying the learning, making use of it and getting value from it within their own departments. This is a very different focus for evaluation activities from the more traditional ways of evaluating courses by looking at them retrospectively. A technique called 'figure of eight' evaluation has been developed (see Jones, 1981)which ensures that evaluation **looks outwards into the results in the organization.**

CONCLUSIONS AND IMPLICATIONS

If the trainer whose main responsibilities include management development intends to develop his role along this more interventionist path, then the implications are manifold. First of all he needs to get the **balance** of his own activities more appropriately geared to getting it right and making it stick. This may mean developing a whole lot of new skills. Then, he will need to redefine his **boundary** from training and development, the training school and his training programmes so that it embraces the whole organization. His **interest** must now encompass the process, systems, relationships and goals within the organization, as well as the individual managers and their training needs. His **focus** shifts from concentrating on individual managers and their development to developing groups of managers and whole departments to meet their particular organizational goals. His **language** becomes the manager's language of management rather than the trainer's language: fluent in both, he becomes an effective **translator**. Finally, he learns to deal in organizational currencies, in achievements and results of the organization and not only with training and learning currencies and achievements within his training events.

Eventually he becomes not the trainer to whom managers go to be developed, sometimes sceptically and reluctantly, but the **resource whom they invite in** to help them with their organizational problems. Although that may sound like a promised land far beyond the reach of many management trainers, more and more are beginning to tread the path towards it. Our taxonomy offers some signposts along that path.

NOTE

1. See the series of articles in *European Training Journals*, 4(5) (1975); G. S. Odiorne, 'Training to be Ready for the 90s', *Training and Development Journal* (December 1980).

REFERENCES

Argyris, C. (1970) *Intervention Theory and Method* (Reading, Mass.: Addison-Wesley)

Bennis, W. (1969) *Organization Development* (Reading, Mass.: Addison-Wesley)

Binsted, D. and Stuart, R. (1979) 'Designing Reality in Management Learning Events', *Personnel Review*, 8(3)

Honey, P. and Mumford, A. (1986) *The Manual of Learning Styles* 2nd edn (London: Honey).

Huczynski, A. and Logan, D. (1980) 'Learning to Change', *Leadership and Organisation Development* Journal, 1(3).

Jones, J. A. G. (1981) 'Figure of Eight Evaluation – A Fundamental Change in the Trainer's Approach', *The Training Officer*, 17(9) (September)

Kolb, D. (1984) *Experiential Learning* (Englewood Cliffs, N.J.: Prentice-Hall).

Manpower Services Commission (MSC) (1979) *First Report of the Training of Trainers Committee*

Zender, J. (1980) 'The Painful Turnabout in Training', *Training and Development Journal* (December)

21

Evaluation

Peter Bramley

The idea of the training department as a passive provider of a menu of courses appears to be giving way to the concept of training as a **management function** which contributes to the growth and development of the organization. As a result, the role of the training manager is changing and the skills of **boundary management** (for instance, acquiring resources, building relationships and coordinating activities with other functions) are becoming more central to the survival of training departments as the latter become more exposed.

There is a growing trend for all institutions – political, educational or even medical – to be required to provide evidence of their **effectiveness**. With training departments, this evidence has usually been provided by established reputation – of the trainers, the training manager, and of repeat business – and not by indices of changed participant behaviour or of increases in organizational effectiveness, but when it becomes necessary to compete for resources, established reputations do not offer such a strong case as **evaluated contributions to effectiveness**.

Evaluation can provide this sort of information, and thus be used to build up a sound track record. The act of following up training and developmental activities also helps to improve relationships with line managers, and these can become central to any decision whether to expand or cut the training department. There are also obvious benefits for the trainers in that the information collected provides a more accurate appreciation of the training need, as well as indicating strengths and weaknesses of various parts of the programme and any problems in transferring back to the workplace.

Why is it, then, that so few training departments evaluate their work? It is certainly difficult and time-consuming to do so, but that is probably not the main problem. My opinion is that the philosophy of evaluation requires a reappraisal of what the **purpose of training is**: a change from conceptualizing it as meeting training needs to thinking of it as an attempt to improve organizational effectiveness. This chapter is based upon that philosophy.

EVALUATING THE TRAINING PROCESS

The process by which training is delivered, and the model on which this is based, can be evaluated against examples of good practice. Some models assume that useful learning takes place as a result of **interaction with other people**; some are based on the principle that, as job performance is judged by the assessment of skills, the function of training should be to **improve these**; other models focus on improved effectiveness in the **job context**. It is surely worth considering whether the model on which a training activity is based is consistent with the purpose, but my experience is that this is not often done.

Individual training models

Training of individuals has its origin in craft apprenticeships where a young person learned, over a period of some years, to imitate the skills of the master. Technical training has been greatly influenced by this tradition of teaching skills to individuals in the belief that they will later find a use for them. The model which is in use here looks like Figure 21.1.

The focus is on **individuals**, and the process is one of encouraging them to learn something which is thought **likely to be useful**, and then expecting them to find **uses** for the learning. In attempting to evaluate training based on this model, it is sometimes very difficult to identify changes in work performance. With most forms of technical training, where the equipment used in training is very similar to that in the workplace, the changes in skills levels achieved during training will

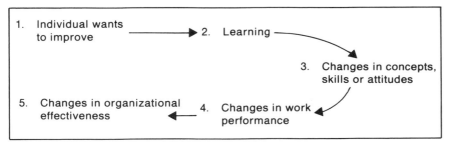

Figure 21.1 Individual training model

usually transfer quite easily into the job (provided there is an opportunity to practise them there). The model is, however, being used for
other forms of training. With most supervisory and management
training, the work situation does not closely resemble that simulated
in the training, and the changes achieved in the training programme
are not necessarily reflected in changes in work performance. The
latter will often mean changing the ways in which **things are done
within the organization**, and the model shown in Figure 21.1 is inappropriate for that purpose.

As Katz and Kahn (1978) point out, attempts to change parts of
organizations by using models like this have a 'long history of theoretical inadequacy and practical failure' (p. 658). The logic of the
approach is that, as organizations are made up of individuals, it must
be possible to change the **organization** by changing the **members**. This
is, however, a great simplification of organizational reality: an organization will have objectives, priorities and policies; it will also have a
structure and accepted ways of doing things. All of these **situational
factors** will have some effect on shaping the behaviour of members of
the organization within their work; often the 'changed' individual is
not able to change these situational factors.

It is important to investigate this further, as it is central to an
understanding of why training sometimes **fails to have any effect**. The
work context can be represented as an interaction between the situation and the people in it; if this interaction is not as effective as it might
be, then changing the people by training might be considered as a way
of improving things. However, this will be successful only if the people
are sufficiently autonomous to change the interaction, and thus the
work situation. This may be the case where people are trained to use a

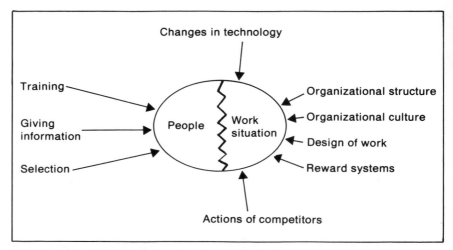

Figure 21.2   Changing the way the work is done

piece of equipment like a keyboard or a lathe, but there is no reason to assume that it is the case with a supervisory problem. Other factors affect the situation, and they may have more influence over the way in which the work is done than the skills of the supervisor (see Figure 21.2).

Factors like the **structure** of the organisation (who reports to whom, how many levels and whether people can communicate horizontally); the **culture** (in what spirit people relate to each other, to what extent individuality is valued), the **design** of the work (the extent to which this is frustrating or stress-inducing); and whether good performance is actually **rewarded** (by recognition, praise, and promotion, as well as financially) will all affect the job situation. It will often be necessary to change some of these as well as to train the people, as their effect on the interaction may be more powerful than the ability of the individuals to innovate in the job.

Increased effectiveness model

Changing the performance of people **in the job** is often more complicated than Figure 21.1 would suggest and it may be more useful to consider the implications of a model which is based on **changing effectiveness** rather than on educating individuals. A possible model is

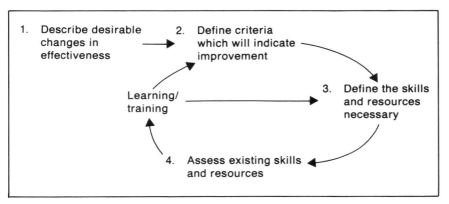

Figure 21.3   Increased effectiveness model

offered in Figure 21.3. The process starts in a part of the organization with a decision about what **level of effectiveness** is desirable; the second stage is to define **criteria** by which changes towards the more desirable state can be measured (i.e., 'How will we know if we are getting there?'). In defining the **resources** necessary (stage 3 of the model in Figure 21.3), aspects of the job situation other than the skills of the people will be considered and it may be that changing some of these will achieve the desired improvements without training. If training is thought to be necessary it is delivered, and the extent to which any learning is useful will be monitored by **changes in job performance** – not, as is usually the case with the model in Figure 21.1, by changes measured **during the training**.

This model is much more appropriate for the kind of work where people have some **discretion about what they do** or where they have the ability to **negotiate priorities**.

Training as organizational change

A rather different cycle is suggested by considering training as a way of enhancing organizational effectiveness. The process starts with an analysis of the existing situation, as suggested in Figure 21.3. The needs identified will be phrased in terms of **new work practices** which will enhance the effectiveness of the particular part of the organization. The senior management of that part of the organization must be

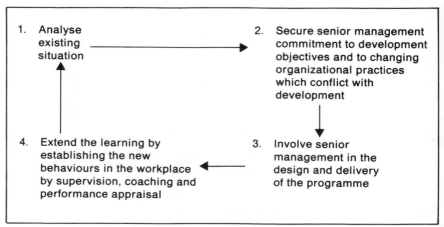

Figure 21.4   Training as organizational change

involved at all stages, and be committed to changing organizational structures or practices which conflict with the new practices which are being introduced. In almost every case, this will imply that these managers are involved in the **design and delivery** of the training; they will also be responsible for encouraging the new behaviours in the workplace by appraising performance and coaching or supervising as necessary to ensure that the learning becomes **incorporated in standard work practices** (see Figure 21.4).

Note that this model is profoundly different to that shown in Figure 21.1; the intention is the same – to change the way that individuals work – but now the new behaviours are **embedded in the organizational context**. In the earlier model, they were encouraged in a training context, and it was hoped that individuals would apply them in their work.

Consider these two models as possible ways of changing part of the organizational culture – say, trying to achieve a more participative management style. Would training individual managers and supervisors and returning them to an unsuspecting workplace as suggested by the model in Figure 21.1 be likely to succeed? Would the procedure suggested by Figure 21.4 be more or less likely to succeed? (The evaluation of the process by which training is delivered is more fully discussed in Bramley, 1990).

EVALUATING CHANGES DUE TO TRAINING

Changes in organizations occur at many levels, and take many forms. Consequently, developing criteria by which changes can be evaluated may result in a range of indices. A good place to start is by establishing that learning has taken place at the **individual level**; this is one of the necessary conditions of those strategies of organizational change which focus on people. It cannot be assumed, however, that individual changes will lead to a change in **effectiveness**, and this will need to be evaluated in its own right.

Changes in levels of knowledge

All jobs require the holder to have some knowledge. What type of knowledge is required? How can this be analysed? It is helpful, in attempting to answer these questions, to have some framework in which to carry out the analysis. One which has proved to be useful is to describe the sort of knowledge required at three levels (this is developed from Bloom, 1956):

- The **basic** level is that of **isolated pieces of information** – ability to recall simple lists or state simple rules, knowing a range of simple facts about the job area
- A **higher** level is to be able to arrange a good many of the pieces of information into **procedures** – how to do things, how to order sets of actions: for instance, starting up a processing plant involves a series of actions which must be done in a certain sequence
- **Higher still** is the knowledge with which to *analyse* any particular situation for its key elements, and thus to make a decision about whether procedure A is more likely to be successful than (say) procedure D; this is essentially the skill to be able to **select** the most appropriate procedure or method of doing something, given the nature of the problem, the organizational context, etc.

This is an hierarchical set, and it is not possible to achieve the higher levels without knowledge at the lower levels. The function of training could, therefore, be seen as:

- analysing what is **required** at each of the three levels for satisfactory job performance
- discovering what the **trainees know** at each level before they attend the training
- trying to **close that gap**
- communicating to the supervisors or managers of the trainees to what extent they are **below satisfactory job performance levels** at the end of training.

The three levels of knowledge have quite different implications for the training process. Isolated pieces of information can be quite easily transferred by lectures to large groups or by paper-based texts or by programmed packages. All of these methods are relatively inexpensive. Procedures, too, can be learned fairly cheaply by using checklists and prompts plus, perhaps, some supervized practice.

The implications of the third (analytic) level are quite different. If this is to be achieved, the trainees will have to practise in **realistic situations**, and make **decisions** about how to handle them. As this is actually a simulation of some aspects of the job, it will be much more expensive to design and it will take much more training time than work at the lower levels.

The implications for the sophistication of measurement of changes in knowledge are also different. It is relatively easy to test knowledge of isolated pieces of information and of procedures; this can be done by simple testing where the answers can easily be seen to be right or wrong. At the analytic level, the solutions to the problems posed will often have a **qualitative** aspect to them; this will imply that a subject expert will have to scrutinize the solutions and decide which are acceptable and which are not. Testing knowledge is not often carried out in management training, probably because the initial analysis (of what is required for satisfactory job performance) is not done. Knowledge is usually taught in the belief that it is necessary in the job, and evaluation can take the form of following up to discover if the learning has been useful.

A simple questionnaire may well be sufficient for this. Questions like:

- how useful is knowledge of this for your job?
- have you used knowledge of this in the last six months?

- was the reference material given out sufficient?

should be asked for each of the topics covered. Following up by using **interviews** will improve the quality of the information gathered, but it is an expensive procedure.

Attitude change versus behaviour change

When thinking about how training and development programmes might be structured in order to increase the likelihood of achieving their purpose, it is necessary to distinguish **skills** from **attitudes**. The distinction is an important one: indeed, failure to clarify the difference between skills training and attitude change can often result in confusion. This is not to suggest that the two are incompatible, but rather that trainers need to decide which aspects of their programmes are addressed to skills, and which to attitudes; in this way, the process of evaluation can be designed to look at one aspect separately from the other, and to give appropriate feedback. Let us consider a working definition which will clarify this important distinction. An **attitude** is a tendency or a predisposition to behave in certain ways in particular situations, whereas a **skill** is an ability to do something well. Attitudes can be measured directly, but are usually inferred from the things which people say or are seen to do. Changing someone's attitude to something may well change what they say or do, but this will not necessarily follow. People behave in ways which they believe to be appropriate to the situation in which they find themselves, so that other variables in the present situation may be more powerful in selecting behaviour than attitudes previously held.

Attitudes can be measured or discussed early in the programme, and it is possible to reassess them towards the end and thus show **changes** in the expected direction; often this is done in an informal way as an end-of-course discussion of 'what were the most important things for me?'. It is possible to make this more formal by developing **action plans** – 'what will I do more of and what will I do less of when I return to work?'. There are also inventories which can be used early and late in the programme. Useful sources of these can be found in Henerson *et al.* (1978) and also in Cook *et al.* (1981). The inventories will seldom be exactly what is required, but the formats can be used to build up something specific for a particular programme. An alternative method of assessing changes in attitude is by the use of a simple repertory grid technique; Honey (1979) provides a detailed example of how to do this.

Following up attitude-changing activities to discover whether the changes are maintained in the workplace is quite difficult to do, and it is doubtful whether this is actually of value; the assumption is that changing attitudes will change the way that people behave, but this assumption can be avoided by observing the actual behaviour to discover if it has changed. It will usually be necessary to enlist the help of line managers or supervisors in order to do this.

Changes in individual effectiveness

Behaviour scales for assessing change should make explicit **what changes are likely**; it may also be possible to integrate these with annual **performance appraisal** categories. If this can be done, then the employing managers will be able to provide evidence of whether changes have taken place – and, if so, whether increased effectiveness is the result. For instance, a study by Latham and Saari (1979) assessed increased performance by an improvement in ratings on the annual appraisal; they also measured productivity in the sections for which the supervisors were responsible, and were able to show an increase after training.

Another way of facilitating the transfer of learning back to work is by the use of **action planning during the training**. At intervals during the training, the participants are asked to focus on the utility of what has been discussed. Towards the end of the programme they cluster the items into areas and then arrange them in some order of priority. The action plan for (say) the next six months is then drafted by putting some time-frame on each area to be tackled. It will also be necessary to write down against each area likely **countervailing forces**, and how these are to be overcome. The questions which need to be addressed will include the following:

- Will this action have an effect on other people? How will they react to it?
- Whose authority will be necessary to implement this action? How do I ensure that this will be available?
- What organizational constraints are likely to prevent this action? What can be done to ease them?

The action plan is a piece of **positive management**; it forms a set of goals to be achieved, and gives a time-frame and rationale for each of them. It can be lodged with the course tutors, and followed up later. Whether this happens or not, the plan should be discussed with the employing manager, before or after return to work. During the follow-up, some six months later, questions like the following can be asked:

- How much of your action plan have you been able to implement?
- Which actions have been shelved, and why?
- What positive benefits in terms of effectiveness in your part of the organization have resulted from carrying out your action plan?

A specific form of action planning is through the use of action learning with an **organizational project** as the focus for the learning. This project often has as a focus the increased effectiveness of a part of the company, and can show a good return for the investment in training. An example of this was described by Woodward (1975) (the programme investigated was for supervisors and led to a National Examinations Board in Supervisory Studies qualification). There was formal course work, mainly on theories of management, which was examined. There was also a work-based project which was intended to show the advantages of good supervisory practice. Woodward was unable to show any differences in ways of working as a result of the theoretical part of the course; this ought not to surprise us. We have considered good examples of the processes which are needed in order to change the ways in which people do things at work; theoretical input on the nature of management, without role-play or work-based practice, is not one of them. Woodward was able to estimate the benefits of the project work and six of the twelve participants showed positive benefits. Averaged over the twelve, the return on training investment (course fee, travel, subsistence, equipment costs, pay of trainees and covering costs) was 2.9 : 1.

Changes in the effectiveness of teams

Team development is intended to improve the effectiveness of a group of people whose jobs **require that they work together**. It assumes:

- that the group has some reason for existing, some **common goals and problems**
- that **interdependent action** is required to achieve the goals or solve the problems
- that it is valuable to spend time in trying to understand and improve the way in which group members **work together** to achieve their tasks.

Team development activities may focus on working relationships or on action planning. There are three main models; problem-solving, interpersonal, and role-identification.

- The **problem-solving model** encourages the group to identify problem areas which are affecting the achievement of group goals. Action planning is then used as a method of tackling the problems. **Quality circles** offer the best-known example of problem-solving groups and can give a return on training investment. Robson (1982) quotes the average return as being between 5:1 and 8:1.
- The **interpersonal model** attempts to improve decision-making and problem-solving by increasing communication and cooperation on the assumption that improving **interpersonal skills** increases the **effectiveness of the team**. Groups regularly report improvements in agreeing goals, increasing cooperation and reducing conflict; there is not so much evidence that these improvements can be linked to higher levels of organizational effectiveness.
- The **role-identification model** attempts to increase effectiveness by increasing understanding of the **interacting roles within the group**; Belbin (1981) describes ways in which this can be done, and some criteria for evaluation.

It is, of course, possible to combine the different models. For instance, the Blake and Mouton (1969) managerial grid is a combination of problem-solving and interpersonal approaches.

Changes in organizational effectiveness

Organizational effectiveness is not a simple concept with only the balance sheet at the end of the year as the criterion to be assessed;

there are many ways in which one can look at it, and many writers have offered sets of criteria. One of the early attempts was that of Georgopolous and Tannenbaum (1957), who evaluated effectiveness in terms of productivity, flexibility and the absence of organizational strain. More familiar is the approach of Blake and Mouton (1964), which seeks the simultaneous achievement of high production-centred and high people-centred methods of management. Katz and Khan (1978) argue for growth, survival and control over the environment.

Another classification has been offered by Cameron (1980), who considers that almost all views on organizational effectiveness can be summarized under four headings – goal-directed, resource-acquiring, satisfying constituencies and internal processes.

Goal-directing

Product goals Many organizations have basic measurements of work output, for instance:
- **Quantity**: produced, completed, processed, sold, turnover, etc.
- **Quality**: rejects, scrap, error rates, etc.
- **Variety**: diversity of products, etc.

It is sometimes possible to evaluate training events against this sort of criterion (for instance, Latham and Saari, 1979, showed that the groups working for trained foremen were more productive than those working for 'untrained' foremen) but it is necessary to control for variations in organizational performance which have nothing to do with training. This means that the output of a comparable part of the organization, where training has not yet been given, is monitored on the same time series of measurements as the group under examination. Often this is just not possible; if the organization believes that the training is likely to be useful it will be reluctant not to give it to the 'control' department–branches, etc. simply to set up an experimental comparison. It is also very difficult to set up a **true control group**: there is usually some incidental learning involved in the process of measurement and via the organizational grapevine; this may affect levels of performance and thus obscure the effect of the 'official' learning achieved on the programme.

System goals Most organizations have systems goals like:

- **growth** in assets, sales, manpower
- **deadline rates**, percentage of quota achieved, on-time shipments
- **reduction** of stoppages, machine down-time, overtime worked.

Provided techniques of assessing these have been developed within the organizations, they can be used as criteria against which to assess management learning. Once again, however, some sort of control will be necessary to isolate the effect of the learning from the peaks and troughs of organizational performance. If the techniques of assessing system goals do not already exist, it is doubtful whether the evaluator will be able to develop them within a reasonable cost, for the evaluation. One way of trying to achieve system goals (and also product goals) through learning is to adopt a problem-solving or project-based approach. What little is known about motivation in adults suggests that they are eager to solve what they regard as important problems; it would thus seem likely that learning experiences which enable them to tackle current problems would be well received (see Chapter 13 above). This may account for the growing popularity of self-development and action-learning approaches to management learning. Certainly, problem centred approaches can give good return on training investment. Woodward (1975), noted above, is a good example.

Acquiring resources

Effectiveness can be assessed by the extent to which the organization acquires needed resources, the emphasis being on **inputs** to increase competitiveness rather than on outputs; the criteria for evaluation are usually long-term comparisons and it is difficult to isolate the effects of learning activities. However, aspects of resource acquisition which can easily be related to training output are:

- Increasing the pool of **trained staff**
- Increasing employment **flexibility**
- Developing skills and abilities for **future job requirements**.

Satisfying customers

Many organizations survey customer satisfaction in some way, and it may be possible to relate this to learning activities; care must be taken to control for **variations in image** which have nothing to do with training. For instance, in the late 1980s British Rail was training staff in customer relations, and advertising on television to tell the public that this was happening; if the initiative results in fewer complaints, it will be extremely difficult to decide how much of the reduction is attributable to training.

If the 'organization' is defined as the workgroup or department, then how well this satisfies those who contact it can be more directly related to training. Surveys of things like 'confidence in', 'loyalty to' and 'what they do which obstructs things which we want to do' can be carried out before and after training. Ford Europe carried out a large-scale organizational development project based upon this sort of approach; the heads of the various functions were asked to write down what the other functions did which **helped** them, and what they did which **hindered**. These lists were assembled into wall displays and, for the first time, the top few managers in each function were able to see how each of the other functions valued their contribution. The training input was largely a facilitation of group problem-solving so that functions could draw up plans for how to improve their 'image'.

Internal processes

'Effectiveness' can be defined in terms of smooth information flows, lack of internal strain, clear definitions of roles, good cooperation between functions or effective teamwork. Efforts to improve indices of these might be evaluated in terms of hard data like grievances, disciplinary actions, absenteeism, sick rates, or turnover, but are more likely to be assessed by use of subjective opinions of 'how we were' or 'how we would like to be'. A whole range of survey instruments to measure attitudes in this area has been produced within the organizational development movement; a useful source of such instruments is Cook *et al.* (1981).

I have found Cameron's classification to be very useful when discussing evaluation of training events with line managers. It is possible to consider effectiveness at levels lower than that of the whole organisation and thus to build up a matrix like that in Figure 21.5. The matrix in Figure 21.5 can be used to discuss desirable changes in effectiveness which might accrue from training or development events; these should be identified by **type** of effectiveness, and the **level** at

	Individual (my work)	Work group (my section)	Function (my dept)	Regional level	Organizational level
Goal-directed					
Resource acquiring					
Satisfying constituencies					
Internal processes					

Figure 21.5   The organizational effectiveness matrix

which they will be measured. You may like to try using the matrix by mapping onto it the changes in effectiveness which you might expect from a particular programme; these can be at the level of the **individual**, the **group** or one of the **higher levels** (the higher the better). The changes may be expected in more than one category of effectiveness.

I have also found this exercise to be useful when discussing with line managers exactly what is supposed to change as a result of a training programme, and how this change is to be **measured**. This is likely to be one of the problems in trying to use the training model which is shown in Figure 21.3. It is also interesting, as a theoretical exercise, to attempt some mapping of possible changes for different kinds of courses. I suggest that you try it for yourselves with a programme which is designed for individuals at a certain level in the organization – say, 'Principles of Management' for junior managers, and then again with a programme which is 'tailor made' for improving the effectiveness of a particular individual or group at work. What criteria can you measure? Which kind of programme do you find easier to evaluate?

PURPOSES FOR EVALUATION

The discussion so far has been about how to evaluate the process by which training is delivered, and how to measure the changes which are

Evaluation of training should be:								
Helping the manage-ment to inspect training	1	2	3	4	5	6	7	Helping the trainers to develop activities
An assessment process which leads to recom-mendations	1	2	3	4	5	6	7	Non-judgemental and therefore likely to pose questions
Statistical and scientific, as its primary concern is with objective mea-surement	1	2	3	4	5	6	7	Anecdotal and descrip-tive, as its primary concern is with subjec-tive interpretation
A carefully planned pro-cess with a set agenda	1	2	3	4	5	6	7	Changing throughout as the focus changes during the process
Estimating the worth of training activities to the organization	1	2	3	4	5	6	7	Providing feedback to the training department
Based on large samples and asking quite simple questions	1	2	3	4	5	6	7	Based on small samples and using in-depth questioning
Part of the process for all training activities	1	2	3	4	5	6	7	Carried out only when there is some doubt about a programme

Figure 21.6   Evaluation of training (Adapted from an idea by Len Gill of the CPU).

expected to result from it. Now we turn to the more 'political' aspects of evaluation, the various purposes which it can serve and the approaches through which these purposes can be met. Before we become too deeply involved in this, it would be valuable for you to consider what your views are with respect to evaluation. What sort of process do you think that it should be? Figure 21.6 offers a set of seven-point scales with anchors at each end. I suggest that you select a point on each scale line which represents your position with regard to the process of evaluation.

The left-hand side of these scales represents a view that the main purpose of evaluation is 'control' – that it should assess the worth of training to the organization and that this is best done by **quantitative** methods. The left-hand side is quite close to research on methods of learning, where the **quality of the experience**, as reported by those involved, is the main focus. Many trainers oscillate between these two positions and hope that evaluation will satisfy both purposes. As we shall see, this is difficult to achieve. Particular forms of evaluation can be designed to meet particular purposes, but it is necessary to be clear about what the **purpose** is before embarking on the **process**.

Goldstein (1986) defines evaluation as 'The systematic collection of descriptive and judgemental information necessary to make effective decisions related to the selection, adoption, value and modification of various instructional activities'. I think this definition sound, and would argue that it implies that evaluation is a set of **information-gathering techniques** – and, further, that the **selection** of a particular stratety or technique, or of the particular aspect of the learning process which is examined, will vary with the **purpose** for which the evaluation is intended. Various purposes have been proposed by different authors; I prefer to group them into five main categories – feedback, control, research, intervention and power games.

Feedback

Feedback evaluation provides quality control over the **design** and **delivery** of training activities. Feedback to the participants during training will be an essential part of the learning process. Timely feedback to the trainers about the effectiveness of particular methods and about the achievement of the objectives set for the programme will help in the development of the programme currently being run, and those planned for future occasions. The information which needs to be collected for feedback evaluation is:

- **before and after measures** of levels of knowledge, concepts used, skills, attitudes and behaviour
- sufficient **detail** to be able to review each topic covered during the learning event and each learning situation
- evidence of **transfer of learning** to the workplace.

The main purpose of what we are calling 'feedback evaluation' is the **development of learning situations** and **training programmes, improving what is being offered**. There is a secondary aspect, as identifying what is good (and what is not so good) improves the professional ability of members of the training department; reports based on feedback evaluation tend to have conclusions in them which the training department can consider and act on (or not).

Control

Control evaluation relates training policy and practice to organizational goals. There could also be a concern for the **value** to the organization of the contribution of the training function, as well as its **costs**. Careful control evaluation might also answer questions like 'Will a main focus on training give a better solution to the problem than restructuring the department or redesigning some of the jobs?' The information required for control evaluation is therefore:

- that required for **feedback** (and listed above)
- some measures of the **worth** of the output of the training to the organization
- some measures of **cost**
- some attempt at a **comparative study** of different mixes of methods for tackling the problem.

Control evaluation is quite close to the left-hand side of the scales in Figure 21.6; it is something that an organization might require of a training manager or might impose through the creation of a group of people responsible for evaluation: there is a strong tendency for this kind of evaluation to result in a report which is full of recommendations, some of which will require changes to be made.

Research

Research evaluation seeks to add to knowledge of training principles and practice in a way which will have more general application than feedback evaluation; studies of ways in which people learn or studies of factors which facilitate transfer would be examples. Research evaluation can also serve to improve the **techniques** available for other purposes like feedback, control and intervention. Research evaluation requires some form of experimental design to counteract threats to **internal validity** – the confidence with which conclusions can be drawn from the data, and the extent to which alternative explanations can be ruled out (i.e., be attributed to the procedure described rather than to some variables which have not been controlled). It also needs some **external validity** – the extent to which the findings can be generalized to other situations. Research evaluation into training within organizations is difficult, as there is seldom the opportunity to set up true control groups and time series of observations. There are not many examples in the literature, but a notable exception is the study by Latham and Saari (1979) which was referred to above.

Intervention

It is a mistake to believe that the process of evaluation is one of applying some **objective measuring instrument, external** to and **independent** of the programme being evaluated; the evaluation is actually likely to affect the way in which the programme is viewed, and can be used to redefine the sharing of responsibility for the learning between the trainers, trainees and employing managers. **Planned intervention** through evaluation can:

- involve the line manager in the **pre/post measurement**
- involve the line manager in the extension of training after the event, by debriefing and helping with the **implementation** of the action plan
- change the way in which the employing managers **selects** and **briefs** people before the learning event
- cause the training department to rethink the **deployment of trainers** to functions within the organization and strengthen the liaison role.

It can thus be a powerful method of intervening into the human resource procedures within an organization.

Power games

Perhaps all information is powerful, but certainly evaluative information about training events can be used within organizational political games; it is not possible to avoid this and perhaps it is not desirable to do so. It does, however, place a burden on the evaluator to make sure that the evidence which is being used is based upon a sound study. People often make up their minds on **anecdotal evidence**: for instance, much of the bad press which sensitivity training received was at the level of 'Did you hear about what happened on the . . . programme last week?'.

APPROACHES TO EVALUATION

Having decided on a purpose (or set of purposes) for the evaluation, the next phase is to select a **suitable approach**. Most authors describing evaluations appear to suggest that the approach which they are advocating is unique. In a sense this is true – no one ever exactly replicates an evaluation – but it is possible to classify approaches into five types – goal-based, systems, goal-free, responsive evaluation and quasi-legal.

Goal-based

Goal-based evaluation starts from the position that training activities are **cyclic**. First, needs are identified and then precise, specific (and preferably **behavioural**) objectives are set. The cycle ends with assessments of the extent to which the objectives have been attained, of the relationship between amounts of learning and methods employed, and of the extent to which the objectives achieved contribute to **meeting the need identified**. This approach is almost universally recommended by trainers for trainers, and there have been numbers of attempts to describe various levels at which the objectives should be set. Table 21.1 is an attempt to cross-classify the better known approaches. The framework used on the left is chronological, based on the sequence of events in learning and then trying to apply the learning in the workplace.

The most comprehensive and convincing of these frameworks is that proposed by Hamblin (1974). The five levels of evaluation are linked by a cause and effect chain:

	training
leads to	**reactions**
which leads to	**learning**
which leads to	**changes in behaviour**
which leads to	**changes in the organization**
which leads to	**changes in the achievement of ultimate goals**

which can break between any of the levels.

Few trainers carry the logic of the goals-based approach through to asking about how **worthwhile** the training was. When this is done a

Table 21.1 Levels at which objectives can be set

Areas	Components	Kirkpatrick (1967)	Warr et al. (1970)	Glossary (1971)	Hamblin (1974)
Within the training	Judgements of the quality of trainee's experiences	Reactions	Reaction		Reaction
	Feedback to trainees about learning				
	Measures of gain or change	Learning	Immediate	Internal validation	Learning
	Feedback to trainers about methods				
At the job after training	Relevance of the learning goals			External validation	
	Measures of use of learning or change of behaviour	Behaviour	Intermediate		Job behaviour
	Retrospective feedback to trainers				
Organizational effectiveness	Measures of change in organizational performance	Results	Ultimate	Evaluation?	Organization
	Implementation of individual action plans or projects				
Social or cultural values	Measures of social costs and benefits			Evaluation?	Ultimate
	Humman resource accounting				Ultimate

number of problems arise, as it is difficult to demonstrate clear linkages between the objectives of higher and lower levels in the organization, and hence to establish the link between training objectives and organizational goals. This is particularly true of management training, where there may be no clear connection between job tasks, nominal training objectives and training content. The choice of appropriate objectives may also be complicated by the coexistence of both **official** goals and **actual** goals which govern behaviour and rewards. It is also the case that in some 'training' events the **symbolic importance of attending** becomes more important than the content; in this case, evaluation against objectives would be irrelevant.

There is a clear bias within this chapter towards the idea that successful training is based upon a fairly precise specification of aims and objectives; this does not imply that 'development' is not worthwhile, rather that there should be some **clarity** in the **expectations** of the parties involved in the process. For instance, some management programmes are habitually justified by managers and trainers as providing a 'broadening experience'; when pressed to explain the concept of 'broadening', most responses can be classified into two areas:

1.   improving contacts **across functional boundaries**
2.   learning to work in **teams** rather than as an individual.

At this level of conceptualization, it is possible to write **objectives**. What is being suggested is that trainers have to tread a path between setting aims so vague that no one can tell whether or not they have been achieved, and setting behavioural objectives so tightly drawn that no room is left for unintended outcomes and the complexity and subtlety of human behaviour.

Systems

Systems evaluation sets out to answer questions like:

- Is the programme reaching the **target population**?
- Is it **effective**?
- Is it **cost effective**?

These sorts of questions are posed by policy-makers looking for 'hard' data, and they largely exclude the opinions of those involved. The main difficulty in applying this approach (which is widely recommended for evaluating social and educational programmes) to training is to decide on **criteria of effectiveness**; effectiveness criteria which satisfy accountants are hard enough to find in technical training, they are virtually impossible to find in management training. This approach is used in some organizations, and training departments must take some responsibility for it; many of them produce statistics each year which represent the 'business' that they are doing in terms of numbers on courses. This may be the only format in which senior management can understand the contribution of training but using this 'headcount' as the sole form of evaluation is tantamount to abdicating and leaving the field to accountants.

Goal-free evaluation

Objectives or goal-based evaluation yields a **measure of intent**, and this may not be all that has been achieved. The evaluator measures what he **expects to find**, and tends not to recognize (or value) **unanticipated** learning and behaviour change. Goal-free methods of evaluation overcome this problem. They have usually been proposed as a reaction to the ubiquity of goal-based evaluations, but their value to trainers is more likely to be in the ways they can complement rather than challenge that approach.

The evaluator sets out, deliberately unaware of the objectives for the programme, to talk to participants about whether some of their needs were met. It is thus possible to pick up **unintended effects** as well as those expected by the programme organizers. It is also possible to discuss, with the participants, alternative ways in which their needs might have been met.

Goal-free methods emphasize **opinions** and they have the problem of gaining consensus on the criteria by which opinions can be judged. They are worth considering when it is necessary to evaluate management learning activities where reasons for attending vary widely and where the participants go back to a variety of jobs. The strategy of goal-free methods can also complement goal-based evaluations where the participants are being followed-up in interviews. Questions about the individual's needs when attending, to what extent they were met, and alternative ways of meeting them, can clearly add valuable information. It is more likely that this information will be wide-ranging if these questions are asked **before** the participants are focused on the intended goals of the programme.

Responsive evaluation

The term 'responsive evaluation' was first used by Stake (1975) to describe a strategy in which the evaluator is less concerned with the objectives of the programme than with its effects in relation to the concerns of **interested parties** – the 'stakeholders'.

In conducting a responsive evaluation the evaluator first talks to the main clients, to staff organizing the programme, and to a sample of those who will be affected by it, both trainees and line managers, to gain a sense of their posture with regard to the programme and the purposes for the evaluation. The evaluator then makes personal observations of the programme to get a direct sense of what it is about. He or she then has begun to discover the **purpose** of the programme, both **stated** and **real**, and also the **concerns** that various stakeholders may have, and is in a position to conceptualize the issues and problems which the evaluation should address.

The design of the evaluation takes place next, and it should be noted that this is well into the process of evaluation; it cannot be designed before the evaluator can specify the kinds of **data** and **information** which will be needed to satisfy the various issues and concerns. The evaluator selects whatever methods and instruments are most appropriate, and collects data. The information collected is organized into **themes**, and the evaluator matches issues and concerns to audiences in deciding what form the report will take (as there may be different reports for different audiences). It is worth noting the **iterations** implicit in this process: at any stage the evaluator may reformulate what is being done, and there is no certain way of predicting the outcome of the evaluation.

Parlett and Hamilton (1977) describe a form of evaluation which has some similarities to responsive evaluation and recommend it for educational research. The primary concern of 'illuminative evaluation' is with **description** and **interpretation**, rather than with measurement and prediction. The suggested method by which to achieve this is 'progressive focussing', which means the systematic reduction of the breadth of the enquiry to give more concentrated attention to the **emerging issues**. A key value which is apparent in the work of Parlett and Hamilton is that they reject the classical evaluator's stance of seeking an objective truth that is equally relevant to all of the parties, in favour of acknowledging the **diversity of questions** posed by different interest groups.

Legge (1984) also arrives at a position which is quite close to that of responsive evaluation from a quite different route. She discusses the research on evaluation of planned organizational change and criticizes it on two main grounds. The first of these is that evaluation research which is rigorous enough to be acceptable to an academic is almost always too trivial to be useful to decision-makers as the designs are so restrictive that most of the things which are of interest are controlled out. The second is that most of the research is so badly designed that it is unacceptable to an academic because threats to internal validity have not been controlled and there is little confidence in the conclusions drawn. Legge suggests that, rather than attempting evaluation as rigorously-controlled research a 'contingent approach' be adopted. This essentially consists of asking the major stakeholders four major questions:

1.   Do you want the proposed change programme to be **evaluated**?
2.   What **functions** do you wish the evaluation to serve?
3.   Which (of a number of possible alternatives) approach best matches the **functional requirements** of the evaluation exercise?
4.   To what extent are **constraints** on the planning and implementation of the change programme (which will be necessary because of this approach to evaluation) **acceptable**?

Responsive evaluation is gaining ground as the most favoured method for evaluating educational and social programmes in the USA. It has obvious strengths as a procedure for evaluating training and development activities within organizations because it attempts to take into account the interests of various groups rather than just the sponsors of the programme. It also has a rationale for collecting information – the **needs of the various stakeholders**.

Quasi-legal evaluation

To adopt this approach, a **tribunal** is set up and **witnesses** are called to testify, and submit evidence; great care is taken to hear a wide range of 'evidence' (opinions, values and beliefs) from the organizers of the programme and the 'users' as well as accountants. Such an approach has been used to evaluate social programmes but not, to my knowledge, for learning activities sponsored by organizations. It might, however, be suitable for something wide-ranging – for instance, a full review of the purpose, strategy and value of management training and development.

OBJECTIVITY OF EVALUATION

It should be obvious, from a consideration of the various strategies available, that evaluation will never produce **absolute truth**; the objectives and systems approaches lead to the collection of 'hard' facts which can be reliably measured, but the evaluators hold values which determine which pieces of information are collected. The other approaches are subjective in their method of collection information but attempt to get at a wider 'truth'.

The evidence produced in an evaluation report should be both **credible** (i.e., have some reliability of measurement) and **useful**. It is a mistake to concentrate on reliable, objective facts if they convince no one. It is better to use more subjective methods of data collection and relate conclusions and interpretations to the data in a way that can be defended as 'fair'. The objectivity comes from a certainty that if someone else had carried out the evaluation he or she would have come to similar conclusions.

PRESENTING AN EVALUATION REPORT

The final stage of most evaluations will be the presentation of the report. The extent to which this will be accepted and acted upon will depend to a large extent on what took place at the beginning of the study. It is crucial to identify the major stakeholders, and to try to discover what **agendas** they have; many of those who have a long-term interest in the programme will have strong views on the desired outcomes of the study, and it is essential to keep such people informed during the evaluation and to involve them in key decisions if they are to 'own' (and therefore **act on**) the results. This is not to imply that the evaluator must produce the findings which they are expecting, rather that their views must be incorporated and they must be kept informed. It is, of course, also essential to establish that the people receiving the report have the **power to implement** the changes being suggested. One way of overcoming some of the problems in presenting the report is to discover what kind of report the major stakeholders expect. In Figure 21.6 you were asked to decide what it was that you meant by 'evaluation'. Making a decision on each of the scales makes explicit what kind of process evaluation is thought to be. Before embarking on an evaluation, you might consider asking the major stakeholders to fill in a set of attitude scales like those in Figure 21.6. You will then know what kind of data **they think that you ought to collect**, and something about **how they expect you to present it**. That should at least alert you to some of the problems if their views are very different from your own; in most cases, we think that it will greatly assist in putting the case and helping them to make changes. It is, of course, possible to make this a major feature of the evaluation by adopting a responsive approach.

The way in which the findings are communicated **during** the study will depend upon organizational style. Some organizations prefer written memoranda, but in many the important decisions are actually made in face-to-face discussions. The presentation of the report itself is not the time to 'defend': if there is some bad news, those concerned should be aware of it before the presentation. This area of the problems of presenting evaluative reports has been rather neglected in the literature, but interesting discussions may be found in Patton (1978) and Easterby-Smith (1986).

DO YOU REALLY WANT TO EVALUATE YOUR TRAINING?

If it is to become the integral part of training and development activities which has been suggested in this chapter, evaluation requires the expenditure of **energy and time**; the costs can be heavy and, if the evaluation is to be justified as an investment, some selection of the programmes seems to be indicated. Some training events are essentially social (for example, the one-day get-together where people from different functions meet and hear a series of briefings on the work of other parts of the organization); evaluation of such events would hardly be worth the cost involved.

The importance of the programme is a further criterion for consideration. Usually evaluation of one-off programmes would not be considered worthwhile; however, if the programme is intended to help with the solution of some important problem then evaluation is indicated. Similarly, if the consequences of **not ensuring that the training has been effective** (for instance, with safety training) are important, then evaluation should be considered.

The data produced in an evaluation study are likely to be a **source of**

power; this will certainly be the case where the primary purpose of evaluation is that of control – for example, central evaluation of decentralized training, or management commissioned evaluation. Most evaluative data should be useful rather than threatening, but training can never be evaluated without some judgements being made about the trainers reponsible. This could account for the widespread defensiveness among practitioners when faced with proposals for evaluation. My reply would be that there are important benefits in increasing the quality of the training, and thus the effectiveness of the training department.

Evaluation can also improve the relationship between the training department and the rest of the organization by producing evidence of real worth to the organization, by linking training events to improved organizational effectiveness, and by changing the relationship with line managers. Training departments have largely avoided the challenge of evaluating their activities; the consequence may be that, by default, they will be assessed only in terms of their cost to the organization.

REFERENCES

Belbin, R. M. (1981) *Management Teams: Why they Succeed or Fail* (London : Heinemann).

Blake, R. R. and Mouton, J. S. (1964) *The Managerial Grid* (Houston: Gulf).

Blake, R. R. and Mouton, J. S. (1969) *Building a Dynamic Corporation through Grid Organization Development* (Reading, Mass.: Addison-Wesley).

Bloom, B. S. (1956) *Taxonomy of Educational Objectives* (New York: Macmillan).

Bramley, P. (1990) *Evaluating Training Effectiveness: Translating Theory into Practice* (London: McGraw-Hill).

Cameron, K. (1980) 'Critical Questions in Assessing Organizational Effectiveness', *Organisational Dynamics* (Autumn) pp. 66–80.

Cook, J. D., Hepworth, S. J., Wall, T. D. and Warr, P. B. (1981) *The Experience of Work* (London: Academic Press).

Easterby-Smith, M. (1986) *Evaluation of Management Education, Training and Development* (Aldershot: Gower).

Georgeopolous, B. S. and Tannenbaum, A. S. (1957) 'The Study of Organisational Effectiveness', *American Sociological Review*, 22, pp. 534–40.

Glossary of Training Terms (1971) Department of Employment (London: HMSO).

Goldstein, A. P. and Sorcher, M. (1974) *Changing Supervisor Behaviour* (New York: Pergamon).

Goldstein, I. L. (1986) *Training in Organisations* 2nd edn (Cal.: Brooks/Cole).

Hamblin, A. C. (1974) *Evaluation and Control of Training* (London: McGraw-Hill).

Henerson, M. E., Morris, H. and Fitzgibbon, C. T. (1978) *How to Measure Attitudes* (Beverley Hills, Cal.: Sage).

Honey, P. (1979) 'The Repertory Grid in Action', *Industrial and Commercial Training* (September).

Katz, D. and Khan, R. L. (1978) *The Social Psychology of Organisations* (2nd edn) (New York: Wiley).

Kirkpatrick, D. L. (1967) 'Evaluation of Training', in Craig, R. L. and Bittel, L. R. (eds) *Training and Development Handbook* (New York: McGraw-Hill).

Latham, E. P. and Saari, L. M. (1979) 'The Application of Social Learning Theory to Training Supervisors Through Behavioural Modeling', *Journal of Applied Psychology*, 64, pp. 239–46.

Legge, K. (1984) *Evaluating Planned Organisational Change* (London: Academic Press).

Parlett, M. and Hamilton, D. (1977) 'Evaluation as a New Approach to the Study of Innovative Programmes', in Hamilton, D., Jenkins, D., King, C., MacDonald, B. and Parlett, M. (eds), *Beyond the Numbers Game* (London : Macmillan).

Patton, M. C. E. (1978) *Utilization-focussed Evaluation* (Beverly Hills, Cal.: Sage).

Robson, M. (1982) *Quality Circles: A Practical Guide* (Aldershot: Gower).

Stake, R. E. (ed.) (1975) *Evaluating the Arts in Education: A Responsive Approach* (Columbus, Ohio: Charles E. Merrill).

Warr, P., Bird, M. and Rackham, N. (1970) *Evaluation of Management Training* (Aldershot: Gower).

Woodward, N. (1975) 'Cost–Benefit Analysis of Supervisor Training', *Industrial Relations Journal* 6(2), pp. 41–7.

22

Team-building*

Bill Critchley and David Casey

It all started during one of those midnight conversations between consultants in a residential workshop. We were running a team-building session with a top management group and something very odd began to appear. Our disturbing (but also exciting) discovery was that for most of their time this group of people had absolutely no need to work as a team; indeed, the attempt to do so was causing more puzzlement and scepticism than motivation and commitment. In our midnight reflections we were honest enough to confess to each other that this was not the first time our team-building efforts had cast doubts on the very validity of teamwork itself, within our client groups.

We admitted that we had both been working from some implicit assumptions that good teamwork is a characteristic of healthy, effectively functioning organizations. Now we started to question those assumptions. First, we flushed out what our assumptions actually were. In essence it came down to something like the following.

We had been assuming that the top group in any organization (be it the board of directors or the local authority management committee or whatever the top group is called) **should be a team** and ought to **work as a team**. Teamwork at the top is crucial to organizational success, we assumed. We further assumed that a properly functioning team is one in which:

*First published in *Management Education and Development*, 15 (2) 1984.

1. people care for each other
2. people are open and truthful
3. there is a high level of trust
4. decisions are made by consensus
5. there is strong team commitment
6. conflict is faced up to and worked through
7. people really listen to ideas and to feelings
8. feelings are expressed freely
9. process issues (task and feelings) are dealt with.

Finally, it had always seemed logical to us, that a team-building catalyst could always help any team to function better – and so help any organization perform better as an organization; better functioning would lead the organization to achieve its purposes more effectively.

The harsh reality we now came up against was at odds with this cosy view of teams, teamwork and team-building. In truth, the director of education has little need to work in harness with his fellow chief officers in a county council; he or she might need the support of the chief executive and the chair of the elected members' education committee, but the other chief officers in that local authority have neither the expertise nor the interest, nor indeed the time, to contribute to what is essentially very specialized work.

Even in industry, whilst it is clear that the marketing and production directors of a company must work closely together to ensure that the production schedule is synchronized with sales forecasts and the finance director needs to be involved – to look at the cash flow implications of varying stock levels – they do not need to involve the *whole* team; and they certainly do not need to develop high levels of trust and openness to work through those kinds of business issues.

On the other hand, most people would agree that **strategic** decisions, concerned with the future direction of the whole enterprise, should involve all those at the top; strategy should demand an input from every member of the top group, and for strategic discussion and strategic decision-making, teamwork at the top is essential. But how much time do most top management groups actually spend discussing strategy? Our experiences, in a wide variety of organisations, suggest that 10 per cent is a high figure for most organizations – often 5 per cent would be nearer the mark. This means that 90–95 per cent of decisions in organizations are essentially operational – that is, decisions made with departments based usually on a fair amount of information and expertise. In those conditions, high levels of trust and openness may be nice, but are not necessary; consensus is strictly not an issue and in any case would take up far too much time. There is therefore no need for high levels of interpersonal skills.

Why then, is so much time and money invested in team-building, we asked ourselves? At this stage in our discussions we began to face a rather disturbing possibility. Perhaps the spread of team-building has more to do with team-builders and **their** needs and values, rather than a careful analysis of what is appropriate and necessary for the organization. To test out this alarming hypothesis we each wrote down an honest and frank list of reasons why we ourselves engaged in team building. We recommend this as an enlightening activity for other team-builders – perhaps, like us, they will arrive at this kind of conclusion: team-builders work as catalysts to help management groups function better as open teams for a variety of reasons, including the following:

1. They like it – enjoy the risks
2. Because they are good at it
3. It is flattering to be asked
4. They receive rewarding personal feedback
5. Professional kudos – not many people do team-building with top teams
6. There is money in it
7. It accords with their values: for instance, democracy is preferred to autocracy
8. They gain power; process interventions are powerful in business settings where the client is on home ground and can bamboozle the consultant in business discussions.

All those reasons are concerned with the needs, skills and values of the **team-builder** rather than the management group being 'helped'. This could explain why many team-building exercises leave the so-called 'management team' excited and stimulated by the experience, only to find they are spending an unnecessary amount of time together discussing other people's departmental issues. Later on, because they cannot see the benefit of working together on such issues, they abandon 'teamwork' altogether. Such a management group has been accidentally led to disillusionment with the whole idea of teamwork and the value of team-building.

We began to see, as our discussions went on through the small hours, that there is a very *large* proportion of most managers' work where teamwork is not needed (and to attempt to inculcate teamwork is dysfunctional). There is, at the same time a very *small* proportion of their work where teamwork is absolutely vital (and to ignore teamworking skills is to invite disaster). This latter work, which demands a team approach, is typified by strategic work but not limited to strategic work. It is any work characterized by a high level of **choice** and by the condition of **maximum uncertainty**.

Most people find choice and uncertainty uncomfortable. Many senior managers attempt to deny the choice element by the employment of complex models and techniques. We do not think most people's management experience teaches them to make choices about the future, for instance – it puts the main emphasis on establishing as many facts as possible and reviewing options in the light of past experience. That is why models like, for example, the Boston portfolio model and the General Electric matrix are so popular; they provide comforting analytic frameworks for looking at strategic options, but they are appealing really to our operational mentality. The hope often is that they will somehow come up with a solution to the strategic question; but of course they cannot make choices for people and they do not throw any light on the future.

The top team of an organization, if it is to achieve quality and commitment in its decisions about future directions, will need to pool the full extent of each individual's wisdom and experience. That means something quite different from reacting to a problem in terms of their own functional knowledge and experience; it means exposing fully their **uncertainties**, taking **unaccustomed risks** by airing their own subjective view of the world and struggling to build some **common perceptions and possibilities**. This is where that much abused word 'sharing' really comes into its own. In this context, it is not merely a value-laden exhortation, it is vital to the future of the organization. Ideas and opinions are all we have to inform our view of the future, but if we are to take a risk with a fragile idea or opinion, unsubstantiated by facts, we will take it only if the climate is right. Conversely, if we take the risk and the sheer airiness and vulnerability of the idea attracts a volley of ridicule and abuse, then it will die quickly and be lost forever.

Most functional executives, brought up in the turbulence of politics and interfunctional warfare, find the transition from functional to strategic mode very difficult to make; they do not always see the difference – and if they do, they are reluctant to leave their mountain top, the summit of knowledge, experience and hence power, for the equality and shared uncertainty of strategic decision-making. And yet this is one area where real team-work is not only necessary but vital.

We had by now got ourselves thoroughly confused. We seemed to be forcing team-building on groups which had no need to be a team and missing the one area where team-work is essential – because choice and uncertainty are at a maximum and for this very reason managers were shying away from the work – work which can be done only by a team. We resorted to diagrams to help clear our minds, and these new diagrams form the basis of the next section of this chapter.

THEORETICAL CONSIDERATIONS CONCERNING MANAGEMENT GROUPS

We found these kinds of discussion taking us farther and farther away from team-building and closer and closer to an understanding of why management groups work, (or do not work), in the ways they do. In the end, we developed two basic diagrams, showing the relationships between a number of variables which operate in management groups:

1. the degree of **uncertainty** in the management task
2. the need for **sharing** in the group
3. **modes** of working
4. different kinds of **internal group process**
5. different levels of **interpersonal skills**
6. the role of the **leader**.

We would now like to present these two framework diagrams as diagnostic tools, which general management groups have found very useful in coming to terms with how they work, and why. These simple diagrams are helping groups see **what kind of groups they are**, and when (and if) they want to be a team, rather than jumping to the conclusion that all groups need team-building.

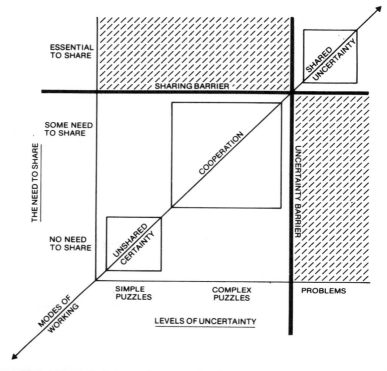

Figure 22.1   Uncertainty and group sharing

Throughout the discussion, we will be talking about the management group – that is, the leader plus those immediately responsible to him or her, perhaps five to ten people in all, at the top of their organization or their part of the organization. The first diagram (Figure 22.1) shows the relationship between the level of uncertainty inherent in any group task and the need for members of that group to share with each other. Expressed simply: 'The more uncertainty – the more need to share'. Everyday examples of this truism are children holding hands for comfort in the dark or NASA research scientists brainstorming for fresh ideas on the frontiers of man's knowledge: any uncertainty – emotional, physical or intellectual – can best be coped with by sharing.

However, the converse is also true – where there is less uncertainty, there is less need to share. The same children will feel no need to hold hands round the breakfast table where all is secure; the NASA scientists during the final launch will each get on with their own well-rehearsed part of the launch programme in relative isolation from each other. Only if something goes wrong (uncertainty floods back) will they need to share, quickly and fully. It took us a long time to realize the full significance of this in terms of the need to share in a management group.

We are dealing here only with the top group of the organization where **task** is the dominant imperative; there are other situations in which other objectives demand sharing – for instance, if one is dealing with the whole fabric of a complete organization and attempting a global shift in attitudes, then **culture-building** may become the dominant imperative and sharing at all levels in that organization may become necessary. But that is a different situation – we are looking here at the top management group where task must be the dominant imperative.

In Figure 22.1 we have used Revans' powerful distinction between problems (no answer is known to exist) and puzzles (the answer exists somewhere – just find it) to describe different levels of uncertainty (see also Chapter 12 above): deciding about capital punishment is a problem for society; tracking down a murderer is a puzzle for the police.

Work groups dealing with genuine problems (of which strategy is only one example) would be well advised to share as much as possible with each other. They should share feelings to gain support, as well as ideas to penetrate the unknown. Figure 22.1 shows two shaded areas. These shaded areas must be avoided. The shaded area on the right indicates the futility of tackling real problems unless people are prepared to share; the shaded area at the top indicates that there is no point in sharing to solve mere puzzles.

Two 'barriers' appear on our model; they indicate that a positive effort must be made if a breakthrough to a new level of working is to be accomplished. For instance, the uncertainty barrier represents a step into the unknown – a deliberate attempt to work in areas of ambiguity, uncertainty and ambivalence. To avoid the shaded areas and arrive in the top righthand corner, the group break through **both** barriers at the **same** time. This is the *only* way to solve genuine problems. Most management groups stay behind both barriers in Figure 22.1 and handle work which is in the nature of a puzzle – and to achieve this they **co-operate**, rather than share, with each other. As long as they continue to limit their work to solving puzzles, they are quite right to stay within the sharing and uncertainty barriers of Figure 22.1.

As team-builders, we now see that we must spend time identifying in which **modes of working** any management group operates. The three modes of working come out in Figure 22.1 as the diagonal, and we would like to describe each mode, by working up the diagonal of Figure 22.1 from left to right:

Mode of unshared certainty

The proper mode for simple puzzles of a technical nature in everyday work, where every member of the group is **relatively competent within his or her field** and speaks from the authority of his or her specialism: ideal when the work issues are independent of each other – as they often are. A healthy attitude is: 'I will pull my weight and see that my part is done well.' Attitudes can become unhealthy if they move towards 'my interests must come first'.

Mode of co-operation

The appropriate mode for complex puzzles which impinge on the work of several members of the management group. In this mode (very common in local authorities), group members recognize the need for give-and-take, co-operation, negotiation and passing of information on a need-to-know basis. The attitude is: 'I'll co-operate for the good of the whole and because other members of this group have their rights and problems too.' Sharing is restricted to **what is necessary**, and each group member still works from the security (certainty) of his own professional base, recognizing the professional bases of his colleagues.

Mode of shared uncertainty

A rare mode; partly because it is appropriate only for genuine problems (such as strategy) where **nobody knows what to do**, uncertainty is rife and full sharing between members is the only way out; partly because, even when it is the appropriate mode, many management groups never reach these professional heights. The attitude of members has to be: 'the good of the whole outweighs any one member's interest – including mine. I carry an equal responsibility with my colleagues for the whole, and for this particular work I am not able to rely on my specialism, because my functional expertise is, for this problem we all face, irrelevant.'

Clearly, this top mode of 'shared uncertainty' is extremely demanding, and it is not surprising that many management groups try hard to avoid it. We know several Boards of directors, and even more local authority managements 'teams', who have devised a brilliant trick to avoid handling genuine problems requiring genuine sharing in the top mode. Quite simply – they turn all **strategic** problems into **operational** puzzles! How? There are very many variations of this trick available; for example:

- appoint a working party
- ask a consultant to recommend
- recruit a corporate planner
- set up a think-tank; etc.

To make sure the trick works, the terms of reference are: 'your recommendation must be short and must ask us to decide between option *A* or option *B*.' Choosing between *A* and *B* is an operational puzzle they *can* solve and it leaves them with the comfortable illusion that they have actually been engaging in strategic problem-resolution work, whereas the truth is they have avoided uncertainty, avoided sharing their fears and ideas, avoided their real work, by converting frightening problems into management puzzles. And who can blame them! We do not feel we have the right to censure top groups for not working in the top mode of shared uncertainty. We do feel we have the obligation to analyse quite rigorously how top groups actually work, before we plunge in with our team-building help.

In Figure 22.1, the size of the box for each mode indicates very roughly how frequently each mode might be needed by most management groups. Sadly, we see many management groups working in modes which are inappropriate to the work being done; it is not just that many top groups fail to push through to the top mode; many management groups get stuck in the bottom box quite a lot of the time, when they should be working in the middle mode. On the other hand, other groups go through a pantomime of sitting round a table trying to work in the middle mode, but in truth feeling bored and uninterested because the middle mode is inappropriate and each member of the group could carry on separately with his own work, without pretending to share it with his colleagues, who do not need to know anyway. In other words, their appropriate mode is unshared certainty, and attempts at sharing are boring or frustrating facades.

Our diagram shows an arrow on both ends of the diagonal, to illustrate that all three modes of working are necessary at different times, and effective work groups can (and should) slide up and down the diagonal. We do not see any management group working in one mode all the time – the really effective group is able to move from mode to mode as the **task** requires. Although it may think of itself as a management 'team', a top group will be truly functioning as a **team** only when it is operating in the **top mode**.

We use the word 'team' here, in the sense used in the first part of this chapter, which we believe is the sense used by most team-builders in team-building work. Because we now believe that working in the top mode of shared uncertainty is called for infrequently – by the nature of the work – and is actually practised even less frequently, we now doubt the value of team-building work with most management groups, when there is so much more urgent work to be done with these groups. We found in Figure 22.1 that when we plotted the level of uncertainty in the work, against the need to share, we discovered three modes of working, on the diagonal of Figure 22.1. These three modes of working were

1. unshared certainty
2. co-operation
3. shared uncertainty.

We now want to go on to answer the question 'How does a management group work in each of these modes? What **processes** are needed, what **skills** are required, and how does the **leader** function?'

The format of Figure 22.2 is the same as Figure 22.1, only the variables are different. The vertical axis of Figure 22.2 is the diagonal lifted from Figure 22.1 (modes) and two new variables are introduced – **processes** on the horizontal axis and **interpersonal skills** become the new diagonal.

Processes

To start with the horizontal axis – processes. We distinguish three levels of process in any group. At the most perfunctory there are **polite social processes**, very important to sustain the social lubrication of a healthy group but not focused on the work itself. The work is accomplished largely via **task processes** – the way work is organized, distributed, ideas generated and shared, decisions made, and so forth. The third level of process concerns people's feelings (**feelings processes**) and how these are handled by themselves and by others.

Reference to Figure 22.2 will make it clear that as the mode of working becomes more difficult, ascending the vertical axis, from unshared certainty towards shared uncertainty, so the processes needed to accomplish this more difficult work also become more difficult, as the group moves along the horizontal axis from simple basic social processes, through task processes, towards the much more difficult processes of working with people's deeper feelings.

Many groups never reach the top mode of shared uncertainty, where people's feelings are actually **part of the work** and all is uncertainty, excitement and trust.

The shaded areas are to be avoided (as in Figure 22.1). The right-hand shaded area indicates that it is absurd to indulge in work with people's feelings if the group is working only in the two lower modes of unshared certainty and co-operation – to engage in soul-searching to accomplish this kind of work is ridiculous and brings team-building into disrepute; the top shaded area indicates similarly that there is no need to share deeply when only the two lower levels of processes (basic social processes and task processes) are operating.

However, a management group faced with the need to tackle uncertainty can either 'funk' the whole thing, by staying safely behind the barriers (which is what most management groups appear to do), or it can have the courage to break through both barriers simultaneously, arriving (breathlessly) in the top right-hand corner, where the mode of working is shared uncertainty and the necessary processes are task **and**

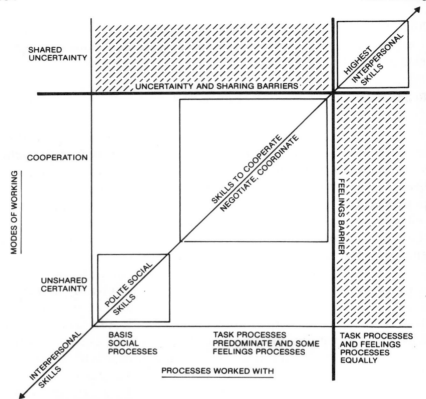

Figure 22.2   Modes of working and methods of cooperation

feelings processes together. Those few management groups which accomplish this become *teams*.

Interpersonal skills

The final variable is the diagonal of Figure 22.2 'interpersonal skills', and clearly, there is an ascending order of skill from the lowest (but *not* least important) level of polite social skills to the highest possible level of interpersonal skills 'required in the rarified atmosphere of highest uncertainty and real teamwork. But, for the middle mode, a solid raft of straightforward interpersonal skills is needed by all managers – empathy, cooperation, communication, listening, negotiating, and many more. We have come to believe that here is the greatest area of need.

The leaders' role

The group leader and group leadership have not been mentioned so far, in an attempt to keep things simple. The whole question of 'leadership' is fundamental to the operation of all management groups and we would like to make some observations now.

Leader's role in the mode of unshared certainty

The leader is hardly needed at all in the unshared certainty mode and, indeed, the social lubrication process of a group working in this mode may well be carried out much better by an informal leader – there is nothing so embarrassing as the formal group leader bravely trying to lead the group through its Christmas lunch in the canteen! Some local authority chief executives (so called) suffer an even worse fate – they cannot find a role at all, because the members of their management team (so called) steadfastly refuse to move out of the bottom mode of working, tacitly deciding *not* to work together and denying the chief executive any place in the organization at all! This is not uncommon.

Leader's role in the mode of co-operation

The leader's role in the central (co-operation) mode, is well established in management convention. For example, a clear role at meetings has been universally recognized to enable the leader to manage the task processes in particular; this role is of course the chairperson. Coordination of the task is at its core, and most group leaders find this role relatively clear.

Leader's role in the mode of shared uncertainty

No such role has yet been universally recognized to deal with the processes in the highest mode, of shared uncertainty. In Britain, we have the added difficulty of our cultural resistance to working with feelings (in action learning language 'No sets please, we're British'). In this sophisticated mode of working, the word 'catalyst' seems more appropriate than the word 'chairperson' and often a team-builder is invited to carry out this role. But where does this leave the group leader? All management group leaders have learned to be the chairperson, very few have yet learned to be the catalyst. And in any case, to be the catalyst and the leader at the same time, is to attempt the north face of the Eiger of interpersonal skills. It can be done, but not in carpet slippers. If, on the other hand, the role of catalyst is performed by an outsider, the leadership dynamic becomes immensely complex, and adds a significant overlay of difficulty when working in a mode which we have already shown to be extremely difficult in the first place. No wonder team-building often fails.

CONCLUSIONS

Many team-builders are unaware of the shaded 'no go' areas and dreamily assume that any progress towards open attitudes, free expression of feelings and genuine sharing in any management group, is beneficial. This is not so – to be of benefit there needs to be a very delicate and deliberate balance between what **work** the group has decided to pursue (what level of **uncertainty**), and the degree of sharing and expression of feelings the group is prepared for, to accomplish that work. Only if the balance is right will the management group be able to aim accurately at the top right-hand corner of Figures 22.1 and 22.2 and succeed in breaking through all the barriers at the same time to experience **real team-work**. Attempts to push through only **one** barrier (trying to handle uncertainty without sharing; sharing for the sake of sharing; being open for the sake of being open) will fail, and in failing will probably make things worse for that management group.

Strategic planners are often guilty of pushing management groups towards handling uncertainty without the concomitant abilities to share and work with feelings. Team-builders are often guilty of the converse sin – pushing management groups to be open and share their feelings, when the group has no intention whatever of getting into work where the level of uncertainty is high. Neither will succeed. It is no coincidence that both strategic planning and team-building can fall quickly into disrepute; it may be too late to save strategic planning from the management scrapheap – it is not too late to save team-building.

FURTHER READING

Adair, John (1986) *Effective Teambuilding* (Aldershot: Gower).
Belbin, R. M. (1981) *Management Teams: Why they Succeed or Fail* (London: Heinemann).
Hastings, C., Bixby, P. and Chaudhry-Lawton, R. (1986) *The Superteam Solution* (Aldershot: Gower).
Woodcock, M. (1989) *Team Development Manual*, 2nd edn (Aldershot: Gower).

23

Choosing resources

Michael Abrahams

This chapter outlines the resources available to a management development specialist (MDS), and some methods which the writer has
found to be practical in making a choice of suitable development
suppliers; it will cover:

- Business schools
- Management colleges
- Consortium programmes
- Management consultants
- Management consultancies
- Public training courses
- Training packages.

The comments made in this chapter presume that a careful analysis of
development **needs** has been undertaken, as described by Andrew
Stewart in Chapter 3: choosing a course or other development activity
for reasons other than need is unlikely to prove useful. The decision to
use external resources to address training or development needs is
usually taken with care; serious discussions may have led to a realization that the organization does not have sufficient trained or qualified
personnel capable of providing the knowledge and skills required for
all their management. The care taken in arriving at the decision to use
external resources is often in direct contrast to the random way in
which actual resources are finally chosen.

A plethora of claims is contained in mail shots from individuals and from prestigious business schools: words such as 'new', 'unique', 'tried', 'tested', etc. are part and parcel of their marketing pitch. It is of little use to initiate discussions with human resource development suppliers (HRDS) in response to the number of colours used in their brochures or their geographical proximity to the client organization. Equally, to choose to use a resource simply because the chief executive had some 'good experiences' with it in the past may be politic, but it will not be a decision based on up-to-date knowledge. There is in the human psyche a deep desire to codify, categorize and label behaviour. The work done by psychologists to encapsulate characteristics of behaviour and personality within psychometric tests and the willingness of organizations to buy the latest thinking in order to improve their selection processes are tributes to hope rather than acknowledgements of reality. Similarly if the MDS were to administer psychometric tests to a putative HRDS there is likely to be little correlation between forecast and outcome. Evidence of past successes (provided by the use of written material, references and observations) are essential, and the following sections aim to provide guidance on how to obtain this evidence, and to suggest ways in which that evidence may be used to make the best choices. Sometimes the material gathered will be contradictory and on occasion it will be difficult to decide: the choice then open to the MDS will be decided by the 'chemistry' that exists between the MDS and a supplier.

There has been a significant increase in the availability and quality of HRDS during the 1980s; institutions of management teaching became far more rigorous than in the past and the growth of large training and organizational development consultancies went a long way to ensuring a measure of integrity; nevertheless it still pays to be choosy and the first step should be to contact organizations who can give advice about HRDS. The organisations listed below will supply information. Those marked* are not without interest in supplying HRDS themselves but they maintain a professional distance when asked for advice.

The Association of Management Education & Development
21 Catherine Street
London WC2B 5JS

British Institute of Management,*
Management House
Cottingham Road
Corby
Northants NN17 1TT

Brunel University*
BIOSS
Uxbridge
Middx UB8 3PH

The Institute of Personnel Management*
IPM House
Camp Road
Wimbledon
London SW19 4UW

The following provide data on a variety of courses in the UK, Europe and the USA.

Brickers Executive Education Service
425A Family Farm Road
Woodside
California 94026 USA

Directory of Management Training
Hoskyns Education
Hoskyns Group Plc
5 Kerley Road
Bournemouth BH2 5DE

The Management Courses Index
7 Princes Street
London W1R 7RB

The experience of other MDSs or management trainers within the public and private sectors cannot be discounted; networks of MDSs exist and their knowledge and skills in choosing HRDSs can be useful to an individual in the early stages. It is a worthwhile exercise to make contact and to tap into various professional groupings, possibly by joining one such as the Association of Management Education & Development. Initially, there will be a tendency to accept the judgement of others; it must be remembered, however, that one HRDS may be meat to one organization and poison to another.

BUSINESS SCHOOLS

For a given level of management, business school programmes can look similar. The objectives are almost interchangeable and the core content, which accounts for something like 70 per cent of the offering, is predictable. Each institution will claim that its faculty and visiting faculty is excellent, and indeed the aim of excellence, in terms of genuinely wishing to provide a worthwhile educative experience, is maintained throughout a wide spectrum of business schools; the problem for a MDS lies in choosing the best programme to fit the objectives of **prospective participants and their organization**. For example, a business school programme with a strong bias towards industrial marketing will not necessarily benefit an individual from a service industry such as insurance – it may be of interest and it may be filed away for future reference, but any application of technique or knowledge may never take place simply because the fields of endeavour are so diverse. The appropriate programme would need to show that a member of the faculty had had some experience in marketing services such as banking (or, preferably, in this instance, insurance).

Another example of a possible mismatch between participant and programme would be where a programme shows a distinct leaning towards the behavioural sciences with elements of personal exposure implicit in the objectives. Little benefit will accrue to an individual whose expectations are geared towards improving his or her financial knowledge, decision-making skills or powers of business analysis. The questions to be asked by a MDS before choosing a business school programme should therefore include the following:

1. What does the organization **require of its managers** in **the next five–ten** years that a business school programme might help to fulfil?
2. What, then, do managers need for their **development**?
3. Have we undertaken a proper **analysis of their individual needs**?

4. Do they require an intensive **educational** programme, or a **skills** programme?
5. Is the best **timing** this year, or next?
6. How does their **experience** shape the type of programme to be used – are they specialists that need to know more about their specialization, or about another one?
7. Are they managers whose experience has been in a limited number of functional areas, and do they therefore need exposure to a **range of issues** facing the organization?
8. Do any of the managers require exposure to an **international** faculty or participant group?

The other important aspect of this analysis is to **engage** the **manager(s) involved with the choice of programmes**; in this way the outcome is more likely to succeed and the individual will not so easily fall into the trap of saying 'I was sent on this course'.

HOW TO CHOOSE A BUSINESS SCHOOL

Having determined the specific educational requirement for an individual and decided to use a business school, the MDS may find the following series of actions and questions useful (experience will enable a MDS to eliminate a number of the following points).

Collecting data by post

Brochures outlining courses are the marketing and public relations side of a business school; their function is to sell and to give outline information: the more prestigious the school the more the emphasis there is on the quality and experience of the faculty, and on course structure and content to ensure that applications are from suitably high-calibre management. Less prestigious business schools may stress uniqueness and novelty and it is not unusual for some institutions to promote the setting of their colleges or the age of the buildings in order to establish an aura of retreat, tradition and learning.

Objectives

The course objectives will indicate whether the **level of managers targeted** is correct – for example, if objectives outline strategic thinking, macroeconomics, international takeovers but suggest that the course is aimed at middle management, then the course is patently misdirected. The brochure should indicate the **interrelationship** between the different **levels** of courses offered, and will therefore give clues on the thinking and house style of the school.

Content

The course content (or programme overview) will indicate the time allocated to the **operational and corporate level** of business. As suggested previously, the course content should match the objectives and any programme which suggests (for example) that the objectives are to increase an individual's capacity to comprehend strategic decisions but apportions 90 per cent of its time to finance and management accounting is unlikely to reach those objectives.

Faculty

A list of **faculty members** should form part of the information in the brochure. The list may indicate whether the faculty is full-time, part-time, visiting, etc. and indicate the mix of nationalities. Brief study will also show the **alma mater** of each member of faculty, and therefore whether there is a preponderance of US-trained professors and lecturers or if there is a balance between New World-trained and the European or Asian-educated faculty; a balance is particularly useful if the school is European and the intending participant is to be based in Europe. Many American managers posted to Europe bemoan the over-emphasis placed on US-trained faculty in European business schools and the over-use of US case study material. However many European business schools (particularly INSEAD) have built up an impressive number of cases based on European and Pacific Basin organizations.

Teaching methods

The **teaching methods** should also be indicated in the brochure. Some schools use case study only, following the lead given by Harvard; it has been suggested that this method is designed to teach people to analyse business problems and make theoretical decisions whilst divorcing them from reality. It must be said that the method does not suit all managers; the reading work load of sometimes two or three cases a day for between fourteen and seventy days, depending on the length of the course, can be onerous and could therefore make learning more difficult. Equally some schools use a high number of lectures, say three or four per day; this method can be numbing both to mind and rear end! Some schools have accepted that teaching methods need to be varied, and use case study, lectures, real-life consultancy, simulation, role-play and advanced audio visual presentation techniques to make teaching points.

Participants

A list of **recent participants** will enable the MDS to assess the levels and backgrounds of the managers attending programmes. It should be noted if a high proportion of the participants hailed from one sector of endeavour (say, merchant banking); if this is obvious and the MDS is employed by a plastic containers producer then the course is likely to be less than fruitful for the production manager. Similarly if the majority of participants came from one geographical area (e.g., Scandinavia or Nigeria) then the benefit of a mixed international flavour would be diluted. The level of management attending programmes can be gauged by the job titles given, but it needs to be remembered that vice-presidents abound in American companies and that there appear to be a large number of senior executives in merchant banking who are disarmingly young and inexperienced! Contacting the MDS in a company shown to have had a manager as a participant on a course, or contacting the manager personally in order to discuss his or her view of the programme will be time well spent.

Publications

It is useful to obtain a list of **recent research publications and articles**; this will give the MDS an idea of the research strengths of the school and whether some of the published material might be applicable to the MDS's own organization, thus indicating the possibility of members of faculty having a closer understanding of the MDS's organizational needs.

MBA programme

If the school has an MBA programme it will be necessary to get information on the curriculum, the number of students, the programme demands, the average age, conditions of entry, breakdown of nationalities, drop out rate, etc.; these can form the basis of discussion on a subsequent visit to the school. Information of the type outlined above can all be obtained by post.

Timing

It is not unusual for the ideal programme to be run at a less than ideal time for the prospective participant! In fact, it is probably a truism that most managers or executives who attend business school programmes find it difficult to release themselves from their responsibilities to attend a programme. The organization may also find that its manpower planning has been less than effective, as it is unable to replace the individual even on a temporary basis! Detailed knowledge of the course and its likely benefits are essential for the MDS in these circumstances, and can help to persuade the manager of the opportunity being offered. The MDS could also suggest that one manager's absence is an **opportunity to develop another manager**, acting as a temporary replacement.

Geography/cost

The geographical position of the offering business school is a strong factor in determining its acceptability. **Proximity** can be a positive factor but so too can the **distance** from the prospective candidates' work-place. (It has been said that for organizations based in the UK, a business school programme increases in its perceived value in direct proportion to its distance south of Calais or west of Cork, hence the popularity of programme in the USA or Europe!) The cost of a programme is not inconsiderable and the closer to the home base it takes place, the lower the overall bill.

Briefing and debriefing

This is an activity 'more honoured in the breach', as it can be time-consuming and the benefits not immediately observable. However, with the financial investment associated with management development the return is worthwhile. There has been a variety of published material which will give MDS's ideas on what briefing needs to be done. The most important aspect associated with any senior management business school or management college programme is the need to ensure that the manager attending has either a **different job** on his or her return, or that the present job requires **restructuring** in such a way that he or she can bring into effect some of the ideas taken on board whilst on a programme. The writer has seen a considerable number of senior managers who having been on a management programme leave their nominating companies, not because they were badly briefed, debriefed or had no briefing/de-briefing at all, but because no allowance had been made for their 'growth' on their return.

VISITING A SCHOOL

The most effective method of choosing a business school is to visit a selection in order to build up a picture and to get an understanding of **methods** and **quality**. The following questions should be asked of directors, staff faculty and participants; some suggested areas to **observe** are also noted.

Management structure

- Where are the decisions made?
- What is the level of independence of the faculty?
- Do they match their material to the needs of the client company?
- Is there an advisory Board?
- What is its function?
- Who are represented?
- How is it structured?

Short courses

- What is the percentage of standard programmes (i.e., off-the-shelf') to 'in-company' programmes?

- What changes in the profile of courses has taken place over the past five years?
- What is the most supported course(s), and as a corollary the least supported course(s)?
- What are the candidates' entry qualifications for a particular course?
- How many applications does a school refuse?
- What are the average numbers of people on courses compared to the targeted number?

The last is an important question: some schools have in the past accepted too many people for a programme, either because they did not wish to disappoint or because they wished to maintain income. Conversely some courses have too few people on them, and should have been cancelled.

MBAs

- What percentage leave for immediate employment?
- What is the percentage of 'funded' students?
- How may 'drop out' (or are asked to 'drop out') during a programme?
- Is there a counsellor for the students?
- What is the pass rate?
- Is there an alumni of MBAs? How does it support the school?

General indicators

- Which teaching area is particularly strong?
- Which research area is particularly strong?
- What is the academic turnover rate?
- What proportion of an academic's time is given over to consultancy?
- Do any of the faculty hold directorial appointments in business?

Observation points

1. Sit in on a class; observe and listen to the **level of participation**. If the class is being conducted in English, do any of the participants

have difficulty with the language? (If so, the question to the directing staff can be 'What steps do you take to ensure that a candidate who has English as a second or third language is fluent?': there are tests available such as TOEFL, the Test of English as a Foreign Language.)

2. Are there any **'course clowns'** or **'sleepers'**? These will indicate either a disaffection with the subject or the teacher, or it may mean simply that the individual should not be on the programme and that the admission committee was lax.

3. Are the teaching methods **appropriate to the subject?** To give a lecture with no visual aids or participation on the subject of capital evaluation techniques does not bear thinking about, but it happens.

4. What **'energy level'** do the participants display for the subject? Talk to a cross-section of participants and get views on the course and faculty (and, where possible, comparisons with other courses that individuals may have attended earlier in their career).

5. How many participants **turn up late** for class? This is often a measure of disaffection with the tutor or the programme.

6. Who does **most of the talking** in a case study class? If it is the tutor, then the class has not done enough work on the case, or has not understood it.

7. How often does the programme director appear to have **contact with participants?** Little is gained if the director introduces the programme, disappears for its duration and then turns up to take brickbats or plaudits at the end.

8. Is there a confusion between **working hard** and **learning well**? They are not necessarily one and the same thing.

9. Have the faculty **talked to each other** before the programme? It can be evident that overlaps have occurred because some tutors have failed to discuss content.

The principal

It is often useful to meet the Head of the School and if possible pose the question: 'What in the school's view are the critical problems facing management education, and how will the school respond?' Reactions will indicate whether the actions being considered are innovative and responsive. The principal of a school can have great or little influence on the institution, and it is useful to check out his or her record in innovation and steering by having discussions with experienced MDSs.

Business schools are usually amenable to visits from MDSs. It is significant that for all the number of organizations represented on the 'rolls of honour' as having had participants in programmes, very few MDSs from those organizations visit programmes and talk with the faculty or directing staff. An investment in time and money of up to £30 000 for a senior manager to undertake a business school programme without a specialist visiting and undertaking some of the questioning and observations shown on the checklist will not serve the interest of the nominators – or, indeed, the business schools.

MANAGEMENT COLLEGES

Such institutions are mainly a UK or European phenomenon. The USA is far more geared to pre-experience education (70 000 MBAs vs 2000 in the UK in 1989), and therefore accreditation is more advanced in the USA; the situation in the UK is changing, and more emphasis is being placed on the middle management MBA (possibly to the detriment of the British equivalent, the accountancy degree). Colleges provide short courses on general management, specific disciplines and management skills, essentially for post-experience managers; the work is usually sound but needs to be approached with caution if senior managers are being considered for placement. The faculty will usually have had previous management experience or have been management consultants. The approach recommended for business schools (i.e., the questions and observation notes), apply equally to management colleges such as Ashridge or Henley. The question about directorial appointments is particularly apposite for anyone considering a management college MBA: it is not unheard of for faculty members of some of the 'lower order' management colleges to be attending MBA programmes at business schools (as participants!) and then teaching their students directly on their return.

Management colleges in the UK have been active in linking up with their European mainland equivalents to provide an international perspective. This may be due to a lack of international faculty in the respective institutions, but the idea is positive and will do much to benefit the choice available to MDSs.

CONSORTIUM PROGRAMMES

The advantages of consortium programmes can best be described by an examination of the relative merits and demerits of internally-run programmes and those of business schools or management colleges.

Internal programmes

The advantages of any programmes mounted by an individual organization are that:

1. Programme **objectives** will be in line with company aims
2. **Content** can be carefully scrutinized to ensure applicability and usefulness
3. Faculty can be chosen for their **match and skill** in delivering what is required; the level will therefore be of uniform excellence.

The disadvantages are that:

1. The participants will not be able to match themselves against **similar level managers** from a variety of **other organizations**
2. There will inevitably be a 'cross-fertilization of self-ignorance'.

External programmes

The advantages of an external business school or management college programme are that:

1. The participants will usually be drawn from a **wide range of enterprises**, both national and international, which increases the value of a programme
2. Managers or executives often find time to **reflect on their job, careers and the totality of their lives** when they are taking structured time off the job, they often return refreshed and energized.

The disadvantages of this type of programme are that:

1. The MDS has little control over the **aims and objectives** of any programme
2. The **faculty** can vary from brilliant to third-rate
3. The participants can be **wrongly selected**, including the MDS's own participant!

The consortium approach eliminates most of the disadvantages and capitalizes on the advantages of external and internal programmes. This is done by agreeing with a variety of organizations on the objective of a programme, choosing a disinterested 'chairman', picking an ideal faculty and ensuring that the level of participants assures a high level of participation and intellectual stimulation. Amongst the first of these was one set up by the writer in 1975 when working with Marks & Spencer. The participants included Dunlop, IBM, Barclays Bank, the Cabinet Office and a number of others. It is still operating at a senior and middle management level.[1]

CONSULTANTS

'People who borrow your watch to tell you what time it is and then walk off with it' (Robert Townsend, author of *Up the Organisation*, describing management consultants).

The type of consultants dealt with in this section are not those who collate the collective wisdom of employees, feed it to the Board in a large report and then walk away after making a number of recommendations that everyone knew they would make. Human resource development consultants do speak to the people within the organization, but on the whole they stay to carry out their recommendations themselves. Consultants can be private individuals who work on their own or occasionally with other consultants, or they can be part of a consultancy group or associates. Sometimes they are people who are encouraged to act as consultants as part of their contract at a business school, management college or in some cases are from private commercial organisations.

The decision to employ an external consultant is often made because an organization's own specialists are fully engaged, or do not have the expertise. A consultant can be an advantage because he or she will be seen as **neutral**, and have no involvement in the internal politics of the organization; at the same time, the external consultant is likely to have greater experience and, more importantly, greater credibility than many internal consultants (it is well known that 'a prophet is not without honour save in his own land'!).

Before contracting to employ an external consultant, it is as well to check out their work either by seeing them in operation if they conduct courses, or by talking with the MDSs of those organizations where a consultant's work has been successful. The consultants will always refer an enquiring MDS to where they have had successes; the secret is to tease out where success has **not been achieved**. No one likes to advertize their failures but if the consultants are experienced, assured and successful they will not wish to appear omnipotent and will, if questioned, volunteer organizations where in their early days, when 'cutting their teeth', they had a number of experiences they would not wish to repeat. Check out successes and check out failures. It is also useful if, before making a choice, the MDS arranges to meet a number of consultants. The MDS should use a similar format for each encounter, and check out the responses and reactions of each consultant. The MDS should also check **their own reaction** to the consultant, as they will be working closely with him or her.

Another criterion for the MDS to apply is whether the consultant is someone who would be acceptable **within the culture of the organization** in terms of their training style; a training consultant who uses psychodrama or bioenergetics may not be suitable in an organization whose managers expect training to be conducted in a more cognitive mode. It is necessary to know what **methods** the consultants favour, and how **flexible** they are within their repertoire.

It is worth mentioning at this stage that discussions should be concerned with contracts with an **individual**, not a consultancy: problems often occur if the MDS has built a rapport with a consultant, only to find that he or she then sub-contracts to someone who may not be as experienced, or as acceptable to the organization.

The final points that must be clarified before employing a consultant are: What will it cost? What time will the consultant be able to devote to the proposed assignment? A useful measure is to check out **how many projects** a consultant has on his or her books at any one time – three would appear to be optimum. After initial discussion of the problem, the consultant should be asked to send a note setting out what he or she understands to be the **issue or problem** in question, and outlining a **course of action** that he or she would propose to take. If the consultant has understood the MDS – which should be evident from the clarity of the proposal – and if the outline is acceptable, with only some 'fine tuning' required, then there is a likelihood of a working arrangement being achieved.

CONSULTANCIES

As mentioned above, I have found that the relationship with an individual consultant is far more likely to prove successful than the relationship with a group of consultants. The arguments about the faculty of a business school apply equally to the 'faculty' of a consultancy: there is no guarantee that good working relationships will ensue simply because the consultancy has a 'good name'. There has been a growth in recent years of consultancies seeing themselves more as 'corporations' in their own right. This is manifested by the increasing size of this type of organization and the fact that many of the old-established management accountancy consultancies have merged. (Many of the consultancies now being formed will be seeking a quotation on the Unlisted Securities Market.) For the MDS, this will mean less choice of consultancies, but possibly a greater chance of finding good people within one consultancy. An exception could be demonstrated in the following advertisements (Figures 23.1 and 23.2), which appeared in the professional press in 1990. They reveal the calibre of consultants required by some consultancies, and underline

---

STRESS MANAGEMENT CONSULTANTS
Join our successful team. OTF £30 000.
Commission only.
Self-employed consultants required all parts of the UK. No previous experience required. Full-time/part-time, flexible hours. Full training whilst working over 18 months. Over 25 and ideal for mothers returning to work, retired teachers, nurses, policemen/women, ambulance workers.
Personal stress management is a growth industry. 40 000, clients have benefited from our programmes. Successful applicants may enter our structured training programme for advancement while earning, which is located in the London and Midland areas. For a personal interview, call or write, etc.

Figure 23.1   Consultants' advertisement

Ms X has moved from education where she had considerable experience working with pupils with special educational needs and in developing in-service training courses for teachers. She is a partner in a consultancy specializing in organizational change, training and recruitment. Her particular strengths are in communication skills, creativity, problem-solving, stress management and team-building.

Figure 23.2   Consultant's advertisement

the necessity to check the CVs of people being employed by consultancies. Figure 23.2 in particular demonstrates one still prevalent state of 'unconscious incompetence' present in a surprising number of consultants.

Questions for a consultant or consultancies

1. What experience have you had with **my type of organization** or **sector**?
2. What experience have you had with the type of **contract** we have in mind (e.g., training in process or content)?
3. What experience have you had working at the **level of management** we have in mind, and with the **volume** we are expecting?
4. Can you give me evidence of **results** within other organizations?
5. **Who else** in the consultancy might be working on the assignment? What evidence do you have of their competence?
6. Are you willing to make **modifications** to the work as we proceed?
7. What methods of **evaluation** can you recommend, and will you be involved with them?
8. Can you cope with the expected **volume of work**?
9. How much will it **cost** my company – broken down by consultant days and an outline of expenses charged?
10. What will the **potential cancellation costs** be?

PUBLIC TRAINING COURSES

These are courses offered by profit-making organisations who offer to give participants expertise in a number of areas such as training skills, stress management, time management, etc. Courses associated with technical expertise (computers, textile technology, engineering, etc.) where individuals are being technically trained or updated on the 'state of the art' are not the subject of this section.

Public courses and training packages abound with 'the elixir effect', which claims to have the ultimate solution to all human resource development problems. There is no standard by which these courses can be assessed. That is not to say that there should not be, or that it would be difficult to institute one; it would make the job of choosing a suitable course very much easier and would rid the market of some disreputable operators: a Sale of Services Act, perhaps?

Choosing a course

Some course providers are producing timetables of events covering a wide variety of subjects. An interesting (if somewhat tedious) activity is to count the number of times a trainer's name appears at the bottom of the programme as a course leader or tutor; it often stretches credulity that any one individual is so skilled and knowledgeable that they are able to tutor such a wide range of subjects. The area which an MDS should be more concerned about is course providers who fail to give **any information about the tutors** they are using; it is not unknown for jobbing trainers to be called in to run public programmes that have been over-subscribed in order that two programmes can be run in parallel, thus increasing income for the training company at the expense of any quality control.

Course objectives

- What are the course **objectives**? What will participants know – and, more important, **do** – that they did not know (or do) before the course? If this area is not clear, then the likelihood is that the content will be woolly as well.
- What **methods** are employed? The methods should recognize that learning is not entirely a listening process, but a talking, doing, practising activity as well.
- The objective, content and **methods** must be in **harmony**. The objectives should be limited to **achievable** and **quantifiable** behaviourial or learning targets; the content must be adequate to

cover the objectives but must not be a huge list of words and phrases designed to flag the erudition of the trainer; the methods must be **appropriate** to the subject (i.e., behaviour modification is not achieved by lecture, and marketing strategy analysis is unlikely to be learnt using interpersonal process recall).

- The **quality of the course tutor** is critical. There are some very charismatic seminar leaders, particularly in the marketing field where bravura performances are applauded, but they are not necessarily good at **facilitating learning**. On the latter subject the grapevine of MDSs can be consulted as can the **Management Courses Index**. The problem is, as ever, that one person's evaluation of an individual can be widely different from another and there is no agreed criterion.
- **Price is no guide**. A more expensive course means only that the course is more expensive. There are courses available, often mounted by polytechnics and university departments, which are professionally tutored, well run and inexpensive.

The final check on a public course is either to send a suitable candidate whose judgement can be trusted or for the MDS to attend the course personally. If the candidate or MDS is satisfied that the objectives of the programme are met, that the content is appropriate and that the course leader is able, then the course could prove worthwhile.

TRAINING PACKAGES

Training packages which contain 'all the trainer needs to conduct effective training at every level' can be attractive to a new MDS. Indeed, they can be a useful adjunct to development activities already in operation, or they can form the basis of a whole range of associated activities.

Their **ease of use** can be their failing if an MDS is not concerned (or knowledgeable) about the **underlying theoretical framework**. Participants on any such programme soon see through hollow trainers who mouth words from the course manual and are not able to answer questions, think on their feet, read the group and respond to it.

Some organizations who promote training packages offer to train trainers in their use, but what they often fail to do is check whether the packages will be appropriate to the MDS's **own organization**. They claim that their training package can easily be assimilated within any current training or development activities; this needs careful analysis, for the following reasons:

1. Many packages originate in the USA, and changing 'sidewalk' to 'pavement' or dubbing a Home Counties voice on a video will not necessarily **bridge the culture gap**
2. 'Ra, Ra' training may suit the marketing development of a floor polish company but not a firm of accountants
3. Packages which provide all materials down to flip chart workings and notepaper and which do not allow the buyer to 'personalize' or 'customize' them are inflexible and show that they are not **sensitive to the needs of the purchasing organization**.

Computer Aided Training (CAT) is becoming increasingly sophisticated, and with the advent of reasonably priced expert systems this form of training and development will grow; it will again be necessary for the MDS to check with previous users on the effectiveness of the systems offered.

SUMMARY

The choice of who will provide human resource development is often left to chance – the whim of the chief executive, the proximity of an organization to an institution or even shared experiences between the MDS and the HRDS. In the final analysis the question to be asked is: Does the development activity provided by the HRDS offer **positive results** to the organization which the MDS represents? If the results achieved are positive – and **observable** or **quantifiable** by whatever means deemed appropriate – then the supplier will have been effective.

NOTE

1. For further information, contact International Management Development, St Johns Innovation Centre, Cowley Road, Cambridge CB4 4WS.

FURTHER READING

Huczynski, A. (1983) *Encyclopaedia of Management Development Methods* (Aldershot: Gower).

Moulton, H. (annually) *The CER Evaluation Guide to Executive Programmes* (Fairfield, Iowa: Corporate Education Resources Inc.).

Oliver, J. (1990) *Developing Managers. A Guide to Executive Programmes in Europe and the USA* (London: Economist Publications).

Rogers, J. (1988) MBA: *The Best Business Tool? A Guide to British and European Business Schools* (London: Economist Publications).

Steverink, L. (annually) *European Management Education Guide* (Bibson: IMEC Nederland).

Townsend, R. (1971) *Up the Organisation* (London: Coronet).

Index